Introduction to

Human Resource Management

Introduction to
Human Resource Management

Paul Banfield & Rebecca Kay

OXFORD
UNIVERSITY PRESS

OXFORD
UNIVERSITY PRESS

Great Clarendon Street, Oxford ox2 6DP

Oxford University Press is a department of the University of Oxford.
It furthers the University's objective of excellence in research, scholarship,
and education by publishing worldwide in

Oxford New York

Auckland Cape Town Dar es Salaam Hong Kong Karachi
Kuala Lumpur Madrid Melbourne Mexico City Nairobi
New Delhi Shanghai Taipei Toronto

With offices in

Argentina Austria Brazil Chile Czech Republic France Greece
Guatemala Hungary Italy Japan Poland Portugal Singapore
South Korea Switzerland Thailand Turkey Ukraine Viernam

Oxford is a registered trade mark of Oxford University Press
in the UK and in certain other countries

Published in the United States
by Oxford University Press Inc., New York

British Library Cataloguing in Publication Data

Data available

Library of Congress Cataloging in Publication Data

Banfield, Paul.
Introduction to human resource management / Paul Banfield & Rebecca Kay.
p. cm.
ISBN 978–0–19–929152–6
1. Personnel management. I. Kay, Rebecca. II. Title.
HF5549.B2593 2008
658.3–dc22
2007043082

Typeset in 9/13pt Akzidenz Grotesk BE by Graphicraft Limited, Hong Kong
Printed in Spain
on acid-free paper by Graficas Estella

ISBN 978–0–19–929152–6

1 3 5 7 9 10 8 6 4 2

This book is dedicated to two inspirational researchers, teachers, and writers who have had a profound influence on our understanding of organizations, employment, and management – Richard Hyman and Tony Watson.

Contents in Brief

Contents in Full

xiv

List of Case Studies

About the Authors

Paul Banfield

Is Programme Director of Human Resource Management and International Development at Newcastle Business School, Northumbria University. Paul has been a lecturer in HRM for many years, combining this with the development of postgraduate and corporate programmes in HRM and general management in the UK and overseas. He has extensive experience of teaching HRM in European universities in Italy, Germany, Croatia, and the Czech Republic and has acted as a consultant to organizations in the UK and abroad, recently completing an assignment for the British Council in Uganda where he worked with African managers on leadership development and Performance Management issues.

He has been heavily involved in the CIPD for over 15 years and is currently a member of the Quality Assurance panel and a national examiner for a specialist Learning and Development module. He acts as an external examiner for Hull Business School, Plymouth University, and London Metropolitan University.

Rebecca Kay

Is HR Director of Cooper Lighting and Security Limited where as a member of the board she is jointly responsible for delivering business objectives and strategy. Her role is predominantly concerned with translating business objectives into HR strategy and practice.

Rebecca has worked in HR since graduating from the University of Liverpool with a BSc in Psychology in 1989. Her initial 12 years in HR were based at Northern Foods where she held a number of site-based roles, she then spent two years coordinating their Graduate Training Programme and was latterly employed as HR Manager at one of their larger manufacturing sites.

Prior to joining Cooper Industries she worked in HR for Stanley Tools and at this time was also a guest lecturer at Sheffield Hallam University. She is also a fellow of the Chartered Institute of Personnel and Development.

About the Book

Most authors claim that their book is different, and by implication, better, than many others currently in use. Often however, the differences, where they exist, are more superficial than substantial and tend to relate to the choice and range of HRM subject areas rather than way these areas are treated. We feel that many contemporary introductory HRM books are very similar in terms of style, approach, and coverage and that many are written by academics in an academic style that fails to reflect the realities, uncertainties, and challenges facing those with responsibilities for HRM. This led us to believe that there was a need for a book on HRM that approached the subject in significantly different ways.

What seemed to us to be missing from much of the literature available to tutors and students was a perspective on HRM that combined a strong academic underpinning with a realistic and informed understanding of the challenges faced by HR professionals and line managers in delivering their objectives. We also wanted to adopt a much more critical approach to the relationship between HR activities and their associated outcomes (often taken for granted), and in doing so, question the unproblematical way in which HR contributions to employee behaviour and business performance are often presented.

It is one thing to have a concept of the book that you would like to write – one that aspires to overcome the gap between 'theory' and 'practice' – but quite another to produce one that actually achieves this and provides students with a set of analytical tools and frameworks that are academically rigorous but also offers important insights into the realities, uncertainties, and compromises that HR practitioners and line managers are faced with on an almost daily basis. Only our readers will be able to say whether we have achieved our objective, but we believe that we have reached our goal for the following reasons:

1. It is jointly written by a lecturer in HR and a senior HR practitioner who worked closely together on all the chapters. The result is a fusion of both academic and practical insights which explore how HR is actually practised and experienced in the workplace, and thus overcomes the idealistic and partial insights of many other textbooks.

2. We take a holistic and integrated approach to HRM which avoids presenting HRM as a series of separate activities and as a separate management function detached from wider organizational and business interests and priorities.

3. The text offers an abundance of real-life examples. All chapters offer a range of challenging student activities, mini-cases, and end-of-chapter case studies which cover a range of organizational and business contexts, both in the UK and overseas.

4. The text actively engages students in their own learning and understanding of HRM by presenting them with real-life situations that can be discussed either in a seminar/group context or on private study basis.

5. The three chapter-long, real-life case studies at the end of the book provide detailed insights into the role of HRM in three different business scenarios: the opening of a new hotel; the closure of a factory; and the reform of the HR function within a NHS hospital. These chapters draw on the topics covered earlier in the text such as planning, recruitment, selection, redundancy, learning, and training but relate the decisions taken in these areas to the achievement of strategic organizational objectives.

6. The extensive Online Resource Centre provides all the teaching and learning materials needed to support each chapter, removes the need for lecturers to look for additional class and test materials, and gives students the resources they need to build their understanding and to check what actually happened in many of the real-life case studies.

How to use this Book

Key Terms

Each chapter begins with clear definitions and explanations of important terms which are explored fully later in the chapter. Understanding these terms from the start makes the ideas and arguments more accessible.

Key Terms

Hiring or employing The overall process of taking on new staff from outside the organization.

External recruitment The process of identifying and attracting potential employees to an organization to fill current or future vacancies.

Internal recruitment The process of identifying current employees who may be suitable for newly created vacancies or for replacing staff who leave.

Learning Objectives

Each chapter establishes the important learning objectives that you can achieve as a result of reading the text, engaging in the different activities, and using the Online Resource Centre.

Learning Objectives

As a result of reading this chapter and using the Onlin

- understand what is meant by 'health and safety' and the different approaches taken to health and safety management;

- explain the importance to organizations of health and safety measures;

- identify the key requirements of organizations

Student Activities

All chapters offer several Student Activities that are clearly linked to the preceding text and enable you to learn through practice. They are often research based and problem-solving, allowing you to develop your skills through group activities and presentations.

STUDENT ACTIVITY 3.5 Looking at

Consider a selection of recruitment adverts fr

1. Identify the qualities that make some adver

2. Produce a checklist of items that must be covered in a r not essential, and the pros and cons of including these.

3. Rank the adverts according to the favourable impression

HRM Insights

Each chapter offers a number of mini-case studies that present different scenarios and challenges experienced in the real world of business. They address a varied range of HR problems and requirements to show how HRM operates in practice. They are accompanied by questions which often ask you to imagine that you are involved in the case in order to develop your ability to diagnose situations and produce appropriate solutions or actions.

HRM INSIGHT 5.1 The case of the Qu

In March 2004, the Queens Medical Centre s surgery, who had 18 years' experience. The s vidual had taken a second helping of soup in t stated that he had simply added more croutons to his soup pension had their operations postponed. One week after his incident was featured in the national media throughout the w willingness to comment.

Questions

1. Why was it considered necessary to invoke the hospital'

2. What alternative forms of action might the HR function h

3. What was the overall impact of this incident likely to be i Medical Centre?

Key Concepts

Throughout each chapter, where new concepts are introduced, they are brought out and explained to give the text a strong theoretical and analytical grounding. These key concepts have specific meanings and are part of the language of HRM.

KEY CONCEPT Stagnation

This term relates to the detrimental effect on c... relying largely, or entirely, on the existing wo... from outside, which can bring new ideas, cha... to the long-term decline of an organization tha...

Signposts

Signposts are used throughout the book to indicate where similar HR activities are addressed in other sections in a complementary or a more extensive way. For example, in the chapter on Recruitment and Selection, Signposts are used to take the reader to Chapter 13 which presents a case study on opening a new hotel, where these activities can be seen in a more integrated and operationally important way.

Signpost to Chapter 15: Case Study: Reformi... employment relations

Figure 4.1 is also useful in that it represents a model tha... those that exist within each organization. It can be used

End-of-Chapter Case Studies

Each chapter finishes with a substantial case study and accompanying discussion questions. These case studies illustrate organizational practice and associated outcomes or create scenarios which present you with problems and challenges. They incorporate many of the key issues and activities covered in the chapter and integrate these in a more holistic way.

CASE STUDY

Unauthorized breaks at Brown Pac...

David Brown Packaging is a small, but highly e... industry. David, who is both the owner and man... the years, his business has expanded and n... addition to a growing number of overseas orga... quality products, produced to high technical sp... system. This means that the company has to

Review Questions

These are designed to reinforce learning by presenting important questions on some of the main themes and issues raised in the chapter. They can also help focus attention on the key learning outcomes and provide guidance for revision.

REVIEW QUESTIONS

1. What are the respective responsibilities of HR... grievances?

2. What contribution might an organization's CE... managed?

3. How does the philosophy of management aff...

4. What are the features of a working organizati...

Further Reading

The texts listed here are recommend reading to help you gain deeper subject knowledge as well as learn about alternative ideas and contributions to the mainstream treatment of HRM issues and topics.

FURTHER READING

IRS (2001) 'The new reward agenda', *IRS Mana...

Marsden, D (2004) 'The "network economy" a... *Industrial Relations*, 42:4, pp 659–84.

Marsden, D, French, S and Kubo, K (2001) *Does... Performance*.

Rousseau, D (1995) *Psychological Contracts... Agreements*, Sage.

How to use the Online Resource Centre

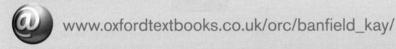

www.oxfordtextbooks.co.uk/orc/banfield_kay/

For Students

Multiple Choice Questions

Each chapter is accompanied by ten multiple choice questions that can be completed online to help test your understanding and aid your revision. These self-marking questions include instant feedback on your answers and cross-references to the textbook to assist with your independent study.

Insights & Outcomes

The reality of HRM is complex and far reaching and much can be learnt from the outcomes of the real-life cases cited in this book. How were these situations actually resolved? What were the developments that followed? How did the company respond? Where indicated in the textbook, HRM Insights and end-of-chapter case studies are followed up online, providing answers to these questions and in-depth analysis of these fascinating examples.

Web Links

Links to websites relevant to each chapter provide a useful hub from which to start your research project or essay.

Flashcard Glossary

Learning the jargon associated with HRM can be a challenge, so these online flashcards have been designed to help you memorize the key terms used in the book. Click through the randomized definitions to see if you can identify which key term they are describing!

For Lecturers

PowerPoint Lecture Slides

A suite of chapter-by-chapter PowerPoint slides has been included for use in your lecture presentations. They focus on the key points from each topic to save you time and make a useful class handout. They are all fully customizable so you can tailor them to match your own presentation style. All the figures from the book are also provided electronically for inclusion in your slides or handouts.

Test Bank

The Test Bank is a ready-made assessment tool that tests your students' understanding of HRM. Twenty questions per chapter are provided in a variety of question styles with automated feedback and grading. This method helps your students understand where they need to improve, as well as informing you of their progress by sending you their scores via your university's Virtual Learning Environment.

Additional Seminar Exercises

Finding new and stimulating ways of reinforcing students' understanding of HRM topics can be difficult. These extra ideas for student activities to run in classes, linked to key topics and arranged by chapter to fit with your module teaching, provide an extra source to boost your repertoire.

Suggested Answers to End-of-Chapter Case Study Questions

Each chapter ends with a longer case study accompanied by questions. These suggested answers succinctly highlight key points that students could consider in their answers to help with your seminar preparation.

Discussion Questions and Suggested Answers

Another resource to help seminar planning, these pertinent discussion questions help focus students on the key issues in each chapter and encourage debate of different viewpoints, thus improving their analytical skills. The suggested answers to each summarize the key points for consideration, as a quick reference guide for you to direct your students' discussion.

Acknowledgements

I would like to acknowledge the many important contributions made to this book, particularly from Frank Sharpe, Claire Wragg, Mags Healy, Christine Johnson, Charles Dolan, Yvonne O'Rourke, Eilish Croke, Dean Royles, Judith Banfield, Fiona Robson, and Chris Atkin.

Special thanks goes to William Beckett whose experiences of running a successful business and managing people informs many parts of the book, and to Helen Adams of Oxford University Press whose unfailing support, guidance, and encouragement kept us both on track when 'the mountain seemed too difficult to climb'.

And finally, I would like to say thank you to Anastasia for her encouraging feedback on some of the book's key chapters, her sterling work in quickly finding so many 'lost references', and in resolving a host of presentational issues.

P.B.

I would like to acknowledge the contribution of my father Neil Kay, and thank him for his pride and encouragement and for his valuable assistance in reviewing this book in the final stages. I would also like to thank my brother, Steven Kay, for his guidance.

I would also like to thank the many people who have inspired and encouraged my development, thinking, and values in delivering a professional HR service and business partnership throughout my career, including Leigh Thomasson, Tony McLoughlin, Sally Cabrini, and Francesca Fowler.

R.K.

The authors and publisher would like to thank the many reviewers for their helpful comments and suggestions throughout the writing process. These include, but are not limited to:

- David Dawson, University of Gloucester
- Gitta Fletcher, University of Central England
- Margaret Heath, University of East London
- Joan McLatchie, Napier University
- Judith Myers, University of Bolton
- Louise Prejet, University of Bournemouth

They are grateful to the following for permission to reproduce copyright materials:

Figure 2.5 reprinted by permission of Harvard Business School Press, from *Human Resource Champions* by D. Ulrich, Boston, MA 1997, p 24, © 1997 by the Harvard Business School Publishing Corporation, all rights reserved; Table 4.1 reproduced from WERS 2004 First Findings © Crown Copyright / ESRC / ACAS / Policy Studies Institute; Table 6.2 reproduced from *Diversity in Business: How Much Progress Have Employers Made? First Findings* (CIPD, 2006), with the permission of the Chartered Institute of Personnel and Development, London; Figure 7.3 Bird & Loftus' *Domino Model of Accident Causation* from Bird FE and Loftus RG 1976 Loss Control Management, used by permission of the copyright owner, Det Norske Veritas, Inc., with all rights reserved; Figure 7.6 *Safety Management Systems from the Health and Safety Executive (2001) A Guide to Measuring Health and Safety* © Crown Copyright / HSE; Figure 8.2 A Competency Model for Overseas Working is taken from *International Recruitment, Selection and Assessment* (P R Sparrow, 2006), with the permission of the publisher, the Chartered Institute of

Personnel and Development, London; Table 9.4 Summary of 2004 Absence Surveys reproduced from *Managing Sickness Absence in the Public Sector – A Joint Review by the Ministerial Task Force for Health, Safety and Productivity and the Cabinet Office,* November 2004 © Crown Copyright / CBI; Figure 10.2 reproduced from Kolb, David A., *Experiential Learning: Experience as a Source of Learning*, © 1984, p 42, Fig 3.1, adapted with the permission of Pearson Education, Inc., Upper Saddle River, NJ; Figure 10.3 adapted from: Kolb, David A., *Experiential Learning: Experience as a Source of Learning*, and Honey, P and Mumford, A 2006, *The Learning Styles Questionnaire*; HRM Insight 10.3 Paul Kearns' Story of an Unhelpful Director, taken from *Evaluating the ROI from Learning* (P Kearns, 2005), with the permission of the publisher, the Chartered Institute of Personnel and Development, London; the Analytical Methodology on p. 312 is reproduced with kind permission of the Hay Group (**www.haygroup.com**); Figure 15.1 reproduced from the Australian Public Service Commission, 2003, © Commonwealth of Australia, reproduced by permission.

Crown Copyright material is reproduced under Class Licence Number C01P000148 with the permission of OPSI and the Queen's Printer for Scotland.

Every effort has been made to trace and contact copyright holders but this has not been possible in every case. If notified, the publisher will undertake to rectify any errors or omissions at the earliest opportunity.

Foundations of Human Resource Management

1

The Management of Human Resources

Key Terms

Dialectics The tension that arises between conflicting ideas, interacting forces or competing interests. The term can also be used to explain the process of reconciling opposing opinions or facts by means of argument and discussion.

Learning Objectives

As a result of reading this chapter and using the Online Resource Centre, you should be able to:

- understand the challenges faced by management in using people as human resources;

- understand the implications of changing environments for the way people are managed;

- develop effective strategies for managing tension and conflict at work;

- explain why an underpinning philosophy is a necessary part of effective people management;

- understand why the emotional dimension of work is critical to the effective management of people.

Introduction

Managing people in the twenty-first century

It might seem strange to begin our analysis of the management of human resources in the twenty-first century by looking back in time, but the reason for this is to do with our ability to learn from the past and to use this understanding to help make sense of the challenges facing management today and in the future. Learning about the way in which people have been, and should be, managed involves using our personal experiences of managing and being managed, and, for the more serious student, it also involves accessing the wealth of ideas, theories, stories and research outputs contained in the numerous books and journals devoted to this subject. Not all of these are contemporary, and while many of the most influential were first published many years ago, these are no less important for that.

Despite peoples' interest in understanding what managing organizations and managing people involves, and the ever-increasing amount of information and knowledge available to us, the enduring paradox is that many of today's managers still find the challenge difficult and frustrating. Even where seemingly major breakthroughs in our understanding of management occur (Peters and Waterman, 1982), it soon becomes apparent that many of the successful companies and managers identified by the authors have been unable to sustain their success in the face of rapidly changing environments and the contradictions inherent in employing and managing people.

It is still surprising, however, that, despite this ever-growing knowledge base, many of the problems that troubled earlier generations of managers are, broadly speaking, the same as those facing today's managers. Without claiming that the example below represents the situation in which all managers find themselves, it probably captures the experiences and sentiments of many. The quotation is taken from Tony Watson's influential book on management and the organization of work, and reflects the experiences, sense of frustration and uncertainty articulated by one manager (Watson, 2002). It is an extract from part of a conversation between the author and a manager.

'So the problem is?'

'It's the people management thing. It's handling the people who work for me. They are a constant headache. I've tried to read the books and I've been on people management courses. I didn't miss one of the OB classes on my MBA course. But I still despair at the difficulty I have with managing the people in my function; sorting out who is going to do what, getting them to do things I want, getting them to finish things on time, even getting them to be where I want them. And that's before I get into all the recruiting, training, appraising and all that stuff.'

(p 3)

It is highly probable that this manager's frustrations with his staff and what managing them involved was mirrored by their sense of frustration and dissatisfaction with him as a manager and the way in which he 'practised' management. Of course, there are many other managers who are more confident about what they do and would claim to be 'good at it', pointing to positive feedback from their staff as evidence of their competence and effectiveness. But the real point of the story is that, despite his efforts — and those of others in a similar position — to learn about managing and to become a better manager, he felt that he hadn't succeeded. Why? Was he looking in the wrong place, reading the wrong books or listening to the wrong lecturers? We don't know why he failed to make progress: like so many others, whether they are students, human resources (HR) specialists or line managers, although he was committed to becoming better at managing people, he just didn't seem to have made much progress.

So, where can answers to the question 'how do we manage people' be found? First of all, it is important to realize that this question is more rhetorical than literal. There are no answers as such, at least in the sense of universal and permanent solutions to the kinds of problem this manager and many others face. But if we are realistic and do not expect the search to be an easy or straightforward one, the fact that there are those who have found managing less problematic and, by consensus, are considered to be 'good managers' suggests that there is much we can learn.

What accounts for such variations in the competence of different managers? One explanation might be linked to the possession of different traits and abilities that are more inherent than acquired, and which lead to certain individuals having the potential to be better managers than others. It might also be because they have learnt to be better managers through reflecting on their personal experiences of managing and because of their sensitivity to the effect that their behaviours have on others. Is good people management something that can be learnt, using the right theories, concepts and practices, or is it, like leadership, a capability that (some argue) you are somehow born with?

On the one hand, this may be too simplistic a proposition because it forces us to choose between one extreme and another, and, more realistically, the answer might lie somewhere in between. On the other hand, it does have the virtue of forcing us to consider the merits of both explanations before we reach our own conclusions.

Managing people is not only about the behaviour and approach of individual managers, but also about the way in which organizations, and the team of managers who influence their philosophy and culture, create particular kinds of environments within which both managers and employees work. When people apply for jobs, not only are they interested in the salary, benefits package and development opportunities, but they also want to know: 'What is it like working here?' The *Sunday Times* carries out an annual survey of the best places to work in the UK and the results provide valuable insights into why the top-ranking companies are voted by their employees as the best companies to work for (**www.bestcompanies.com**) What do these organizations know and do that sets them apart from those that are less successful, or those that struggle to get even the basics right? Why is it that, if those organizations who appear to be at least successful in the short term are prepared to publicize their achievements and allow their employees to explain why they are such good places to work, other organizations can't try to emulate them? Or is the problem not one of learning from what others do, but rather one of managers either not liking or agreeing with what they see, or having difficulty in applying the lessons to their own organization that others seem to have learnt so well?

Of course, the difficulties that contemporary managers appear to face in learning the 'secrets' of managerial success might have a completely different explanation. Could it be the case that the very nature of what managing people involves has changed so much and continues to change at such a rapid pace that what can be learnt from the past and from our contemporaries quickly loses its value and relevance? If this explanation has any merit, it means that today's managers are looking in the wrong place and learning the wrong lessons for the constantly evolving challenges they face now and will face in the future. If the factors that contribute to managerial success are contextually specific and time-limited, as opposed to being universal and enduring, then our knowledge about management quickly becomes redundant and even irrelevant. Alternatively, the challenge may not be one of discovering new answers and creating new knowledge, but rather one of making sense of what we already know and beginning to use this knowledge more effectively.

At the moment, we can only speculate on these questions, and we will return to them later in the chapter, but the point we would make is that much of what needs to be known about managing people already exists: we actually know more than we think we do. The real challenge is to know where to look and what to look for (Pfeffer and Sutton, 2000).

STUDENT ACTIVITY 1.1 Researching the *Sunday Times* Top 100 companies

1. Split the seminar group into three groups.

2. The task of group 1 is to research the top ten best big companies to work for and present their findings to the whole group in the form of a PowerPoint presentation.

3. Group 2 has the same task but focusing on the top ten best small companies.

4. The task for group 3 is to research Peters and Waterman's book, *In Search of Excellence* (1982), and summarize its main conclusions regarding the employment and management of people.

5. In open discussion, explore the findings produced by all three groups and draw appropriate inferences and conclusions.

Connecting the past to the present

The idea that the past has an important contribution to make to understanding the challenges contemporary managers face is grounded in the belief that learning about anything is always built upon what is already known, what has already been tried and what has worked, or not, in particular conditions. While the past provides neither neatly packaged answers nor the secrets of good people management (there aren't any, as such), it does offer insights and reference points that help us to make sense of where we are now and to consider whether the challenges managers face now are the same, different in degree, or different in kind, to those faced by earlier generations of managers.

Try to imagine that you are living in the era of the Egyptian Pharaohs and are sitting on the banks of the River Nile watching the Pyramids being built. What would you have seen? Lots of people would have been toiling in rather unpleasant conditions — the temperature would certainly have been quite hot; different kinds of raw materials would have been moving around the site, and the skills and energy of many different kinds of people would have been used to complete the project to specification. You might even have witnessed the odd accident or two, and have noticed groups of people wearing different clothes, walking around and looking important, and generally checking up on things. It's also conceivable that, instead of watching from afar, you might actually have been one of the thousands of workers engaged in building the Pyramids or even the Egyptian equivalent of an employment administrator, with responsibility for ensuring that the workers were fed, housed and paid (interestingly, contemporary opinion suggests that most workers were in some kind of paid employment as opposed to being used as slaves). Depending on your own skills and experience, you might even have been an overseer — the equivalent of a modern-day supervisor — with responsibility for organizing resources and making sure the workers did what was required of them.

If it's difficult to project yourself so far back in time, consider a more recent period — the industrialization of Britain in the nineteenth and twentieth centuries, and specifically the construction of the country's rail and canal networks. Where did all the workers who built these monuments to Victorian Britain come from? How did they learn the skills they needed, and who determined what and how they were paid? When employers today try to overcome labour shortages in, for example, teaching, nursing and plumbing, by recruiting people from abroad, we should remember that many of the Irish 'navvies', who built the railways and canals, were also brought in because of labour and skill shortages in England. In times of economic expansion, many industries face the same kind of resource problems: where to get the necessary labour resources with the right skills; how to get the most out of those resources; what to do with them when projects are completed or the economic cycle moved in a downward direction. Has anything fundamentally changed?

Whether those who managed people in Egypt in the fourth century BC and nineteenth-century Britain had an easier task than that of managers today is an arguable point, although given that the situation of the twenty-first-century employee has improved beyond all recognition in comparison with that of our historical comparators — the modern-day employee benefiting from a 35-hour week, extensive employment rights, and compensation for being treated unfairly — there might be a few contemporary managers who believe that the task has definitely become more difficult and complicated! There may also be some employees who might look back in time and wonder what life would have been like without workplace stress, but long hours, authoritarian management and dangerous working conditions represent equally unattractive features of employment and work.

A tentative conclusion that emerges from these brief references to previous eras might be that, despite differences in organizational form, the power of managers, technology and social relationships, the challenges that managers faced and the experiences of being employed are not fundamentally different today from the experiences of our predecessors. But, while we have suggested that the fundamentals might not have changed much over time (see **www.accel-team.com**), it is also undeniable that the conditions in which people are employed and managed have changed as our economic, political and social systems have evolved and become more sophisticated and employee-orientated. A direct consequence of this is that the task of managing has become more complicated and problematic, in the sense that success, even when achieved, is never complete or permanent. It is also subject to more constraints and pressures than ever before. If managing people, or rather managing people effectively – there is an important distinction between the two – was never easy, it is certainly more complex and challenging for the manager in the twenty-first century.

Today's managers have to ensure that goods and services are provided profitably and efficiently, while maximizing the productivity of their workforce. They have to do this in an arena of rising expectations from all stakeholders, global competition, and an ever-changing balance of rights, duties and responsibilities. But the challenge to management goes beyond this: they also have to ensure that the individuals and teams creating these goods and services work in environments that:

- are rewarding;
- provide opportunities for personal growth and development;
- generate commitment to the organization;
- encourage employees to use their capabilities and potential to the full and in the interests of the organization.

It might be argued, therefore, that those charged with managing have two distinctive, but related, challenges to meet. Firstly, they have to ensure that the interests and objectives of the organization itself are met; secondly, they must understand, and go as far as possible to meet, the legitimate interests and needs of their employees. For the student trying to make sense of whether these two challenges are equally important, it might be worth noting what one successful employer and managing director remarked. In a conversation with one of the authors, William Beckett, head of a small, but successful, plastics manufacturing company in Sheffield commented:

> ...the relationship between these is clear: if I don't ensure that the company remains competitive and survives, then my employees' interests don't matter – there won't be any employees, or managers for that matter, to worry about.

Many other employers (particularly those in the private sector) would probably share this view, but it is also worth noting that one of the most important developments in recent years has been the increasing prominence and importance given to what might be described as the 'people dimension' of management. The reasons for this increasing recognition that 'people matter' are complex and changing, but a consequence, by which managers in earlier times were probably less troubled, is the tension that is created between the interests of the business and those of the people it employs. Squaring the circle, for managers who are part of this dialectic, is becoming increasingly difficult to achieve.

The basic premise of this book is that, however difficult a challenge managing people represents, some managers and some organizations have been more successful than others, who continue to struggle. Why is this? In trying to answer this question, it is worth remembering that, while many organizations claim to be successful, this success is often short-lived and has little to do with developing sustainable people management practices that are effective over the long term. The rise and fall of management 'fads' is also testament to the attraction of 'quick fixes' and easy solutions to requirements and challenges that are anything but superficial and easy to meet. Yet it is possible to identify organizations, as O'Reilly and Pfeffer (2000) have done, which combine profitability and durability through the successful engagement of the emotional and intellectual resources of their people, even though the authors accept that the companies they identify may not be able to sustain their successes forever. What do these companies do that makes them successful and which, at the same time, results in high levels of employee satisfaction? This is the question that this chapter tries to answer.

Today's challenges

Before we move on to consider the nature of the challenge that all managers face, it is important to consider the impact of contemporary changes in work and employment that have helped to shape the internal and external environments within which managers have to operate. The changes outlined below represent distinctive and influential characteristics of the postmodern age of employment.

● **The rise of self employment and the independent worker**

Many more people are 'free' to work or not, depending on their particular circumstances, than ever before. Those who want and choose to work also have more choice with regards to who they work for, the kind of work they do and for how long they are prepared to work. 'Portfolio working' reduces a person's dependency on an individual employer and creates a workforce more able and predisposed to shape its own careers and lifestyles. These people are also able to exercise greater control over levels of 'discretionary effort' and are willing to engage in negotiations over what has become known as the 'psychological contract' (Hiltrop, 1996; Castells, 2000).

KEY CONCEPT Discretionary effort

Effort or performance that is additional to that which the employee is contractually required to deliver. Discretionary effort, by definition, is determined by the individual employee, or by a group of employees, and can represent a significant additional resource if they choose to make this available to management. It can be thought of as the difference between what employees are minimally required to give and what they are capable of giving.

In much of manufacturing and engineering, discretionary effort is associated with additional payments and is only made available if it is paid for, but this can result in higher labour costs and forward-thinking managers seek to access this by exploring alternative strategies, such as involvement and job satisfaction.

KEY CONCEPT The psychological contract

This term is used to describe the unwritten, often unarticulated and not necessarily shared, expectations that exist between employees and managers (as representatives of the organization), which influence the relationship between the two parties and particularly the behaviour of employees (Coyle-Shapiro, 2000).

● **Changes in the external regulation of employment**

The power of managers to act unilaterally in areas such as hiring and firing, promotion and payment has been reduced by developments in UK and European legislation that give greater rights to employees and create new responsibilities for employers. Particularly important examples of this trend are to be found in the areas of race, gender and age discrimination, employment protection, the treatment of pregnant women and trade union membership. One extreme example of the influence of the law on employment decisions can be found in the recent case in which the Swiss giant Nestlé was ordered by a French court to reopen a loss-making plant, employing 427 workers, which had been closed in June 2005 (Evans-Pritchard, 2005). Despite sustained losses over several years, and a commitment either to find the employees jobs in other parts of France or to offer an early retirement package, the judge ordered the company to restart production and re-employ the workers — a decision that was described by Nestlé as 'unbelievable and unprecedented'. While such extreme cases of legal intervention in business and employment are rare, the trend within the European Union to limit management's freedom to take rational business decisions where these threaten the legitimate interests of employees is increasing.

- **The emergence of new ideas and ways of managing associated with inward investment and the spread of 'new knowledge'**

Since the days when much of UK industry was regarded as beyond hope, with industries such as motor manufacturing associated with unreliable products, outdated working practices, a strike-prone workforce and 'macho management', much of the UK's manufacturing sector has been transformed by the influx of new management thinking and practices. Many of these changes can be linked to massive inward investment and the growing influence of Japanese and German companies, which have introduced radically different ideas to the organization of work and the management of employees. The removal of unnecessary and restrictive differences between managers and employees, the harmonization of terms and conditions of employment, the removal of restrictive labour practices, and the emphasis on a new culture of pride and achievement, represent some of the groundbreaking changes that have permeated parts of the manufacturing sector.

Workers who were previously associated with the worst excesses of industrial conflict and inefficiencies have now become the valued employees of some of the most profitable companies in the country. The startling reality is that this transformation has been achieved, with some notable exceptions, with the same labour force (Wickens, 1987).

- **The challenge to, and replacement of, physical power and manual skills by the power of knowledge, creativity and intellectual capital**

The increasing importance of knowledge-based industries and the corresponding rise in the number of knowledge workers is creating a different kind of labour force, which has different requirements and expectations of work, and different expectations of how it will be managed. The fact that, in 2005, London's financial heartland was responsible for nearly one third of the UK's economic output, in comparison with 25 per cent in 1995, shows how important such industries as finance, banking, insurance, consulting and other parts of the services sector have become. With this growth has come a new kind of employee – the 'knowledge worker' (Swart, Kinnie and Purcell, 2003). Knowledge workers can be seen to be different from other professional groups because, unlike those who draw upon a distinctive body of knowledge and work from this, the knowledge worker works *with* knowledge – not only their own, but that generated and used by others – generated through such mechanisms as 'communities of practice' and professional networks. The implications of knowledge-based work and the growing numbers of knowledge workers for the way people are managed extend to:

- the need to align rewards more sensitively with the motivational characteristics of this kind of employee;
- the nature of supervision and what managing the knowledge worker actually involves;
- the intrinsic importance of work;
- work–life balance issues.

  (Scarborough and Carter, 2000)

- **A diversified labour force**

'Globalization' isn't something that only represents what is happening to 'the world outside'. It also expresses the growing richness and diversity that exists within UK organizations, particularly in relation to the workforce. Similarly, 'multiculturalism' is not simply a description of a new society, but of a culturally diverse workplace. New migration patterns are adding to the demographic mix from which the labour force is drawn; labour market activity rates are increasing among ethnic minorities, and increasing numbers of female and older workers have become economically active. These developments are affecting the need for different employment and working arrangements, with flexible and varied contracts, home working and career breaks becoming well established in certain sectors of the economy.

One of the implications for HR arising from these developments is that a 'one size fits all' approach to rewards, training, communications and performance management is increasingly unsustainable. Flexibility has been one of the central themes of employment and employee behaviour over the past twenty years, and it is now becoming increasingly significant for the practice of HR (Bishop, 2004).

STUDENT ACTIVITY 1.2

Why are some organizations and certain managers more successful in the way they manage their employees than are others? From a learning perspective, knowing what explains relative failure can be as important as identifying the causes of success.

1. Think of an organization to which most group members can relate, and which might be considered to have a good reputation for managing people.

2. List the characteristics of this organization in terms of its human resource practices.

3. On a separate sheet, list the practices and behaviours of a manager who stands out as being effective in the way s/he manages. You may even want to organize both lists in terms of the priority or importance of each point.

4. Repeat the exercise, but this time choosing organizations and managers known (or thought) to be less effective and successful in their approach to managing people.

5. Discuss your findings and draw conclusions.

Fundamental management objectives

The changes affecting the legal regulation of employment, the nature of work and the influence of new ideas about management have undoubtedly transformed the environment within which organizations function and people are employed. But, as was pointed out earlier, the era in which we currently live and work in is not unique in terms of the volume of changes to which managers have had to respond. The particular nature of the changes might be different, or its intensity greater, but managers in previous periods have had to respond to equally difficult challenges and pressures. The 1960s and 1970s saw a rapid increase in the unionization of the workforce and a growth in the frequency and intensity of industrial conflict. The dominant influence of large-scale bureaucratic organizations and mass production techniques created particular types of working environment that influenced management thinking and practice. It can also be argued that the second half of the twentieth century saw the development of the knowledge worker, even though they might not always have been described in these terms. But the crucial question is not that which focuses on the differences in environments, work and workers — these are more appropriately seen as differences of degree than of kind; rather, the question is that which asks us to consider whether the fundamental nature of what managing people involves has changed.

Accepting that the context within which people are employed and managed has changed and will continue to change does not prevent us from attempting to distinguish the underlying objectives that are common to managing people in all productive enterprise, irrespective of size, sector and era. We also need to know how managers try to meet and deliver these objectives. In other words, we are suggesting that there are a number of fundamental and enduring objectives that are common to all organizations (*ends*), which are distinguishable from the way in which these ends are achieved (*means*). These fundamental objectives may change in importance and may impact differently on individual organizations, but it is difficult to argue that they are not universally relevant, or that they have not been at the core of what all managers need to achieve, irrespective of the era in which they operate.

● Ensuring that the supply of labour is in line with demand

Organizations could not begin to generate wealth through the production of goods and services without the necessary numbers and mix of people to engage in productive activities. The key challenges here are to do with ensuring that management is able to deliver the required quantity and quality of people in environments that are dynamic and often unpredictable. It is also critical that managers respond to changes in supply and demand as quickly as possible, so that the organization reduces to a minimum the period over which it experiences an excess or a shortage of labour. Over the long term, organizations generally need fewer people as managers develop more efficient working practices, rationalize or re-engineer production, or, as is becoming increasingly prevalent, outsource production. In such situations, demand for labour falls or is displaced, and the pressure on HR practitioners is to develop labour reduction strategies that bring supply back in line with demand with the minimum of disruption and conflict. In other circumstances, under which organizations are experiencing growth and expansion, the need to increase the supply of labour (not to be confused with increasing the number of employees) emphasizes effective supply management strategies, but restrictive and 'tight' labour markets may limit the supply and quality of labour available to organizations.

In addition, the ability to treat people as 'commodities' — i.e. as factors of production — and to hire and fire as economic conditions change has been limited by legislation, which gives employees increased security of employment and the right not to be unfairly dismissed. Trade unions, where they exist, are also likely to see the preservation of jobs and employment as one of their key objectives. These constraints on management's freedom of action may, but will not necessarily, affect the ability of organizations to maintain a perfect balance between labour supply and demand. Being quick to shed labour when demand falls can involve long-term reputational cost; operating with excessive labour brings with it significant financial cost.

> **Signpost to Chapter 9: HR Planning and Measurement**, which provides detailed explanation of supply and demand strategies

● Utilization

Once acquired, people have to be 'used' — they need to engage in productive activities. An enduring objective for management is the need to 'squeeze' more from any given resource. This search for greater productivity is, in part, responsible for disturbing the equilibrium and stability of workplace relationships as managers react to financial or competitive pressures not only by cutting the number of people employed, but by trying to get those that are left to do *more*, through, for, example, using existing, but underutilized, capabilities or through creating more functional flexibility. The distinction between people *being at* work and what they *do* at work is vital to management's ability to reduce non-productive time and increase labour utilization; employing people and getting them to be at work is a challenge in itself, but so too is the management of their contribution and the extent to which they add value.

KEY CONCEPT Functional flexibility

This is a term used to describe the range and depth of knowledge and skills that someone possesses, which means that they are multi-skilled and can do a range of different tasks related to a particular job or job family (Atkinson, 1984).

> **Signpost to Chapter 11: Managing Performance**, for details of how managers seek to increase employee utilization levels

● Maintenance and development

Using a garden metaphor, managers are also tasked with 'growing' the human resource. People have to be nurtured and developed so that, through becoming more, they can give more, but it does not automatically follow that, if peoples' capabilities are extended, they will necessarily use these in ways that support managerial and organizational interests. If skill levels are low and supply exceeds demand, maintaining and developing the workforce is often less important than utilizing it, but simply consuming labour resources without any regard for their regeneration is both short-sighted and of limited effectiveness. Maintaining the labour force involves ensuring that employees' physical and psychological health is catered for: a sick and stressed employee is unlikely to be a productive one!

● Order and control

One of the inherent disadvantages in employing people as opposed to robots is that people have the capacity to resist what managers want them to do. They can be uncooperative and can resist change, and, if they believe managers have acted wrongly or unfairly, they can take what is euphemistically called 'industrial action'. This means that employees can attempt to challenge 'management's right to manage' through the application of a range of sanctions, such as strikes, go-slows and even sabotage, in an attempt to force management to make concessions or to concede to employee demands. The systematic questioning of managerial authority, of seeking to mobilize power through collective action, imposing costs on the organization by leaving, reducing performance levels and generally acting against the interests of the organization reflect a loss of management control and represent break-downs in workplace relationships. The objective for managers is, therefore, to develop strategies that prevent or limit the ability of employees, either individually or collectively, to engage in practices that challenge management's authority and control, and/or to eliminate the need for such action.

● Generating commitment

Employees who are 'committed' identify with their job, their manager and with the organization they work for, and demonstrate this commitment through expressions of loyalty, higher levels of discretionary effort and a predisposition to stay rather than to leave. Highly committed employees have a qualitatively different relationship with the organization than that of those who are less, or un-, committed: the organization becomes much more than a place of work. Commitment is important to managers because it usually means that employees can be trusted to act in the interests of the organization and rarely need to be subject to forms of extrinsic motivation. The level of commitment, characterized as a quality of the relationship between those employed and those representing the employing organization, changes over time and is thought to be closely related to the nature of the psychological contract (Shepherd and Mathews, 2000).

While managers value a committed labour force, the dynamic nature of the conditions of employment and work means that any given level of commitment is always problematic: it is not a permanent characteristic of a relationship and cannot be taken for granted; it cannot easily be bought, but rather emerges over time from employees' experiences of working and their treatment as employees and human beings.

One final point to note about these objectives is that they are not wholly compatible with each other and relative success in one might prove to be at the expense of relative failure in another. For example, competitive pressures that push businesses to reduce labour costs and increase levels of utilization, even if successful, are likely to result in an increased challenge to management's authority and a weakening of commitment levels as employees reassess their relationship with the organization. To use an expression from the theory of negotiation, successful managers are those who are able to avoid 'win–lose' situations and instead generate 'win–win' outcomes, although the latter can never be guaranteed.

Employee objectives of being managed

One of the distinctive features of this book is the adoption of an employee perspective on employment and management rather than one that exclusively reflects the interests of the dominant stakeholder. There is a good reason for this: the more managers can, metaphorically, inhabit the world of their employees, the greater the likelihood that they will have a more informed and useful understanding of where those employees 'are coming from', i.e. the forces that drive their behaviour. This is not about knowing what employees want and giving it to them, but about being sensitive to their motivations, interests and concerns, and (in so far as it is possible) incorporating these into the decision-making process.

With this in mind, what are employees looking for from their engagement with organizations and their managers? Although it is not claimed to be exclusive, the following list seems to be particularly important.

- **To be treated as a human being: to be known and to be part of something**

    It might be considered to be stating the obvious, but the reality for many employees is that their essential human nature is insufficiently recognized by their managers, who often give the impression that the employee is little more than a number and a factor in production, rather than a complex individual. Years ago, in many manual occupations, vacancy boards would feature the words 'hands wanted' – an expression that highlights the more subconscious attempt to dehumanize work and employment. Even today, particularly in large bureaucratic organizations, the sense of being unknown to all but your immediate colleagues, and of being seen more as a cost, an asset or a resource than a person, can be the defining experience of employment and work. In his seminal work, *The Abilene Paradox*, Jerry Harvey (1996) talks about the fear that people have of being alone, isolated and alienated, arguing that people have:

    > **. . . a fundamental need to be connected, engaged and related and a reciprocal need not to be separated or alone.**

    Understanding this basic human requirement is at least the first step towards creating a working environment that connects the individual to his or her work and to other employees, and avoids the development of a sense of isolation and separation. (More will be said about this later.)

- **To be valued as an employee and to be allowed to work in a secure and safe working environment**

    For many people, their sense of self-worth and self-respect is determined within the workplace. The loss of job and employment is often associated with a loss of self-respect and this can have serious long-term consequences for an individual's psychological health. Even within employment, the failure to recognize the value of an individual's contribution and performance, or its denial, can be equally damaging. People 'are' what they do and achieve, and to deny the opportunity to be valued by others is, for many, a serious and unacceptable condition. Irrespective of their economic value to the organization, most people need to be valued, and this doesn't necessarily mean being highly paid.

    Understanding the importance of this requirement is closely related to the idea that the working environment should be safe and should offer security to the employee, as well as being a place of productive activity. Historically, it was the physical environment that was of concern to enlightened employers, social reformers and legislators, but today the psychological environment is seen as equally important to the employee's well being. Consider the growth in stress-related illnesses and absence. Might these be related to people feeling that they are not valued or that their work is unrecognized? It is not unreasonable to think that the two are in some way connected.

→ Signpost to Chapter 7: Managing Health and Safety, for details on a safe working environment

---

- **To be allowed to grow and develop as an employee**

    The human condition, whether we are aware of it or want it, requires that we evolve and grow into something more than we were at the beginning of our lives; we do not stop this process of becoming more than we were when we reach adulthood. To suppress this inherent force is to deny what is a necessary requirement for a psychologically healthy and well-adjusted human being. Concepts such as continuous and lifelong learning not only reflect the interests of governments and employers for a skilled and flexible workforce, but also express the importance of new challenges and experiences that provide pathways to personal and professional development.

This requirement is increasingly seen in the behaviour of new graduates, who see opportunities for development as one of the key considerations in taking a particular job. Unfortunately, the fact that expectations in this area are not always met is often associated with low retention rates, with many of those who leave within 12 months of joining a company citing lack of training and development opportunities as the main reason. It would be naive to argue that this objective is equally important to all employees, and anecdotal evidence suggests that many people only come to work *to work* and are not interested in responsibility or development. But even though this may be the case, the discovery of the value and liberating effects of learning has been known to change the attitude of even the most sceptical employee (Megginson et al, 1999).

- **To be paid and rewarded fairly**

  People work for different reasons, and it is too simplistic and unhelpful to present the motivation to work only in terms of material rewards. Clearly, people do not work only to earn money, but, for the vast majority of those who are either employed or self-employed, work does represent a source of income and other benefits that help to determine a person's standard of living and social status. To deny this fact would be to understate the relationship between work and valued material rewards. What is more difficult to establish, however, is the precise value that people place on different types of reward, and how the experience of receiving and not receiving rewards of which they had reasonable expectation impacts on their behaviour. To be paid fairly in relation to the job and in relation to what others are paid has long been held to be one of the principles of trade unionism, and most employees have expectations of being treated and rewarded fairly. 'A fair day's pay for a fair day's work' is an aphorism that, even today, resonates with most people. Unfortunately, what constitutes fair pay is both subjective and problematic, and disputes over the unfairness and unacceptability of pay levels and pay increases continue to be a major cause of industrial disputes.

 Signpost to Chapter 12: Managing Rewards, for a review of the importance of different kinds of rewards

The relationship between managerial and employee objectives

The significance of comparing managerial and employee interests and objectives lies in the relationship between the two. Consider the following scenarios.

1. In all cases, the two sets of objectives are incompatible and mutually exclusive. For example, the managerial need to reduce the labour force in conditions of falling demand or increasing labour costs will be difficult to reconcile with the employee's need for employment security and a fair wage/salary. The managerial objective of increasing labour efficiency and productivity sits uneasily with the employee's need to limit work intensification and disruptive changes in the working environment. This juxtaposition of positions suggests deeply rooted differences, and a constant struggle between employees and managers over the primacy and legitimacy of their respective objectives.

2. There is a considerable degree of overlap between the two sets of objectives, and, while there is the potential for tension and disagreement, the opportunities for accommodation and compromise are clear and attainable. For example, the employee requirement for personal growth and development seems to be consistent with managerial needs to increase employee utilization and for a flexible workforce. But such an accommodation may, realistically, need to be understood as fragile, provisional and subject to temporary breakdown. Conflict may not be endemic and inevitable, but it is likely to feature at some time in the relationship between the two parties, and does require effective management to avoid it becoming destabilizing.

3. Organizations have the capacity to deliver both sets of objectives to the respective parties, although not on a permanent basis and not in all circumstances. The commitment made by some employers to provide a high level of employment, as opposed to job security and for as long as trading conditions allow this, in exchange for flexibility suggests that through working together a much longer term accommodation might be possible. Even when labour reductions may become necessary, how these are carried out and the terms associated with job losses may still be compatible with a mutual commitment to support, as far as is possible, the interests and objectives of both parties. This position suggests that any differences between the interests of capital and labour are superficial, and can easily be dealt with by appropriate managerial practices. Conflict, if it does occur, can then be interpreted in terms of unreasonable and irrational behaviour or the commitment by a minority to an outdated and discredited political ideology.

Signpost to Chapter 4: Managing Employee Relations, for a detailed analysis of industrial conflict

---

STUDENT ACTIVITY 1.3

Consider your own experience, and the experiences of work and employment of other people you know or can talk to.

1. Establish whether the evidence collected supports any one of the above three propositions.
2. Research the data on industrial conflict, and establish whether its major causes have changed and what the significance of these changes might be for management.

(Beardsmore, 2004)

The fact that conflict is still generated at work, even though its frequency and intensity may have changed in recent years, might suggest that there are enduring tensions, more often latent rather than manifest, between employers and employees, and that these tensions do, in fact, reflect important differences in the respective interests and objectives of the two parties. The rise of the Marxist School of Industrial Relations in the 1970s, led by such writers as Richard Hyman (1975), lent credence to the idea that, because of the nature of class-based and exploitative relations within the economic system, the parties would recognize and pursue separate and opposing interests. Hyman himself pointed out, however, that cooperation, a desire to reach a compromise and accommodation between managers and employees also characterized industrial relations because, despite the existence of ideological and material differences, the two parties had a vested interest in working together to ensure that the interests of both parties were maximized.

What emerged, however ideologically inconvenient for some, was a sense that relationships and behaviour based on a recognition that mutual dependency (*win–win*) rather than adversarial independence (*win–lose*) was the only sensible long-term strategy that served the interests of both parties.

In trying to make sense of the underlying dynamics that influence the way in which employment relationships evolve, the position adopted here is that outbreaks of conflictual behaviour — whether formal or informal, or collective or individual — can be viewed as 'abnormal' and atypical. Most employees and managers would probably see breakdowns in relationships as relatively infrequent experiences and, as such, it can be argued that most of the main stakeholders see employees and managers *working together* rather than working against each other as the normal and preferred state. This is the position taken in this book. It is recognized, however, that sustaining this feature of the employment relationship depends on factors that are often outside the control of both parties and changes, particularly in the economic environment, can result in severe strains on the stability of this relationship.

Deconstructing human resource management

Before we can begin fully to understand the challenges facing the HR professional and line managers, it is necessary to look more carefully at the component parts of human resource management and to consider each element separately. Human resource management is not simply a label, an approach to managing people, or a convenient abbreviation. It actually represents something far more complex, the understanding of which is profoundly important to those with managerial responsibilities. We need to extend our understanding beyond the superficial and ask the question: 'What does "human resource management" actually mean'?

Employees as human beings

Peoples' objectives of work and employment have been briefly touched upon earlier; it is now necessary to explore the nature of what 'being human' means in ways that help to explain how and why, in their role as employees, people behave in the ways that they do. A useful starting point is to examine the assumptions made about people that are used, often unconsciously, to help managers make sense of what managing people involves. Perhaps the most well-known contribution to our understanding of the attitudes and behaviours of employees comes from the work of Douglas McGregor (1960). McGregor presented a dichotomy of the assumptions made about people, which he labelled 'Theory X' and 'Theory Y'.

Theory X assumptions are based on a belief that:

- the average human being has an inherent dislike of work and will avoid it if he/she can;
- because of their dislike of work, most people cannot be trusted to do a good job, and therefore need to be controlled and closely supervised;
- people generally prefer to be directed, dislike taking on responsibility, will not change much beyond what they already are and desire a high level of security.

As a result of these assumptions, under Theory X, managers need to develop working environments and organizational controls that reflect the unreliable and problematic nature of their employees.

Theory Y assumptions, on the other hand, are based on a different view of people and the way in which they are likely to behave at work. They reflect a view that:

- people enjoy work as a natural and necessary part of the human experience;
- tight control and the use of punishments are not the only, or most effective ways to make people work;
- employees are capable of self-motivation and self-direction, and can, under certain circumstances, show a high level of commitment to management and the organization for which they work;
- the average person is capable of learning and changing, and will be prepared, under certain circumstances, to take and exercise responsibility for his/her and others' actions.

The conclusion reached by McGregor is that, because of the existence of Theory X-based management practices, which he argues are based on a simplistic and partial understanding of people at work, there is a significant gap between what people are doing and giving at work, and what they are capable of. This is a point taken up by O'Reilly and Pfeffer (2000), who argue that, because of Theory X assumptions or the inability and reluctance to create environments that reflect a Theory Y view of their workers, many organizations are failing to unlock the hidden value and potential that their employees offer. They claim that:

> . . . this 'hidden value' is not scarce or unique, but rather can be found in all companies. It resides in the intellectual and emotional capital of the firm and is in the minds and hearts of its people. Although organisations we describe have used this potential, to achieve great success, most companies squander this resource even as they bemoan its scarcity.
>
> (p 8)

The significance of this argument can hardly be overstated: it is quite simply that there is, in most organizations, a productive potential that managers are failing to access and utilize because they base their approach to management on mistaken assumptions about the nature of employee motivation. Moreover, because of the assumption that most people fit McGregor's 'Theory X' description, management practice based on this belief also becomes a self-fulfilling hypothesis: employees treated as if they are 'Theory X people' will conform to the stereotype.

McGregor's emphasis on the human side of work is part of a long tradition of managing thinking linked to the Human Relations Movement. With its origins in the famous Hawthorne Studies, carried out at the Western Electric Hawthorne Works in Chicago between 1924 and 1927, this movement emphasized the importance of understanding the social and psychological dimensions of employee behaviour. Arising from the work of people such as Elton Mayo (2001), a set of beliefs emerged that transformed our understanding about work and what people expect from it:

- work is a social activity involving people working together in groups and teams;
- the need for security, sense of belonging and recognition is more important for morale and performance than the physical working environment;
- an employee is a person whose attitudes and effectiveness are conditioned by social expectations that exist both within and outside the place of work;
- when employees complain, the complaint may have some basis in fact, but can also be seen as a symptom that reflects changes in their status or sense of self-worth.

The so-called 'Hawthorne Effect', which is arguably as relevant today as it was when it was first used, suggests that treating employees as human beings — showing that management has an interest in them and cares about them — will, under most conditions, result in behaviour that is associated with higher levels of production and performance than would have been generated had management failed to demonstrate this concern and consideration. It can be argued, therefore, that the Hawthorne Effect is a consequence of applying Theory Y assumptions to the management of people, and can be seen as representing further evidence to support the belief of Pfeffer and Sutton (2000) that many organizations are failing to access and utilize employee potential (see **www.accel-team.com**).

William Ouchi's contribution to the debate about how underlying assumptions influence the way in which managers manage people is found in what he terms 'Theory Z' (Ouchi, 1981). In his work, Ouchi takes as his starting point the need to adopt a Theory Y perspective, arguing that workers:

- are capable of demonstrating a strong sense of loyalty;
- will respond positively to working in teams because they are social animals;
- if trusted to work in a demanding, but not coercive, environment, can and will reflect the interests of the organization, as well as their own.

Ouchi's description of the management practices that flow from this conceptualization reflect what can be described as modern Japanese management, which emphasizes:

- personal responsibility and accountability;
- collaborative working;
- devolved decision making;
- harmonized working conditions.

The debate about whether Theory X or Y accurately reflects the nature of people as employees is often presented in terms of whether people correspond to one or the other sets of characteristics. This is both unhelpful and simplistic. It seems to us much more useful to accept the fact that people have the capacity to be both, and that whether they display the negative characteristics of a Theory X employee or become a more valued and desirable Theory Y employee is driven by their experiences at work, particularly those that relate to how their managers treat them, and the extent to which they see this treatment as reflecting a genuine concern with their social and psychological needs. Whether managers are dealing with Theory X or Theory Y people is not, therefore, a function of any inherent and deep-rooted differences between people, but rather reflects their experiences of being managed and the environment in which they live and work. Put simply, many (although not all) employees behave as Theory X predicts, but do so because of their experiences of work and of being managed in particular ways. It follows, therefore, that these people could become Theory Y employees if the way in which work is organized and the way in which managers control them reflects a different set of assumptions about people and their motivations.

HRM INSIGHT 1.1 **The Men's Warehouse**

This case study is based on ch 4 of O'Reilly and Pfeffer's book, *Hidden Value* (2000). It has been chosen because it represents an example of an unfashionable company that achieved success through its distinctive people-orientated business philosophy and, through this, was able to access the full potential of its employees.

The Men's Warehouse is an American clothing retail business founded by George Zimmer in 1973. In a market that faced little or no growth, the company achieved a five-year annual growth rate of 26 per cent in revenues and 29 per cent in net income between 1995 and 1999, a period during which other retail clothing chains closed stores or suffered financial hardship. Why was The Men's Warehouse so successful?

A significant part of the answer can be found in its founder's underpinning humanistic philosophy, which is expressed in the following statement (found on p 86):

Our mission . . . is to maximise sales, provide value to our customers, and give quality customer service while still having fun and maintaining our values. These values include nurturing creativity, growing together, admitting to our mistakes, promoting a happy, healthy lifestyle, enhancing our sense of community and striving to become self-actualised people.

O'Reilley and Pfeffer accept that this people philosophy and the need to develop them to be the best they can be is at odds with the prevailing view held by other American retailers and most other industrial companies. It is a philosophy and an approach to managing people that would be difficult to copy, but it is an approach that has worked for this company. In trying to tease out the lessons that can be taken from the case study, O'Reilly and Pfeffer make one powerful statement: in an industry that is not known for the quality of its employees or management concern with their interests, The Men's Warehouse stands out precisely because it didn't treat its people badly! They claim (on p 97) that:

By exceeding peoples' expectations concerning the chances they will be given, the dignity and respect with which they will treated, and the opportunities they will have, the company builds an incredible sense of loyalty and commitment. Doing the unexpected — doing more than is expected — earns the company extraordinary performance from its people. If there is a lesson here, it is the power of treating everyone as if they are important and matter.

Questions

1. Why might this philosophy of managing people be so difficult to copy in other companies?

2. In the light of this philosophy, what do you think the company's approaches to training and compensation are?

3. What is the company's recruitment and selection strategy likely to be? What will it be looking for in new employees?

People, pain and toxicity

A more recent contribution to our understanding of employees as people and of their behaviour at work comes from Peter J Frost (2003) and his pioneering study of the emotional dimension of work. Frost accepts that what he describes as 'toxicity' or emotional pain is a normal by-product of organizational life and that the generation of emotional pain is an inevitable part of 'doing business'. He argues that 'normal' levels of toxicity rarely cause long-term damage because of workers' coping strategies, such as the abilities to rationalize, to empathize with each other and to engage in pressure-releasing behaviours, which, together with the positive effects of 'toxin handlers' means that, more often than not, there is an acceptable level of emotional pain that is time-constrained and is 'fixable'. According to Frost, emotional pain itself is not toxic: what determines whether its long-term effects are positive or negative is how the pain is handled.

In a comment echoing the belief expressed by Harvey (1996), Frost, after recounting a story of an employee who had experienced what she considered to be a lack of understanding and compassion from her manager during a difficult period in her life, talks about how unfeeling responses can:

> ... undermine peoples' confidence, esteem, dignity and sense of connection to others. It disconnects them from the capacity to respond competently to their painful situation.
> (Frost, 2003, p 18)

We would argue that the need to be 'connected', and the importance of a person feeling his or her self to be 'part of something' and valued, is fundamental to what being human means. Many employees are motivated to avoid the psychological damaging effects of excessive work-related pressure and the effects of 'organizational toxicity', although we accept that individuals vary in relation to their ability to cope with such pressure and 'toxins'.

While the concepts of organizational toxins and emotional pain are relatively new, the same cannot be said for their consequence – stress. While it is undoubtedly the case that certain people seem to prosper in stressful working environments (although for how long is more problematic), and that a certain level of pressure is both necessary and stimulating, stress, when it reaches levels at which people find it difficult to cope, becomes dysfunctional and damaging.

According to the Stress Management Society (**www.stress.org.uk**):

- stress affects one in five of the working population;
- it is now the single biggest cause of sickness absence in the UK;
- it costs UK industry £3.7bn each year.

(See Stress Management Society web page 'Stress at work'.)

If these statistics are to be believed, a concern with the human consequences of stress and emotional pain, and action to alleviate this, is not only consistent with an organization recognizing its responsibilities to its employees as people, but will also have a beneficial effect on the well being of the organization.

STUDENT ACTIVITY 1.4 Toxic environments

Research and discuss the following questions.

1. How can the place at which people work be capable of 'poisoning' them?
2. What are the toxins that are generated at work and how do they affect employees?
3. What is the role of 'toxin handlers', and how do they work to reduce the impact of toxic environments and emotional pain?
4. What are the main causes of work-related stress?

People as a resource

From an economic and business perspective, rather than employees being seen as people, people are seen as employees or workers. Employees represent an input to the productive process; they are seen as an economic resource. People are employed not because of employer altruism or because they deserve a job, but because they possess valued physical and intellectual capabilities that are needed in the production of goods and services. People, as employees become, in one sense, commodities; i.e. they have a value that expresses their importance to the productive process, which is reflected in the fact that they have a job and are given a wage or salary. When their economic value as productive resources falls, they may well lose their jobs or experience pressure for wage/salary reductions.

As a commodity, people have no rights as such, although, as human beings in employment, they enjoy varying degrees of protection from the ability or desire of managers to treat them as a commodity. But even these rights do not prevent managers from terminating the employment contract for reasons to do with changes in the need for, or value of, an individual. As the demand for the goods and services falls, or the costs of production become excessive, then the rationale for employing people is removed or is displaced from one location to another.

The current trend towards outsourcing the production of goods and services from the UK and other Western countries to the Far East reflects the economically rational decision of companies to move from employing high-cost workers to employing — at lower cost — workers abroad, who may even be more compliant. These economic forces and business imperatives may take time to work through and affect the demand for labour in the UK, and managers may be constrained in how quickly they can respond to them, but only in the most protected of environments can they be ignored for long. However much we want to be treated as people, this underlying dynamic means that we are also a useable and disposable factor of production.

This acceptance that each individual has an economic value commensurate with his or her capabilities partly explains why some people are paid more than others. But does this also mean that some people are more important than others, and does it justify managers treating some differently and more favourably than others whose value to the organization is less obvious? From an economic perspective, the answer must be 'yes'. While we, as employees, all share the same or similar requirements to be treated as human beings, as an economic resource and providers of productive inputs, we do have different values to the organization because the value of our contributions differs. This is an important point because it provides a rationale for the application of *differentiated employment policies*, under which certain groups or individuals are treated differently with regard to rewards, training and development opportunities, and promotion.

Although not well developed in the UK, the emphasis on the quantitative and financial aspects of employment, under which costs and asset values become key employment criteria, is very much part of mainstream HRM in the USA and is recognized as an academic discipline in its own right, with the titles of 'human resource accounting' and 'personnel economics' (Fitz-Enz, 1990; 2000).

People as assets

The interest in, but difficulty with, 'seeing' people as commodities and treating them in the same way as other tangible assets is that they do not fit the strict definition of an 'asset'. According to Mayo (2001), employees have to be seen as intangible assets because:

- they cannot be transacted — i.e. bought and sold at will;
- their contribution is individual and variable;
- they cannot be valued according to traditional financial principles.

The inability, or reluctance, of many organizations to value their 'human assets' can, however, have important consequences. Firstly, managers who are unable to estimate or calculate an individual's worth or value to the organization are also unable to develop HR practices that reflect these differences in employee performance and contribution. This effectively inhibits the development of an individual or of a differentiated approach to the management of people, with the implication that the 'one size fits all' mind-set will continue to be adopted, almost on a default basis. Secondly, returns on investments in training and development will be difficult to calculate because of managerial inability to measure any changes in employee value, through increased competency, that might follow from such an investment.

The re-emergence of this interest in the economic value of people as resources and assets, through the growth in what has been described as the 'expense model' of human resource accounting (Fitz-Enz, 2000; Mayo, 2001), confirms the importance to organizations of finding ways of allocating financial value to employees' asset value, and of being able to calculate the value of employing people through the systematic measurement and evaluation of their costs and the value of their contributions. This is by no means an easy task, but it is nevertheless one that is seen as increasingly important if HR is to engage with, and support, an organization's economic and financial agenda.

The enduring paradox that managers struggle to resolve and which is fundamental to understanding the challenge they face is that employees are both people, with human requirements and sensitivities, *and* economic resources, with differentiated and changing asset values. This dilemma, faced by successive generations of managers, is perfectly captured by Henry Ford, who once asked why he always had to deal with the whole person when he had only hired a 'pair of hands':

Hands were what he hired, but troublesome bodies with querulous minds were what he so often got.
(Clegg et al, 2005, p 56)

Management

Countless books and articles have been written on, and about, management, to the point at which it can be difficult to identify and to make sense of the myriad of different approaches and traditions. Our advice is that you select a number of authors, whose work is recognized as distinctive, insightful and original, and become familiar with their ideas and contributions. We have been particularly influenced by such people as Peter Drucker, Tony J Watson, David Ulrich, Jeffrey Pfeffer and Henry Mintzberg in recent years, but earlier works by Weber, Barnard, Elton Mayo (see references at end of ch 1 in Hannagan (2002)) and McGregor also stand out for their distinctive contributions to our understanding of how organizations function and how people are, and should be, managed. Consistent with our view that students need to take control of their own learning and development, it is recommended that you agree a personal 'contract' to engage with some of this literature, and to reflect on its relevance and value to your own understanding of what management is about.

As a starting point, consider our earlier references to the building of the Pyramids in Egypt, and of England's canals and railways. Would 'managers' have been found there, doing the same kind of things that today's managers do? Even though the word 'manager' may not have been used, the functions that are generally associated with management — directing and controlling resources — would almost certainly have been understood. As a function, defined as 'what needs to be done' or the 'nature of the contribution required to achieve stated objectives', management, despite its complexities and different traditions, can be understood as being about:

- clarifying objectives;
- planning and organizing;
- directing and controlling.

According to Clegg et al (2005), this functional and rational approach to management, associated with such people as FW Taylor, Henri Fayol and Henry Ford, not only identifies key management activities and responsibilities, but also explicitly excludes employees from any meaningful part of what management does. Organizations based on hierarchy, centralized decision making and a belief that employees were incapable of anything more than following orders produced managers and an approach to management that is associated with Scientific Management and Fordism, significant elements of which are still influential today.

KEY CONCEPT Scientific Management

Scientific Management is sometimes called 'Taylorism' after the American employer and writer, Frederick Winslow Taylor, with whom it is closely associated. This theory of management involves the application of precise procedures and approaches to the management and control of work and workers, in contrast to the use of tradition and 'rule-of-thumb' decision making. Scientific Management seeks to provide a 'one best way' approach to improving labour productivity.

KEY CONCEPT Fordism

Fordism was the dominant method of production over the last century and is associated with mass production techniques, extreme forms of the division of labour, and assembly line techniques, reflecting a Taylorist (i.e. Scientific Management) approach to the control of work.

But this historical emphasis on functionality and rationality needs to be put into a more contemporary context, in which:

- as change and increasing complexity become the norm for those organizations exposed to competition and a dynamic external environment, these core functions may, in themselves, be insufficient to deliver all of the required outcomes, and so new management activities may emerge (e.g. the need to communicate, to consult and to motivate);

- because these functions are essentially technical in nature – they demand specialist knowledge and skills to carry them out to the required standard – who carries them out, i.e. who is seen to or can act managerially, becomes a question of competency rather than of hierarchical position. This conception of management, reflected in the concept of 'empowerment', means that, as the workforce becomes better educated and technically equipped to manage, there is less need for people in formally designated management positions. Such a realization is associated with the notion of self-management, self-direction and self-control;

- challenges emanating from postmodernists raise questions about the effectiveness of traditional approaches to management in delivering sustained economic success in the context of rapidly changing environments. One of the important outcomes of this debate has been the realization that understanding what management involves requires us to accept not one, but several different types of rationality.

What these points actually mean is that the 'old' ideas that management is the province of only those with managerial responsibilities, that it is only done 'to people', and that employees can easily be organized, directed and controlled, while still retaining some support, are not the only ways of understanding what management involves. For those with responsibility for managing organizations, it is important to consider the limitations of the first conceptualization and also the implications of the second.

As an example of this more 'unconventional' thinking, Cloke and Goldsmith (quoted in Mullins, 2005, p 235) claim that '*managers are the dinosaurs of our modern organizational ecology*' and that '*the age of management is ending'*. They base their argument on the rapid advances in information technology and knowledge growth, increased environmental influences and the continuing search for improvements in productivity, which are forcing organizational leaders to find alternative and more effective ways of controlling activities and regulating behaviour. They believe that organizations which do not understand the need to respond to these dynamic forces, and to share decision-making power and responsibility with their employees, will lose those employees; they also believe that the biggest changes in the history of management are the decline of hierarchy and bureaucracy, autocratic management, and the expansion of collaborative self-management and organizational democracy (see Mullins, 2005, p 215).

In his influential books, *In Search of Management* (2001) and *Organising and Managing Work* (2002), Tony Watson reaches similar conclusions to those of Cloke and Goldsmith, but by a different route. In the first chapter of his ethnographical study of a manufacturing company, Watson offers a powerful and persuasive analysis of the meaning and practice of management that is derived from his own observations, from discussions with managers in the company and from his own theoretical insights. One of his more interesting conclusions is that, however much conventional thinking about management is based on the belief that what needs to be managed can, in some mysterious way, be completely captured and appropriated from the working environment and packaged into management jobs, this belief is a fiction.

Support for many of the conclusions reached on the changing nature of management in the twenty-first century is given by the findings of The Tomorrow Project (Moynagh and Worsley, 2001), which reported on conditions of work and employment until 2020. It found that:

- there will be more self-management;
- outsourcing will create these opportunities;
- higher skilled jobs will increase employee discretion;
- managers will develop new ways in which to supervise and delegate work;
- people will want greater responsibility;
- more mundane jobs will be transformed to make employment feel more like self-employment.

To support their conclusions, the authors quote the example of a just-in-time car plant at which many middle manager jobs have been taken over by assembly workers, who manage day-to-day scheduling, machine set-up, work, discipline and quality control (Moynagh and Worsley, 2001, p 96). In a similar vein, Richard Scase (2000) refers to Toyota's Takaoka plant, at which individual workers can stop the assembly line if they see a problem with the production process.

This brief and necessarily limited analysis of the nature of management and its relevance for the management of people at work does, however, allow us to conclude this section with the following observations.

- The traditional divide between those who manage and those who are managed is becoming narrower, increasingly blurred and, in certain cases, reversed, with the number of managers being reduced and their responsibilities passed to individuals or groups of employees.

- Changes in the nature of work, illustrated by the growing number of knowledge-based jobs, makes traditional ideas of what managing involves increasingly inappropriate. The knowledge owned by such workers cannot be easily appropriated or replicated, and this means that organizations cannot control and motivate the workers as easily as they believed they could when dealing with a less skilled and more dependent workforce.

- Social and technological changes have resulted in much more complex and varied working patterns, with an increasing number of employees working from home or away from the office for long periods. Inevitably, such changes have resulted in managers and HR specialists having to redefine what managing such staff involves.

A philosophy of management

KEY CONCEPT Philosophy

A set of beliefs about how things work; an interest in knowledge and knowing; a way of making sense of the world, so that how we act can be seen as rational in relation to what we believe and what we 'see'.

The final section of this introductory chapter considers the importance of philosophy for the management of people and seeks to answer the question: 'Is the existence of a coherent and sustained philosophy of management correlated with effective and successful organizations?' Earlier, we rejected the notion that some special ingredient or single factor might explain why some managers were consistently better than others in managing people as being too simplistic and misleading — but what explanation can be put forward that explains the success of certain organizations while not of others? The contribution of such writers as Pfeffer and Sutton (2000) and Jim Collins (2001) suggests that something to do with philosophy may represent at least part of the answer.

A philosophy of management is far more than a single ingredient — that 'something extra' which explains why some managers seem to be able consistently to outperform their contemporaries — but there is extensive anecdotal and empirical evidence that a particular type of philosophy is associated with managerial effectiveness and organizational success, and that this philosophy is deeply rooted in beliefs about people and their behaviour.

O'Reilly and Pfeffer (2000) emphasize the importance of philosophy and the assumptions managers make about people, and provide detailed accounts of the management styles and practices of eight successful American companies which share a similar approach to managing people, in which managers identify with a distinctive set of values and principles that influence and give consistency to what they do. They quote George Zimmer, founder of The Men's Warehouse, who described how the company's strategy and how it operates comes from a philosophy or world view based on humanistic principles. Zimmer's humanistic philosophy allows him to see the power of untapped human potential, which, when realized, allows win–win outcomes to be achieved, within which the interests of all the key organizational stakeholders can be met.

Collins' 2001 book, *Good to Great*, is also full of references to the values and beliefs held by the leaders and managers of companies he identifies as going beyond being only 'good' and becoming 'great'. Whether these represent a coherent and articulated philosophy of management is less important than the fact that they provide successive managers with a framework for action; within which consistency, rigour and a belief that their way is right for them sustains an environment within which the right kinds of people can prosper, grow and outperform competitors. Collins and his team of researchers were not interested only in identifying great companies; they wanted to identify the underlying reasons for sustained success, or, as Collins puts it:

I think of our work as a search for timeless principles — the enduring physics of great organizations.

(p 15)

STUDENT ACTIVITY 1.5

Consider the three examples from Collins' book (2001) presented below, and reflect on their application to management decisions and objectives. What do these statements mean for selection, motivation and people strategy?

1. *'When in doubt, don't hire – keep looking.'* (p 63)

2. *'Spending time trying to motivate people is a waste of effort. The real question is not, "How do we motivate our people?" If you have the right people, they will be self-motivated. The key is to not de-motivate them.'* (p 89)

3. *'The executives who ignited transformations from good to great did not first figure out where to drive the bus and then get people to take it there. No, they first got the right people on the bus (and the wrong ones off the bus) and then figured out where to drive it.'* (p 41)

In one of the most eloquent contributions made on the importance of values and beliefs, Thomas J Watson Jr (2003), argued that great organizations owed their success not only to the power of their beliefs, but also to the appeal these beliefs had to their employees:

> . . . I believe if an organization is to meet the challenge of a changing world, it must be prepared to change everything about itself except those beliefs as it moves through corporate life. In other words, the basic philosophy, spirit and drive of an organization have far more to do with its relative achievements than do technological or economic resources, organizational structure, innovation and timing. All these things weigh heavily in success. But they are, I think, transcended by how strongly the people in the organization believe in its basic precepts and how faithfully they carry them out.

Perhaps the most significant conclusion that emerges from this statement is the importance of getting the people that organizations employ to understand and support the values and beliefs espoused by their managers. Too often, managers make the mistake of assuming that simply publicizing mission and value statements is sufficient and that commitment automatically follows. This rarely happens: *living* a philosophy is much more difficult and demanding that articulating and publicizing one!

Reference to the importance of an underpinning and integrating philosophy can also be found in the HR literature. In their important, but largely unrecognized, work on personnel managers, Buckingham and Elliot (1993) argued that simply possessing basic competencies is not a sufficient condition for generating managerial success. This, they suggest, is much more a function of the concepts they use, their values and how they relate to others. Underpinning their personal characteristics and how they work is what they describe as a conceptual mindset, which they define as:

> . . . a perspective on their role and its purpose that is significantly different from their less highly rated colleagues.

They equate this mindset to a philosophy of personnel management that is:

> . . . strongly rooted in clear perceptions about, and a real commitment to, the value of good employees and of their contribution to the company.

Buckingham and Elliot found that those personnel managers who were rated more successful than others subscribed to a personal and professional philosophy that helped to shape their thinking and the way in which they discharged their responsibilities. This, combined with an ability to conceptualize and mobilize a range of more effective personal characteristics, was seen as the reason why they were considered to be successful HR managers — a finding that lends further support to the belief that those involved in the management of people need to underpin their behaviour as managers with a clear set of values and beliefs about the employment of people and their relationship to the organization.

Summary

The purpose of this introductory chapter has been to present our analysis about the employment and management of people within a broader framework of work, organization and productive activity. The chapter also serves as a reference point for those that follow, by which we mean that any particular area of HR — whether recruiting and selecting staff, or training them — needs to be carried out in ways that reflect the interests of the organization and those of the people who constitute its 'human resources'. Recognizing this duality of concerns does not imply that they have to be given equal emphasis, but rather that it is in management's long-term interests to understand and, wherever possible, reflect the things that are important and which matter to employees in the way in which 'the business' is run.

While it is accepted that external forces influence the degree to which management can act on this requirement, it is also important to recognize that these forces do not determine how people are managed. It is clear from references made to those organizations which stand out for being successful 'businesses' *and* which also enjoy enviable reputations for being 'good places to work' that there are choices to be made about how people are managed, and that these choices have consequences for such things as the quality of employee relations, employee satisfaction, and performance and retention rates.

The final point to note is that treating employees as people and as economic resources is not a mutually exclusive proposition — it is neither one nor the other — but getting the balance right, in the context of each organization's circumstances, represents a fundamental and enduring challenge that not all managers seem capable of meeting.

 Visit the Online Resource Centre that accompanies this book for self-test questions, weblinks, and more information on the topics covered in this chapter.
online resource centre **www.oxfordtextbooks.co.uk/orc/banfield_kay/**

REVIEW QUESTIONS

1. To what extent is organizational success a function of the 'human dimension'? What is the evidence that that supports your conclusion?

2. What are the current and future challenges that organizations face with regards to the way in which they manage people?

3. What might happen that will increase the level of conflict between employers and workers? If conflict does increase, is this likely to be because of what employers and managers do, or do not do, or is it likely to be generated by factors outside their control?

4. Why is a philosophy of management important and where can this be found?

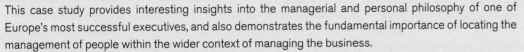

This case study provides interesting insights into the managerial and personal philosophy of one of Europe's most successful executives, and also demonstrates the fundamental importance of locating the management of people within the wider context of managing the business.

This is a story about the merger, in 1987, of two engineering companies — Brown Boveri from Switzerland and the Swedish firm ASEA — and the role of one of Europe's most well-known and success-ful chief executives, Percy Barnevik. It is taken from the book *ABB — The Dancing Giant*, by Kevin Bareham and Claudia Heimer (1998). ABB was chosen because it represents an example of a company that enjoyed phenomenal growth, financial success and an international reputation for its ability to oper-ate a highly decentralized international business. It is described by Bareham and Heimer as a '*globally connected corporation operating a loose-tight network of processes, projects and partners that is held together by highly committed people and strongly held principles*'. Its approach to business, the way in which it is organized and the approach taken to the management of its employees, certainly in the 1990s, set it apart from many of its contemporaries and brought it to the attention of management writers such as Warren Bennis, who were interested in Barnevik's leadership style and global/local business model (Bennis, 1993).

Always recognizing that further improvements might be made, the company emphasized the crucial role played by its employees, particularly its cadre of managers, and the importance of creating a culture of:

> ...continuous learning and change, wherever higher targets and constant transition are seen as normal and positive, not threatening and negative. We will make it happen only by instilling a creative and entrepreneurial attitude in all our employees who welcome change as a challenge.
> (Bareham and Heimer, 1998, p xii)

In addition to his personal qualities and business acumen, Barnevik also had a strong commitment to the company's people, and was able to articulate a distinctive philosophy of management and organization. In ch 11 of the book, entitled 'Developing ABB's people and corporate glue', Barnevik is quoted as saying:

> It is fantastic how much business is really about people issues. You never cease to be surprised whether you are a lawyer or an engineer, or if you have a business education, that the question really is: can you communicate, ignite people, be believable, build trust? We talk about having bright strategies. But at the end of the day it comes back to execution. Can you create a culture, leadership, make people buy in, and feel part of it?
> (p 317)

Barnevik's successor as CEO, Goran Lindahl, has a similar belief in the importance of the company's human resources, with a particular emphasis on attracting and developing new talent, a role that is seen as being the prime responsibility of line management.

What comes through clearly is the way in which ABB makes strong demands on its people: it is not a company that offers its employees an 'easy ride'. According to Bareham and Heimer, employees — and par-ticularly management—are expected to work extremely hard, perform well and be technically very good. The existence of internal competition and profit-and-loss centres means that business unit performance is regularly reported, and this has the effect of encouraging people to feel ownership and of meaningful autonomy deep down within the business.

The company also sets high standards in its recruitment of new staff, with all newly appointed profes-sional staff expected to have:

- a good education;
- strong analytical skills;

➜

27

- good communication skills;
- an interest in, and openness to, other cultures;
- energy, to drive the business.

As far as developing people is concerned, ABB has a very simple approach: after recruiting talented people, give them early responsibility and subject them to a range of informal and formal development strategies. The line drives both sets of activities, with the personnel function supporting the line with leading-edge development strategies rather than with complicated models and elaborate processes. As the head of the corporate management resourcing function, Arne Olssen, is reported to have said:

> **Exposing talented people to demanding assignments and providing feedback and support – this is the key to management development.**
> (p 326)

Olssen articulates ABB's management development philosophy very clearly, when he states that managers develop:

- 70 per cent on the job;
- 20 per cent by the influence of others;
- 10 per cent as a result of courses and seminars.

Without it being explicitly stated, it is reasonable to assume that the same principles and philosophy also applied to the development of the company's non-management employees.

Questions

1. Do you think ABB would be a good company to work for? If so, why?
2. What are the distinctive features of the company's culture and what effect do these have on employee behaviour?
3. What specific examples of management development practices would fit with the company's approach to this activity?

 Insights & Outcomes: visit the Online Resource Centre at www.oxfordtextbooks.co.uk/orc/banfield_kay/ for an up-to-date summary of issues related to talent management.

FURTHER READING

Davenport, TH (2005) *Thinking for a Living: How to Get Better Performances and Results from Knowledge Workers*, Harvard Business School Press.

Heil, G, Bennis, W and Stephens, DC (2000) *Douglas McGregor, Revisited*, John Wiley and Sons.

Pink, DH (2002) *Free Agent Nation: The Future of Working for Yourself*, Business Plus.

Sparrow, P and Cooper, CL (2003) *The Employment Relationship: Key Challenges for HR*, Butterworth-Heinemann.

REFERENCES

Atkinson, J (1984) 'Manpower strategies for flexible organisations', *Personnel Management*, Aug, pp 28–32.

Bareham, K and Heimer, C (1998) *ABB – The Dancing Giant*, FT/Pitman.

Beardsmore, R (2006) 'International comparisons of labour disputes in 2004', *Labour Market Trends*, 114:4, pp 117–28.

Bennis, W (1993) *An Invented Life: Reflections on Leadership and Change*, Addison-Wesley Publishing Co.

Bishop, K (2004) 'Working time patterns in the UK, France, Denmark and Sweden', *Labour Market Trends*, 112:3, pp 113–22.

Buckingham, G and Elliot, G (1993), 'Profile of a successful personnel manager', *Personnel Management*, 25:8, pp 26–9.

Castells, M (2000) *The Rise of the Network Society*, Blackwell, ch 4.

Clegg, S, Kornberger, M and Pitsis, T (2005) *Managing and Organisations*, Sage.

Collins, J (2001) *Good to Great*, Random House Business Books.

Coyle-Shapiro, J and Kessler, I (2000) 'Consequences of the psychological contract for the employment relationship: a large-scale survey', *Journal of Management Studies* 37:7, pp 903–30.

Evans-Pritchard, A (2005) 'Nestlé forced to reopen loss-making coffee factory', *Daily Telegraph*, 27 August, available online at www.telegraph.co.uk.

Fitz-Enz, J (1990) *Human Value Management: The Value-Adding Human Resource Management for the 1990s*, Jossey-Bass.

Fitz-Enz, J (2000) *The ROI of Human Capital*, American Management Association.

Frost, PJ (2003) *Toxic Emotions at Work*, Harvard Business School.

Hannagan, T (2002) *Management: Concepts and Practices*, FT/Prentice-Hall.

Harvey, JB (1996) *The Abilene Paradox and Other Meditations on Management*, Jossey-Bass.

Hiltrop, JM (1996) 'Managing the changing psychological contract', *Employee Relations*, 18:1, pp 36–49.

Hyman, R (1975) *Industrial Relations: A Marxist Introduction*, Blackwell.

Mayo, A (2001) *The Human Value of the Enterprise*, Nicholas Brealey Publishing.

McGregor, D (1960) *The Human Side of Enterprise*, McGraw-Hill.

Megginson, D, Banfield, P and Joy-Mathews, J (1999) *Human Resource Development*, 2nd edn, Kogan Page.

Moynagh, M and Worsley, R (2001) *Tomorrow's Workplace*, The Tomorrow Project.

Mullins, LJ (2005) *Management and Organisational Behaviour*, Pearson Education.

O'Reilly, CA and Pfeffer, J (2000) *Hidden Value*, Harvard Business School Press.

Ouchi, W (1981) *Theory Z: How American Management Can Meet the Japanese Challenge*, Addison-Wesley.

Peters, TT and Waterman, RH (1982) *In Search of Excellence: Lessons from America's Best-Run Companies*, Harper and Row.

Pfeffer, J and Sutton, RI (2000) *The Knowing–Doing Gap*, Harvard Business School Press.

Scarborough, H and Carter, C (2000) *Investigating Knowledge Management*, CIPD.

Scase, R (2000) *Britain Towards 2010: The Changing Business Environment*, ESRC/Foresight.

Shepherd, JL and Mathews, BP (2000) 'Employee commitment: academic vs practitioner perspectives', *Employee Relations*, 22:6, pp 555–75.

Stress Management Society web page, 'Stress at work', available online at www.stress.org.uk.

Swart, J, Kinnie, N and Purcell, J (2003) *People and Performance in Knowledge-Intensive Firms*, CIPD.

Watson, TJ (2001) *In Search of Management*, Thomson Learning.

Watson, TJ (2002) *Organising and Managing Work*, FT/Prentice Hall.

Watson, TJ (2003) *A Business and Its Beliefs: The Ideas That Helped Build IBM*, McGraw-Hill Education.

Wickens, P (1987) *The Road to Nissan: Flexibility, Quality, Teamwork*, Macmillan.

2

HRM: An Academic and Professional Perspective

Key Terms

Personnel Management The name given to the specialized management function responsible for an organization's employees.

Human Resource Management (HRM) A more recent approach to the management of employees, which sees people as a key organizational resource that needs to be developed and utilized to support the organization's operational and strategic objectives.

Human Resources (HR) An alternative to 'people' and also the name used by many organizations to describe the specialized department that deals with the administration and management of employees.

Learning Objectives

As a result of reading this chapter and using the Online Resource Centre, you should be able to:

- understand the origins and evolution of Human Resource Management;

- explain the reasons for the change in emphasis from Personnel Management to Human Resource Management;

- engage in a critical exploration of HR and its contribution to individual and organizational performance;

- explain why the role of the line manager is critical to the management of human resources.

Introduction

The aims of the previous chapter were to introduce students to the more general themes and issues that have a bearing on the employment and management of people, and to put these in the context of how organizations function – particularly the way in which their internal and external environments shape and influence the way in which people are managed at work. This chapter continues to explore how organizations have responded to environmental change in the ways in which they manage employees, but with a particular emphasis on the development of the specialist management functions that were established to help organizations deal with the more complex and difficult employment and management issues that began to emerge in the second half of the twentieth century.

One of the key conclusions that emerges from the analysis of how organizations operate is that, while there are choices to be made about how to manage people, and managers enjoy a significant degree of discretion in the selection and application of human resource strategies, very few organizations can escape from the logic of organization, competitive market forces, the importance of efficient production, and the need to achieve and sustain financial stability.

Organizations experience differences in the degree to which these forces impact on the ways in which they function and on how they are managed – differences that reflect size, sector, competitive pressures and technology, as well the kind of people the organization employs. Almost all, however, experience pressures to use their productive resources efficiently and productively, and to meet financial and performance targets. It would be difficult to argue that, in an increasingly global economy, these pressures are not likely to increase.

Depending on the kind of organization in which they work, the impact of these forces will be experienced differently by the employee. Some will feel protected from external threats and will enjoy relatively stable working lives, but in situations in which change and instability have become the norm rather than the exception, very few are immune to the effects of globalization, legislative and regulatory changes, market upheavals and financial pressures.

An inevitable outcome of these developments is that management itself has become more complex and demanding, particularly in terms of the responsibilities of managers in managing people. While the 'managers' in charge of building the Pyramids and the UK's canal and rail networks were not without their problems, including those relating to the people they employed, it would probably be fair to say that they enjoyed more power and control over their employees, and used these effectively to impose their own will and interests in preference to those of the workforce. In contrast, managers in the twenty-first century are subject to a growing number of regulations and restrictions that limit their freedom to act unilaterally, and are faced with much more volatility and unpredictability in their external environments. The following case study, based on events in 2006–07 illustrates how environmental change can affect an organization's business and its human resource strategies.

> **HRM INSIGHT 2.1 William Beckett Plastics Ltd**
>
> This company was set up by the owner/proprietor some 25 years ago and employs 56 people in a manufacturing unit on an industrial estate in Sheffield. From modest beginnings, the company has grown steadily over the years, with turnover now at just over £3m. It makes and sells plastic components to over thirty countries, and its reputation for product innovation and customer service has enabled the company to remain competitive and to increase its product and customer base. It represents, by any criteria, a successful small to medium-sized enterprise (SME). The company does not have an HR department – its size makes this an unrealistic proposition. Responsibility for HR lies with its owner and its team of senior managers, who have a genuine understanding of the importance and role of their employees, and who are considered to be fair and reasonable in the way in which they deal with HR issues.
>
> Management employs a specialist firm of solicitors to provide legal advice on employment matters, has developed a number of innovative practices to retain experienced employees, and operates a modest bonus system
>
> →

that is linked to company profitability. As seen in Chapter 1, William Beckett, the owner, has a very simple, but balanced, view about his employees and the role of HR. He believes that, without a healthy and successful business, there wouldn't be jobs to be filled and employees to manage; while the people are key to the business, they *are not* the business, and there have been times when it has been necessary to dismiss staff for disciplinary reasons, to make people redundant and, in extreme situations, to reduce the wages of all employees, including management. These have all been decisions made in the best interests of the company and its long-term future.

In 2006, after a successful year during which production and profits grew, the company decided to apply for economic development grants that would allow it to move to new, custom-built premises and to expand its production facilities. Such a move would also mean that new employees would need to be hired and that staff could have confidence in the company's, and their, future. Discussions with various government agencies had progressed well, and considerable management time and money had been invested in the project, when the company heard informally that its biggest customer, part of an international engineering toolmaking business, was to be closed and production transferred to Brazil. The reason given by the parent company was that the business no longer fitted into its international strategy.

The loss of the contract, which represented a significant part of its turnover and an even greater proportion of profits, meant that William Beckett Plastics had to terminate discussions over the new premises and, rather than looking to hire new people, it was faced with the inevitability of making some of its existing employees redundant. Literally overnight, the company's environment had changed and its plans for the future had to be abandoned.

Questions

1. Should the company have tried to retain its employees in the hope that growing demand from other companies would compensate for the loss of its biggest customer?

2. What might the effects have been on employee morale and performance of the news about the lost business, and what short-term action might management have taken to alleviate any negative effects?

3. What longer term action might management take to alleviate the damage done by the loss of the contract?

Insights & Outcomes: visit the Online Resource Centre at www.oxfordtextbooks.co.uk/orc/ banfield_kay/ for an explanation of how the company responded to its changing environment.

The challenge in managing people

There is a wealth of anecdotal evidence to support the view that, while technology, product/service development and organizational change challenges managers, the challenge with which managers at all levels seem to have the most difficulty is managing people. These are the challenges that can consume a disproportionate amount of management time and energy, and, paradoxically, despite the sustained investment in management education and training, there is little evidence that today's managers feel confident that they have found the answers to the questions and challenges that face them.

But what are these questions and challenges? Without being exhaustive, the following list represents arguably the most common and persistent questions with which managers are struggling.

- 'What makes employees "tick" and how can they be motivated?'
- 'What do people want from work and what is the best way to reward them?'
- 'Where am I going to get well-qualified staff from and what do I have to do to keep them?'
- 'How I am going to get my workers to be more flexible and deliver higher levels of discretionary effort?'
- 'How can I find the right balance between treating my workers fairly and with consideration, but at the same time ensuring that wider organizational interests are not compromised?'
- 'How can I reduce or eliminate the causes of conflict and build a loyal and committed workforce?'

If, as is argued here, these are questions that are relevant and important to *all* 'managers' — from charge-hands and supervisors, up to the most senior executives in both public and private sector organizations — how do they relate to Personnel Management and Human Resource Management, as specialized approaches to the management of human resources?

One way of making the connection is to see the emergence of a specialized people management function as an expression of the difficulties and problems 'general' managers faced in the second half of the twentieth century, as the work environment became more volatile and the pace of change began to accelerate. As management, in general, became more differentiated and specialized, the people management aspect began to acquire a distinctive identity, developed more specialist roles and became increasingly professionalized. Either as a consequence, or a cause, of these changes, a distinctive, but provisional area of responsibility and set of activities began to be acquired by the new 'personnel managers'. This new domain reflected the specialist expertise and knowledge claimed by this new breed of manager and the ceding of responsibility for people management matters by line managers, who felt unable or unwilling to take the lead in dealing with many of the questions highlighted above.

Figure 2.1 illustrates the shift from the line manager towards the personnel specialist during the latter part of the twentieth century. Interestingly, one of the key changes in the early part of the twenty-first century has been a reversal of this trend and a redefinition of the relationship and responsibilities of the line manager and personnel specialist.

The debate about the respective roles and contributions of line managers and people management specialists has been an enduring feature of the literature on HR, and the work of Hutchinson and Purcell (2003) has been particularly influential in exposing the tensions and contradictions in the relationship between the two. In its extreme form, this late twentieth-century practice of moving responsibility for key aspects of people management away from the line and into centralized personnel departments effectively disenfranchised line managers, and became one of the most important sources of criticism levelled

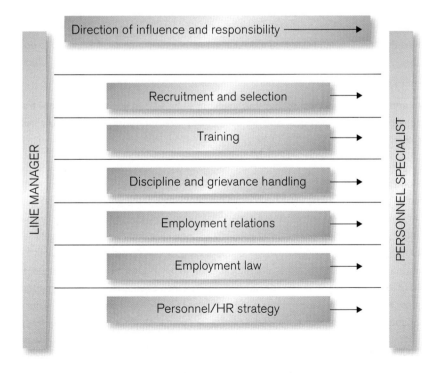

Figure 2.1 Diagrammatical representation of the shift in responsibility from the line to personnel specialists in the 1970s and 1980s

at people management specialists. More recent research (CIPD, 2005) has found evidence that this loss of responsibility for HR by the line may have had serious consequences because:

> ... front line managers played a pivotal role in terms of implementing and enacting HR policies and practices ... where employees feel positive about their relationship with their front line managers they are more likely to have higher levels of performance or discretionary behaviour.

The importance of the line to the way in which people are managed and the outcomes that are generated is also recognized by Tyson and Fell (1986), who argue that:

> All managers of people are 'personnel managers' in the literal sense, that is they have a personnel function to perform.

This means that (using the more contemporary expression) all managers can be seen to be human resource managers because part of their responsibility involves managing resources, of which human resources are a constituent and vital part. Managers who do not, therefore, recognize and fulfil their human resource management role can be said to be failing to meet the full range of their managerial responsibilities.

Confusion surrounding the question 'who is responsible' and the controversy accompanying the role of centralized HR departments are fundamental problems that still face HR. It is not a problem that can ever entirely be resolved and remains a potential source of tension between line managers and HR professionals. Will the centralized HR department, staffed by HR specialists prove ultimately to be the preferred model or will its alternative, based on the key role of line managers, come to dominate thinking and practice? In his 1997 article, 'Where is human resources?', Christensen argues that the future of HR lies in the importance of being able to:

> ... differentiate between human resource management and the human resource department.

He also describes the situation in which, after asking for the HR strategy or plan, senior managers are often presented with a description of current and future activities of the Personnel/HR department, which, he argues, more often that not has little obvious connection to the business. He goes further in this differentiation between the Personnel/HR department and what can only be interpreted as the 'real HR' when he claims that '*the Human Resource Plan doesn't necessarily have anything at all to do with the HR Department*', arguing that the HR plan belongs to the business. Accepting that there is a lack of clarity in terms of who is responsible for human resource management, he offers the opinion that:

> Managers and HR professionals of the future will understand that line managers are the 'people managers' of their organisations and as such, they are ultimately accountable for human resource management.
>
> (p 22)

The conclusion that can be reached at this point is that the growth of a specialist people management function – the question of what it is called is considered later – has the potential of making major contributions to the way in which people are recruited, selected, trained and rewarded. While these specialists may have a key role in the design of policies and procedures, however, it is the line managers who have the responsibility *for delivery* and this can never be taken or given away. As a consequence of this realization, the trend over the past ten years or so has been for the line to re-engage more explicitly and directly in the management of its employees, with HR specialists playing a less executive, and more supportive, role.

A consequence of the line re-engaging directly with employees – and one that has major implications for the size of specialist HR departments and for those working in them – is that fewer HR professionals will be needed in this new HR 'architecture'. Reilly and Williams (2006) refer to British Airways halving its HR department in 1989, devolving much of its HR responsibility to line management, and to the BBC, who more recently cut over half of its specialist HR jobs. Clearly, there is an ongoing tension and dynamic between the line and HR specialists, with some organizations abandoning centralized departments altogether in favour of a decentralized and devolved approach to the management of people; others, particularly in the public sector, continue to retain well-resourced HR departments and a key role for the HR specialist.

But arguably the most important question that emerges from the growth of specialist 'people managers' and different approaches to the way in which people are managed is not about differences of definition and conceptual models, but rather about *what* works and *why*. Tyson and Fell (1986) articulate this concern when they pose the question:

> **Given that the appointment of these specialists is one answer to the question of how to manage people, how effective is it?**
>
> (p 7)

Personnel Management – origins and influences

The origins of the approaches to people management that we now call 'Personnel Management' and 'Human Resource Management' can now be understood to lie in the trend towards a greater degree of specialization in the people management function as organizations and their environments became more complex and demanding. (Note that the upper case versions relate to specialized management activities and responsibilities, often associated with specialized departments. The lower case versions relate to the technical function associated with employing and managing people, and the associated generalized and diffuse management responsibilities.) In the latest edition of their book, Torrington et al (2005, p 11) explain that the origins of Personnel Management can be seen to be an expression and an outcome of the work of nineteenth-century social reformers and Quaker employers, such as Cadbury, Rowntree and Boot, whose concerns for the well being of employees led to the creation of the first specialist personnel management role – the welfare officer. Such people were employed by owners of mills and factories to provide basic canteen facilities, social activities and occupational health services for their workers. The motivation for what, at that time, were original and innovative practices is usually expressed in terms of the employers' religious beliefs or their commitment to social justice, although a complementary, if not alternative, explanation might be that a concern for the well being of workers made 'good business sense', in that it helped to build positive working relations, and a loyal and healthy workforce.

Over the course of the twentieth century, as the first personnel departments emerged in larger organizations, welfare officers became an integral part of this growing specialist management function and were still in existence even as late as the 1960s and 1970s. Interestingly, the origins of the Chartered Institute for Personnel and Development can be traced back to this concern with employee welfare, with the formation in 1917 of the Central Association for Welfare Workers, which led, in 1924, to the establishment of the Institute of Industrial Welfare Workers Incorporated.

The demise of welfare officers and of the welfare movement can be seen to be linked to the emerging post-war welfare state, which removed the need for individual organizations to provide traditional welfare services to their workers, but also to developments in occupational health and safety, which absorbed part of the role of the welfare officer (Niven, 1967). World War I gave a boost to this fledgling management function through the army's use of more systematic selection methods; World War II provided further encouragement and focus to this development, as the wartime use of psychometric testing and specialized training techniques spilled over into civilian life.

But at least as important to the growth of Personnel Management as were these societal and organizational changes was the impact of Scientific Management and the work of writers such as Frederick Taylor and Henry Fayol (Smith and Boyns, 2005). The emphasis they gave to an essentially rational approach to management in general and to the management of employees in particular, covering such areas as organizing, planning, work measurement, training and the use of financial incentives, led to a much more detached and 'scientific' approach to work and to the control of workers. The 'industrial engineer' began to replace, or at least challenge, the welfare officer as the operationalized expression of what Personnel Management was becoming. The emergence of the 'manpower planner' and the use of quantitative resource planning models in the 1970s represented a further step forward, at least chronologically, in the evolution of this specialized management function.

The re-emergence of trade unionism in post-war Britain gave Personnel Management — the status of which was officially recognized in 1946 with the formation of the Institute of Personnel Management — a new focus and direction. The so-called 'challenge from below', expressed through strikes and other forms of industrial conflict, represented a direct threat to management authority and control: a threat that, in more extreme cases, was ideologically, rather than materially, based. At the forefront of this struggle for control over much of the country's manufacturing and heavy industries were the industrial relations officers, whose job it was to negotiate wage increases, to develop effective consultative and communication strategies, and to address emerging issues, such as equal pay and union rights at work. But their main role was, through the process of negotiation, to engage with shop stewards and full-time union officials to establish a level of stability and order that allowed production to continue. The defining characteristic of Personnel Management in the 1970s and 1980s — certainly as far as manufacturing, heavy industry, transport and communications, and parts of the public sector were concerned — was the struggle for influence and control between trade unions and management. The institutions of industrial relations and the conflict that was generated as a result of this struggle for control, rather than relationships at the individual level, defined the agenda of those involved in Personnel Management until the legislative changes introduced by the Thatcher government and the effect of economic recession began to change the external context of employment in the 1980s. These combined to undermine significantly the collective power of trade unions and, with the rise of Human Resource Management, to re-emphasize the importance of individual employee relations (see CIPD, 2004).

One final development influencing the practice of Personnel Management in this period was the growing importance of training. As is the case today, Britain's relatively low skills and productivity levels were factors affecting economic competitiveness, and this resulted in governmental intervention through the Industrial Training Act of 1964, which created a network of Industrial Training Boards. The system of levies and grants through which the Boards sought to encourage companies to address skill deficiencies meant that organizations had a financial interest in developing training programmes. The 'game' at the time was to ensure that the value of training grants received from the relevant Training Board was at least as much as the cost of levies, which were based on a fixed proportion of the company wage bill. Training officers grew in number and influence largely because the system of grants and levies provided a financial incentive to train employees and managers; once this institutionalized system ended, the number of trainers fell dramatically, with predictable consequences for the level of commitment given to training.

The rise of Human Resource Management

The term 'Human Resource Management' has its origins not in the UK, but in the USA during the 1980s, and is associated with the work of such writers as Tichy et al (1982) and Beer et al (1985). For some, it came to represent a fundamentally different approach to the management of people, based on new assumptions about employees, about the changing nature of work and about how best to maximize the potential of an organization's human resources. Many UK organizations were quick to embrace this new development and many personnel departments became, almost overnight, departments of human resources (HR); personnel officers were transformed into HR officers and managers. Not all organizations embraced HRM, in that they preferred to retain the 'personnel management' title on the grounds that this avoided the impersonal association with their employees as 'human resources', but, over time, more and more specialized 'people' departments became known as HR departments.

There is, however, still argument and disagreement over what this new development actually represented, although most of the argument and debate has been confined to academics. Those actively involved in the management of people appear to have been less concerned about titles, concerned more with practice and with the effects on employee behaviour and performance of new ideas about commitment, involvement, resource utilization and the role of the line manager.

The academic debate is, of course, not without interest or relevance for those who practise HR and a number of important contributions to this debate need to be analysed. The key issue – that of whether HRM is, or is not, different to Personnel Management – is considered by Hoque and Noon (2001), who quote both David Guest, arguing that the HRM label *does* represent something new and distinctive, and John Storey, who suggests that there are 27 points of distinction between the two. Yet Karen Legge (1995) begins her chapter on 'Human Resource Management' by quoting a caller on BBC4, who described HRM as:

> ... a posh way of describing a personnel manager ... but it goes a bit further than that.

In trying to make sense out of what appear to be quite different views, Hoque and Noon argue that:

> ... the key issue is whether departments that have adopted the HR title operate differently from those that have retained the personnel title.
>
> (2001, p 6)

They suggest that, based on numerous anecdotal evidence, the introduction of the HR title has meant little more than a '*change on the door*'.

Gennard and Kelly (1994) researched the views of personnel directors and came to the conclusion that the debate over differences between Personnel Management and HRM was largely sterile: many of the organizations from which they had gained information displayed evidence of fundamental changes in employment and management practices, but many did not adopt the HR label to indicate or justify these changes. In other words, practitioners were embracing many of the ideas of HRM, but were not necessarily adopting the label or changing the departmental title. Simply looking for evidence of difference by focusing on nominal changes in department titles is not, therefore, likely to be particularly helpful.

In a later telephone-based survey of a wider sample of practitioners, Grant and Oswick (1998) found that 50 per cent of their sample was convinced that HRM was something different to Personnel Management; 37 per cent believed that there was no difference. In Chapter 15, John Harper is very clear about this question: he believes very strongly that HRM does represent a very different, and more effective, approach to the management of people. In general, however, there remains an interesting lack of consensus on this question.

Signpost to Chapter 15: Case Study: Reforming the HR Function for further analysis of HRM in practice

---

A further source of confusion lies in the way in which HRM is split into two forms, with a distinction made between 'hard' and 'soft' types of HRM. The *hard* approach emphasizes the quantitative, strategic aspects of managing people as organizational assets. A *soft* approach instead highlights the importance of communication, motivation, leadership, and the mutual commitment of employees and employers. Unfortunately, using such simplistic terms to represent complex phenomena not only has the effect of trivializing the debate, but also of presenting the practitioner with a choice: which form of HRM should be adopted? More realistically, a combination of both 'hard' and soft' versions is likely to have a greater impact on employee behaviour and performance than the selection of one or the other.

Despite the differences between, and within, these approaches, it is important to try to capture some of the most important differences between the two, which Figure 2.2 summarizes overleaf.

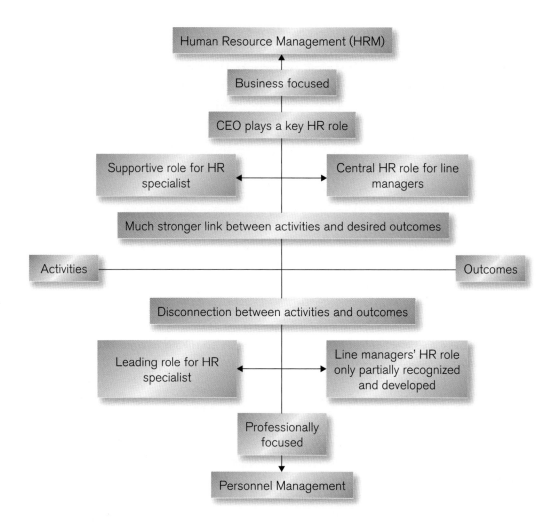

Figure 2.2 A comparison of Personnel Management and HRM

For students coming to this debate for the first time, the attempt to understand the debate about Personnel Management and HRM, and to make sense of the ambiguous language and sometimes inaccessible arguments, can be a frustrating experience. Tony Watson (2002) recorded the story of one student, who was left confused, and an abbreviated version is presented in the following HRM Insight.

HRM INSIGHT 2.2 The story of Sue Ridgebridge

This story is told in detail by Tony Watson (2002). The essence of the story is the confusion and frustration experienced by a student being 'taught' Human Resource Management at a UK university.

The student, Sue Ridgebridge, starts her story by explaining that, when the organization she worked for changed the title of the specialized people management function from 'personnel' to 'human resources', it represented little more than a continuation and development of what had previously been done under the personnel banner. She speculated that the reasons behind the change were more to do with being fashionable and the need to be seen to be moving away from the welfare tradition of Personnel Management towards something more business-orientated.

As far as the experience of being taught HRM was concerned, Sue had a particular problem: she was confused about whether HRM is to do with the general business of managing people or represented a particular approach. She had real difficulty in understanding what one of her tutors meant when he said that 'Human Resource Management Is a particular approach to human resource management'! As someone who had spent most of her working life in a personnel department, she also felt aggrieved when her tutors emphasized that the distinctions between Personnel Management and Human Resource Management were to do with the former's

- short-termism;

- tendency towards a reactive, firefighting approach to problems;

- association with collectivism;

- inability to move away from transactional, towards transformational, management;

- lack of a strategic dimension.

When presented with John Storey's list of 27 differences between Personnel Management and Human Resource Management (Storey, 1992), her response was to cross out HRM and retitle the table '27 differences between good personnel management and bad personnel management'.

The point about this case study is that it highlights the problem that students can experience when being introduced to the subject for the first time, and illustrates the difficulties they have in understanding the terms and labels used by academics, many of which tend to confuse rather than enlighten. It also provides justification for Watson's comment that:

> ...these criticisms are well founded and...there is a serious ambiguity in the HRM literature about its analytical and prescriptive elements.
> (2002, p 374)

What complicates the search for a greater degree of clarity in the characteristics of, and relationship between, these two approaches to the management of people is that academic writers rarely make it known to the reader whether they are offering:

- definitions and descriptions based on *practice* — in other words, whether they are studying these two approaches empirically and making comparisons between the two based on observed/discovered differences;

OR

- presenting what are known as *analytical or conceptual models*, with each approach associated with certain practices and characteristics based on assumed or conceptualized differences.

What adds to the confusion is, as Storey quite rightly claims, the fact that writers often fail to explain which position they are adopting, and — more worryingly — fail to tell the reader when they switch from one position to another.

Storey also sets out to establish the defining characteristics of HRM, which set it apart from Personnel Management at the philosophical, or belief, level. A more detailed list of 27 different dimensions between the two approaches can be found on p 34 of his book. He argues, however, that the following four key elements express the essence of the concept.

- HRM represents the belief that people, or human resources, are the key to organizational successes. The majority of employees, in the way they contribute and work for the organization, can make the critical difference between success and failure, and management needs to understand the employees' value to the organization.

- HRM embodies a much greater understanding and awareness of the strategic importance of the human resource. Its management cannot and should not be delegated to, and reserved for, human resource professionals, but must involve the direct and ongoing involvement and leadership of senior management.

- HRM, unlike Personnel Management, is central to organizational performance and, as such, must involve all managers with line responsibility. HRM is seen as being delivered primarily by and through line management, who are supported and advised by HR specialists.

- HRM reflects the belief in the importance of integration, both vertical and horizontal, and the use of particular strategies to improve and reward employee performance in pursuit of enhanced organizational performance.

KEY CONCEPT Vertical integration

This relates to the linkage between the policies and practices associated with the management of people, and the wider business or organizational strategies and objectives. Vertical integration can be based on the cascading down of corporate priorities and objectives, which then inform and give direction to HR priorities, policies and practices. Alternatively, it can be based on representatives of HR informing senior management of the current and future state of human resource capacity and capabilities, which helps to ensure that corporate strategy is grounded in a realistic understanding of what is, or will be, available to deliver the strategy.

KEY CONCEPT Horizontal integration

This relates to the linkage between different HR activities and practices, and emphasizes the importance of looking at what HR does holistically, rather than as separate and disconnected elements. The concept also expresses the need for consistency in the sense that the way in which the activities are carried out reflects understood and agreed strategic objectives. For example, adopting an individualist, rather than a collectivist, approach to the management of people implies the use of individual reward and development practices if consistency in practice is to be achieved.

Whether these defining features of HRM are actually delivered and experienced in practice — that is, whether they become operationalized — is another matter. These differences suggest, at least, that HRM is an approach that is, or should, involve a more systematic and sophisticated engagement with employees and managers as part of the process of adding value to the organization through the efforts and contributions of all of its employees.

Table 2.1 A summary of the main analytical differences between Personnel Management and Human Resource Management

Personnel Management	Human Resource Management
Emphasis on collectivity	More emphasis given to individuals
Generalised HR solutions	More tailored and bespoke solutions
Centralisation of HR responsibility	Greater devolution of authority and responsibility for managing people
Increasing role for HR specialists	Senior managers and those in line positions seen as key to delivering effective HR 'solutions'
Associated with maintaining status quo and stability	Associated with maintaining stability and driving through changes in structures, practices and capabilities
Associated with trade unionism and managing conflict	Associated with capabilities, performance and outcomes
'Can't do' mindset	'Can do' mindset
Thought to be reactive	Associated with a more proactive orientation
Associates employees primarily as an economic resource and a cost	Much more emphasis on employees as a source of resourcefulness
More operationally orientated	Operates at the strategic and operational levels
Lacking in sufficient integration of activities	Strong emphasis on vertical and horizontal integration

Although, in one sense, it matters little what label is used to give an identity to these underlying beliefs, because it is the beliefs themselves that are important, for many practitioners the label *is* important because it symbolizes the departure from one approach to the management of people and the adoption of another. This other approach is considered to be more in tune with changes in the nature of work, the organizational pressures to 'deliver', and the need for a more flexible, committed and productive labour force.

And then came Strategic Human Resource Management (SHRM)!

One of the questions inevitably asked by students of HR is: 'If Human Resource Management represents, among other things, a more strategic approach to the management of people, what is Strategic Human Resource Management (SHRM) about and how is it different?'

This is a question that has merit and deserves a considered answer. The first thing to say is that SHRM is not a third distinctive and different approach to the management of people, with its own 27 differences that help to establish its separate identity. For many who use this term, it means little more than recognizing the strategic dimension of HRM. In this sense, as Boxall and Purcell (2000) state, when the adjective 'strategic' is applied to HRM, in many cases, it means nothing at all.

On the other hand, SHRM, for some academics and practitioners, does represent something more than the strategic dimension of HRM and this 'more' can be explained in three ways. Firstly, SHRM is concerned with the way in which the management of people is critical to, and contributes towards, organizational effectiveness. It therefore represents a level of thinking and a set of activities that connect the domain of HRM more explicitly to the strategic needs and interests of the organization. Put in a slightly different way, this means that, while HRM is associated with the integration of its activities at the horizontal level, SHRM is more concerned with integrating HRM activities vertically, ensuring that these 'fit' with the strategic direction in which the organization is moving.

Figure 2.3 and HRM Insight 2.3 help to illustrate and explain the concepts of vertical and horizontal integration.

HRM INSIGHT 2.3 Introducing a leadership training programme at Midshire University

Midshire, one of the UK's 'new' universities, had been structured around ten departments, each with its own management team and administrative support. Central functions, based on finance, marketing, the registry, facilities and HR, coordinated a series of common services and procedures for all of the academic departments, with the 'centre' operating very much as a bureaucracy, exercising hierarchical control over its constituent parts.

Over time, the HR department had grown from rather modest proportions to what had now become a large and influential part of the university, employing approximately sixty staff, split evenly between professional and administrative employees. Its main operational role was in maintaining good relations with trade unions, providing advice to the senior management teams within the departments, managing grievance and disciplinary cases, and providing a centralized, course-based training service. Its reputation within the university ranged from being seen as an expensive overhead, through being seen as a well-managed but largely administrative service, to, for the majority of university staff, a somewhat remote and detached set of people who didn't have much interest in, and experience of, what most staff actually did and the environment in which they worked.

As a result of a major reorganization in 2002, which resulted in the merger of the ten academic departments into three new super-colleges, it became apparent that many of the newly appointed senior managers lacked the strategic management skills that they needed to take on these important leadership roles. In addition, the results of the annual staff survey indicated that many employees, in both academic and non-academic roles, had considerable concerns about the quality of leadership in general and felt that this was an important matter that had to be addressed if the aspirations of the university's vice chancellor were to be met.

Responding to a request from the vice chancellor, the head of HR contacted an external provider of leadership training and held discussions about what would represent the most appropriate way of dealing with this problem. What emerged was a sophisticated course in leadership, delivered off-site and consisting of three separate two-day sessions using a mixture of both experiential and classroom-based learning.

The reaction of those who participated in the training was that, while the experience of being on the course had been interesting and developmental, the big problem was that little, if anything, had changed in the university and that the course on its own was not able to address the problem of a lack of leadership among management. The results of the staff survey the following year confirmed that staff continued to feel that the university had a serious leadership problem.

Questions

1. What action should have been taken and by whom prior to, during and after the course to ensure that there was a high level of integration within the whole learning experience?

2. What other HR and management changes might the HR department have made to ensure that the new leadership course was horizontally integrated?

3. What should have been the respective contributions of the HR specialists and line managers in making sure that the investment in both time and money delivered the necessary outcomes?

The second way of understanding the significance of SHRM is to link it to what is known as the 'resource-based view of the firm' (Kamoche, 1996). According to this view, organizations can be conceptualized as consisting of a set of tangible and intangible resources and capabilities that have the potential of generating competitive advantage and organizational success. Barney (1991), for example, considers that an organization's resources include all of its assets, capabilities, processes, attributes, knowledge and information, and, from a SHRM perspective, this means that the key human resources — particularly the competences and knowledge associated with employees — are both developed and used to create new capabilities that help to deliver organizational success.

A third way of understanding SHRM is to see it in terms of strategic choice. Strategic choice is about making critical decisions in the key areas of managing people, such as rewards, relations, training and development, recruitment and selection, and performance management, and involves management deciding on:

- whether to commit to an individualist approach to employee relations or to recognize and negotiate with trade unions;

- whether to reward employees on merit, performance and potential, or on the basis of the jobs they do and their length of service;

- whether to employ only talented people or those that are available;

- whether to base the development of employees on learning or training;

- whether to adopt a 'one size fits all' approach to the development of HR practices or to develop more tailored and individualized policies and practices.

SHRM might, in the context of strategic choice, be seen to represent the processes and decisions that shape the organization's philosophy towards its employees and how they are managed in relation to the above strategically important areas.

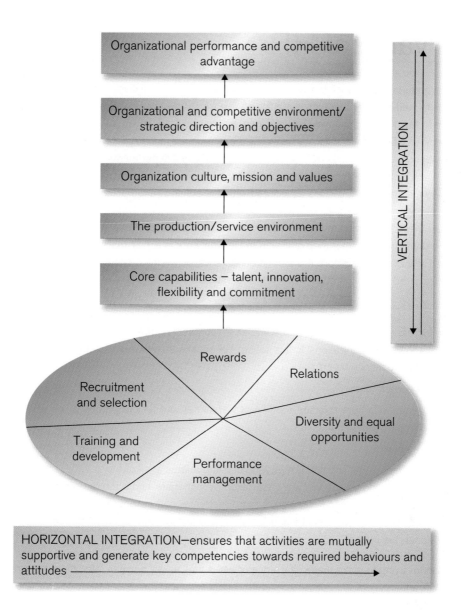

Figure 2.3 A diagrammatical representation of the horizontal and vertical dimensions of HRM

One final way of making sense of SHRM, and one that is not unconnected to the previous three, is to see it terms of the development of what Becker et al (2001) call the 'strategic HR architecture'. This concept expresses the full range of HR activities, interventions, policies and practices, and links these to the effect they have on the value-creating potential of all employees, and how this added-value potential is actually measured and utilized.

The critical point that emerges from this brief review of key contributions to the meaning of SHRM is that the management of people *must* have a strategic, as well as an operational, direction, but what this actually means and how it is expressed is likely to differ between organizations, which need to express their own unique needs and requirements in determining what SHRM means to them. Whatever their chosen form of expression, one thing that they are all likely to have in common is the need to ensure that what HR does is connected to, rather than disconnected from, the wider organizational context.

The value of HR

One of the enduring features of the academic debate on HR is the criticism that has been levelled at HR professionals and the HR function for failing to live up to the expectations of those who were told, or believed, that HR was the key to unlocking the potential of an organization's human resources (Hammonds, 2005). Many of these criticisms are well founded, although it would be wrong to suggest that they apply to all those who work in HR. Equally, many HR departments enjoy a positive reputation and are valued by line managers for the contributions they make to the management of people; others, unfortunately, do not and are more associated with the administration of employment rather than the effective management of people.

Because these criticisms are serious rather than superficial, and are as much to do with the nature of the HR function itself rather than only with those who work in it, it is important that they are properly considered and evaluated. Before this can be done, however, we must ensure that the meanings of the key terms referred to in this section are clearly understood.

- **HR**

    This is increasingly used to refer to the human resources department or section that exists in many medium and large organizations. In this sense, 'HR' means the HR department, or the department of human resource management.

- **Personnel departments**

    Some organizations have retained the title of 'personnel', but for our purposes, we can equate the personnel department to that of HR.

- **The HR function**

    This has two meanings. The first is a general one and relates to all of the activities and contributions involved in managing people that are undertaken by managers, and often by employees, throughout the organization. The second meaning is more restrictive and essentially relates to the specialized department, which can be called HR or personnel, within which HR/personnel administrators and professionals are based.

The reason for trying to make these differences clear is that, as will be seen later, there are almost 'two' kinds of HR and many of the criticisms made by academics and managers relate to only one of these (Banfield, 2005).

Karen Legge (1978) comments that:

> **On a daily basis personnel managers are confronted by ambiguities that arise out of problems in defining personnel management... and which lie at the heart of personnel specialist's perennial concern with the issue of credibility.**

This suggests that many of the criticisms levelled at HR are not to do with lack of professionalism or an inability to operate at a strategic level, but reflect deeply rooted issues and problems that may not, in fact, be resolvable. The ambiguities that Legge identifies are:

- the problem of demonstrating unequivocally that HR/personnel, as an organizational activity, can and does make a significant contribution to the behaviour and performance of employees. This is because, as we will see Watson argue later in this chapter, employees, as people rather than resources, are capable of independent thought and action — they are not simply passive 'things to be managed', and behave in ways that reflect their unique individuality and a wide range of influences from within and outside the organization. This means that is difficult to prove conclusively that either desirable or undesirable employee behaviour — for example, low productivity or high absenteeism — *is the result* of good or bad personnel/HR management. Legge goes on to state that:

Difficulty in demonstrating a direct relationship between personnel management activities and valued organisational outcomes presents particular difficulties for the personnel department. (1978, p 22)

● because all managers, whether specialists in HR or on the line, are in an important sense 'managers of people', i.e. human resource/personnel managers (note the significance of the lower case), the contributions that each party makes to desired and undesirable outcomes is difficult to separate out and measure. This means that it is possible for one party to blame the other when things go wrong and to claim the credit when things go well. Much depends, of course, on the nature of working relationships between specialists and line managers, and the way in which the HR/personnel department operates, but the problem of causal relationship between what one party does and its effects is an enduring one;

● although nominally offering an advisory service, the HR specialist can be seen by line managers to be taking on executive responsibilities and introducing practices and policies that, although in the interests of the organization as a whole, can be perceived as intrusive, unhelpful and having little relevance to the line manager's priorities and agendas. In seeking to develop their functional expertise and professional identity, those who work in HR can become detached from 'the needs of the business', and, as a consequence, run the risk of being seen as 'marginal' and adding little of value. An example of this tendency might be the increasing emphasis HR give to diversity issues, which, while of general importance, can be perceived by line managers as having little direct relevance to matters of production or to 'bottom-line performance'.

STUDENT ACTIVITY 2.1 **The business case for diversity training**

1. Research the literature on the business case for managing diversity.

2. Taking the role of a team of HR professionals, prepare a PowerPoint presentation, to be delivered to the CEO of an organization of your choice, which presents your findings and recommendations.

3. Faced with a sceptical and pressurized group of line managers who have responsibility for delivering a product or service – you can pick your own industry/organization – what would you say that would convince them that HR has not jumped on yet another bandwagon and that the investment in learning about diversity issues is justifiable?

4. What desirable or value-added outcomes would you be able to identify from such an investment?

The sense that HR is somehow 'failing to deliver' is a central theme in the writings of a number of influential American writers. Jeffrey Pfeffer (1997), for example, writing about the future of Human Resource Management, suggests that it would be wrong to conclude that the growing interest in HR and Human Resource Management necessarily means that the future of the HR function (in its departmental form) is bright:

My advice is to resist the temptation to believe that HR managers and staff in organizations have a rosy future, or a future at all, because there are some profound problems facing human resources as a function within organizations, as contrasted with the study of human resources as a topic area, that makes its viability and continued survival problematical. (p 190)

Posing the question, '*where is the HR function in the debate about flexibility, contingent working arrangements and the implementation of high performance working practices?*', he suggests that the tentative answer is, '*largely absent*'. He continues:

To the extent it has a presence, HR is frequently an accomplice in a number of trends such as downsizing and contingent work arrangements that promise to actually undo much of the progress made in managing the employment relationship in the past several decades. (p 191)

Pfeffer is particularly critical of the lack of leadership shown by HR professionals in demonstrating the relationship between HR practices and organizational performance, and he believes that many are unaware of the empirical business case for managing people effectively. Despite these criticisms, he believes that HR professionals do have a future, but only if they change their roles and acquire new skills. Above all, he argues, they need to learn how to add value to the organization.

Dave Ulrich, one of the most influential writers on HR, has levelled similar criticisms at the HR profession. In his 1998 article, 'A new mandate for human resources', he asks whether we should do away with HR, justifying this by referring to the serious and widespread doubts about HR's contribution to organizational performance. But before we progress his arguments, it is worth noting that many of the earlier and indeed current definitions of Personnel Management and HRM – he is not distinguishing these from what he means by HR – do not include any explicit reference to organizational performance. In their most recent edition, Torrington et al (2005) retain, with only slight modifications, the same definition of 'Human Resource Management' as they gave for 'Personnel Management' in 1979:

> **Human Resource Management is a series of activities which: first enables working people and the organisation which uses their skills to agree about the objectives and nature of their working relationships and, secondly, ensures that the agreement is fulfilled.**

Nowhere in this definition is there any reference to HR supporting the business, contributing to organizational performance or adding value; whether any of these could be implied in the wording or sentiments expressed in the definition is, at best, arguable. And this is Ulrich's main point: he claims that it is precisely because HR is still associated with traditional activities, rather than with outcomes, and with a concern with consensus, rather than with delivering valued contributions, that many still see HR, as:

> **... often ineffective, incompetent, and costly; in a phrase, it is value sapping.**
> (Ulrich, 1998, p 124)

On reflection, his answer to these criticisms is not, in fact, to '*do away with HR*', but to '*create an entirely new role and agenda for the field*', with HR not being '*defined by what it does, but by what it delivers – results that enrich the organisation's value to customers, investors, and employees*' (p 124).

It's interesting to compare the Torrington et al definition of Human Resource Management with that of a comparable American text. Denisi and Griffin (2001) provide a definition much closer to that with which Ulrich would feel comfortable. They argue that human resource management (the wider function *and* the specialized approach) can be understood as:

> **... the comprehensive set of managerial activities and tasks concerned with developing and maintaining a qualified workforce – human resources – in ways that contribute to organisational effectiveness.**

The need for HR – and again it is important to understand that Ulrich uses this to refer to HR professionals and the work of the HR department, not the wider HR function–to ensure that its activities are connected to the 'real work' of the organization led him to develop his model of a new HR, which would contribute to organizational competitiveness and performance. This model is summarized in Figure 2.4.

The four key roles that HR professionals need to play to deliver the contributions outlined in the model are as follows

● A partner in strategy execution

This doesn't mean that HR should take responsibility for HR and business strategy, which is rightly the domain of the chief executive, but that the head of the HR department should be an equal partner with other senior managers and should 'have a seat at the top table'.

● An administrative expert

This is about getting the basics right and adopting a much more instrumental approach to the use of procedures. The emphasis needs to be on the efficiency of the HR department – reducing its cost base and speeding up its cycle times, without compromising on quality or effectiveness.

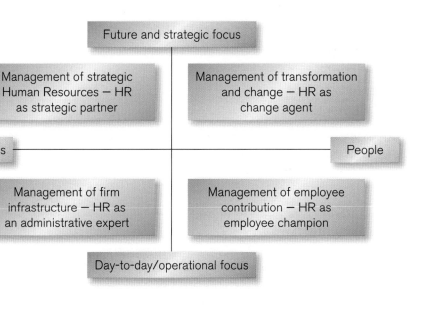

Figure 2.4 A framework for understanding HR roles and contributions

- An employee champion

    This is about HR recognizing that work intensification and an increased sense of insecurity are becoming the new reality for many people and that this is associated with weakened levels of employee commitment. This, in turn, affects the preparedness of employees to contribute more than their contracted level of effort and performance. The role of HR here is to ensure that employees remain engaged and committed, or become re-engaged, either directly through the activities of HR or by HR working with line managers to ensure that they can create a positive psychological and emotional working environment.

- A change agent

    According to Ulrich (1997), this role involves HR in building the organization's capacity to embrace and to capitalize on change. Given that change is the norm for most organizations, the ability to implement and manage the change process is seen as critical to the organization's ability to function during the change process and to reap the benefits from the changes that have been made. Reducing resistance to change is seen as a key HR contribution.

Interestingly, Ulrich is aware of the danger of oversimplifying the roles that HR professionals need to play in order to gain credibility for themselves and the HR function: it isn't simply a question of moving from the operational to the strategic, or from a reactive to a proactive, orientation. The reality is that HR roles are multiple, changing and complex, involving them in policing *and* partnering, and delivering operational *and* making strategic contributions. He concludes:

> **For HR professionals to add value to their increasingly complex businesses, they must perform increasingly complex and, at times, even paradoxical roles.**
> (1997, p 24)

In a more recent work, Ulrich and Brockbank (2005) refine Ulrich's model of HR roles to reflect a more sophisticated understanding of what HR professionals need to be and to contribute to in the next two decades, compared to the situation in the 1990s. The revised role model emphasizes the importance of the HR professional becoming:

- a developer of human capital;
- an employee advocate;
- a functional expert;
- a strategic partner;
- a leader of the HR function.

The main changes are in the incorporation of the change agent role within that of the strategic partner and the recognition of the importance of leadership in HR.

STUDENT ACTIVITY 2.2

In his book, *Human Resource Champions* (1997), Ulrich compares what he calls the old myths associated with HR with the new realities facing HR professionals. Working in groups, your task is to fill in the 'new realities' part of the table without referring to the book. Only make reference to the original table on completion of the exercise.

Myths and misconceptions	The 'new realities' *(Complete this part of the table)*
People want to work in HR because they like people Anyone can do HR HR is woolly and too people-focused HR is about controlling the line and telling them what to do HR is about rules and procedures and enforcing these HR is the conscience of the organization HR is full of fads and jargon HR is staffed by nice people HR is HR's business	

Rationality in HR

Ulrich's criticism that HR is over-concerned with activities at the expense of outcomes and value-adding contributions is, in one sense, important because it puts the emphasis on what HR actually achieves. But there remains the question of what HR does or should be doing – i.e. its activities – and how these actually produce desired and valued outcomes. Outcomes have to be linked to inputs or activities – they do not happen in isolation!

What has emerged so far in this critical perspective on HR is that many of the activities that HR professionals engage in appear not to be valued by managers and employees. This is because there is either no evidence that the activities actually achieve things that matter or because it is very difficult, as was pointed out earlier, to prove that what HR does actually results in improvements in behaviour and performance. If the latter is the reason, then the task of HR is to look carefully at the way in which it measures and evaluates effectiveness; if the problem is more to do with what HR does and how it carries out these activities, then the challenge it faces is more fundamental.

This is something about which Tony Watson (2003) has written extensively and Watson is one of the relatively few writers on HR who confronts the often taken-for-granted assumptions associated with HR activities, and their effects and consequences.

The relationship between what can be understand as the *means* employed by those associated with the HR function (i.e. activities, instruments and processes) and the *ends* actually achieved, rather than expected, is often seen as unproblematical. But what is too frequently ignored is the existence and effect of powerful mediating factors within the organization that 'interfere' with, and undermine the impact of, many HR interventions. Simply carrying out an activity does not necessarily mean that the intended outcomes are actually achieved; often with HR, the outcomes and consequences that are experienced are more unintended than intended!

To illustrate this point, let us consider one of the most widely used HR practices, the performance appraisal process, which provides an interesting example of how many mainstream writers fail to give sufficient critical attention to what is *actually* achieved from this and many other HR activities.

In her popular textbook, Maund (2001) presents a list of the advantages of an appraisal system, which include the positive nature of formal appraisal meetings between appraiser and appraisee, and the generation of valuable feedback. She is not alone in claiming that performance appraisals offer advantages to the organization; most other mainstream HR textbooks make similar claims. The problem, however, is that there is no recognition that the claimed advantages for performance appraisal *might not* be experienced by those involved in the process or by their organizations.

Taking a more realistic stance, the starting point has to be that many of these claimed advantages are, in fact, potential rather than actual, and — more worryingly — may not, in fact, be experienced by the majority of those involved in the process. This is the basic premise of Coens and Jenkins (2000), who, in their book *Abolishing Performance Appraisals*, quote numerous writers who claim that performance appraisals, in whatever form, are at best likely to have a limited effect on individual performance, but are actually more likely to result in the *undermining* of employees' morale and performance by their experiences of the performance appraisal processes. They refer to a comment made in the *Wall Street Journal* by TD Schellhardt, who said that:

> **If less that 10% of your customers judged a product to be effective, and seven out of ten said they were more confused than enlightened by it, you would drop it, right? So, why don't more companies drop their annual job-performance reviews?**

The very clear implication is that, in the opinion of this particular commentator at least, one form of performance appraisal was not seen to deliver particularly valued outcomes. But the important point is not only about whether performance appraisal itself is not valued as an activity and fails to deliver improvements in employee performance, but about whether HR is seen to be the driving force behind this activity. As Coens and Jenkins state, as a result of the failure of most performance appraisal schemes, rather than abandon them:

> **HR staff finds itself policing, refereeing, and collecting a lot of paper that doesn't mean much to most people.**
> (2000, p 2)

This, of course, does little to enhance the credibility of HR.

Yet Maund claims that appraisal, regardless of which system is used and because it is part of the employee development process:

> **Has to be perceived, therefore, as useful to everyone concerned.**
> (2001, p 574)

This is far too simplistic a position to take and is not consistent with the experiences of many people involved in the performance appraisal process, nor is it consistent with the research quoted by Coens and Jenkins. Moreover, it is a position that suggests that there is an unproblematical link between what HR does and what results from its interventions. Using performance appraisal as a specific example helps us to reach the more general conclusion that many HR activities do have an effect on employee and managerial behaviour, but that these effects can be negative as well as positive. However unpalatable it might be to those who are professionally associated with HR, the possibility has to be acknowledged that HR, rather than representing the solution to the challenges of managing people, can, in certain circumstances, be part of the problem.

Watson's analysis of how organizations operate offers an insight into this problem of why what appear to be valued and useful activities do not always deliver desired outcomes. He observed that modern organizations are more or less based on bureaucratic principles, and place a heavy reliance on rational techniques and processes, particularly in the way in which employees are used as resources in the pursuit of organizational goals. Accepting that people, as resources, are also human beings, who have their own interests and can be assertive when they perceive that these interests are being undermined by the activities of the dominant stakeholders, he argues that managers generally — but particularly those involved in the HR function — are subject to what he calls the 'paradox of consequences'. He describes this concept as:

> **The tendency for the means adopted by organisational managers to achieve particular goals to fail to achieve these goals since these 'means' involve human beings who have goals of their own which may not be congruent with those of the managers.**
> (2003, p 90)

This paradox — which potentially exists in all organizations, although its strength and significance may vary — is closely linked to the Weberian concepts of formal and material rationality. An appreciation of what these two concepts mean for HR is critical to understanding the problematical nature of the means—ends relationship and the experience of unintended consequences.

KEY CONCEPT Formal rationality

This refers to the choice and use of planned and sensible techniques and processes to control and manage employees by those in positions of authority. These include workplace rules, processes used in recruitment and selection and performance management, many of the methods used in training, and methods of incentivizing staff. Collectively, these would be defined as 'means'. There is an important sense that these rules, interventions and activities will work and will have the desired effect because they are theoretically or formally attractive and sensible.

KEY CONCEPT Material rationality

This refers to what actually works: results that confirm that the intended consequences following any intervention or action have actually been met. The test of whether any intervention or activity meets the criteria of material rationality is whether it works 'in practice' and generates the desired 'ends' or outcomes.

Because of the effects of the paradox of unintended consequences, the rules and 'ways of doing things' associated with HR, which can often be seen as being formally rational ways of operating and managing, can fail to meet the criterion of material rationality. This helps to explain why many performance appraisal systems, as an example, don't improve performance, but instead undermine it, and don't improve motivation, but instead weaken it. An exclusive reliance on formal rationality also explains why certain types of incentive scheme result in a long-term decline in productivity, and why the use of certain training methods and techniques fail to generate the required learning outcomes.

What is the future for HR?

When considering the answer to this question, it is important to understand that it relates primarily to the HR department and the role of HR professionals, rather than being about human resource management, and it is in this context that the debate is continuing. As far as human resource management is concerned, there is no equivalent question and debate. As Meisinger (p. 189, 2005) asserts:

> The good news is that today the mantra 'people are our most important asset' is not just rhetoric. For most leaders , it's the reality.

Not everyone would agree that each employee has the same value or potential as every other, but the view that employees are critical to organizational success is now generally accepted. In this sense, managing the human resource effectively has become even more important in the twenty-first century because, of all of the resources that organizations utilize, this is the one that is the most difficult to replicate and is that which represents an organization's unique competitive advantage.

Looking for and recruiting the most talented people available, giving them meaningful and rewarding jobs to do in a supportive environment, and developing and utilizing their competences in ways that deliver in whatever jobs they are in, will become more, rather than less, important. But the crucial question for HR professionals is what will their role be in these vitally important areas?

Rucci (1997) holds the view that HR is a profession at the crossroads. While accepting that there are those who believe HR to be on the ascendancy, based on continuing progress in helping to develop innovative people practices that support organizational objectives, he holds a different view: one that sees HR as a separate 'entity' and profession ceasing to exist.

He presents two scenarios for the demise of HR. The first results from HR's failure in:

- promoting change;
- understanding and becoming integrated within the business;
- relating to customers;
- addressing the issue of costs and efficiency;
- emphasizing and ensuring organizational values are 'lived'.

Recent research in the UK suggests that Rucci's 'demise by failure' scenario is a definite possibility. Whittaker and Marchington (2003), for example, found that line managers complained about HR:

- being out of touch with business realities;
- constraining line managers' freedom of action;
- being unresponsive and slow;
- developing policies that are good in theory but which don't work well in practice (i.e. that are lacking material rationality).

Rucci's second, and more positive, scenario for the demise of HR is based, paradoxically, on HR becoming more business-focused, managing change well, developing good leaders and promoting values. According to Rucci:

> . . . the milestone of HR's effectiveness will not be its ability to survive and do these things for the organisation, but rather its ability to transfer these into the responsibilities and accountabilities of managers at all levels.
> (1997, p 198)

The implication of this position is that HR, *as a source of expertise*, has to move out of centralized departments and into the line, where it is needed and where it will have the greatest impact. This may be achieved through developments in the HR business partner role, which involves HR professionals working directly with designated line managers, or through line managers themselves acquiring this expertise as a result of their own development and the redefining of the responsibilities of line management roles to include explicit reference to managing people.

But where does that leave HR's strategic contribution? It seems increasingly likely that the requirement for a strategic HR plan for the organization, as opposed to a strategic plan for HR, will increasingly be owned by CEOs and other senior managers. This trend reflects the view that human resource management is too important to be left exclusively to HR and that this will particularly be the case at the strategic level of activity.

As far as the bulk of HR's administrative responsibilities are concerned, the outsourcing of these to specialist organizations is continuing and is likely to grow in its frequency. The Work Foundation (2003) found that occupational health services, payroll, pensions and training were the most common HR activities being outsourced. This picture is supported by the Department of Trade and Industry's Workplace Employee Relations Survey 2004 (WERS 2004), which found that training was cited by 27 per cent of respondents as being outsourced, with 25 per cent citing payroll and the sourcing of temporary employees, and 14 per cent citing other recruitment. Factors influencing the outsourcing of HR administration are likely to be:

- the high cost;
- concerns over efficiency levels;
- the availability of new technology.

HR departments that retain responsibility for HR administration are likely to be under pressure to reduce the amount of time and resources allocated to this aspect of their work — there is a high opportunity cost associated with this — and to deliver a reliable and efficient service; those that don't face outsourcing and a loss of credibility.

According to Reilly and Williams (2006), the future of HR is linked to its ability to combine administrative efficiency with operational and strategic effectiveness, and a heightened level of professionalism. They argue that HR professionals have to learn to work with, and through, line managers at all levels, but to do this, they need new skills and capabilities. Where it still exists, the 'old' HR mindset associated with centralization, remoteness, rules, procedures and regulation needs to be replaced by one that emphasizes the importance of a business orientation, partnership, results and generating competitive advantage through maximizing the contributions that employees make to the organization. Reilly and Williams suggest that:

> HR should not spend too long trying to divine an abstract meaning to their work. Rather, in doing their job well — helping connect people and business — they will be adding value, demonstrating their worth and indicating their USP [unique selling point].
> (2006, p 49)

Conclusion

There is little doubt that HR, as a specialist management function, faces a challenging future: a future that, for some, involves something of a metamorphosis. There also seems to be a general consensus that it has to change before it can meet the requirements and expectations of other organizational stakeholders, and be accorded the status and credibility that the function is seeking. Whether the change, as Rucci (1997) believes, will involve its demise is more problematical and contentious.

What are the changes to which HR needs to commit in order to preserve its future? They can perhaps be expressed in relation to the following.

- Acquiring and applying a much stronger *business orientation* in designing and delivering HR activities and services

This has major implications for the skills and mindset of HR professionals and in relation to their recruitment and selection. The employment of people from outside of the HR profession to senior HR positions is a trend that is likely to continue.

● Being clearer about the *priorities* they pursue and why certain activities have been prioritized

This will inevitably mean than the HR agenda and the deployment of HR resources is influenced, if not determined, by the 'users' of HR — i.e. by employees, line managers and senior executives, as well as HR professionals.

● Developing their *functional expertise*

This involves developing skills and competences that allow HR to deliver 'solutions' and to offer advice and support to managers that is founded on a body of professional theory that has been tested and refined in countless situations. If line managers retain a degree of dependence on HR experts, then the expertise offered has to deliver the contributions and outcomes that those line managers need.

● Building *personal credibility* and a reputation for reliability and professionalism

In their article on what distinguishes successful from less successful HR managers, Buckingham and Elliot (1993) found that those rated as 'above average' in performance were associated with:

- the ability to motivate others;
- the ability to build relationships;
- the ability to seek and build commitment;
- the possession of a conceptual mindset, and a clear perspective on their role and its purpose.

They conclude:

> **This mind set may be defined as a philosophy of Personnel Management and a conceptual ability to define the significant contribution that the personnel professional can make to the organisation. This philosophy is strongly rooted in clear perceptions about, and a real commitment to, the value of good employees and of their contribution to the company.**

The future of HR will undoubtedly be influenced by developments in technology, in organizational forms and in relation to the capability of line managers in taking on much more responsibility for the management of their staff. It might also be argued that its future is in the hands of those who work in HR and whether they can rise to the challenges confronting the profession.

STUDENT ACTIVITY 2.3 Identifying HR competences

This final activity involves researching the kind of competences needed by HR professionals and can be the basis of a group project or presentation.

1. Research the literature on HR roles and their associated competences, and summarize your findings. You may also be able to collect data from within organizations to help build this picture.

2. On the basis of your findings, devise a strategy for developing these competences, showing, in a practical way, how a newly recruited graduate to HR might acquire these competences.

3. Explore how the competency and effectiveness of HR professionals might be measured.

Summary

This chapter has deliberately adopted a more questioning and critical approach to the role and contribution of HR in organizations than is found in some other HR textbooks. The reason for this is that HR professionals are under increasing pressure to 'deliver' and those who cannot, or do not, understand what this means will not be considered credible. The departments within which they work are likely to be reorganized and parts of their responsibilities outsourced: this is the new reality.

HR also operates in an often-unpredictable external environment, which can undermine existing practices and priorities, and transform what the organization expects HR to do. In Chapter 14, the Oliver's case study involving plant closure is an example of what this can involve. The conclusion is, therefore, that HR and those who are associated with it need to become flexible and adaptable, and be comfortable with uncertainty and ambiguity. To be able to do this requires new skills and competences, and the effective recruitment and development of HR staff is becoming increasingly important and challenging.

 Signpost to Chapter 14: The Role of HR in Closing a Factory

Finally, to secure its long-term future as a specialist management function, the evidence from many of the academic contributions on HR suggests that it must become much more 'business-orientated' and deliver value-adding contributions to the business. What this actually means has to be determined within each organization, but it will inevitably involve accepting that the HR agenda has to be more business-led. Those who work in the HR department, meanwhile, must recognize that human resource management has become far more important than Human Resource Management.

 Visit the Online Resource Centre that accompanies this book for self-test questions, weblinks, and more information on the topics covered in this chapter.
online
resource
centre **www.oxfordtextbooks.co.uk/orc/banfield_kay/**

 ## REVIEW QUESTIONS

1. What are the contributions of HR professionals and line managers to the behaviour and performance of employees?

2. What is the difference between human resource management and Human Resource Management?

3. In the context of the knowledge economy, what particular employment and HR practices will be necessary if organizations are going to maximize the performance and contributions of knowledge workers?

4. What will be the issues and pressures affecting HR in ten years' time?

CASE STUDY
Reforming the HR function at the Royal Mail

The material for this case study is taken from a presentation given at the CIPD national conference in 2005.

The Royal Mail, prior to recent changes, employed over 200,000 people and had been a national institution for over 300 years. In the early part of this century, however, it began to suffer serious performance and financial problems. It was known for poor industrial relations and accounted for nearly 50 per cent of working days lost because of strikes. It was a business that was near to insolvency, and was renowned for low pay and long hours, and an overreliance on agency workers. It was, in other words, a business that had failed to adapt its internal structures and culture to a rapidly changing external environment in which increasing competition was the most important development.

The HR function, defined in terms of those who worked in and for the specialized HR department, was costing the business £200m each year. Approximately 3,700 people were employed in HR, which meant that the ratio of HR staff to total employees was near to 1:55 (i.e. for every 55 employees, there was one member of HR). The primary role of HR was in relation to the trade unions, which defined the state of the company's employee relations. But, increasingly, HR had become associated with numerous policies and procedures covering almost every aspect of the employment and management of people. Unfortunately, the increasing influence of the centralized HR function had led to a defranchising of line managers, who felt unable to engage directly with their staff.

The need to transform HR as part of changing the culture of the organization was based on a clear understanding of how the 'people' side of the business needed to change. It involved:

- an overall reduction in costs;
- a modernization of employment processes and procedures;
- the professionalization of the HR function;
- a change in the relationship with trade unions;
- adding more strategic value;
- empowering line managers;
- driving change.

The transformation was achieved by creating a new HR architecture, based on a very clear distinction between the different contributions that HR was required to make. The 'new' HR was based on three distinctive domains:

- establishing functional expertise that supported the line;
- creating business partners that worked with the line;
- a shared service capability that delivered administrative efficiency.

The transformation was not achieved without considerable investment in the development of HR staff, supplemented by the injection of new talent to lead the changes. The newly appointed 'Business Partners' were assessed against a demanding competency framework and there was an emphasis away from 'doables to deliverables', with a new focus on how HR could add value to the business.

The results of the transformation were both impressive and challenging. The ratio of HR staff to employees rose to 1:130. A new attitude and relationship with the trade unions resulted in a reduction in industrial disputes and restrictive work practices, and a reduction in headcount of 34,000.

The clear message, however, was that this was the beginning rather than the end of a process. Further competitive pressures meant that Royal Mail needed to become more competitive, leading to increasing pressure on jobs and the need to raise productivity levels even higher. For HR, there was 'no hiding place', but its key contributions could only be made as a result of a very different HR architecture and a new relationship with line managers.

Questions

1. What particular competencies do the organization's HR 'Business Partners' need to be able to work effectively with line managers?
2. What are shared service centres and how do they operate?
3. What needs to be done to allow line managers to take direct responsibility for managing their staff?
4. What happened to those HR staff that were lost to the company?

FURTHER READING

Pfeffer, J (2005) 'Changing mental models: HR's most important task', *Human Resource Management*, 44:2, pp 123–8.

Reddington, M, Williamson, M and Withers, M (2005) *Transforming HR*, Elsevier.

Turner, N (2004) *Achieving Strategic Alignment of Business and Human Resources*, Work Foundation.

Ulrich, D and Beatty, RW (2001) 'From partners to players: extending the HR playing field', *Human Resource Management*, 40:4, Winter, pp 293–308.

REFERENCES

Banfield, P (2005) 'Schizophrenia, Inuits and the Holy Grail: a brief reflection on the search for professional identity', CIPD South Yorkshire Branch Newsletter (visit the Online Resource Centre to view the article).

Barney, JB (1991) 'Firm resources and sustained competitive advantage', *Journal of Management*, 17:1, pp 99–120.

Becker, B, Huselid, MA and Ulrich, D (2001) *The HR Scorecard*, Harvard Business School Press.

Beer, M, Spector, B, Lawrence, P, Quinn Mills, D and Walton, R (1985) *Human Resource Management: A General Manager's Perspective*, Free Press.

Boxall, P and Purcell, J (2000) 'Strategic human resource management: where have we come from and where should we be going?', *International Journal of Management Reviews*, 2:2, pp 183–203.

Buckingham, G and Elliot, G (1993) 'Profile of a successful personnel manager', *Personnel Management*, 25:8, pp 26–9.

Chartered Institute of Personnel and Development (2004) *Personnel Management: A Short History*, CIPD factsheet, available online at www.cipd.co.uk.

Chartered Institute of Personnel and Development (2005) *The Role of Front-Line Managers in HR*, CIPD factsheet, available online at www.cipd.co.uk.

Christensen, RN (1997) 'Where is human resources?', quoted in Ulrich, D, Losey, MR and Lake, G (eds) (1997) *Tomorrow's HR Management*, John Wiley and Sons.

Coens, T and Jenkins, M (2000) *Abolishing Performance Appraisals*, Berrett-Koehler, p 1.

Denisi, AS and Griffin, RW (2001) *Human Resource Management*, Houghton Mifflin Co, p 4.

Department of Trade and Industry (2004) Workplace Employee Relations Survey (WERS 2004), available online at www.dti.gov.uk.

Gennard, J and Kelly, J (1994) 'Human Resource Management: the views of personnel directors', *Human Resource Management*, 5:1, pp 15–32.

Grant, D and Oswick, C (1998) 'Of believers, atheists and agnostics: practitioner views on HRM', *Industrial Relations Journal*, 29:3, pp 178–93.

Hammonds, KH (2005) 'Why we hate HR', *Fast Company*, Aug, p 40.

Hoque, K and Noon, M (2001) 'Counting the angels: a comparison of personnel and HR specialists', *Human Resource Management*, 11:3, p 5.

Hutchinson, S and Purcell, J (2003) *Bringing Policies to Life: The Vital Role of Front Line Managers in People Management*, CIPD.

Kamoche, K (1996) 'Strategic Human Resource Management within a resource capability', *Journal of Management Studies*, 33:2, pp 213–33.

Legge, K (1978) *Power, Innovation and Problem-Solving in Personnel Management*, McGraw-Hill, ch 1.

Legge, K (1995) *Human Resource Management: Rhetorics and Reality*, Macmillan Business.

Maund, L (2001) *An Introduction to Human Resource Management*, Palgrave.

Meisinger, SR (2005) 'The four Cs of the HR profession: being competent, curious, courageous and caring about people', *Human Resource Management*, 44:2, pp 189–94.

Niven, MM (1967) *Personnel Management 1913–63*, IPD.

Pfeffer, J (1997) 'Does Human Resource Management have a future?' in Ulrich, D, Losey, MR and Lake, G (eds) (1997) *Tomorrow's HR Management*, John Wiley and Sons.

Reilly, P and Williams, T (2006) *Strategic HR: Building the Capability to Deliver*, Gower.

Rucci, AJ (1997) 'Should Human Resources survive? A profession at the crossroads' in Ulrich, D, Losey, MR and Lake, G (eds) (1997) *Tomorrow's HR Management*, John Wiley and Sons.

Smith, I and Boyns, T (2005) 'British management theory and practice: the impact of Fayol', *Management Decision*, 43:10, pp 1317–34.

Storey, J (1992) *Developments in the Management of Human Resources*, Blackwell, p 35.

Tichy, N, Fombrun, C and Devanna, MA (1982) 'Strategic human resource management', *Sloan Management Review*, 23:2, Winter, pp 47–64.

Torrington, D, Hall, L and Taylor, S (2005) *Human Resource Management*, FT/Prentice Hall.

Tyson, S and Fell, A (1986) *Evaluating the Personnel Function*, Hutchinson Education.

Ulrich, D (1997) *Human Resource Champions*, Harvard Business School Press.

Ulrich, D (1998) 'A new mandate for Human Resources', *Harvard Business Review*, 76:1, pp 124–34.

Ulrich, D and Brockbank, W (2005) *The HR Value Proposition*, Harvard Business School Press.

Watson, TJ (2002) *Organising and Managing Work*, 2nd edn, FT/Prentice Hall.

Watson, TJ (2003) *Sociology, Work and Industry*, Routledge.

Whittaker, S and Marchington, M (2003) 'Devolving HR responsibility: threat, opportunity or partnership', *Employee Relations*, 25:3, pp 245–61.

The Work Foundation (2003) *Outsourcing and Offshoring: Implications for Organisational Capacity*, The Work Foundation.

Operational Challenges

2

Recruitment and Selection

Key Terms

Hiring or employing The overall process of taking on new staff from outside the organization.

External recruitment The process of identifying and attracting potential employees to an organization to fill current or future vacancies.

Internal recruitment The process of identifying current employees who may be suitable for newly created vacancies or for replacing staff who leave.

Assessment The tools and techniques used by an organization to identify and measure, either qualitatively or quantitatively, the skills, knowledge, and potential of applicants.

Selection The process, culminating in the decision to fill a vacancy from internal or external applicants, used by the organization to choose the most suitable candidate from a pool of applicants.

Competency profiles/framework These are statements of what people need to be able to do in order to perform their job to the required standard.

Best practice This terms implies that in carrying out HR activities there is 'one best way' of doing things, irrespective of the context or circumstances.

Best fit This approach decides what should be done and how it should be done based on the unique circumstances that characterize every organization. It links action to specific requirements rather than following an established approach.

Opportunity cost This is the cost associated with not choosing to pursue one course of action in favour of another. This is a difficult calculation but is nevertheless an important consideration when deciding which course of action to take.

Productive capacity/potential Productive capacity expresses what employees can currently do and thus conveys their current value to the organization. Productive potential on the other hand represents employees' future value and contribution based on future learning and development.

Learning Objectives

As a result of reading this chapter and using the Online Resource Centre, you should be able to:

- understand the importance of attracting high-performing employees to an organization;
- define and manage the processes involved in recruitment and selection;
- identify and develop different recruitment strategies for an organization;
- understand the professional and ethical standards that are appropriate in recruitment and selection;
- understand the relationship between recruitment and selection and other HR activities.

Introduction

Figure 3.1 illustrates the relationship between the two connected fields of 'recruitment' and 'selection'. A more detailed 'map', which connects these two central activities to a more strategic understanding of what is involved in the acquisition of human resources, is provided later in the chapter. For the moment, Figure 3.1 shows how the two activities are related and what the key issues are. The bubbles on the left show the types of consideration to be made at each stage and the boxes on the right list some of the

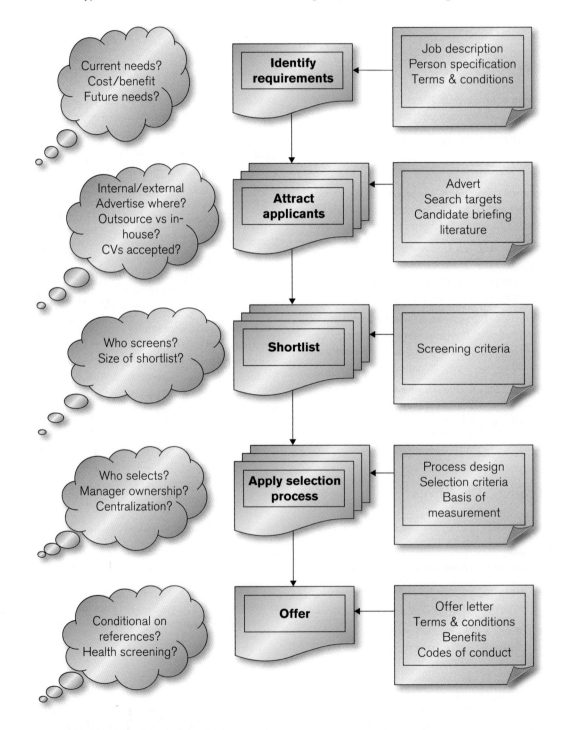

Figure 3.1 The recruitment and selection process

typical documentation required at each stage of the process. As the chapter develops, a more detailed analysis of each of the three intermediate stages will be provided.

Why is recruitment and selection so important?

No matter how sophisticated the systems, processes and technology of an organization, it is the capabilities and commitment of its employees that ensure its success. Without the optimum combination of people at different levels, with appropriate capabilities, knowledge and motivation, individual and organizational performance will suffer. It is therefore essential to the success of the organization to ensure that recruitment and selection is effective, and delivers the highest calibre of employees at optimum cost. As many writers have maintained (e.g. Gratton, 2000; Michaels et al, 2001), by the beginning of the twenty-first century, an increasing number of managers had become aware that the only unique and sustainable source of competitive advantage came from the inspiration, knowledge and effort of employees; i.e. of the organization's 'human capital'. Human capital is a valuable asset for organizations, which resides within the people that comprise the workforce and can easily be lost through people voluntarily leaving the organization or as a result of organizational restructuring. Maintaining and strengthening the human capital base is one of the main strategic challenges facing the human resource professional, and recruitment and selection are key to achieving this goal.

It would be a mistake, however, to see these activities in isolation. Carrying out the various activities that result in the hiring of new employees is a necessary, but not sufficient, requirement. An organization's human capital base is enriched not only by the employment of new recruits from outside, but by the retention and development of the majority of its employees. Nevertheless, there is a strong case to be made for recognizing that recruiting and selecting the 'right' employees is absolutely critical to an organization's ability to grow and prosper. This view is reflected in the work of such writers as Jack Welch, a previous head of GE, who argues that:

...nothing matters more in winning than getting the right people on the field.
(Welch and Welch, 2005, p 81)

But attracting and selecting the 'best' candidates is neither an easy task, nor is it risk free. Burrows (2004) justifiably argues that the challenges of introducing and integrating new recruits from outside a company cannot be underestimated or treated lightly. He also believes, however, that as long as the proper tools are used in the assessment process, applicants' ambitions and personal motivations are understood, and coaching is used to ensure the rapid integration of new recruits, the chances of meeting these challenges will be much greater than if these requirements were ignored or misunderstood. Notwithstanding this, mistakes can be made and the 'wrong' people hired, with unfortunate implications for the organization and for the employee.

→ Signpost to Chapters 10 and 11: Learning and Development and Managing Performance, for implications of underperforming staff

Collins (2001) offers an opinion on the importance of being as sure as one can about a person's suitability before making the job offer:

When in doubt, don't hire, keep looking...A company should limit its growth based on its ability to attract enough of the right people.
(p 63)

Pressures to fill positions quickly can often result in the wrong decisions being made — decisions that are not always easily rectified. The following HRM Insight illustrates very clearly why it is preferable not to hire until a thorough assessment of each candidate's suitability has been completed.

HRM INSIGHT 3.1 **Recruiting the wrong person at ABC Logistics**

Margaret Bailey had recently been appointed head of HR for ABC Logistics – a newly formed business based on the merger between a distribution company and a national retail group. The new greenfield site offered state-of-the-art logistics management systems and an attractive working environment for its employees. Margaret's main responsibilities since being appointed were to lead on the recruitment of the workforce, and to ensure that those employed not only had the necessary experience and competence that would enable them to meet challenging job performance requirements, but also 'fitted in' to the new culture that the senior managers were trying to build.

Building her own team of talented and committed HR professionals was key to being able to implement the recruitment strategy and also to delivering the wider HR agenda, and Margaret had been trying to recruit like-minded professionals to join her team. As with all new projects, time was a critical factor and she needed to recruit an additional HR person to contribute to the demanding departmental workload. As she remarked:

We were under real pressure to get someone in as quickly as possible.

Alan Hudson seemed a reasonable candidate. He had several years of general HR experience behind him and had said all of the right things in his interview. The decision to appoint him at first appeared to have been uncontroversial, but it wasn't long before the first worrying signs began to appear. It wasn't anything specific, but more of a general lack of urgency and commitment in his work. He was taking much longer than other members of the team to complete his work assignments and he showed little evidence of self-motivation.

Margaret's initial response was to have an informal meeting to establish how he was feeling and whether there was anything in particular about which he was concerned. But, despite this meeting, little changed and, in subsequent meetings, the question was raised of whether he had made the right decision, in career terms, in joining ABC Logistics. After three months, he submitted a holiday approval request to Margaret, which was refused on the grounds that insufficient notice had been given and the department could not afford to be understaffed. Alan accused Margaret of bullying and went off 'sick'. On his return, Margaret convened a formal meeting with Alan to review his performance and made it clear that, unless this significantly improved, further action would be taken. Alan subsequently submitted his notice and it was agreed that he could leave immediately.

Questions

1. What selection shortcuts might have been made in Alan's appointment?

2. Estimate the costs that the company incurred as a result of Alan's appointment.

3. Devise and present an assessment strategy for applicants applying for the recently vacated HR position at ABC Logistics.

If recruitment and selection is not risk free and may result in mistakes being made, can the assessment and selection of applicants be carried out in such a way that the 'best', or the 'right', person will always be identified, and the 'wrong' people kept out of the organization? The answer to this is, unfortunately, that 'no', it cannot be guaranteed. Recruitment and selection is not an exact science and, no matter how thorough and objective the processes undertaken are, there is always a possibility that the chosen candidate will not perform to the expected standard. Extraneous pressures can interfere with the decision-making process, and subjectivity and bias can undermine procedural rigour. It is important to recognize, however, that much better decisions and fewer mistakes can be made if a thorough process is followed, involving the gathering of as much relevant and objective information as possible, and using the expertise and judgement of different stakeholders. Consider the following HRM Insight, in which an important and costly mistake was avoided only by the timely intervention of an HR professional.

HRM INSIGHT 3.2 **The legal practice that nearly got it wrong**

Celia Johnson had been employed by Richard Curtis, senior partner in the law firm Curtis, Bowers and Smith, to bring some structure and order to the firm's HR provision. Up to her appointment, the HR function had effectively been limited to a part-time administrator and Curtis, who looked after all recruitment and reward matters. In an increasingly competitive recruitment environment, the firm had been struggling to attract and retain experienced lawyers, some of whom, in addition to their fee-earning roles, also had to manage different departments within the firm. Richard, aware of the need to strengthen his managerial team, was always on the lookout for new staff.

The firm had no recruitment strategy as such: recruitment was very ad hoc and relied on word of mouth, external networks, and on following up enquiries and the CVs submitted by lawyers seeking to develop their careers. The firm didn't advertise positions and had no formal selection procedures, relying instead on informal mechanisms to hire new recruits.

This was of concern to Celia, who felt that even one bad appointment might have serious implications for the harmonious working relationships that characterized the firm. She wanted to replace the existing approach to hiring new staff with one that offered more rigour, checks, and a shared responsibility for the assessment and selection of candidates.

One Monday morning, not long after she arrived in the office, Richard called her to say that he had received a CV from someone who looked really promising and who would be worth having. As well as having a good track record as a fee-earner in a similar-sized law firm, Richard thought he might be useful in acting as temporary head of section for one of the partners who was about to go on maternity leave. Richard told Celia that he would give this person a call and ask him to come in to talk about the possibility of a job. Unfortunately, Celia could not be present at this meeting and was concerned when, after the two had met, Richard began to enthuse about the person's background and experience, concluding:

He looks perfect. I'm sure he'll fit in and do a good job for us.

Unknown to Celia, it appeared that the first informal discussion had turned into a formal interview and that Richard was about to make an offer of employment. To pre-empt this, she suggested to Richard that this first meeting should be seen very much as the informal and preliminary stage of a more thorough selection process, and that the next stage should be a formal interview, preceded by a presentation on the applicant's strategy for enhancing the firm's fee-earning capability. Richard reluctantly accepted her advice and the necessary arrangements were made to invite the applicant back the next week. This gave Celia time to talk to the other partners and senior managers about the applicant's CV and whether they had an opinion on his suitability. She also arranged for one of the other partners to join her and Richard to hear the presentation and to interview the candidate.

The candidate's presentation turned out to be superficial and limited. Moreover, he failed to impress in the interview, coming over as one-dimensional and inflexible. This was despite the impressive list of achievements that he had claimed in his CV. In the discussion that followed the candidate's departure, Celia told the two partners that one of the firm's senior managers had spoken to her about the candidate and had said that 'he shouldn't be touched with a barge pole': it was alleged that, in one of his previous jobs, his behaviour had resulted in other staff leaving. Moreover, his claimed experience was, to say the least, clearly exaggerated.

A very different picture had now emerged from that which had originally been acquired by Richard Curtis and all three agreed that a letter would be sent informing the candidate that, in the light of all of the available evidence, it was not considered appropriate to offer him a position.

Questions

1. What are the particular difficulties associated with recruiting knowledge workers?

2. What might the firm do to develop a more effective and reliable recruitment strategy?

3. What costs might the firm have incurred if the candidate had been offered a position?

Why is it important to make the right recruitment and selection decisions?

Apart from the obvious importance of attracting talented people into the organization, why is the recruitment and selection process so important? It is important because:

- each employment decision can add to, or subtract from, the overall quality of the workforce;
- the ability of managers continuously to generate greater levels of added value from each employee is heavily influenced by what each new recruit brings into the organization and what each is capable of becoming;
- as a result of the increase in employment protection rights, it has become more difficult to correct mistakes in employment decisions once a person has been offered, and has accepted, a contract;
- employees who fail to meet the performance and behavioural expectations of managers can have a detrimental impact on the performance of others;
- the process of correcting a hiring mistake can be difficult, prolonged and costly to all those involved;
- employing new and better qualified staff to replace those that are unwilling or unable to adapt to new requirements is often the only effective long-term strategy for improving the operational performance of functions and departments.

The aphorism 'if you can't change people, change the people' helps to explain the extent to which the introduction of new people with different attitudes, competency profiles and, above all, a stronger work ethic can bring about transformation in performance capability throughout the organization.

 Signpost to Chapter 15: Case Study: Reforming the HR Function, for an example of replacing HR personnel

In summary, the solution to many so-called 'people problems' is often associated with improving the effectiveness of the recruitment process, discriminating between potential stars and potential problem employees, and providing a workforce that delivers against current and future requirements (Ryan and Tippins, 2004). It is against this background that the role and contribution of the HR professional will be judged and evaluated. And if this is the challenge to be faced, there must be a debate about the way in which these objectives can be met, and about the specific practices and techniques that meet the criteria of 'best practice' or 'best fit', about which more will be said later in the chapter.

Alternative challenges and perspectives

While an approach to recruitment and selection reflecting an overtly economic rationality, based on differences in individual productive capacity, is a persuasive one, it is not the only approach that the HR practitioner can adopt. For many organizations, the search for skilled and productive recruits takes on a more strategic and demographic perspective. For example, a report by the Women and Work Commission (2006) raised the issue of female under-representation in the science and engineering sectors, and the importance of developing strategic recruitment initiatives to overcome expected shortages in skilled engineers. The report also linked this under-representation to poor-quality career advice in schools, to continued male domination of the engineering profession, and to persistent pay differences between men and women. The objectives and challenges faced by those managing the recruitment process in this context are fundamentally different from those experienced when an employer is seeking to replace an employee who has left the organization or is advertising for a new position.

The use of recruitment as an instrument of social engineering, particularly in the public sector, can also be seen in the way in which police forces have been tackling issues of ethnic minority representation and accusations of institutional racism. As an example, The Sussex Police Race Equality Scheme makes an explicit commitment to increase the proportion of ethnic minorities in its workforce from the current levels of 2.1 per cent of police staff and 1.2 per cent of police officers, to 3.5 per cent for each by 2010. This represents a strategic commitment to developing new and more effective recruitment policies and practices, and suggests that major challenges will have to be overcome in understanding and managing labour markets, communication media, and the limitations of existing selection procedures and standards. Such a commitment will also have implications for the design and implementation of support and access mechanisms, and for the training requirements of those who will be directly involved in assessment and selection decisions. (See www.sussex.police.uk for more information.)

> Signpost to Chapter 6: Equality in Employment, for more information on racial equality at work

Other kinds of recruitment challenge may also exist. Specific organizations may be suffering from serious and structural shortages of skilled labour that might well be sector-specific or countrywide. Such shortages may be related to demographic change, shifts in career patterns, inflexible employment conditions and perceptions of low pay, and may not easily be overcome by conventional recruitment strategies or by exploiting existing labour markets. The shortage of nurses within the National Health Service in the early years of this century is a case in point and illustrates the scale of the recruitment challenge faced by the NHS. Its response was to develop a four-part strategy to solve the labour shortage, involving:

- increasing the supply of trained nurses by expanding the number of training places available;

- working to increase retention rates and attract nurses who have left the NHS back into employment;

- addressing the pay problem by improving salaries;

- mounting an international recruitment strategy.

By the end of 2004, evidence was emerging of the scale of overseas recruitment and its impact on nursing numbers (Batata, 2005). From his analysis of international nurse recruitment, Batata found that, in 2001, nurse recruits trained overseas exceeded the number of new UK-trained recruits on the UK nurse register for the first time, with healthcare service providers increasingly relying on overseas nurses to fill the void.

But foreign recruitment comes at a price, particularly for the countries from which the nurses are recruited. Source countries suffer from their own nursing shortages and experience distortions in their healthcare provision. In some situations, recruitment strategies involve exploiting new labour markets and the migration of large numbers of skilled workers, and the issues and implications associated with these strategies extend beyond the assessment and selection of candidates (Department of Health, 1999; Buchan, 2004).

STUDENT ACTIVITY 3.1

Prepare a presentation outlining the advantages and disadvantages associated with the recruitment of overseas nurses, as well as the implications of such a strategy, and consider the ethical issues involved in this recruitment practice.

A summary of different recruitment situations

It should be clear by now that the recruitment and selection challenges facing management not only vary in their scale and complexity between organizations, but change over time and differ in terms of their rationale. Without necessarily being complete, the following list represents the situations most likely to be encountered by the HR professional.

- Replacement recruitment

  This might involve recruiting to replace any kind of employee, from the managing director of a plc to a manual worker in a factory.

- Recruiting for a new position/job

  The scale of this challenge may also be limited to one person, but because someone is needed to fill a new or revised position, the processes and implications are not identical to those of recruiting a replacement.

- Recruiting for a new build

  In this situation, the whole organizational unit is new — a new hotel or factory for example — and this creates differences in scale, complexity and timescales.

- Recruitment needs that reflect long-term distortions in the supply and demand for labour

  These needs are often sector-specific or geographical in nature. Responses may involve developing new, and often overseas, labour markets and may feature an ethical, demographic and political dimension.

- Recruitment that is used as an instrument of social engineering

  The challenge in this situation is less linked to labour shortages, but to desired or enforced change in the composition of the labour force and its political and social acceptability.

An economic perspective on recruitment and selection

The ability to differentiate between applicants, in terms of their suitability and 'fit' with a person specification and the organization's culture, is at the core of what recruiting and selecting involves. But this still leaves unanswered the question: 'What difference does it make and can these differences be quantified?'

Cook (1988), in considering what the value of good employees actually means, offers an insight into the economic and financial dimension of employment decisions. His statement that '*The best is twice as good as the worst*' and, by implication, the idea that the best adds at least double the economic value to the organization of a poor recruit has two important implications:

- decisions about employing new staff can have either long-term financial costs or benefits for the organization. This means that the difference between the value of the contribution of the person employed, compared with that of one who was rejected, can be either positive or negative, depending on whether the 'right' employment decision was made. Of course, it is impossible to know precisely what the value of the contribution someone rejected might have made. It was explained earlier, however, that many organizations experience the negative outcomes of employing the wrong person, and have to bear the costs and losses of having to rectify decisions that, when taken, seemed rational and defensible. In economic terms, this is what is known as an 'opportunity cost' and, in extreme cases, such costs can be very high;

- it becomes even more important to understand both the 'real' costs of recruitment and selection, as opposed to those associated with direct expenditure, and the longer term financial consequences that follow from the selection decisions.

According to Cook, failing to discriminate between the 'productive potential' of different potential employees can be detrimental, should the 'productive capacity' of employees differ greatly. He poses two questions to illustrate this:

- how much do workers vary in their productive capacity and value to the organization?
- how much are these differences actually worth?

As far as the first question is concerned, Cook believes that good workers do twice as much work as poor workers. In terms of the value of these differences, his opinion is that it roughly equates to the wage or salary that they are paid. In this context, the direct costs of recruitment and selection, the time of those involved and the value of production lost while positions remain unfilled must all be included in an overall cost–benefit calculation.

According to Edward P Lazear (1998), however, the best and most productive employees are also likely to be the most expensive in terms of their recruitment and employment costs. This presents an interesting dilemma: is it better to employ the best people, irrespective of the costs involved, because their long-term value to the organization will be greater than the costs of recruiting and paying them, or is it better to employ the cheapest people and minimize recruitment and selection costs, irrespective of the quality of those employed? Decisions on whether a cost reduction or productivity maximization strategy is to be adopted can only be made within a specific context and if the implications of adopting one or the other have been fully explored. The reality for most organizations is that a position between the two extreme points on this continuum will be adopted, based on pragmatic considerations. Much will depend on contextual factors.

Fitz-Enz (2002) holds the view that:

> The hiring decision is often made too lightly; few organizations have stopped to figure out how costly the decision to hire a new employee is . . . every time the recruitment system cycles, the company incurs a cost and runs the risk of making a poor hiring decision. Even if the new hire is good, there is a productivity loss as the person moves up the learning curve. Any way you look at it, hiring is expensive, and one cannot ignore the importance of the selection process.

The implication arising from the contributions of Cook, Lazear and Fitz-Enz are obvious. An economic approach to recruitment and selection must reflect the fact that decisions to appoint and reject an applicant will:

- affect the financial value of the contribution directly related to the newly employed worker over the duration of his or her employment;
- involve expenditure and costs.

Over the full period for which an employee remains with an organization, the costs associated with recruitment and selection become proportionately less as the net value of the employee's contribution increases, assuming that the most suitable person was employed. The reality is that few organizations have developed the kind of HR metrics that Lazear, in particular, has developed in the USA, which allow the value of contributions and costs to be calculated reliably.

Calculating recruitment costs

Fitz-Enz (2002) offers the following formula for the calculation of what he calls 'cost per hire' (CPH):

$$CPH = \frac{AC + AF + RB + TC + RE + RC + NC + 10\%}{H}$$

Where:

AC = advertising costs;

AF = agency fees;

RB = referral bonus;

TC = travel costs;

RE = relocation costs;

RC = recruiter costs;

NC = the costs of processing unsolicited CVs;

H = the number of hires.

An alternative costing model, more appropriate to the UK, might be expressed as follows:

$$CPH = \frac{DA + GO + RE + C\ of\ S + RC + EAF + TC + CLP + 10\%}{Numbers\ involved}$$

Where:

DA = direct administration costs — time plus rate of pay;

GO = a proportion of general overheads;

RE = recruitment expenses;

C of S = costs of selection — time of staff involved, selection materials;

RC = relocation costs;

EAF = external agency fees;

TC = training costs;

CLP = costs of lost production.

This is a potentially useful way of understanding and calculating hiring costs. But the other side of the equation involves estimating the net value of each hiring decision, recognizing that this can be negative as well as positive.

 Signpost to Chapter 9: HR Planning and Measurement for a perspective on planning staffing requirements

Checklist

To avoid a situation in which an excessive number of applications are submitted, which can increase the administrative burden and costs of assessment and selection, the following actions are recommended:

- develop clear communications on the kind of person required and set realistically high standards. This will have the effect of limiting responses to advertising to fewer, but more suitably qualified, applicants;

- engage in the rigorous screening of applicants using criteria that have been validated against job performance measurements. For example, according to Lazear (1998, p 48), the ability to perform well at school and the ability to perform well on the job are highly correlated, although this is more likely to be true in white-collar than in blue-collar jobs. The implication is that some measure of school performance — with an appropriate standard, such as aggregate qualification points — will help to screen the weaker from the stronger applicants;

- use validated assessment techniques after the shortlisting stage. This not only means that criteria validated against job performance will be used, which are likely to differ from those employed at an earlier stage, but that people with suitable experience and training in their use will be involved in making final selection decisions;

- employ contingent contracts. Under this type of contract, a successful applicant is offered an initial temporary or fixed-term contract, with the assumption of permanent status conditional on the outcomes of performance reviews;

- use probationary periods to allow initial employment decisions to be checked against behavioural and performance standards, with those newly employed applicants who fail to meet the set standards being dismissed.

STUDENT ACTIVITY 3.2

1. Test the validity and acceptability of the formula for calculating recruitment costs by asking organizations for information on how, if at all, they calculate overall hiring costs. Be prepared to amend the formula, in the light of what is found, to improve its usefulness.

2. Generate estimated or actual information on financial values for the above variables and calculate the CPH value for specific recruitment exercises.

As an example, one of the author's postgraduate students, completing a similar calculation but not necessarily using the same formula, came up with a figure of £6,000 as the cost of replacing a single administrative worker in a local authority. It doesn't take much imagination to realize that organizations which are growing organically, creating new productive units or which have high turnover rates are likely to experience very substantial, and possibly recurring, hiring costs. Whereas recruiting in the context of the first two situations (replacement and new positions) can be considered to be necessary and an opportunity to invest in new and talented staff, recruitment that is linked to excessive rates of labour turnover is an unnecessary and unjustifiable cost.

The CIPD Recruitment, Retention and Turnover Survey 2007 provides more authoritative data on the economic costs of hiring. The survey found that the average cost of recruitment (i.e. of hiring someone) is estimated to be £4,333, rising to £7,750 when the full impact of turnover, training and induction are taken into account. It also found that 47 per cent of organizations do not even measure the direct costs of recruitment. Whatever the methodology used, being able to put reasonably robust and consistently applied financial values on this important area of HR is becoming less an option, and more a requirement, if the 'true' economic costs of finding new and replacement labour are to be recognized fully.

Labour markets

Labour markets can be virtual or physical, and they are important because they represent the source of an organization's supply of labour. External labour markets can be thought of as geographical areas within which potential employees are economically active. This means that these people are either in employment or unemployed and seeking work. The markets can be local, regional, national or international in size, depending on the degree of scarcity and specialization of the skills and experience required, but many, particularly for professional, technical and managerial work, are more virtual than real, with both applicants and employers using web-based recruitment practices. Historically, the physical limits of external labour markets were determined by travel-to-work times but, because work can now, for many, be from home and because many professionals are prepared to commute long distances, such physical limitations are less important than they used to be. Depending on the type of work and the degree of flexibility that an organization allows, potential employees can be found almost anywhere. Having said this, for many manufacturing businesses and 'lower level' service industries, the local or regional labour market represents the only realistic source of new and replacement labour.

The concept of the internal labour market, originally developed by Doeringer and Piore (1971), focuses attention on an organization's existing workforce and the extent to which this represents an alternative or complementary source of labour supply. Whether this is the case depends on the rules and procedures governing internal movements and transfers, and the extent to which an organization offers employees defined career development paths.

For most large-scale organizations, particularly those in the public sector, the internal labour market is an important source of applicants for newly created vacancies or those that result from the need to replace people. Many organizations have a deliberate policy of either looking first within for applicants, or prefer to recruit from within if at all possible, but much depends on the managerial philosophy that shapes the organization's recruitment strategy. In the DTI-sponsored *Sunday Times* survey of the '100 Best Companies to Work For' (2006), there are numerous examples of companies which inspire employees, and secure committed and satisfied workforces. Many of these have a strategy of promoting from within, and there is a strong association between encouraging staff to develop and to apply for positions that become vacant and the very positive attitudes expressed by those staff.

Kwik-Fit Financial Services, for example, is a company within which all of its managers have been promoted internally, but yet within which staff can earn £1,000 by recommending friends for vacant positions, a practice that accounted for 45 per cent of new recruits in 2004 (Oasis, 2005). In cost terms alone, the savings to the company are significant: the cost of advertising and agency fees, which can be anywhere from 10 to 30 per cent of an employee's annual salalary, would be far in excess of rewarding existing employees for finding new recruits.

ScS Upholstery is another company that made the *Sunday Times* Top 100 in 2006. With over a thousand employees working at eighty different sites around the country, it has to rely on different local labour markets for many of its sales staff. Most of its middle and senior managers have been promoted from within and this is linked to a strong philosophy of staff development. Mark Dawson, himself the product of internal promotion, is quoted as saying: '*I think if you can develop someone from within then you should.*'

The case for using the internal labour market rather than various external sources of labour is, however, by no means conclusive. One of the complicating factors is the increasing importance of contingent or flexible working arrangements. As a result of the growing numbers of temporary, fixed-contract, casual

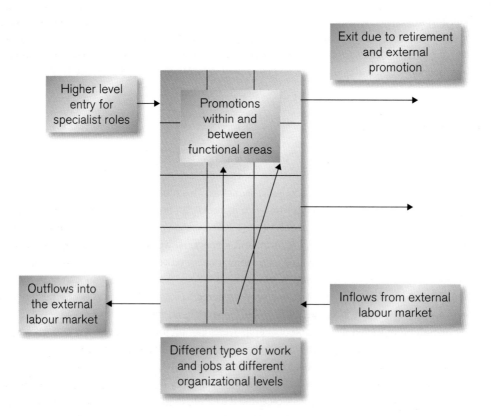

and agency workers, not only are organizations faced with the need to recruit more often, but the ability to rely on the internal labour market may be restricted by policy considerations. It has been estimated that, within the total labour force, 13 per cent of men and 45 per cent of women are in other than full-time, permanent employment (ONS, Labour Force Survey, 2005). And too much internal recruitment can cause instability, lead to reduced job performance and incur high transactional costs as a result of a constant process of applications, selection and movement of staff.

According to Fitz-Enz (2002, ch 6), most organizations rely on the external labour market to fill higher level positions, with more lower level jobs being filled by existing staff who have the necessary skills and experience to move upwards or laterally, or who have the potential to develop into the new job. Whether this happens is, however, very much dependent on:

- the existence of an effective HR information system that contains up-to-date details on the skills and personal profiles of every employee;
- a reliable and fair method of communicating internal vacancies and promotion opportunities;
- the deployment of efficient procedures for receiving and processing applications and selecting applicants;
- line managers who are supportive of a system that can involve frequent internal losses of valued staff.

However attractive, in terms of cost and time, an organization's internal labour market might be, there are dangers in over-relying on this source of recruitment. The main one can be expressed in terms of stagnation.

KEY CONCEPT Stagnation

This term relates to the detrimental effect on creativity, change and originality that is associated with relying largely, or entirely, on the existing workforce to fill job vacancies. The lack of 'new blood' from outside, which can bring new ideas, challenge and vitality into an organization, can contribute to the long-term decline of an organization that is too inward-looking in its search for new talent.

As Burrows (2004) argues, in the context of the pharmaceutical industry:

> ... many organizations will not survive without the injection of new talent from outside, bringing world-class skills and track records of addressing some of the challenges facing the industry.
> (p 390)

His argument that familiarity can become more important than real competence represents a clear warning of the danger of adopting a conservative and complacent approach to recruitment. Developing a strategic and flexible approach to recruitment not only involves searching for the best qualified and talented staff, wherever they might be found, but understanding and managing the different stages and activities of the whole process, from deciding a vacancy exists and needs to be filled, to the decision to hire and the induction of new employees. Figure 3.3 builds on Figure 3.1, presented at the beginning of the chapter, and provides a more comprehensive and integrated picture of what these stages and activities involve. The pre- and post-employment activities emphasize the importance of seeing recruitment and selection as connected to other areas of HR, such as the planning of human resource requirements and developing effective induction and development practices.

From the perspective of the HR practitioner, the danger that must be avoided is to see recruitment and selection as a set of discrete and isolated activities. An inability to see that success in HR is linked to managers taking a holistic, rather than a fragmented, perspective is the reason often used to explain why training often fails to meet the legitimate expectations of both employees and managers. This is often because the importance and effective management of the pre- and post-training stages are either

Pre-recruitment phase

- Decide on scale of project and timescales
- Decide whether demand for labour can be met by increasing flexibility and utilization of existing workforce
- Liaise with other stakeholders to develop strategy
- Prepare and agree on employment package and degree of discretion in wage or salary
- Agree on contractual details, such as probationary period

Key recruitment activities

- Carry out job analysis and produce up-to-date job descriptions
- Choose between internal and external labour markets
- Decide which communication medium to use
- Decide on standards to be applied and 'ideal' person specification

Key selection activities

- Prepare competency statements and frameworks
- Decide on which selection approaches and instruments to use
- Decide on shortlisting criteria
- Build checks and safeguards into selection decisions
- Document and store selection criteria and applicants' profiles against these
- Train staff in interview, questioning and feedback techniques

Post-selection activities

- Check references and consider any other relevant evidence for contra-indicators
- If appropriate, carry out medical and employment eligibility tests
- Prepare employment offer documents
- Keep on file records of those not offered position but who may be suitable for alternative job
- Provide feedback for unsuccessful candidates, which creates positive feeling towards the organization

Post-employment activities

- Prepare appropriate socialization and induction experiences
- Design opportunities for informal discussions and formal review of performance at appropriate time
- Confirm or terminate employment at end of probationary period
- Attempt to validate selection criteria, score against key criteria and measure of job performance
- Agree training and development programme
- Cost whole exercise and produce useful metrics, in terms of time, money and other resources used
- Learn from the whole experience, share and agree on this learning, and use it in subsequent recruitment and selection exercises

Time line

Figure 3.3 A strategic overview of recruitment and selection

ignored or misunderstood, and as a consequence, badly managed. The outcome of recruitment and selection can be equally disappointing, and for exactly the same reasons.

This importance of integrating recruitment and selection into a wider HR and business agenda has been supported by research conducted by Reed Executive, one of the country's leading recruitment firms (Carrington, 2004). The survey found that more than one in three of the organizations that responded admitted that their recruitment strategy was not aligned to business goals and nearly one in three said that recruitment had failed because it was not aligned to the internal motivation and retention of staff. Only 17 per cent said that recruitment strategies failed because of external skills shortages.

The role of fairness in recruitment

It is important that the recruitment and selection processes adopted by an organization are fair. This means that processes need to be as objective as possible and that only information relevant to the situation should be required. Decisions at all stages should be based solely on the merits of applicants and their suitability for the position in question. Employers have a legal responsibility to ensure that processes do not allow either direct or indirect discrimination to occur on the grounds of race, religion or belief, sex, sexual orientation, disability and age.

The law allows for some exceptions to the above, known as 'genuine occupational qualifications', such as recruiting a male attendant for the male changing facilities at a swimming pool. Discrimination on the grounds of disability can, in some circumstances, be shown to be justifiable, but organizations are obliged to consider making reasonable adjustments in the work that needs to be done before excluding any such applicant for a job. A wheelchair user, for example, may have difficulties operating checkout facilities. It may be justifiable not to employ this person, but only if it can be shown that consideration was given to ways of altering the environment to allow the work to be done by a wheelchair user. A larger organization would be under a greater obligation to make this type of adjustment than would a small local shop, due to the relative affordability of such changes.

⊙ Signpost to Chapter 6: Equality in Employment, for more information on discrimination

Identifying recruitment requirements

In most organizations, the costs associated with employing the required number of people represent a significant proportion of the organizational budget. Having too many people in a particular section will quickly impact upon either the profitability of the organization or its ability to deliver requirements within the specified budget. When a vacancy arises, it is therefore important to consider whether the need for the tasks carried out has changed, whether or not a different skill set may be required, whether or not tasks might be redistributed among others in the organization and whether forthcoming changes may impact upon requirements. (Further consideration of the issue of how to establish staffing requirements is discussed later in the text.)

⊙ Signpost to Chapter 9: HR Planning and Measurement, for information on staffing requirements

As well as HR and the line manager, the person leaving the job and their colleagues may have a valuable contribution to make in reaching the decision about recruitment requirements. Contributions from these groups may be a useful consideration when deciding to update or amend the job description and person specification for the role.

STUDENT ACTIVITY 3.3

1. Consider the contribution that different stakeholders can make to decisions about recruitment requirements.

2. In avoiding an automatic decision to replace an employee, what criteria might be applied to justify the decision to recruit a replacement?

Defining recruitment requirements

There are often two important documents that are used to define recruitment requirements. The *job description*, sometimes referred to as the 'job specification', gives details of the purpose or the job, and of the tasks and responsibilities or areas of accountability that are assigned to the jobholder. The *person specification* details the skills, knowledge and attitudes that should ideally be possessed by the jobholder to ensure he or she can meet objectives, while feeling that the job holds sufficient challenge and opportunity for growth.

Job description

A job description, or job specification, is the document used to record what it is that an employee should be doing. At more junior levels, it is likely to be primarily concerned with the tasks that the postholder is required to carry out on a day-to-day basis. At more senior levels, however, it becomes harder to define the exact details of actions required and job descriptions at this level are more likely to be primarily concerned with the overall responsibilities or areas for which the employee is accountable. Job descriptions are considered to be useful when jobs are relatively routine, if the work people do and the contributions they make are clearly defined and uncomplicated, and if organizational change is not a major factor. If these criteria are not met, however, then the value of the job description is more uncertain.

One of the questionable practices found in certain public sector organizations, in which there are many similar kinds of job, is the use of *generic* job descriptions. This has the advantage of simplifying the process of producing and amending job descriptions, but its disadvantage is that the distinctiveness and unique characteristics of each job are ignored. Does this practice also mean that generic job descriptions result in generic person specifications? If so, this has significant and worrying implications for the selection process, because effective teams need a balance of people with differing, but complementary, skills.

Fitting the person to the job or the job to the person?

The routinization and bureaucratization of recruitment and selection, under which conforming to established rules and procedures is often more important than the outcome of the process, can make it difficult for managers to appreciate the choice they have in how they define the nature of the task they face. Organizations that are highly structured, inflexible and hierarchical invariably see the task as finding a suitable person to fit any given job. It becomes a matching exercise, in which the job is seen as constant and 'known', and the role of those involved in selection is to filter out those who clearly, in their eyes, do not 'fit' the requirements of the job, expressed through the person specification. The rarely articulated assumptions underlying this approach are worth considering:

● that there is a consensus about what the job involves and that this does not change;

● that the process of agreeing on a job description is purely technical and involves no political dimension;

- that the job specification is sufficiently flexible and is not so narrowly applied that good candidates are excluded;
- that assessors have the skills and experience to be able to develop accurate profiles of candidates, and are free from bias and have open minds.

The reality is often that these assumptions are not valid, or are only partially so. In such situations, the final decisions to employ and reject candidates may well be compromised. This is not to deny that many hiring decisions are subsequently seen to be 'good' ones, but, equally, it cannot be denied that there are numerous examples of a decision to hire subsequently turning out to be 'wrong', for any of a number of reasons.

One assumption that is particularly rarely articulated is to do with the existence of political cliques and groupings that function to serve the interests and purpose of their members (Bozionelos, 2005). His argument is that:

> **Consideration of organizational politics is of prime importance, because an understanding of political processes within organizations will assist in accounting for decisions, attitudes and behaviours and outcomes that cannot be fully accounted for by the rational approach to management.**

This suggests that what might appear to be essentially 'technical' and objective processes, involving the collection and presentation of information about jobs and people, are almost certainly influenced by political and interest group considerations.

An alternative approach to selection is to start off with the objective of recruiting talented people, even though there may not be a current vacancy or an applicant might not match the person specification as closely as might others. Often jobs are created for those who clearly offer distinctive and valued competences and personal traits, but who may not correspond to the requirements of a specific job. The skills and flexibility needed to break out of a particular recruitment and selection mindset, and to find and mould jobs to fit the talents of outstanding applicants, are not always appreciated, but are increasingly seen to be vital to an approach that recognizes the benefits of hiring the best people in the market as well as hiring those that 'fit' existing person specifications.

Of course, for practical reasons, hiring to a specific job description and person specification may be the appropriate and preferred approach in the majority of recruitment situations, but there are times when this is too restrictive and limiting, and needs to be replaced by a more flexible and creative recruitment and selection mindset.

This creative approach is advocated by Jack Welch (Welch and Welch, 2005, ch 6), in the context of hiring what he describes as 'leaders'. For this type of recruitment, while consideration is certainly given to experience and technical ability, it is the personal traits and characteristics of the person that come under the closest scrutiny. Welch believes strongly in the importance of looking for evidence that candidates possess the following qualities.

- Integrity

  This quality is about honesty, admitting to mistakes and fixing them, taking responsibility, and playing to win but by the 'rules of the game'.

- Intelligence

  Intelligence does not equate to education, but is about essential cognitive skills, such as problem solving, analytical ability, reasoning and an intellectual curiosity.

- Maturity

  Maturity is not about age, but is expressed in an ability to handle pressure and setbacks, to enjoy successes, to understand and respect others, and a display of confidence in how he or she operates.

Based on these initial requirements, Welch also emphasizes the importance of what he calls the '4-E Framework', which can be incorporated into any assessment and selection process. The personal characteristics he describes are as follows.

1. **Positive** *energy* **or a strong work** *ethic*

   This is about a strong internal drive and energy source. It refers to self-motivated people, who enjoy and thrive on work.

2. **The ability to** *energize* **others**

   This involves taking others in the direction you need them to go. It's about setting examples, working with others and even inspiring them.

3. **Having the '***edge'*** to take important and often challenging decisions**

   This quality emphasizes recognizing that all of the information about something will never be available — that people are depending on you to use your judgement and understanding of what needs to be done and to make the decision for the right reasons.

4. *Execute* **– the ability to get the job done**

   This is about achieving results, meeting targets and overcoming problems.

The person–organization fit

The idea that the assessment and selection process allows managers to identify someone from among those remaining 'in the pool' who is the 'best qualified for the job' informs the thinking of many HR professionals. 'Best' is, however, a relative term, and while the objective might be to eliminate weaker candidates and be left with the 'best', being the 'best' may not, in fact, mean that this person has the necessary personal and technical competences to perform the job to the required standards. An alternative approach to selection, often described as 'criterion-referenced selection', is based on the principle that the 'best' of applicants may not possess the required competences for the job. If this approach is taken, it is much more likely that a decision to appoint will not be made because none of the applicants meets the required standards. Such an approach is often associated with the re-advertisement of positions, after none of the original applicants have been considered suitable.

Both approaches fundamentally involve 'fitting' the person to the job and, in each, either the 'best fit' or the 'right fit' is chosen at the end of the process. This notion of fit can be seen as both attractive and yet, at the same time, worrying. It is attractive because it implies that, with sufficient preparation and care, it is possible to match the person to the job with the minimum of disruption and friction to the social fabric of the organization. It is worrying, however, because it implies that, as with physical objects such as machines, human beings can be treated as the equivalent of machine parts and somehow 'fitted' into the organization (i.e. the 'machine'). The belief that organizations can be understood as machines and managed as such is associated with the widespread use of the organization-as-machine metaphor, within which order, predictability and control mechanisms are believed to result in efficient and non-problematical employee performance (Morgan, 1997). But the complex, and often unpredictable, nature of human behaviour and the high level of subjectivity that still surrounds the recruitment and selection process, despite its procedural regulation, means that seeing candidates as the equivalent of pieces in a jigsaw puzzle is both simplistic and unhelpful.

Part of the problem is not simply associated with the dangers of seeing organizations as machines, but with limiting the notion of 'fit' exclusively to the job. Fitting people into the organization, in terms of its culture and values, as well as into a job makes this task even more challenging. The identification of personal characteristics associated with being an effective part of a dynamic and challenging working environment is, arguably, of equal importance to the assessment of applicants against a more specific set of job competences. The emphasis on certain personal traits and strengths, described above by Welch and Welch (2005), suggests that, in some organizations, more importance is given to the ability of applicants to fit into the organizational culture and value system than is given to their fitting the requirements of a specific job. It has also been found that selecting someone who 'fits' both job and organization is even more problematical when the approach to hiring is opportunistic rather than planned (Levesque, 2005).

Person specification

In many cases of recruitment and selection, the person specification takes the form of a document that records the qualities of the ideal candidate for the job. The qualities are often prioritized in terms of importance, as shown in Table 3.1. Typically the person specification will describe the skills, knowledge and attitudes required to carry out the job, the level and amount of experience necessary, the level of education and training required and the personal qualities and competence of the ideal candidate. These are often prioritized in terms of essential and desirable characteristics. Care should be taken to ensure that criteria actually reflect requirements. For example if 10 years experience is not necessary and 3 or 4 will suffice, requiring 10 years could result in a claim of unfair age discrimination as this would automatically rule out younger candidates. More importantly, the best candidate may be excluded from the process for no good reason.

Once a person specification has been agreed upon, this then becomes the basis of the assessment process, where evidence about applicants from different sources is assessed against the requirements and standards contained with the person specification.

STUDENT ACTIVITY 3.4 Producing a job description

1. Consider a role with which you are familiar in an organization of your choice, and produce a job description and person specification for that role.

2. What additional information would you want to know about the job and the ideal person to help you in the process of sifting applications and the assessment of shortlisted applicants?

Table 3.1 Person specification for a payroll administrator

PERSON SPECIFICATION	
Payroll administrator	
Grade 4	

Essential	*Desirable*
Skills, knowledge, attitude	
Numerate	Motivated by repeated routine tasks
Accurate	
Teamworker	
Trustworthy	
Works well to a deadline	
Experience	
Must have a minimum of one year's experience in an office environment, working with computers and entering/processing data	Experience in a payroll, accounts or HR environment
Education and training	
A good standard of education, including GCSE or equivalent in maths and English	Training or qualification on tax and pay systems
Personal qualities	
Polite	
Helpful	
Able to relate to people at all levels	
Articulate	
Patient	

Attracting the right applicants

A recruitment and selection strategy that focuses on hiring well-qualified high performers, or at least those with the potential to be this type of person, is likely to be more demanding and challenging than one under which lower standards are applied, or under which selecting the 'best' from a set of applicants is seen as the objective of the exercise. Even when unemployment levels in the external labour markets are relatively high, better workers are less likely to be unemployed or will only temporarily be so. The challenge of attracting them becomes, therefore, much harder than when recruiting less qualified people. This is because high-potential and top-performing candidates who can deliver the best results are often:

- well recognized, valued and nurtured by their current employers;

- unlikely to be looking for another job, because they will have high current levels of job satisfaction;

- attractive to many employers when they do look and will often get more than one offer when they start looking;

- given a counteroffer to stay with their current employer;

- hard to convince that it is worth their while to move to a new job in an unknown organization.

The process of attracting the right candidates is that activity within which the HR function needs to give serious consideration to marketing the organization to potential candidates. There are many channels that can be used to make potential candidates aware of current and future vacancies, and these vary in degrees of formality and expense. Figure 3.5 shows the types of option available and the main features associated with each method. It should be noted that, while informal methods of recruitment, such as word of mouth and the use of 'now recruiting' banners, can be very cost-effective, they may limit the pool of applicants. The Commission for Racial Equality and the Equal Opportunities Commission warn specifically against the dangers of indirect discrimination inherent to word-of-mouth recruitment should the workforce consist predominantly of one gender or racial group.

KEY CONCEPT Employer of preferred choice

This is a status that certain employers seek to attain in relation to prospective applicants. It means that, through its successful marketing of the organization, the development of challenging and supportive working environments, and the opportunity to enjoy good reward packages, applicants are attracted to the prospect of being employed by the organization. As a consequence, there is a natural flow of predominantly high-calibre people towards these organizations, which has the effect of reducing the time and costs of recruitment.

Research into the effectiveness of different recruitment strategies offers interesting insights into what appears to work and what doesn't (CIPD, 2007). Horowitz et al (2003), in their study of knowledge workers, found that highly effective attraction strategies included:

- very competitive total reward packages located in the upper quartile range;

- internal talent development strategies;

- a positive reputation as an employer of preferred choice;

- the use of proactive recruitment initiatives.

Their research also found that other strategies were less effective, at least for this type of worker, with the implication that they were less cost-effective. Such strategies included:

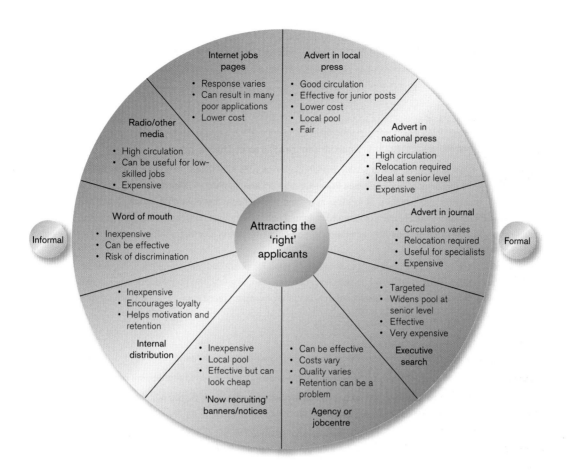

Figure 3.4 The recruitment 'wheel' – where and how to market vacancies

- online recruitment;
- advertised vacancies;
- headhunters;
- recruitment fairs;
- planned recruitment visits/student interviews.

Despite finding that potential applicants would not consider visiting a company's website unless they were made aware by some other means about a vacancy and that online recruitment was found to be one of the less effective strategies, the increase in the use of online recruitment and selection is difficult to ignore (see www.changeworknow.com and Kent, 2005). Kent's article makes reference to several industry-based surveys showing its growing popularity, even going so far as to describe online recruitment as no longer an extra tool in the recruitment toolkit, but as the toolkit itself (Kent, 2005, p 38).

The important point to note about these different approaches and media for communicating with and attracting prospective employees is that, depending on the numbers of people being recruited, the level and type of worker, and the importance of time and costs, different organizations will develop and use a mix of techniques and methods that works for them. All have potential advantages and disadvantages, and it is unrealistic and misleading to think that there is any 'right' way in which to recruit. What *can* be said is that, through experience and the ability to relate outcomes to the methods used, HR professionals should be able constantly to reduce the costs involved and improve the quality of employees hired.

But recruiting new staff continues to pose problems and challenges, as the two following HRM Insights illustrate.

HRM INSIGHT 3.3 **Recruitment practices at Thompson**

CW Thompson is a privately owned business with over 2,000 employees. The vast majority of its recruitment is via referrals from existing staff and customers. Many new recruits are, in fact, the friends and relatives of existing staff, and the manager believes that this is one of the reasons why there is a strong sense of loyalty and team working. Thompson is based in an area with a high ethnic minority population, but the manager has only employed three people in the last four years from an ethnic minority – and three of these have left.

A local resident submits a complaint to the Commission for Racial Equality, which investigates and, on the basis of the evidence that is available, decides to prosecute the company. The business' defence is that it cannot afford to advertise all vacancies in the newspaper and that changing recruitment practices would displease the existing staff.

Questions

1. What low-cost options might the manager have used to advertise more fairly?

2. How might the manager ensure that staff are not displeased by changes to recruitment practices?

3. Given that the business employs over 2,000 employees, to what extent do you feel that the cost of advertising should be taken into consideration?

4. What might explain the decision of the three people to leave?

HRM INSIGHT 3.4 **The case of LLT Solutions**

LLT Solutions had a vacancy for a computer network administrator manager at one of its most prominent call centres, managing calls for global retail customers. The call centre was also a 'European hub', responsible for transferring queries to other European call centres. As this was a key role, the position was advertised nationally in the most widely recognized journal for network personnel and a thorough selection procedure was followed to select the preferred candidate.

The successful candidate accepted the offer and submitted one month's notice to his employer. That employer made the candidate a generous counteroffer, increasing his salary by 20 per cent, to beat the offer made, and promising to make a number of changes to the role to address previously unresolved concerns about issues such as effective communication and involvement in corporate decision making and projects. The candidate consequently withdrew his acceptance of the newly offered post three days before he was due to join.

Because no other suitable internal candidate was available, the position was re-advertised the following month with a suitable closing date. The originally successful candidate applied again for the post, sending in an accompanying letter that explained that the promises made by his present employer had not been fulfilled and that he continued to be interested in joining the new business.

Questions

1. What are the pros and cons of making a 'counteroffer' if an employee resigns after an offer of employment is made by another organization?

2. In this example, what are the pros and cons to the recruiting organization of considering the same applicant a second time around?

3. What options does the recruiting company have in handling this application?

4. What would you do and why?

Recruitment advertising

Perhaps the most widely used method to attract applicants is the recruitment advert. Adverts are typically placed in either — or a combination of — local or national press, and appropriate trade or professional journals. The size, colour design and text for adverts varies enormously between organizations and types of role, as do the costs and circulations of different publications.

Unless you are very familiar with the most reliable publications to use for an area, it may be advisable to employ the resources of a specialist agency that can advise on the choice of media. Many recruitment firms will offer a service that includes writing, designing and placing adverts as part of a range of recruitment solutions including shortlisting, interviewing, managing applicants and searching for candidates. Of course, all of this comes at a premium and consideration must be given to whether the organization has sufficient in-house expertise on these matters and whether the cost of 'buying in' external services can be justified.

The most effective adverts are those that are eye-catching and give sufficient accurate details, without being too lengthy, to attract interest. Care needs to be taken to ensure that the wording is not discriminatory. Words such as 'young', 'mature' and 'recently qualified' may be regarded as indirect age discrimination, while 'energetic and lively' might potentially discriminate against people with certain disabilities.

Some adverts will have a telephone number or contact details for informal enquiries and encourage an informal approach, while others may be more formal. The effect of the wording and any informal contact that might be encouraged will have an important effect on an applicant's perception of the job and the employing organization. Consider what impression might be made should the words 'previous applicants need not apply' be included in a job advert: this suggests a re-advertised job, for which recruitment may have previously failed — or for which a preferred candidate turned down a job offer. Another phrase sometimes used is 'interviews will take place on [a certain date] and applicants not contacted before this date should assume that they have not been shortlisted': does this suggest that the organization 'can't be bothered to respond'? What lasting impression might be created in the mind of someone who has spent a considerable amount of time in completing an application form, but receives no acknowledgement or response? The message is simple: think carefully about the way in which information about the job and the company is communicated in any advertising material.

STUDENT ACTIVITY 3.5 Looking at recruitment adverts

Consider a selection of recruitment adverts from a journal or newspaper.

1. Identify the qualities that make some adverts stand out more than others.

2. Produce a checklist of items that must be covered in a recruitment advert, items that are often included but not essential, and the pros and cons of including these.

3. Rank the adverts according to the favourable impression they create and justify your decision.

CV or application form?

A curriculum vitae (CV), or résumé, is a document prepared by the candidate as part of his or her application, giving personal details, education and employment history, and other relevant information.

In any advert, details of how to apply should include whether to send a CV or to ask for a standard application form. It might be argued that an application form ensures that only objective and relevant information is gathered, and that it is fairer to consider similar information from all candidates. In practice, a tribunal claim for unfair selection is extremely unlikely to arise in relation to, let alone be found in favour of, a claimant on the strength of requesting only a CV. An application form does, however, make the life of those screening much easier because all data is in a similar format. For lower level jobs — for which applicants may be unlikely to have access to a computer or the necessary guidance to complete a CV — application forms can help to attract a wider candidate pool.

It cannot be denied that the first time writing a CV is time-consuming, but it is quick and easy to update, and few people relish the prospect of repeatedly filling in lengthy application forms. Particularly for senior roles, it is the recruiters that need to do the work to attract high performers, so applications via CV may be preferable.

Handling applications

Before applications begin to arrive, the organization should consider how these are going to be handled. It is good practice to acknowledge all applications and often organizations will send a candidate pack, either upon first enquiry with the application form, or to those candidates who are shortlisted for interview.

It is important to consider and decide in advance on the process for shortlisting applications, and on the final assessment and selection stages. Larger organizations, particularly those from the public sector and those with large numbers of applications, are likely to use a scoring system based on agreed criteria, which are applied at the shortlisting and final assessment stages, or both. Often, this involves the allocation of points and the use of scoring matrices to express differences in applications/candidates in quantitative terms. If there are fewer applicants, it may be easier simply to rank the applications based on the closeness of the match with the person specification and chose an appropriate number for interview.

Other checks

Organizations may have other obligations for checks, such as criminal record checks, checking eligibility to work in the UK, checking references and health screening. Checks such as these can occur at different stages in the recruitment process, but they should always be applied consistently and fairly to avoid the risk of indirect discrimination. For example, checking eligibility to work in the UK should be handled consistently, to avoid a claim of racial discrimination, and health checks should be job-relevant, to avoid risking claims of disability discrimination.

Assessing and selecting

Assessing the suitability of applicants at each stage of selection, starting from reviewing application forms or CVs, to evaluating psychometric test results and rating performance in interviews, is central to the process not only of hiring, but of hiring the right kind of people. As a result of 'knowing' how well applicants match up to the requirements of a person specification or competency framework, the next stage in the assessment process can be planned. This involves the use of techniques and tools that are designed to discriminate between shortlisted applicants, using legal, relevant and predictive criteria. The requirement to assess and distinguish is both challenging and difficult, and the people involved need to apply a range of skills to the task. It is also important to understand that the ability to make the 'right' selection decisions is as much of an art as it is a science, with, ultimately, professional judgement based on experience playing an important part.

Evidence from research carried out in the USA suggests a move away from restricting the assessment of specific applicant characteristics, such as educational attainments or cognitive ability, to a more holistic approach, as part of which assessors are interested in the 'whole person' and the full range of competencies that each person offers (O'Leary et al, 2002). Recognizing that effective job performance may be linked to other, perhaps less well-understood, skills and competencies is associated with the ideas of writers such as Daniel Goldman (1995; 1998), whose work on emotional intelligence has provided new insights into the relationship between what people are and how they behave, and job performance.

The importance of predictive validity

According to O'Leary et al (2002), the most important property of the assessment instruments used to measure or assess applicants against set criteria is their ability to predict future job performance, or job-related learning. In other words, does someone who scores well on the assessment instrument perform better on the job than someone whose score is poor? If the instruments and techniques are sufficiently reliable — meaning that they produce consistent results — the degree of predictive validity indicates which instruments and techniques are useful. Differences in test scores or ratings can then be used to identify which candidate is likely to be a better performing employee. This is the evidence upon which distinguishing between candidates is based. The challenge for managers is, therefore, one of identifying the degree of predictive validity for the assessment instruments in use, or of those that might be used.

One of the difficulties for those involved in using assessment instruments is, as Ryan and Tippins (2004) argue, that many of the research findings on recruiting staff have not been widely embraced by HR professionals. There are several reasons for this, including the failure of researchers to present their findings in an accessible and understandable way. The main reason, however, is perhaps that those using assessment instruments may have inaccurate beliefs about the predictive powers of the instruments they use. For example, in their USA study, Rynes et al (2004) found that 72 per cent of the HR managers they surveyed thought that the degree of applicant conscientiousness was a better predictor of job performance than intelligence, whereas the reverse is true. They argue that evidence shows that structured selection processes are better than less structured ones and suggest that, often, those involved in making selection decisions rely too much on what they call 'gut instinct' and 'chemistry'. This is a complex and difficult issue, and however much evidence is presented that emphasizes the use of one or a combination of assessment instruments, it remains the case that the actual selection decision will involve some element of judgement and the application of personal experience of previous selection decisions.

As a result of reviewing a number of studies, Rynes et al found the following statistical relationships between commonly used assessment instruments and predictive validity.

Assessment instrument	Predictive validity
Work sample tests	0.54
Cognitive ability tests	0.51
Structured interviews	0.51
Job knowledge tests	0.48
Unstructured interviews	0.31
Biographical data	0.35
Assessment centre results	0.37
Reference checks	0.26

In the earlier study by O'Leary et al (2002), those instruments found to have significantly lower levels of validity included the following.

Assessment instrument	Predictive validity
Job experience	0.18
Training and experience	0.11
Years of education	0.10
Graphology	0.02
Age	−0.01

These findings suggest that those instruments that have a high predictive validity relative to others should be used, but this is an assumption that ignores the influence of contextual factors. For example, the skills and experience of interviewees will affect the actual level of predictive validity, with the use of inexperienced interviewers and deviations from 'best practice' resulting in considerably lower validity levels. What we need to emphasize here is not simply the use of particular instruments, but the way in which they are used, the qualities and experience of those involved, and the way in which different contributions to an assessment of the whole person are generated, evaluated and combined with the judgement of the decision makers to produce a final selection decision.

An applicant perspective

One of the distinctive features of this book is the emphasis given to making sense of HR from an employee perspective. In bringing this chapter to a close, it is necessary to ask the question: 'What does recruitment and selection mean to the person searching for a job?'

Inevitably, almost all of the research on this subject and, indeed, the approach taken by many writers of HR textbooks essentially reflect a managerial perspective. This managerialist tendency is understandable and justifiable, but without considering the applicants and how their behaviour and attitudes are influenced by the experiences they are required to go through, it is a one-sided and limited perspective.

Chambers (2002) makes the important distinction between factors that influence behavioural reactions among applicants and the consequences that follow from these reactions. This distinction is important because it shows that the consequences of positive or negative experiences, particularly at the selection stage, continue after the selection decision has been taken. As an example, consider the situation in which an internal applicant has received negative feedback from the chair of an interview panel, who is also his or her line manager. The effect, while not inevitable, is likely to be a degree of demotivation and possibly a questioning of self-worth; the long-term consequences may involve rethinking the 'psychological contract', reduced levels of job performance and a worsening of interpersonal relationships.

→ Signpost to Chapter 4: Managing Employee Relations, for more information on psychological contracts

---

Research quoted by Chambers (2002, p 318) points to the way in which applicant reactions to selection procedures are related to whether the procedures are perceived by the applicants as fair and just. The suggestion is that, if applicants perceive their experiences as unfair, unprofessional or uncaring, they will take the decision not to continue with an application and to seek employment elsewhere. This reaction applies equally to internal and external job applications.

Chambers distinguishes between what he calls 'distributive justice', which is concerned with the perceived fairness of the outcome itself — for example, receiving or not receiving a job offer — and 'procedural justice', which is concerned with the perceived fairness of the procedures used to reach the outcome. This is to do with feeling that the procedures used in assessment and selection have been valid, fair and managed in a professional manner. He also offers a further form of justice, which he describes as 'interactional justice'. This relates to the interpersonal treatment of applicants as procedures are enacted and the manner in which information is conveyed and managed.

The important point to emerge from this brief consideration of an applicant perspective on recruitment and selection is that managers and HR professionals need to recognize that applicants are human beings, who will become emotionally engaged in, and affected by, the way they are treated and what they are required to do. Decision making is not something that only managers do; applicants are constantly evaluating their experiences and can decide at any point whether to continue with the process, up to, and including, declining the offer of a job. In tight labour markets and with an increasing proportion of knowledge workers in the labour force, traditional patterns of dependency, within which managers were 'in control', are being eroded, to the point at which talented employees with high performance potential are more selective about who they work for and the kind of work they do. The consequences for an organization that fails to understand this and bases its approach to recruitment and selection on twentieth- rather than twenty-first-century practices will almost certainly be costly and recurring.

Summary

This chapter, in addition to offering insights into what constitutes effective practice in recruitment and selection, highlights the importance of taking a holistic view of either filling vacant positions or of hiring people into new posts. Hiring new staff cannot be seen in isolation from an organization's wider HR and business strategy, nor can it be seen only from the viewpoint and interests of managers and HR professionals. Being able to visualize the experience from an applicant/employee perspective is a necessary part of being aware of, and sensitive to, the lasting effects that these experiences can have on those who are selected and those who are not. These experiences can be positive and rewarding, but can also result in negative perceptions of the organization and of individual managers.

Even though the process may be well managed and carefully controlled, mistakes in selection can still be made, and the ability to recognize and correct these mistakes is as important as any other part of the whole process. Failure to do so simply stores up problems for the future should unsuitable and potentially disruptive people be allowed to stay and prosper. And finally, despite advances in assessment instruments and high levels of procedural regulation, the final decision to hire or not remains, in many ways, a subjective one. It is likely to be more effective if inputs from different stakeholders are built into the assessment and selection process.

 Visit the Online Resource Centre that accompanies this book for self-test questions, weblinks, and more information on the topics covered in this chapter.
online resource centre www.oxfordtextbooks.co.uk/orc/banfield_kay/

87

REVIEW QUESTIONS

1. Who should be involved in recruiting and selecting staff, and why? What roles will they play and why?

2. What are the arguments for fitting the organization to the person rather than fitting the person to the organization?

3. What do the concepts 'reliability' and 'validity' mean, and why are these important?

4. Making the right selection decision does not guarantee that the new recruit will stay — but what does?

5. From your own personal experiences of being recruited and selected, what can you add to this chapter?

CASE STUDY
The Midlands Spring Company

The Midlands Spring Company manufactures a wide range of springs for the engineering and automobile industries. It was established by David Wheeler in 1986 and employs some 35 skilled and semi-skilled workers in its Peak District factory. David recently passed over management responsibility to his daughter, Jenny, and her husband, Alan Johnston. David comes in to work a couple of days a week but his main interests now lie outside the company. Jenny and Alan have been effectively running the business for the ➔

last 12 months and, while they have made considerable progress in sorting out some of the problems they faced, they are still struggling to deal with all of the issues that are preventing the business from developing. Alan has concentrated his energy on the sales and marketing side of the business, while Jenny has worked hard to develop the office and administrative systems. They are currently in the process of applying for the ISO 9000 standard, which is critical to getting orders from new customers who will only do business with suppliers who have been awarded the standard.

The main challenge is in the production area. Much of the plant and equipment is old, and maintenance costs are high. While the workforce is reliable and hard-working, there is little flexibility between the machine setters and production workers, all of whom are male and are full time. The packers and dispatchers are female, and work under a variety of full- and part-time contracts. Quality has been a problem for some time, with scrap levels, waste and faulty products worryingly high. Without significant and sustained improvements in production planning and control, and quality standards, the company faces a difficult future.

One of the first decisions Jenny and Alan made was to appoint a quality manager to work on the ISO 9000 application, and to introduce the necessary quality checks and procedures in the factory. Chris Openshaw had been recommended to them by a recruitment agency in Sheffield, and they appointed him after considering his CV and a short interview. Neither of them had any previous HR experience nor did they involve anyone else in the decision. In addition to having to pay the agency fee of £7,000, the appointment has proven costly. Despite his CV, which originally impressed them, it soon became apparent to Alan and Jenny that the appointment of Chris had been a mistake. He spent most of his time in his office working on statistical control procedures and showed little interest in the shop floor, where these measures would need to be implemented. He didn't understand the importance of developing good working relationships with either Jenny and Alan or the shop floor staff. Progress with the ISO 9000 application has been slow and the submission document is far from being complete.

Knowing what to do was key to making the right decisions. Jenny and Alan needed to address the issue of Chris' appointment and get help with finding someone else who could combine the quality role with that of production manager. They decided to terminate Chris' contract and gave him one month's notice. In fact, he hadn't been particularly happy in his job and the parting wasn't acrimonious. He decided to leave after two weeks. The second problem was addressed by talking to their local Training and Skills Council, who arranged for an experienced recruitment consultant to work with them on finding a replacement. After discussing their requirements, the consultant suggested that they create a new post of works manager, and develop a more effective recruitment and selection strategy than that used before. Jenny and Alan agreed, and went through a rigorous job analysis with the consultant. This resulted in a job description and person specification. They now had to decide on how to recruit and on the selection process. They knew another bad appointment could mean the end of the business, so they were determined to take advice from the consultant and work with him.

Questions

1. Where would the kind of applicants the company was looking for be found and how would you go about contacting them?

2. Using the information provided, plus further details on what similar jobs in the engineering and related sectors involve, prepare a person specification for use in the selection process.

3. Consider and decide upon a selection strategy, identifying the selection tools/instruments you would recommend that the company use if you were in the role of the consultant. Justify your recommendations.

4. What would be the key criteria you would use in producing a shortlist?

5. Who would take the final decision and what criteria would you use to establish whether the appointment was a success?

6. Produce an estimate of the costs of the whole process.

Insights & Outcomes: visit the Online Resource Centre at www.oxfordtextbooks.co.uk/orc/banfield_kay/ to find out what the recruitment and selection strategy was and the outcome of the process.

FURTHER READING

Advisory Conciliation and Arbitration Service (2006), *Recruitment and Induction*, advisory booklet, available online at www.acas.org.uk.

Chartered Institute of Personnel and Development (2007) *Recruitment Retention and Turnover Survey*, CIPD survey report, available online at www.cipd.co.uk.

Cook, M (2003) *Personnel Selection: Adding Value Through People*, 4th edn, Wiley.

Dale, M (2004) *A Manager's Guide to Recruitment & Selection*, 2nd edn, Kogan Page.

Sims, J (2005) 'Weathering recruitment', *People Management*, 8 Dec.

REFERENCES

Batata, AS (2005) 'International nurse recruitment and NHS vacancies: a cross-sectional analysis', *Globalization and Health*, 1:7, available online at www.globalizationandhealth.com.

Bozionelos, N (2005) 'When the inferior candidate is offered the job: the selection interview as a political and power game', *Human Relations*, 58:12, pp 1605–31.

Buchan J (2004) 'International rescue? The dynamics and policy implications of the international recruitment of nurses to the UK', *Journal of Health Services Research & Policy*, 9:1, pp 10–16.

Burrows, C (2004) 'Enriching the talent pool: injecting new blood from outside the industry', *International Journal of Medical Marketing*, 4:4, pp 390–2.

Carrington, L (2004) 'Laws of attraction', *People Management*, 17 Jun, p 26.

Chambers, BA (2002) 'Applicant reactions and their consequences: review, advice, and recommendations for future research', *International Journal of Management Review*, 4, Dec, pp 317–33.

Chartered Institute of Personnel and Development (2007) *Recruitment, Retention and Turnover Survey*, CIPD survey report, available online at www.cipd.co.uk.

Collins, J (2001) *From Good to Great*, Random House, ch 3.

Cook, M (1988) *Personnel Selection and Productivity*, John Wiley and Sons.

Department of Health (1999) Guidance on International Nursing Recruitment, available online at www.dh.gov.uk.

Doeringer, PB and Piore, MJ (1971) *Internal Labor Markets and Manpower Analysis*, Heath & Company.

Fitz-Enz, J (2002) *How to Measure Human Resource Management*, McGraw-Hill.

Goldman, D (1995) *Emotional Intelligence*, Bantam.

Goldman, D (1998) *Working with Emotional Intelligence*, Bantam.

Gratton, L (2000) 'A real step change', *People Management*, 16 Mar, pp 26–30.

Horowitz, FM, Heng, CT and Quazi, HA (2003) 'Finders, keepers? Attracting, motivating and retaining knowledge workers', *Human Resource Management*, 13:4, pp 23–44.

Kent, S (2005) 'Get on Board', *People Management*, 28 July, pp 38–40.

Lazear, EP (1998) *Personnel Economics For Managers*, John Wiley and Sons, ch 2.

Levesque, LL (2005) 'Opportunistic hiring and employee fit', *Human Resource Management*, 44:3, Fall, pp 301–30.

Michaels, E, Handfield-Jones, H and Axelrod, B (2001) *The War for Talent*, Harvard Business School Press.

Morgan G (1997) *Images of Organization*, 2nd edn, Sage.

Oasis (2005) *Report on the Kwik-Fit Financial Services and Microsoft Presentations on CSR*, 30 June, available online at www.oasisedinburgh.com.

Office for National Statistics (2005) *Labour Force Survey*, Apr 29, available online at http://www.statistics.gov.uk/.

O'Leary, BS, Lindholm, ML, Whitford, RA and Freeman, SE (2002) 'Selecting the best and brightest: leveraging human capital', *Human Resource Management*, 41:3, Fall, pp 325–40.

Ryan, AM and Tippins, NT (2004) 'Attracting and selecting: what psychological research tells us', *Human Resource Management*, 43:4, pp 305–18.

Rynes, SL, Colbert, A and Brown, KG (2004) 'HR professionals' beliefs about effective human resource practices: correspondence between research and practice', *Human Resource Management*, 41, Summer, pp 149–74.

Sunday Times (2006) 'Top 100 Best Companies to Work For', 5 Mar.

Welch, J and Welch, S (2005) *Winning*, HarperCollins.

Women and Work Commission (2006) *Shaping a Fairer Future*, Department of Trade and Industry.

Managing Employee Relations

4

Key Terms

Trade union An organization that is independent of an employer and funded by member contributions, the function of which is to represent worker interests in relations between workers and employers.

Collective bargaining The process of negotiation between trade union representatives and employers, or employer representatives, to establish by agreement the terms and conditions of employment of a group of employees.

Collective agreement A written statement defining the arrangements agreed between a union and employer, and the terms that will apply. Such agreements are only legally enforceable if this is expressly stated or if the collective agreement is referred to in individual written terms and conditions of employment.

Psychological contract The obligations that an employer and an employee, or group of employees, perceive to exist between each other as part of the employment relationship, comprising both expectations of each other and promises made to each other.

Learning Objectives

As a result of reading this chapter and using the Online Resource Centre, you should be able to:

- understand the importance of maintaining good relations with employees, through involvement, and through effective communication and consultation;

- recognize the importance of the psychological contract at work and how to manage this to support organizational objectives;

- be able to evaluate the contemporary role of trade unions and how to manage effective union relationships through partnership;

- understand the difference between consultation and collective bargaining, and how to avoid disruption due to collective disputes;

- understand and apply key theoretical and conceptual contributions to the analysis of individual and collective behaviour.

Introduction

The relationship between an employer and its employees lies at the heart of what makes an organization effective. The employees of an organization have the power to allow an organization to meet and exceed its objectives, or to fail. Highly motivated employees work more productively and, if they feel engaged with their employer, will make a greater contribution towards its overall direction and success. Demotivated employees, on the other hand, can also have an impact on the organization, but in different and more negative ways. This can include individual and less visible expressions of dissatisfaction, such as high absenteeism, poor timekeeping and low productivity, as well as collective action, such as strikes and working to rule, all of which undermine the organization's ability to ensure its financial health and long-term competitiveness.

While the long-term decline in British manufacturing can, in part, be explained by the emergence of low-cost economies in the Far East, it is also worth remembering that those industries which experienced a rapid and close-to-terminal decline in the 1970s and 1980s — the most well known of which were motor manufacturing, shipbuilding and steel production — were industries that were renowned for 'bad' industrial relations, low morale and high levels of industrial conflict. As a general statement, organizations that are able to establish and maintain good relations with employees and their representatives are those that will not only avoid the weakening effects of an underproducing and uncooperative workforce, but gain the advantages that result from a workforce that is motivated and committed. The expectation is that this workforce will understand that its long-term interests are better served by working with management, rather than by challenging them in the pursuit of its own short-term interests. This theme of working with or against management, which is central to the whole of this text, will be explored in more detail later.

It is important to recognize that getting an organization's employment relations 'right' does not have the same significance as having an effective recruitment or training strategy. It is actually of *more* importance, because the state of an organization's individual and collective employment relations has a pervasive influence on how the other aspects of managing people are carried out. It is inconceivable that strategies to drive performance forward, initiatives to increase the level of employee utilization and attempts to access the world of discretionary effort will be successful if the general state of employment relations is poor and unsatisfactory, and if there is little trust between managers and employees. Effective employee relations provide a framework conducive to, and a positive psychological environment within which, performance discussions and other employment matters can take place. As a result, employees should be confident about expressing their views, in the expectation that these will be taken into account when final decisions are taken. But to be able to manage performance or gain employee support for change, an employer must first have a constructive relationship with its employees.

→ Signpost to Chapter 11: Managing Performance, for perspectives on maximizing performance

The origins and scope of industrial (or employment) relations

What is now called 'employment relations' or 'employee relations' was originally known as 'industrial relations' and has its origins in the 1960s as a separate discipline or field of study in the 1960s. As was explained in Chapter 2, the importance of industrial relations in the second half of the last century shaped and influenced the development of personnel/human resource management as a specialist management function, and the agendas of those who had responsibilities in this area. But this does not mean that interest in the relationship between employee and employer is a relatively recent phenomenon. The contractual relationship that is at the heart of employment has been of interest to economists, sociologists and lawyers since at least the middle of the nineteenth century and, arguably, since even earlier.

This contract provides a set of rights, responsibilities and obligations that structure the behaviour of both parties, and represents the basis of what constitutes the normative system of regulation and control within the workplace. For many writers on political economy, the perceived and actual inequalities between the individual worker and his or her employer, based on the ownership of the means of production (*capital*), is closely associated with the rise of the trade union movement in the latter part of the nineteenth century. Even today, it is seen as being at the heart of what many believe to be the source of conflict between employers and workers (Clarke and Clements, 1977).

After the end of World War II, and in the immediate aftermath of reconstruction and readjustment to post-war conditions, trade unions and employers re-established relationships and proceeded to build new frameworks for the collective regulation of industrial relations, although many of those that came into being owed much to pre-war antecedents. The system of Whitely Councils, for example, established after the end of World War I to provide a comprehensive collective bargaining framework for a range of industries, survived well into the second half of the twentieth century, although almost all of those that remained were in the public sector. This fact reflects the way in which trade union presence and activity has become concentrated in public sector institutions, with only relatively few pockets remaining in the private sector (mainly in transport and communications).

What became a feature of post-World War II industrial relations was the increase in industrial conflict, particularly strikes, experienced by companies in heavy engineering, manufacturing and, increasingly, in parts of the public sector. The so-called 'Winter of Discontent' of 1978−79 was the culmination of trade union activity in pursuit of pay claims that were higher than government pay policy allowed and began in private industry, before spreading to local authorities and other public sector employees.

The incidence and frequency of strike action were not on the same scale as that which was experienced in the 1920s, but, nevertheless, the disruption caused to production, competitiveness and to public service were considered to be serious problems that needed urgent attention The so-called 'British Disease', represented by a strike-prone and inefficient workforce, became an uncomfortable, but not entirely unjustified, description of what was wrong with industrial relations at that time (Metcalfe and Milner, 1991).

The influence of academics

The 1960s saw the emergence of a group of academics who had a particular interest in trade unions and industrial relations. Among the most influential were John Dunlop (1958), Richard Hyman (1975), Alan Flanders (1970) and Alan Fox (1966). These, and others who shared their concerns about the state of industrial relations, were interested in trying to identify the underlying dynamics and structural forces that were 'determining' worker behaviour. They were particularly concerned with developing theoretical contributions that offered insights into:

● the political and institutional role of trade unions, and the impact that trade union activity had on employment and wages;

● the relationship between trade union leaders and members;

● the causes of strikes;

● the role and influence of management and employers in shaping the way in which industrial relations developed.

Dunlop (1958) developed a theory of industrial relations that saw industrial relations as a subsystem of society, on a par with the economic and political subsystems, which overlapped and influenced each other. Although the suggestion that industrial relations was equivalent in importance and impact to the two other societal subsystems is much more contentious now that it was in the 1960s, the central components of his theory are still relevant. They provide important conceptual and explanatory tools that can be used by those who are trying to interpret the way in which the 'system' functions, and can be summarized as:

- what he describes as 'actors' in the system. These are the representatives of management, employees and their representatives, and specialist government agencies that have an industrial relations function;
- the context or environment within which the actors operate and which determines the material conditions of work and employment;
- the ideology or belief systems that each 'actor' possesses and is influenced by, and which help to determine the way in which particular groups relate to other 'actors' within the system;
- the system outputs, which are expressed in terms of rules, that give the system a degree of stability and maintain order, although these should be seen as provisional and conditional rather than as permanent.

The importance of rules and rule-making processes are central to understanding the primary 'function' of the industrial relations system. One way of understanding why rules are important is to consider the limitations inherent in the formal contract of employment. By this, we mean that, while the employer agrees to the rate of pay, fringe benefits, holidays and other conditions of employment, the commitment of the employee is quite different. He or she agrees to accept a role that is subordinate to that of management, in the sense of accepting managerial authority, and to carry out the duties associated with the job for which he or she been employed. But there is an important area of indeterminacy in the formal contract of employment, in terms of levels of job performance that will be delivered and sustained, and in acceptance of specific management orders. As Hyman and Brough (1975) argued, an employee makes a commitment to obey:

> Yet such a promise is neither unambiguous nor conditional; and its interpretation is thus a source of potential conflict.

They quote Gouldner (1954), who asks:

> Which commands has the worker promised to obey? Are these commands limited to the production of goods and services only? Under the terms of the contract, may an employer legitimately issue a command unnecessary for production? Who decides this anyhow, worker or employer?

This recognition that there is a degree of indeterminacy in all employment contracts means that one, or both, of the workplace actors, or an external third party, must establish rules to ensure that there is the necessary level of normative order, and therefore stability, within the national or local system. If this does not happen, the tendency will be for the lack of normative regulation to lead to higher levels of uncertainty, instability and conflict than would otherwise have been the case.

Rules in employment relations

Rules in employment relations fall into two main categories, as follows.

Procedural rules

Procedural rules are those that establish how the actors in the system will respond and behave in given situations. For example, if managers and union representatives fail to reach agreement about annual pay increases, they may have already agreed on ways in which to resolve the impasse and avoid industrial conflict. This may involve third-party intervention, a cooling-off period or some other mechanism for facilitating agreement. These rules fulfil the important role of maintaining system stability and avoid either party taking arbitrary action.

There is, however, a second category of procedural rules that has a quite different function. In this case, rules are agreed that determine how other kinds of rules will be determined. Again, a simple example will illustrate how these rules work: consider the important issue of what employees will be paid for the work that they do. Payment can be based on hours worked, production achieved or performance attained – but who makes this decision? Is this something that management alone is to determine, or should it be decided by the employees themselves or through the intervention of a third party? These are important questions, the answers to which will have an important impact on the economic health of the organization and on the quality of the relationships between managers and employees. These rule-making processes are at the heart of any employment relations system and can be expressed in terms of:

- *unilateral regulation*, under which either managers, unions or employees create rules that regulate a particular part of the employment relationship. For example, on the question of overtime and what will be paid for such time, managers might feel that this is something that they alone need to regulate;

- on the other hand, trade unionism is based on the belief in, and commitment to, what is called *joint regulation*, more usually known as 'collective bargaining', under which both parties meet and, through the process of negotiation, reach a joint decision on rules, such as those that regulate the allocation and payment of overtime working, as well as other matters of importance. Unions have consistently strived to extend the application of joint regulation to as many aspects of the organization as possible, in an attempt to increase the protection they can provide to their members and to enhance their own influence;

- procedural rules that originate outside of the employing organization or national institutions of the employment relations system can be created through *legal and judicial processes*. The British Parliament, the European Union and associated judicial bodies make and interpret laws that regulate work and employment. In fact, it might be argued that the relative importance of each of these rule-making processes has changed significantly over the past fifty years, with the influence of judicial processes increasing, while that of trade union unilateral regulation and joint regulation has been decreasing in both frequency and influence. This view is consistent with the evidence of the relative decline in trade unionism and the increasing difficulty that unions experience in maintaining the idea and practice of joint determination, particularly those that represent workers in the private sector. Think about the Working Time Regulations (WTR) and the National Minimum Wage (NMW) as examples of how complex sets of rules over working time and payment are made by external parties rather than by unilateral or joint regulation.

Substantive rules

These are the rules that are generated by rule-making processes, such as joint determination and unilateral decision making. Once again considering pay as an example, these types of rule determine how pay rates and levels are determined, but represent the actual rules that say what a person's basic pay will be and what any additional payments for extra work done might be. As was explained above, the 'working week' – an area of particular importance for both employees and employers – is now, for many workers, regulated by the EU and the substantive rules that have been established take preced-ence over any that were agreed by collective bargaining or imposed by employers. Substantive rules regulate how much people get paid, their hours of work, holiday entitlement and so on. Many of these are contained in the formal contract of employment but, as explained earlier, this only regulates certain aspects of an employee's behaviour and performance at work. In a constantly changing environment, new conditions and situations arise that need to be regulated and, through the processes for creating new rules or amending old ones, the body of substantive rules is constantly being amended.

Table 4.1 summarizes the findings of the 2004 Workplace Employment Relations Survey (DTI, 2004) about the way in which rules are established and the degree to which management involves employees in the rule-making process.

Table 4.1 Joint regulation of terms and conditions of employment

Issue	Management decides	Informs	Consults	Negotiates
Pay	70 (16)	6 (10)	5 (13)	18 (61)
Hours	71 (18)	5 (10)	8 (20)	16 (53)
Holidays	71 (19)	9 (17)	5 (13)	15 (52)
Pensions	73 (22)	11 (25)	6 (16)	10 (36)
Staff selection	78 (42)	10 (26)	9 (23)	3 (9)
Training	75 (36)	10 (24)	13 (31)	3 (9)
Grievance procedure	69 (15)	9 (20)	14 (36)	9 (28)
Disciplinary procedure	69 (15)	9 (21)	13 (35)	8 (29)
Staffing plans	75 (33)	11 (26)	12 (34)	3 (7)
Equal Opportunities	72 (22)	10 (23)	14 (40)	5 (15)
Health and safety	69 (17)	9 (19)	17 (49)	5 (15)
Performance appraisal	75 (33)	9 (20)	12 (33)	4 (14)

Source: *WERS 2004 First Findings*. © Crown Copyright/ESRC/ACAS/Policy Studies Institute.

(Note that the figures in brackets represent the managerial responses in workplaces that recognized trade unions.)

KEY CONCEPT Managerial authority

The concept of managerial authority is central to understanding the sources of tension within employment relations and the ongoing struggle between managers and trade unions, in particular over the 'rights' and authority of each party. 'Prerogative' means the right to make decisions and to establish rules that are essential in allowing the production system to operate efficiently and effectively, and, historically, managers have tended to guard their prerogative and have tried to prevent trade unions from eroding it. If trade union power has increased as a result of economic or political change, and has strengthened their representative and negotiating role, managerial rights have been eroded and pushed back; if trade union power has been weakened by the movement of capital and restrictive legislation, managers have been able to reassert their rights 'to manage' and to restrict trade union involvement in the decision-making process. In extreme cases, this has involved the removal of recognition and the restriction or elimination of bargaining rights. This is an aspect of employment relations that is never completely resolved, but is rather in a state of dynamic tension.

STUDENT ACTIVITY 4.1

1. Summarize the information contained in Table 4.1 and compare it with the results of previous Workplace Employment Relations Surveys on the same subject.

2. Explore the implications emerging from this comparison.

3. Consider the inferences that can be reached about changes in trade union influence and the significance of collective bargaining (negotiating) in contemporary employment relations.

Rules and legitimacy

There is one further category of rules that needs to be explained, and this concerns the form that the rules take and their legitimacy. The idea that people at work operate within two organizational environments has long been recognized (Handy, 1993). At one level, the environment represented by the formal organization consists of the formally approved, usually by management, procedural and substantive rules.

These rules are legitimised, through being known and approved by management, and regulate how people are supposed to behave at work.

The concept of the 'informal organization', however, suggests that this informal world, represented by the place of work and the day-to-day interaction between managers and employees, and within employee groups, can develop its own social and work-related norms (rules). These are often unknown to senior managers and may be in conflict with the formal rules that have emerged from 'more legitimate' processes. Such rules may lack the legitimacy of formally derived rules, but can nevertheless exert a powerful influence on the behaviour of the managers and employees affected by them. The reason why it is important to understand the importance of informal rules is that, while much of our behaviour is regulated and controlled in ways known to management, other aspects are not, e.g.:

- levels of discretionary effort;
- output and performance levels;
- the level of cooperation offered to management;
- the degree of employee flexibility.

In situations in which there is a lack of trust between employees and managers, and in which employees exercise control over the production/work process, it is likely that employees, either as individuals or groups, will limit their performance, creating a body of informal and, as far as management is concerned, often unknown rules that regulate what employees are prepared and not prepared to do. The challenge that contemporary managers face is not simply to discover and change these rules, but to understand the reasons why they exist.

STUDENT ACTIVITY 4.2 The Wildcat Strike

Alvin Gouldner's (1954) classic study of an unofficial strike and its causes remains one of the out-standing contributions to our understanding of the interaction between the formal and informal systems of work. The task is to read the first chapter of his text, *Wildcat Strike*, in order to answer the following questions.

1. What is meant by the term 'indulgency patterns'?
2. Why did the original managers appear to allow the workers to break the formal rules?
3. Why was legitimacy an important issue in the conflict that led to the strike?
4. What role did management play in events leading up to the strike?

Figure 4.1 represents a way of understanding the essential elements of an industrial relations system and how, as these change over time, the system produces new institutions, different patterns of rule making, and new ways of preventing and resolving conflict. The important point to note is that the system must be understood as dynamic, rather than static, and as influenced by forces that are often outside the control of the main participants and interest groups. A particularly good example of this inability to control the system can be seen in the way in which the effects of internationalization and globalization have changed the forces of competition in manufacturing and service industries. This has resulted in growth in the knowledge economy and the numbers of knowledge workers, a decline in manufacturing jobs and a corresponding fall in private sector union density. Because the public sector environment has so far remained relatively immune from the employment effects of the globalization of trade and competition, trade union membership and influence in this sector have been preserved. As the private sector increases its involvement in the provision of public sector services, however, and as old labour supply monopolies come under increasing pressure, it is inevitable that the form of regulation, union membership patterns and the influence of trade unions will change.

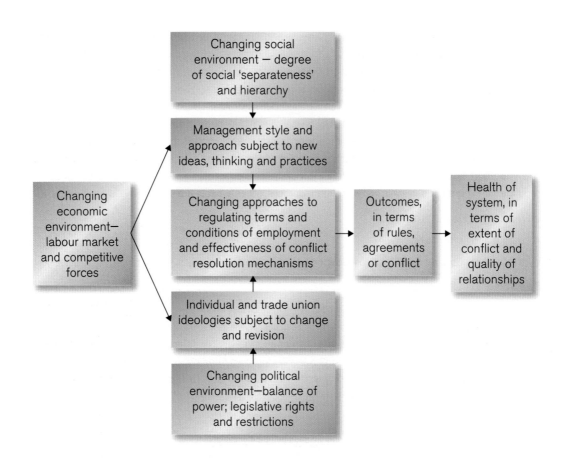

Figure 4.1 A diagrammatical representation of an employment relations system

→ Signpost to Chapter 15: Case Study: Reforming the HR Function, for an example of changing employment relations

Figure 4.1 is also useful in that it represents a model that can be applied both to national 'systems' and to those that exist within each organization. It can be used to explain why:

● the frequency and pattern of industrial conflict changes and differs between sectors and industries;

● new methods of reaching agreement on work and employment have been created;

● trade unions have a history of mergers and reorganization, and of developing new services for their members;

● more emphasis is now placed on individual, rather than collective, employment relations, as employers and managers — many of whom are from overseas — use different and more effective strategies to gain acceptance and commitment from their employees;

● governments periodically intervene in the system in an attempt to 'correct' any imbalances of power and to limit the ability of the main parties to damage the social or economic fabric of society.

Perspectives on employment relations

One of the most important theoretical contributions made by the early industrial relations theorists, summarized by Salamon (2000), is the development of what are commonly known as perspectives on, or approaches to, the study and interpretation of industrial/employment relations. These perspectives are important because they express the different assumptions that academics and others make about the nature of organizations, the fundamental nature of the relationship between workers and employers, and the characteristics of the society within which work organizations exist and function.

The three perspectives that are most frequently referred to are:

- the unitary perspective;
- pluralism;
- the radical, or Marxist, perspective.

The unitary perspective

According to Rose (2001), the unitary perspective represents a view of the work organization — and indeed of society as a whole — in which it is assumed, or seen as preferable, that:

- those who work together, in whatever role and function, are essentially integrated and are working towards shared objectives;
- there is a single and accepted structure of hierarchical authority, and that, within this structure, the role of managers in exercising control is legitimized by those in a subordinate relationship to them;
- the different groups within the organization share the same interests and have a common set of values.

The unitary perspective is important because of the implications it has for the authority of management and its reaction to any challenges to its dominant position. Employers and managers who identify with a unitary perspective believe that it is their prerogative to 'be in control' and to take decisions on how the organization functions. Managers also tend to view any questioning of their right to manage to lack legitimacy and as likely to be 'the work of 'troublemakers', who seek to destabilize and undermine a stable and relatively harmonious working and social environment. This reflects the belief that managers and workers share the same interests and objectives, and that all parties have accepted that those in positions of authority are there because they are owners, or their agents, or are professionally qualified and experienced to manage. There is, in other words, 'a natural order' to the relations between employers and workers, which has to be defended against 'outside interests' that might seek to undermine it.

Such an interpretation has important implications for the status of trade unions, which are seen by employers who subscribe to the unitary perspective as an intrusion and threat to management, and to the stability and status quo that is assumed to exist. It also means that, from a unitary perspective, the management of conflict is often restricted to a denial of its existence and/or the pursuit and removal of individual 'troublemakers', the derecognition of trade unions, and the removal or restriction of representation and negotiation rights.

HRM INSIGHT 4.1 ABC Pharmaceuticals

ABC Pharmaceuticals is a global business with a manufacturing plant in the Republic of Ireland that is responsible for the production of the active ingredients used in a wide range of pharmaceutical products. The site employs over 400 skilled employees and has not had any union representation since the facility was built in the late 1970s. While the company does have union representation at some of its other manufacturing sites in Europe, its vision of the Irish site was that it would stay non-unionized. The decision by senior management not to recognize any union for either negotiation or representational purposes was based on the company's philosophy that its employees' best interests would be served through the creation of a single-status working environment. This would provide an excellent reward-and-recognition package and facilitate communication with employees at all levels.

From an operational perspective, it was also important to create a high level of flexibility in working practices, so that the plant could adapt and respond quickly to the continuing changes in product development, manufacturing processes and market demand, all of which are features of the pharmaceutical industry.

→

To allow for employee representation, the company created the specific role of 'employee representative'. This role provides both individuals and groups of employees who have grievances or other difficulties with a route, involving defined procedure, by which they can raise issues and express their concerns to management. Management will then consult with the representative in solving the problem and in delivering a solution in the way that best meets the employees' and the business' needs.

There is a strong emphasis on communications at the site and it is a multi-level activity, involving crew/team meetings, individual discussions, general employee meetings, a newsletter (both internal and external), and the use of both email and intranet.

Because of the nature of continuous change, any changes that are mooted are discussed within teams that are both directly and indirectly affected, and within specialized forums, such as safety committees. For the majority of employees, this system works very well and representatives play an important part in dealing with a wide range of concerns and issues, very few of which, to date, have required outside intervention of any sort.

There is a small minority of employees, however, who feel that they would like the right to join a trade union and have its presence formally recognized. The effectiveness of the employee representative role and management's engagement with employees has not, however, resulted in any sense of dissatisfaction among the majority of employees about the way in which grievances and concerns have been dealt with.

Questions

1. Is there a case to be made that the interests of employees would be better served by union recognition and negotiating rights?

2. Would recognizing trade unions result in an increase in differences and disagreements between managers and employees? If so, why, and what would they be likely to involve?

3. To what extent are the success of the plant and the stability of employment and wages a function of its non-unionized status?

4. If you were a national trade union official trying to achieve union recognition in the plant, what arguments would you present to management and employees to try to persuade them to accept this objective?

Pluralism

The second of the three perspectives, according to Rose (2001), can be regarded as:

more congruent with developments in contemporary society.
(p 31)

This means that, while the characteristics of the unitary perspective might be attractive to owners and managers (although less so to employees), it is a perspective that is more aspirational than realistic, simply because it does not accord with how society and work organizations are actually structured.

Pluralism literally means 'more than one' and reflects a view of society in which many different groups coexist in a state of partial, mutual interdependence. In the context of employment relations, the distinctive features of pluralism are:

- the existence of different groups/interests, which reflect differences in occupation, role and social ideology;

- that, while the objectives and interests of these groups are not fundamentally different, differences can emerge about how organizations are managed and controlled, and there is a recognition that the objectives of managers and workers can diverge, particularly over such issues as job security, employee rights and pay;

- the acceptance of conflict as an inevitable outcome of this plurality and that it has a degree of legitimacy. Rather than to deny it, or to see it as the work of outside troublemakers, conflict needs to be managed and resolved through the creation of institutional mechanisms, such as collective bargaining, conciliation, mediation and arbitration.

With recent changes in contemporary society, particularly the large-scale movements of people across national boundaries and the emergence of a multicultural Britain, it might be argued that society generally – and the workplace, in particular – has become increasingly 'pluralistic'. The danger of this, however, is that the underlying common interests and identities of employees, based on class and occupation, which have helped to limit the degree of social diversity in the workplace are actually threatened by the extent of differences based on gender, ethnicity, religion and cultural values.

It might, therefore, be argued that this perspective is the most useful in trying to understand changes in the pattern of collective employment relations. This is a view supported by Salamon (2000), who argues that organizations are:

> …in a permanent state of dynamic tension resulting from the inherent tension and competing claims which have to be 'managed' through a variety of roles, institutions and processes.
> (p 7)

As far as system stability is concerned, adopting a pluralistic perspective means that any accommodation or stability that emerges between cooperating and competing groups should be seen as conditional and temporary rather than as permanent.

From an employment perspective, the one common interest that both managers and employees share is the prosperity and survival of the enterprise, which provides both groups with valued social and economic rewards. Those who subscribe to a pluralist view of the workplace believe that the fundamental interests of managers and employees are, if not identical, very similar, and that there is a mutual dependency in ensuring that the organization, which provides jobs and rewards for both parties, is financially healthy and prosperous. But the perspective also allows for, and expects, a degree of transactional conflict to characterize a pluralistic workplace. For example, few workers today articulate a fundamental rejection of their status and role in relation to management, but they may well disagree with management over pay and how employees are treated.

Of course, employee levels of dependency on management fluctuate in line with the state of the labour market, and are affected in the longer term by the growth of portfolio working and self-employment. Nonetheless, for the vast majority of people who are employed, the reality of their situation is that they and their managers have a sense of being united rather than divided. This perception means that their interests are better served by working together and reaching an accommodation, however conditional this might be, than by seeing themselves as in a wholly adversarial relationship. This is the essence of what pluralism means (Beynon et al, 2002).

The radical, or Marxist, perspective

The radical, or Marxist, perspective is the third, and in some ways the most difficult, of the three perspectives to reconcile with what the majority of present-day employees and managers actually perceive and experience. It is founded on the analysis and critique of capitalist society by Karl Marx and other 'left-wing' writers, and has been an important contribution to understanding the dynamic, and often contradictory, forces that shape society and the economy. It was particularly influential in the twentieth century, but appears to be less so today because the ideological conflict between capitalism and communism is, except for those adhering to the political far left, effectively over. The distinguishing features of this perspective are that:

- society is based on a hierarchy within which class, wealth and power determine a person's social status and importance, and these determinants of social standing are replicated in the workplace. This has the effect of creating a situation in which workers are at the bottom of the hierarchy, are subordinate to the agents of capitalism (managers) and are dependent on them for employment and work;

- the inherent inequality between employers and workers is based on the ownership of the means of production and the exploitation of workers in the wealth-generating process, as part of which the surplus value that workers generate through their efforts is appropriated as profit by the owners;

- trade unions are as much an expression of the political interests of workers as of their industrial or employment interests. In pursuit of political change, trade unions are not simply attempting to improve the terms of worker subordination, in the sense of achieving higher pay and better conditions, but are engaged in a struggle to challenge the system of power and control that places workers in a position of social and economic subordination;

- industrial conflict has a political, as well as an economic, purpose and is an instrument that can be used to achieve political change, as well as improvement to the terms under which workers are employed.

The radical perspective, which is associated with those who reject capitalist society and its institutions, sees any accommodation with the interests of employers and managers as problematical. As Salamon (2000) points out:

> **The Marxist perspective sees the processes and institutions of joint regulation as an enhancement rather than a reduction in management's position; or at best, they provide only a limited and temporary accommodation of the inherent and fundamental divisions within capitalist based work and social structures.**
>
> (p 9)

There have, in the past, been periods during which certain UK trade unions have been associated with this perspective and its associated political ideology, and there remain pockets of what might be described as 'militant' trade unionism. For the most part, contemporary trade unions appear to have abandoned or rejected this perspective as largely irrelevant to their perceived role and to the expectations their members have of them. The majority of trade unions and trade union leaders see their role as being to improve the economic terms and conditions of their members, *within* the existing political and economic system, and through working with, rather than working against, management. Evidence of this can be found in the changing pattern and frequency of strikes and of other forms of industrial conflict (Metcalfe, 2005).

What is a trade union?

A 'trade union' is a body that both collectively and individually represents the interests of its members, predominantly in the context of employment. The union is therefore concerned with the relations between workers and their employer. Many organizations formally recognize one, or more, trade unions for representation or negotiation purposes, but equally many, predominantly in the private sector, do not. The form of recognition adopted might be restricted to recognition of a particular union to represent individual employees, or groups of employees, in procedures such as dismissal and grievance procedures, but will often extend to the recognition of unions for collective negotiation over issues such as terms and conditions, including pay. It should be noted that formal recognition comes about when an employer is willing to negotiate, rather than simply to recognize or consult with, a trade union.

Trade unions are a worldwide phenomenon and are associated with industrialization, the fracturing of old social relations and dependencies, and the experience of greater economic uncertainty and insecurity. Their form, practices and ideologies differ between countries. For example, Japanese unions are based largely on individual companies, rather than on national associations, and are known for their commitment to a close working relationship with management. Their fundamental purpose is the same as that of British trade unions, i.e. to offer their members protection and defence from the arbitrary action of management and from the economic system within which they are employed. What is different is the way in which each nation's trade unions try to deliver these outcomes and how successful they are.

Trade unions, in the absence of legal prohibition, thrive in situations in which:

- employees enjoy limited, or no, protection from state or other judicial authorities;

- management show little concern for the interests or well being of their employees;

- individual workers are relatively powerless to challenge management and are unable to restrict their power;

- workers' experience of employment leaves them with a strong sense of grievance towards management, based on a feeling that they are being exploited and treated unfairly.

Of course, the corollary of this is that workers may experience none of the above and, as a consequence, may feel disinclined to join a trade union or to participate in any trade union activity.

Member commitment to the union can therefore be strong or weak, depending on the perceived need for unions and the degree to which members share the ideology of the union leadership. Those who subscribe to a radical and Marxist-informed ideology are likely to have a much more adversarial relationship with employers and managers than will the representatives of a union that adopts a pluralist perspective. It might be argued, therefore, that the contemporary existence of trade unions, and the relationship they have with employers and managers, is as much a function of the attitude and behaviour of employers and managers as it is of any independent motivation that affects the predisposition of workers to join, or to remain outside of, trade union representation. Employees may also have the option, as an alternative to joining a national trade union, of becoming a member of a company- based staff association.

STUDENT ACTIVITY 4.3 A comparison between a trade union and a staff association

This activity involves considerable research, which might include surveying people who are members of both types of representative body as well as looking at the literature on employee representation. Groups can concentrate on either trade unions or staff associations, or both, but the idea is to produce presentations that address the following issues:

- the motivation behind joining trade unions rather than staff associations;

- the functions of the two types of body;

- management attitudes to the bodies;

- the advantages and disadvantages they offer to employees and managers.

The most well-known definition of a trade union was provided by the Webbs, in 1920, when they said it was:

> **... a continuous association of wage earners for the purpose of maintaining or improving the conditions of their working lives.**
> (Webb and Webb, 1920)

A more contemporary definition can be found in the Trade Union and Labour Relations (Consolidation) Act 1992, which defined a trade union as:

> **an organization ... consisting wholly or mainly of workers of one or more descriptions whose principal purpose includes the regulation of relations between workers of that description and employers or employers associations.**

Both definitions are similar and emphasize the union's regulatory and rule-making function, although the purpose of this activity, beyond reference to maintaining or improving the conditions of the working lives of members, is not made particularly clear.

Dunlop (2002), on the other hand, offers a much more helpful definition of what trade unions 'are for' and what this involves them in doing. He argues that, while people join unions for many different reasons, unions are fundamentally concerned with the following.

- Industrial jurisprudence

  This means that unions are involved in grievance and arbitration procedures, rules governing promotion, transfers, discipline and dismissals, and so on. Being able to participate in the regulation of such critically important policies and decisions provides a degree of protection and security from arbitrary action on the part of managers, but also helps to establish a more legitimate normative order. Dunlop calls this the '*human rights aspect of the workplace*'.

● **The economic regulation of employment**

This is concerned with what and how people are paid, the benefits they enjoy, their hours of work and the terms of the wage–work bargain. This aspect of trade union activity is much more a reflection of the resource status of employees, the economic value they generate through using their physical and intellectual capital, and what they can expect in return from managers as rewards for their wealth-creating contributions.

Union recognition

There is no obligation for employers to negotiate with a union. If no voluntary recognition agreement is in place, however, a union can apply for recognition to the Central Arbitration Committee (CAC) if it can show that it has at least 10 per cent membership among the group it wishes to represent and if it can secure a vote in favour of recognition from at least 40 per cent of the workers in that group. While recognition is usually expressed in some form of written agreement, it may be implied by the common practices undertaken by the organization.

It should be noted that the subject of unions, and the extent of their rights and immunities, has swung in different directions throughout recent history, depending on the government in power at the time. As a generalization, however, it might be argued that, since the curbing of trade union power during the years of the Thatcher government in the 1980s, subsequent legislative changes have concentrated on protecting the rights of individual workers and union members rather than on restoring the collective rights and power of trade unions.

STUDENT ACTIVITY 4.4 Analysing changes in trade union membership

There are a number of questions and issues that might be the basis of researching into changes in membership, but finding answers to the following questions will generate important insights into unionisation.

1. Nationally, what are the current patterns of trade unionism and how have density levels changed from those of 25 years ago?

2. What explanations can be offered for changes in unionization and density levels?

3. What is the union situation in the private sector compared to the public sector?

4. Why do have unions have such a limited presence and influence in the private sector?

5. Identify one union that you consider to be particularly successful and explain what the reasons for its success are.

(see Grainger (2006) for help in completing this exercise)

Rights, obligations and immunities of trade unions, members and representatives

Within the law, employees have individual rights, such as the right against discrimination on the grounds of being a union member, and the trade union also has certain rights, obligations and immunities from certain kinds of legal action, such as not being sued by employers in certain circumstances under which the union is representing its employees. These rights, obligations and immunities are summarized in Figure 4.2.

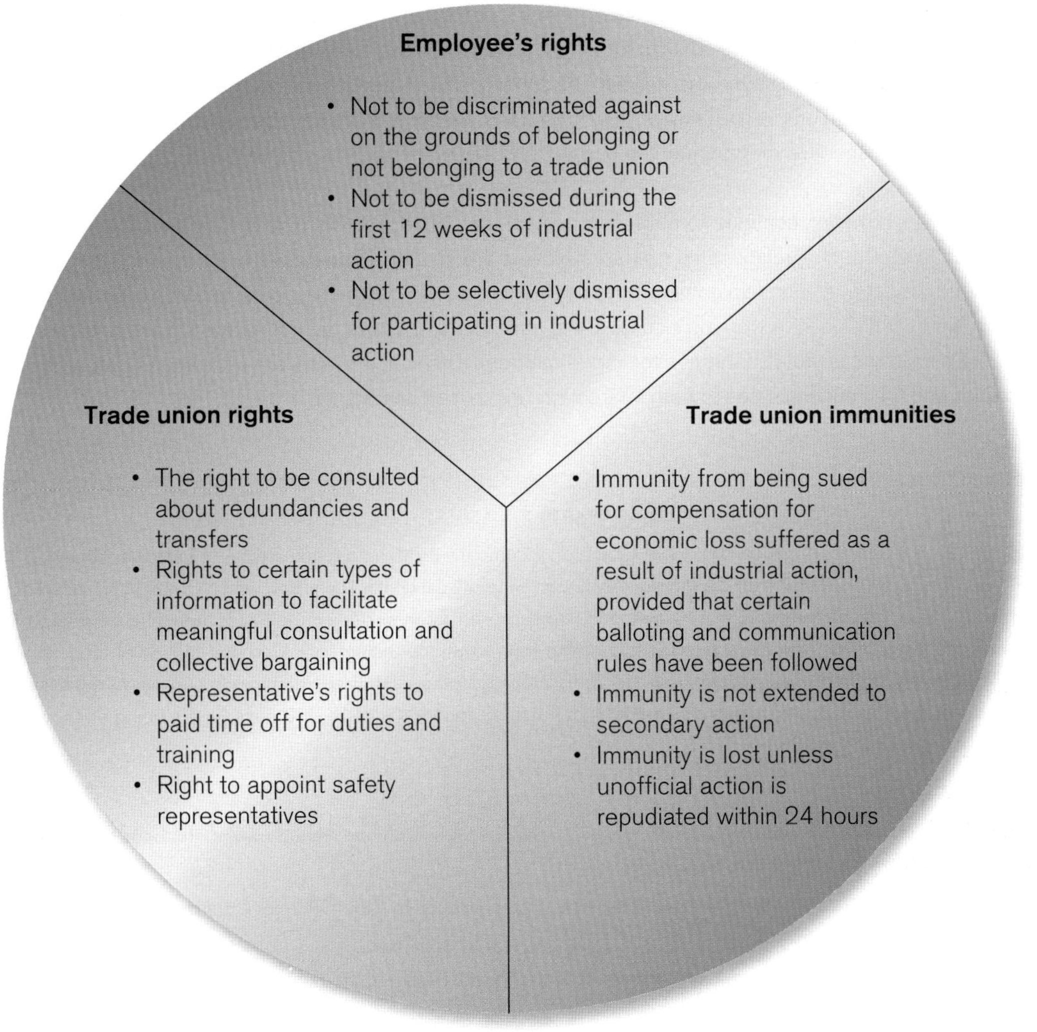

Employee's rights

- Not to be discriminated against on the grounds of belonging or not belonging to a trade union
- Not to be dismissed during the first 12 weeks of industrial action
- Not to be selectively dismissed for participating in industrial action

Trade union rights

- The right to be consulted about redundancies and transfers
- Rights to certain types of information to facilitate meaningful consultation and collective bargaining
- Representative's rights to paid time off for duties and training
- Right to appoint safety representatives

Trade union immunities

- Immunity from being sued for compensation for economic loss suffered as a result of industrial action, provided that certain balloting and communication rules have been followed
- Immunity is not extended to secondary action
- Immunity is lost unless unofficial action is repudiated within 24 hours

Figure 4.2 Individual rights and trade union immunities

The contemporary role of trade unions

Like many organizations, trade unions have had to adjust to a rapid change in the arena of employee relations over the last thirty years. As earlier noted, unions were originally formed to provide a collective voice to assert and defend employee rights; today's trade unions have been forced to find an alternative role because successive governments have introduced legislation to regulate employees' treatment, terms and conditions of employment, benefits and individual rights. In many instances, trade unions have struggled to come to terms with their changing environment and loss of influence, particularly with governments. The traditional and more confrontational approach, associated with the radical perspective, is unattractive to current and potential members who, in today's buoyant and more transitory employment market, can find alternative employment. Many have become less dependent on the unions and/or have been alienated by their ideologies.

If a collective agreement on pay and conditions is in place, union members and non-union members alike benefit from the pay deals negotiated. With the rise in 'no win, no fee' offers of legal assistance from certain firms of solicitors, the legal service offered by unions is less of a concern and many employees may choose not to pay a union subscription even if collective agreements are in place. Unions have, therefore, had to find alternative ways to attract members and have also been faced with the need to control costs, lose jobs and reduce the burden of administrative expenses in much the same way as have many other organizations. In many ways, they have had to become more sensitive and aware of what their members or prospective members actually want, and become more 'business-like' in the way in which they operate.

Unions do, however, continue to play an important and influential role in many organizations and it is important that, if such a relationship exists, employers are careful to manage it in a constructive manner. Managed well, the relationship can promote useful dialogue, and can contribute towards effective decision making and a positive working climate. If the relationship is managed poorly, then the results can be, at best, disruptive; at worst, if there is feeling of mistrust, there can be constant friction and outbreaks of conflict, and the consequences to both interest groups can be damaging.

HRM INSIGHT 4.2 Gate Gourmet

On 10 August 2005, Gate Gourmet, a company producing ready meals for use on aeroplanes, sacked 667 workers for participating in an unofficial strike. The strike, which was illegal, followed the recruitment of 130 seasonal workers and large-scale redundancies from the company's permanent workforce. This is resulted in four flights from Heathrow being cancelled due to lack of food. The following day, an unofficial 'wildcat' strike by British Airways ground staff at Heathrow in support of the Gate Gourmet workers resulted in over a hundred flights being grounded and 15,000 passengers being stranded, with costs estimated at £45m.

Questions

1. What legal considerations would have come into play for Gate Gourmet, Heathrow and the trade union representing the strikers in this example?

2. What practical use was the protection offered by this legislation to Gate Gourmet employees, Gate Gourmet and to British Airways?

3. What options might Heathrow Airport have considered with regard to the ground staff at Heathrow?

More information on this dispute is available online at www.tgwu.org.uk and at news.bbc.co.uk (12 August 2005; 28 November 2005); *see also Personnel Today, 28 February 2006.* Links to these articles are provided on the Online Resource Centre accompanying this textbook.

Why do employees join a trade union?

We have already considered the general reasons why employees join trade unions, but from the perspective of managers who are developing their strategy towards trade unions, a more detailed consideration of their motives is necessary. Historically, the reasons have often been negative, resulting from poor industrial relations and less favourable terms and conditions, leading to employees needing to feel supported by the strength of being part of a trade union. Changes in legislation and the employment market, together with increased awareness among employers of the need to engage their employees and to reward individual contribution, may have contributed to a decline in union membership over recent years.

Unions have, therefore, had to offer a wide range of benefits, and also appeal to a wide audience, in order to find members and hence maintain their funding through membership fees. In many cases, unions have merged to save costs and to offer better services.

Table 4.1 outlines some of the reasons why employees may choose to join a trade union. It is important for employers who maintain a non-union environment, or move to derecognize unions, to understand these reasons and, in so doing, avoid challenges to their non-union status quo.

Table 4.2 Reasons why employees join trade unions

Positive reasons for joining a trade union	Negative reasons for joining a trade union
Legal support	Peer pressure
Representation in formal meetings	Political persuasion
Credit union availability	Perceived lack of security
Cheap deals on insurance and other similar benefits	Lack of trust in employer
To benefit from union communications	To be able to participate in industrial action
Negotiating pay deals	To have support in expressing dissatisfaction
A shared identity and expression of common interest	High membership density

STUDENT ACTIVITY 4.5

This activity comprises two parts (the first comprising questions 1 and 2; the second, question 3) and either one part, or both, can be undertaken. Given the potential research and scope involved, this is better as a collaborative activity, but can be undertaken on an individual basis.

1. Interviewing a number of different people in employment among your contacts, friends and family, establish whether or not they are members of a trade union and the reasons for which they have chosen to join or not to join. Match these to the lists in Table 4.2 to establish the most common reasons for joining trade unions, adding any additional reasons that emerge. Put the reasons in an order that expresses their importance.

2. If people are trade union members, ask them what benefits they enjoy from union membership. Match these to information available on the union websites to establish how popular and widely known the benefits offered are.

3. Interview employers, or use a questionnaire, to establish why employers do, or do not, recognize and negotiate with trade unions. Establish what benefits those employers that do work with unions gain from such a relationship.

Collective bargaining

An employer can recognize unions at a number of levels. We will see in Chapter 5 that all employees have the right to be accompanied by a union representative of their choice in formal disciplinary meetings; this may be expressed in the form of a recognition agreement with a particular union.

 Signpost to Chapter 5: Managing Discipline and Grievance, for further information on disciplinary and grievance meetings

Employers can also recognize a union as the party with which they will consult about information affecting the organization and about issues such as redundancies, transfer of legal ownership and changes to pension provisions, for example.

Some employers also recognize one, or more, unions for the purposes of representing the interests of members in collective bargaining arrangements. The distinction between consultation and bargaining is important and, from a managerial viewpoint, should not be confused. Trade unions will always tend to prefer to bargain, rather than be consulted, because 'bargaining' implies that any important decision has yet to be made, and is subject to trade union influence and, where appropriate, pressure and sanctions. 'Consultation', on the other hand, implies that management retains the final right to make the decision, but wishes to keep representatives informed of its intentions and is prepared to listen to what they have to say.

 Signpost to Chapter 14: Case Study: The Role of HR in Closing a Factory, for an example of consultation over a factory closure

When a union is recognized for bargaining purposes, it has certain rights, which were summarized in Figure 4.2. The information that should be disclosed is covered by the Trade Union Relations (Consolidation) Act 1992 and includes information about the company's business, information relating to the categories of workers covered by the recognition agreement and broader categories of information, such as information which, were it not disclosed, would impede the union ability to negotiate and which it is good industrial relations practice to disclose. There are also exclusions if it might, for example, be damaging to the company to disclose the information. A union can make complaints for failure to disclose information to the Central Arbitration Committee (see www.cac.gov.uk).

Negotiating committees may consist of a number of union representatives, including company shop stewards and full-time regional officials employed by the union. For negotiation purposes, two or more unions may also form a joint negotiating committee. Negotiation may take place at different levels, from local negotiations covering a group of workers at one or more sites, to national-level negotiations, if there is a national agreement in place. Employers may be members of employers' associations and, should the need arise, may draw upon the advice and expertise of experienced management negotiators. There may also be scope to establish a second tier of negotiation, usually involving either more senior levels within the unions or management, or involving external bodies, in an attempt to resolve negotiations should the original negotiating committee fail to reach agreement.

Collective bargaining has four dimensions over which each party has an interest in influencing.

- Scope

    This relates to the range of issues that are subject to joint regulation.

- Form

    This explains whether the bargaining is formal or informal.

- Level

    This relates to whether the bargaining is at company or national level.

- Unit

    This relates to the bargaining unit, which identifies the group of employees covered by the resulting collective agreement. The unit can change, depending on what is being negotiated.

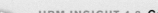 **HRM INSIGHT 4.3** **Goldsmith's Pies**

Goldsmith's Pies employs around 800 people, manufacturing pies and ready meals for the retail sector. The 650 hourly paid employees fall into two distinct groups for collective bargaining purposes. The food manufacturing team are represented by the FBCU. The maintenance team of 25 mechanical and electrical craft employees, who are responsible for maintaining and repairing all of the food processing equipment, are represented by Fidelity, predominantly an engineering union.

Earlier in the year, the FBCU negotiated a pay increase of 3.5 per cent for the manufacturing employees and this was accepted by ballot. The maintenance team negotiations are more problematic. This group feels that it is underpaid. The workers are particularly unhappy with the management team's suggestion that they should become multi-skilled (electricians learning mechanical skills and vice versa) to bring about productivity savings that will fund pay increases. They have also taken exception to new working practices, which include all employees being required to wear wellingtons in production areas and a move away from hairnets and cloth caps to disposable 'mop cap'-style headwear to reduce the risk of hair contamination in the products.

The local representatives of Fidelity have refused to recommend the offer of 3.5 per cent and, as a result, members have rejected this in a show of hands. The management team does not wish to offend the majority of its employees in manufacturing by offering bigger increases to one group compared to another.

Questions

1. What options might Goldsmith's Pies have to resolve this dispute?

2. What might be the potential consequences of industrial action?

3. What recommendations would you make to try and move discussions forward?

4. What recommendations would you make to avoid this type of dispute arising in future?

Industrial action

Industrial action can have a damaging effect on an employer and its customers. It is the ultimate expression of force that a group of workers can inflict upon managers in an attempt to coerce management to agree to workers' demands. Equally, industrial action can have a negative effect on employees through loss of earnings, conflict between employers reflecting differences in the level of support for industrial action, and the possibility that prolonged action will result in job losses.

In organizing industrial action, a union is encouraging its members to break their contractual obligation to attend work and hence, in turn, cause the organization to break its contractual obligation to customers, clients and suppliers. On the face of it, such actions are unlawful and, were it not for the immunities granted to unions in such circumstances, they would be sued for compensation for the economic loss that results from these actions. Interestingly, individual employees have no such protection and are reliant in the avoidance of claims on the fact that it would be difficult to prove the economic loss attributable to each individual.

Procedures required to secure immunity

In order to secure immunity from being sued for damages (known as 'tort'), there are a number of conditions that the union must meet, which include that:

- the action must be taken 'in contemplation or furtherance of a trade dispute';
- the union must conduct a secret postal ballot under strict conditions, involving every member who may be involved in the action;
- there are specific requirements about notifying the employer of the ballot, providing the employer with copies of the ballot paper, and with the numbers and categories of employee to be balloted;
- the ballot paper should state if the union is calling for either strike action or action short of a strike;
- specific conditions must be met with regard to calling action and notifying the employer of action to be taken.

 Further details of requirements can be found online at www.acas.org.uk. A link to this information is provided on the Online Resource Centre accompanying this textbook.

Types of industrial action

- Strike action

    A 'strike' is a temporary withdrawal of labour. This might involve a complete stoppage of work over a number of days or a series of shorter strikes of perhaps a day, or even a number of hours, at a time. Some strikes have lasted months and even years!

    Strikes are often accompanied by a number of employees 'picketing', i.e. standing at the entrance to 'encourage' other employees, customers and suppliers not to enter the premises or to cross the picket line.

- Action short of a strike

    Most types of action short of a strike still consist of a breach of contract. Examples include a 'go-slow', under which employees refuse to carry out a specific task, and 'blacking', under which trade union members refuse to work with another employee. Types of action that do not necessarily consist of a breach of contract include a 'work to rule', under which employees do the bare minimum to meet their contractual obligations or an 'overtime ban', under which employees withdraw from voluntary overtime.

- Unofficial industrial action

    If action is taken by members, or is called by a union representative, and does not follow the strict conditions for balloting for industrial action referred to above, then the union must repudiate or disown it within 24 hours to maintain its immunity. This involves the principal executive committee, president or general secretary of the union writing to withdraw support from the union representatives who called the action and all those involved in the action. Writing to all of these participants deems the action to be unofficial and warns them that there is no protection from unfair dismissal, providing that *all* of those participating in the action are dismissed.

Strategies for improving poor industrial relations

- Be clear on the rules and the distinction between normal working duties and union duties.

- Train, coach and support the union representatives and line managers.

- Communicate directly with employees, as well as with union representatives, to prevent messages being distorted.

- Listen to employee concerns and rectify these wherever possible before the union representatives get involved.

- Apply the same consistent rules to union representatives as to all employees.

- Invite union representatives and managers to participate in joint training.

- Enlist help and support, and encourage senior dialogue with full-time union staff.

- Offer additional observer and participant places at consultation and negotiation meetings to other managers and representatives of non-union members to remove the mystery of such meetings.

- Take responsibility for the negotiations: managerial representatives should be given the authority to act, not be only a messenger.

- Brief managers and staff promptly, and publish minutes and notes following all collective meetings.

- Be consistent and clear.

- Ensure that all first-line managers are well trained to make appropriate decisions to avoid the need for an overruling decision to be made.

- Establish clear scope and objectives, along with joint commitment to outcomes of meetings, before commencing consultation or negotiation.

 HRM INSIGHT 4.4 **The Case of Southlands Hospital**

Southlands Hospital Trust employs a wide variety of different employees. The ancillary hospital staff have a 39-hour working week, compared to a 37-hour working week for nursing and professional staff. Over the last three years, the union, as part of the collective negotiating process, requested a reduction in the working week of ancillary staff from 39 hours to 37 hours, to match those in professional positions, with no loss in overall weekly pay.

Negotiations for this group have previously involved local branch union leaders meeting with senior managers. The series of meetings has lasted several months and, if this has gone beyond the normal settlement due date, increases have been backdated. The hospital trust has resisted this claim in previous years by stating that, in years of low inflation, it is hard to find a way to accommodate this change without the organization incurring significant additional employment costs.

This year, the union supporting the ancillary workers has made it clear that this unfair term must finally be addressed and that, while it does not wish to pursue industrial action, it may have no alternative given the strength of feeling about this disparity among its members.

Questions

1. What mistakes have potentially been made in previous years' negotiations?

2. What options might be available to the Hospital Trust to help to resolve this disagreement?

3. What strategies might be employed over the course of the negotiations to resolve this issue?

4. What recommendations might you make to improve future negotiations?

Table 4.3 Characteristics of good and of poor industrial relations

Good industrial relations	Poor industrial relations
Regular opportunities for dialogue between parties	Each party critical of the other
Accessibility to appropriate levels between both parties	Adversarial relationship between parties
Helpful, impartial and realistic union support for employee in disputes and disciplinary matters	Unquestioning support of union for all employees in all disputes
Understanding of each party's role	Lack of union understanding of organizational objectives
Practical and realistic approaches	
Short, effective and realistic bargaining	Little appreciation among union representatives of potential consequences of poor organizational performance
Open-minded parties	
Readiness of each party to back down and change direction	Lack of trust between parties
	Unions encourage negativity towards organization to build their own power base
Well-defined and clear mechanisms for allowing and managing distinct time off for union duties	Drawn-out, unrealistic bargaining
Organization takes responsibility for joint training and coaching of managers and representatives involved in the relationship	Union representatives see union job as main role and union duties interfere with main job purpose
	Over-reliance of organization on union to train representatives and lack of involvement of managers in training
Rapid resolution of issues at lowest possible level prior to union and senior management involvement	
	Over-reliance of organization on union and senior managers or HR to resolve disputes

Information and consultation

Directive 2002/14/EC of the European Parliament and of the Council of 11 March 2002 establishing a general framework for informing and consulting employees in the European Community was implemented in the UK in the form of the Information and Consultation of Employees Regulations 2004 (ICE). The Regulations, which came into force in 2005, introduced a requirement for businesses to inform and consult with their employees. Introduction was phased to allow smaller businesses time to prepare for the requirements and the Regulations apply to all businesses employing more than 50 people from April 2008.

The Regulations give employees the right to be:

● informed about the business' economic situation;

● informed and consulted about employment prospects;

● informed and consulted about decisions likely to lead to substantial changes in work organization or contractual relations, including redundancies and transfers.

Perhaps the easiest way to meet these obligations is through an existing communications forum, established under either a union recognition agreement or an agreement with, for example, representatives of an existing staff committee. These arrangements must meet the requirements set out in the Regulations, but there can be provisions to ensure that confidential information is protected and that any disclosure does not harm the business.

If no such agreement exists, the concern for managers might be that consultation, defined as '*the exchange of views and establishment of dialogue*' between the employer and employees or employee representatives, may include pay and conditions if these have previously been determined without reference to the workforce. Unless companies in this position take the initiative to set up a voluntary agreement, there is a risk that employees will apply to the Central Arbitration Committee (CAC) to force the company to engage in an extended dialogue.

If businesses operate in more than one European country, there are similar provisions covering the requirement to establish a 'European works council'. These provisions are aimed at larger employers, with over 1,000 employees and 150 employees in each of at least two different European countries. The regulations are complex and the implications are potentially extremely costly, given certain requirements to provide translation facilities at meetings. For more details on works councils, see ACAS' 2004 document, *Employee Communications and Consultation*.

HRM INSIGHT 4.5 Gateway Haulage

Gateway Haulage is a well-established and successful haulage firm, employing over 250 employees in the UK and with a number of distribution and transport contracts throughout the UK. Following its success, it is about to acquire another UK-based haulage business, which also employees 80 people, 20 of which are based at a depot in Holland.

Neither business has any formal union recognition agreement, nor do they have any arrangements in place covering consultation with employees. To date, each has relied on informal meetings held by managers with staff, on an ad hoc basis, to communicate with employees.

Questions

1. What is the risk to Gateway of not having a consultation agreement in place?

2. How does this risk change with the acquisition of the new business?

3. What recommendations would you make for consultation arrangements for Gateway Haulage?

STUDENT ACTIVITY 4.6 Tools and techniques for improving communication and employee relations

Consider the advantages and disadvantages of the following methods of communication with employees. Think carefully about why the workforce would have positive or negative views of each one:

- opinion surveys;
- team briefings;
- staff committees;
- newsletters;
- notice boards;
- regular manager briefings;
- shop-floor visibility;
- suggestion schemes;
- employee participation through 'works councils'.

The psychological contract

We began this chapter by explaining the importance of trust between employees and managers, and how the quality of relations between them impacted on other aspects of human resource management. Reference was also made to the importance of the informal dimension of employment — an idea that captures the day-to-day interaction between people who have to work together to produce goods and services. Both of these aspects of what can be described as the 'human', as opposed to the 'institutional', aspect of employment relations are expressed in the concept of the 'psychological contract' (Hiltrop, 1996).

The psychological contract refers to the obligations that an employer and an employee, or group of employees, perceive to exist between each other as part of the employment relationship, and consists of both expectations of each other and promises made to each other. Rousseau (1995) captured the relationship between the psychological contract, trust and performance when she wrote:

> When two people working interdependently, such as a worker and a supervisor, agree on the terms of the contract, performance should be satisfactory from both parties' perspectives. As individuals work through their understandings of each other's commitments over time, a degree of mutual predictability becomes possible: 'I know what you want from me and I know what I want from you.' Commitments understood on both sides may be based on communication, customs and past practices. Regardless of how it is achieved, mutual predictability is a powerful factor in coordinating effort and planning.

Arguably, the psychological contract is more important as a determinant of behaviour than is the formal contract because of the way it connects to employees' everyday experiences of work and of being managed. Indeed, as the frequency and intensity of strikes and other forms of formal, collective industrial action have diminished, perceived managerial violations of the psychological contract may explain the continued persistence of dissatisfaction and conflict, which is increasingly expressed at the individual and informal level.

The references made in Chapter 2 to the rise in the frequency of stress-related illness and absenteeism, high turnover rates and the withholding of discretionary effort may suggest that conflict has not necessarily been removed from the system but has become expressed in different forms. Moreover, it seems now to be expressed in ways that do not fit easily with the formal and collective mechanisms of conflict resolution that are associated with the 'old' industrial relations.

The extent to which an employee feels 'engaged' with their employer and therefore feels duty bound, morally obliged or genuinely motivated to do all that is within their capability to contribute towards an organization's success is heavily influenced by the psychological contract. Put simply, the psychological contract affects what an employee is willing to do, based upon the belief that, over the long term, the individual and group will be treated fairly by their manager(s) and be rewarded for their performance and contribution, but not necessarily on a day-to-day basis.

→ Signpost to Chapters 11 and 12: Managing Performance and Managing Rewards, for further insight into enhancing employee performance and linking this to reward

---

Good managers, perhaps instinctively, develop psychological contracts that result in high performance from those that report to them, from the first interaction during recruitment, through to all aspects of employment. Ensuring that high expectations are clearly understood and accepted by all employees, and are rewarded with promises about involvement, development and recognition, is the key to utilizing the psychological contract effectively to the organization's advantage. This is perhaps easier to achieve in smaller, more flexible, organizations because managers and employees are more closely engaged in 'production', but the principle applies generally. Organizations that experience low morale, frequent complaints from employees and a general lethargy may well be those within which the psychological contract may be perceived to have been broken by either party, with neither even aware that it has happened!

Research from the CIPD (2005) shows that, while the majority of workers report major organizational change taking place where they work, they are not necessarily hostile to change, unless it is a major change resulting in redundancy. What does cause problems is management's failure to engage in meaningful communication and consultation, and to listen to what employees are saying. Worryingly for the general state of employment relations, the CIPD also found that employee trust in organizations is declining and that most people feel their organization is badly managed, which can be interpreted as a way of expressing dissatisfaction with the way employees are treated.

Table 4.4 Employer/employee characteristics under positive and 'broken' psychological contracts

Party to contract	Positive psychological contract	Broken psychological contract
Employer	Is supportive	Offers only subjective evaluation
	Encourages two-way communication	Pays lip service to employees' views
	Is consistent	Engages only in pseudo-consultation
	Is fair	Is single-minded
	Sets clear standards	Reneges on commitments
	Keeps to commitments	Is lacking in trust
	Offers objective evaluation of performance	Decision making is controlled at senior level
	Engages in meaningful dialogue	Actions are motivated by need for personal approval and acceptance rather than team success
	Offers a high level of empowerment and engagement	
Employee	Has strong sense of obligation	Feels threatened
	Is trustworthy and honest	Questions job security
	Makes maximum use of working time	Lacks loyalty
	Is reliable	Has low expectations
	Is loyal	Considers that appearances are more important than delivery of performance
	Is open-minded	
	Feels secure	
	Is confident	
	Has high expectations	

Summary

What originally was known as 'industrial relations' reflected an era in which 'old industries', the collective institutions of employers and workers, and the management of industrial conflict were the dominant features. This 'area' of human resource management has, for some but not all, changed in important ways. Firstly, the tendency to talk about 'employment' rather than 'industrial relations' represents a broadening of the subject to include all employment contexts, irrespective of whether these involve the collective representation of workers or not. The change in emphasis represented by the renaming of the field meant that unionization and collective relations were no longer assumed to be the norm or the starting point, particularly for HR professionals and line managers. Nor was conflict seen as inevitable and, as new management practices were introduced by Japanese and other overseas companies, a different mindset and approach to relations between managers and employees began to emerge, based much more on a unitary perspective and cooperative attitudes. The notion of 'employee relations' takes this evolutionary trend even further, because of the emphasis this term gives to the primacy of individual over collective relations. This is consistent with the idea that the employment contract and the psychological contract are both important in understanding the dynamic behaviour of relations and relationships at work.

Visit the Online Resource Centre that accompanies this book for self-test questions, weblinks, and more information on the topics covered in this chapter.

online resource centre

www.oxfordtextbooks.co.uk/orc/banfield_kay/

1. Are the causes of industrial conflict post-2000 similar or different to those of conflict in the 1970s and 1980s?

2. What are likely to be the most important consequences for the management of people of an increasing emphasis on the individualization of employment relations?

3. In the absence of trade unions and collective bargaining, what can employers do to ensure that their workers have the ability to communicate with and influence management?

4. What are the essential differences between a 'formal' and an 'informal' approach to employment relations?

CASE STUDY

The claim for union representation

William Beckett Plastics is a small plastics manufacturing business based in Sheffield. It employs 50 people, the majority of whom are shop-floor operatives. The managing director, William Beckett, bought the company twenty years ago and has built it into a £3m business that sells plastic components in over thirty countries. It has never been unionised, and relations between management and employees have always been fairly informal and amicable.

The MD's main contribution to the business was in the development of its business and marketing strategy, and he was heavily involved in expanding its national and international markets. While he maintained strategic control of the business, operational responsibility was in the hands of the production director and production manager, who were in day-to-day control of production and the two shifts of operatives that constituted 35 out of a total of 55 employees.

Unexpectedly, in 2000, William Beckett received a letter from the Transport and General Worker's Union (TGWU), seeking recognition and representational rights on behalf of the company's production operatives. He was initially surprised at the request — he had no idea that there had been discussions among his employees about union representation. Overcoming this, he remained unconvinced that there was sufficient overall support within the employee group for a change from the existing informal and direct model of employee relations, based upon management taking decisions on pay, benefits and other employment matters in the best interests of the company. He decided, therefore, to write to each employee, reminding them of the benefits they had enjoyed in working for a company that, in his opinion, had treated them fairly and with consideration. At the same time, he wrote to the TGWU expressing the view that he did not believe their claim enjoyed sufficient support to be accepted.

In response, the union sought advice from ACAS and made an application to the Central Arbitration Committee for union recognition. After passing the initial CAC test of acceptability, the union was given 20 days to agree on the representational and collective bargaining unit it wished to base its claim on. Believing that, at best, the union had the support of a handful of shop-floor operatives, the MD decided, with the assistance of the Electoral Reform Society, to ballot all 55 employees — a figure that included 34 operatives. He felt that any decision he might take needed to be based on a clear understanding of what all of his staff wanted, not only a small minority of them.

Almost all of the administrative staff voted for the status quo. Of the 34 shop-floor operatives, 24 returned valid ballot papers, of which ten represented a vote for union representation, two for a system of non-union employee representatives and 12 voted for the status quo. As a result of the ballot, the union ➜

115

was disinclined to pursue the matter further, feeling that it had insufficient support from a bargaining unit based on all employees.

On reflection, the MD realized that there must have been something wrong for a significant number of shop-floor workers to feel that they needed independent union representation. After discussing the matter with his senior management colleagues, they all agreed that management had become complacent about the shop floor and had effectively become psychologically disengaged from the workers, even though it was in day-to-day contact with them. To avoid a similar situation occurring in the future, management had to make changes to the way in which employment relations were handled.

Questions

1. What procedures and criteria does the CAC apply in deciding on whether a union claim for recognition and representation rights succeeds?

2. What had management failed to do that resulted in the claim for representation being made and why had this happened?

3. What options were available to the MD in changing the way in which relations with his employees were managed?

4. As the MD, what would you have done and why?

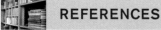 **Insights & Outcomes**: visit the Online Resource Centre at www.oxfordtextbooks.co.uk/orc/banfield_kay/ for an account of the developments that followed the final ballot.

FURTHER READING

Brown, W et al (1998) *The Individualisation of the Employment Contract in Britain*, Department of Trade and Industry/HMSO.

Fabr, H and Western, B (2001) 'Accounting for the decline in unions in the private sector 1973–98', *Journal of Labour Research*, 22:3, Summer, pp 459–86.

Hyman, R (1984) *Strikes*, Fontana Press.

Millward, N, Forth, J and Bryson, A (2000) *All Change at Work? British Employment Relations 1980–98, Portrayed by the Workplace Industrial Relations Survey Series*, Routledge.

REFERENCES

Advisory Conciliation and Arbitration Service (2004) *Employee Communications and Consultation*, available online at www.acas.org.uk.

Beynon, H, Grimshaw, D, Rubery, J and Ward, K (2002) *Managing Employment Change: The New Realities of Work*, Oxford University Press, ch 8.

Brown, W, Deakin, S, Hudson, M and Pratten, C (2001) 'The limits of statutory trade union recognition', *Industrial Relations Journal*, 32:3, pp 180–94.

Chartered Institute of Personnel and Development (2005) *Managing Change: The Role of the Psychological Contract*, CIPD change agenda, available online at www.cipd.co.uk.

Clarke T and Clements, L (1977) *Trade Unions Under Capitalism*, Fontana.

Department of Trade and Industry (2004) Workplace Employee Relations Survey (WERS 2004), available online at www.dti.gov.uk.

Dunlop, J (1958) *Industrial Relations Systems*, Holt and Co.

Dunlop, J (2002) 'Reflections on six decades in industrial relations: an interview with John Dunlop', *Industrial and Labor Relations Review*, 55:2, pp 324–48.

Flanders, A (1970) *Management and Unions*, Faber and Faber.

Fox, A (1966) *Industrial Sociology and Industrial Relations*, Royal Commission Research Paper No 3, HMSO.

Gouldner, A (1954) *Wildcat Strike*, Antioch Press.

Grainger, H (2006) *Trade Union Membership 2005*, Department of Trade and Industry.

Handy, C (1993) *Understanding Organizations*, 4th edn, Penguin.

Hiltrop, JM (1996) 'Managing the changing psychological contract', *Employee Relations*, 18:1, pp 36–49.

Hyman, R (1975) *Industrial Relations: A Marxist Introduction*, Macmillan.

Hyman, R and Brough, I (1975) *Social Values and Industrial Relations*, Blackwell.

Kersley, B, Alpin, C, Forth, J, Bryson, A, Bewley, H, Dix, G and Oxenbridge, S (2005) *Inside the Workplace: First Findings from the 2004 Workplace Employment Relations Survey*, Department of Trade and Industry.

Metcalfe, D (2005) *British Unions: Resurgence or Perdition?*, The Work Foundation.

Metcalfe, D and Milner, S (1992) *A Century of UK Strike Activity: An Alternative Perspective*, Centre for Economic Performance, LSE, CEP Discussion Paper No 22.

Rose, E (2001) *Employment Relations*, FT/Prentice Hall.

Rousseau, DM (1995) *Psychological Contracts in Organisations*, Sage Publications.

Salamon, M (2000) *Industrial Relations: Theory and Practice*, 4th edn, Prentice Hall.

Webb, S and Webb, B (1920) *The History of Trade Unionism 1866–1920*, Longman.

Managing Discipline and Grievance

5

Key Terms

Misconduct Behaviour that transgresses contractual arrangements, work rules, established norms of performance or other standards that can be seen as reasonable and necessary for the effective employment and management of people at work; behaviour that is deemed to be unacceptable by reference to formally established norms.

Discipline The formal measures taken, sanctions applied and outcomes achieved by management in response to perceived acts of misconduct.

Grievance The formalization of a claim that one or more persons, either co-workers or management, have acted wrongly towards another person(s) and, as a consequence, inflicted physical or psychological harm on that person, or others. This may involve an act, or acts, of misconduct.

Exit interviews These are meetings between an employee about to leave an organization and a management representative to establish the employee's reason for leaving.

Learning Objectives

As a result of reading this chapter and using the Online Resource Centre, you should be able to:

- deliver an organization's approach to unacceptable behaviour and misconduct to reflect its wider managerial philosophy and values;

- understand what is meant by, and the role of, discipline and grievance at work;

- apply the law covering employee rights and procedural regulation thoughtfully and with regard to its consequences;

- understand the importance of acting ethically in discipline and grievance management;

- recognize the consequences of failing to manage effectively disciplinary and grievance issues in the workplace;

- develop effective processes for handling grievances at work.

Introduction

Context and culture

The management of discipline and grievance features highly on the HR agenda of most UK organizations. While it is difficult to quantify the frequency of cases involving grievance and discipline at work, the recent growth in the number of employment tribunal cases dealing with claims of unfair dismissal suggests that either employers are initiating more disciplinary cases, or that employees are questioning the legitimacy of such action, or both (Employment Tribunals Service, 2005). Further evidence for the growing importance of this aspect of HR can be found in the limited, but high-profile, number of cases of constructive dismissal, in which alleged failure by employers to respond adequately to employee grievances over issues such as harassment, bullying and sexual discrimination have resulted in damaging and costly claims for compensation. Such cases highlight the danger of ignoring, or failing to investigate, behaviour at work that undermines the contractual, statutory and human rights of employees.

The fact that employees are becoming increasingly aware of their 'rights' is neither contentious nor surprising. The preparedness of many managerial and professional staff to raise grievances over the way in which they have been treated suggests that organizations, and particularly their HR functions, will need to pay particular attention to this growing tendency and to the reasons for it. A report in the *Daily Telegraph* (2007) cites a female city trader who, because of her perception of failure in the grievance procedure of the company for which she worked, is another example of grievances allowed to go unchecked and, despite the existence of a formal grievance procedure, unresolved. The case is to be heard by an employment tribunal at which the employee is claiming £1.35m in damages for a range of alleged breaches of her contractual and legal rights.

Yet it would be unwise to assume that grievances are restricted to professional-level employees and it would be even more simplistic to assume that acts of misconduct resulting in formal disciplinary action are to be found only within the ranks of shop-floor workers and their equivalent. Of particular significance to our understanding of the challenges that management face in responding to both types of misconduct is the recognition that such problems occur at all levels within the organization and involve professional, white-collar and manual employees.

Although small in number, some cases of serious misconduct involving financial irregularities and the breaching of important protocols involve top management. The Enron affair in the USA is a recent example of executive misconduct that led to criminal charges being brought against several of the corporation's top management, leading to new rules on corporate governance (*The Economist*, 2002). It seems inevitable, therefore, that the ability of HR to deal sensitively, but firmly and effectively, with different situations associated with misbehaviour and misconduct will continue to be tested over the coming decade.

Despite the belief that the management of misconduct may become more significant in the years ahead, it would be misleading to suggest that the typical organization experiences more than a handful of cases each year. Factors such as size, sector and employee characteristics have an influence on the actual number of cases that require resolution. Moreover, the preference by most progressive HR professionals for trying to manage grievances, as far as possible, at the informal level further complicates any meaningful attempt to establish the number of incidents of misconduct that actually occur. Even if such cases are limited in number, responding to them can consume significant amounts of management time and resources, and the more difficult and complex cases often generate intense emotional pressures for those directly involved. This may result in psychological damage to individuals who believe that they have been treated unfairly and without proper regard to the circumstances and explanations that led to the action resulting in disciplinary proceedings.

Organizations that consistently fail to act within defined legal and procedural frameworks, and which show scant regard for any wider ethical considerations, can also acquire damaging reputations as a result of the way in which they treat their staff. This, in turn, can affect their ability to recruit and retain top-quality people. The implications and consequences of 'getting things wrong' or, for reasons only known to those managers directly involved, of acting precipitously and without regard to the consequences can go beyond reputational damage. Collective responses, in the form of strikes and other expressions of industrial conflict, can be triggered by a sense of injustice and disproportionality or changes in what Alvin Gouldner (1954) called 'patterns of indulgency'.

KEY CONCEPT Indulgency

This relates to the situation in which managers, either deliberately or by default, allow and condone breaches of works' rules. This is essentially an informal understanding and is often associated with employees 'giving something in return'. Any new managers becoming involved are unlikely to have been party to this understanding and, viewing the behaviour of employees as being in breach of rules procedures, act accordingly. The point is that what is defined as misconduct may not be quite as simple and straightforward as it seems.

STUDENT ACTIVITY 5.1 Indulgency

Using Alvin Gouldner's book, *Wildcat Strike* (1954):

● find out what the term 'indulgency' means in the context of this book;

● consider its significance for alleged employee misconduct;

● establish the relationship between changes in the indulgency pattern and the unofficial strike action;

● think of examples from your own experiences of uncertainty over what management has considered to be examples of employee misconduct.

Failure to respond effectively

The important point is that the consequences of failing to act appropriately in the management of discipline and grievance do matter. Few senior managers will be so cavalier as to disregard these consequences in the lead they offer to those given specific responsibility for this key part of the HR agenda. One of the difficulties faced by HR professionals, however, is that they can never be sure that they are in full control of the situation that they are required to manage. Often, they become involved after an incident, or series of incidents, have already taken place, with initial action having already been taken by line managers. The type of question that a manager may ask, along the lines of 'I've sacked someone: is that ok?', illustrates that HR professionals are often faced with having to recover a situation that may already, by the time they are involved, have become more serious than it needed to be. As will be made clear later, the key challenge facing HR, beyond the procedural management of discipline and grievance, is the ability to influence the actions of other participants, particularly line managers, whose own agendas and interests may take precedence over any wider organizational interests.

While the arbitrary and inconsistent treatment of staff will never be entirely eliminated, there is an increasing awareness among line managers and HR professionals that their organizations need to develop more effective approaches and mechanisms for the management of discipline and grievance. This is not simply because of changing ethical, contractual and legal considerations, but stems from the simple recognition that getting it wrong can result in serious and damaging consequences for all parties.

Choices in the handling of discipline

Organizations that might claim to have efficient and well-used disciplinary and grievance procedures may have less reason to feel self-satisfied than organizations that only infrequently need such procedures to be invoked. In the latter type of organization, it is clear that employee behaviour is such that disciplinary and grievance procedures need rarely to be used. It is important, therefore, to distinguish between two very different situations.

- the causes of misconduct and its severity;
- how cases of misconduct are managed.

The position taken here is that the role of HR is not simply about managing the resolution of discipline and grievance cases, but includes investigating and addressing the reasons that contribute to their existence, however difficult and challenging this may be.

As far as acts of employee misconduct are concerned, the following may be relevant factors:

- deficiencies and failings on the part of the individual;
- external pressures and circumstances that have a temporary effect on individual performance and behaviour;
- management style and practices;
- the working environment;
- personal relationships;
- changes in people's employment status and security;
- misunderstandings and genuine mistakes;
- changes in standards, expectations and social norms, resulting in behaviour that was previously considered acceptable becoming unacceptable.

From an HR perspective, it is important to establish which of the above explanations is relevant to each individual case of misconduct and whether, over time, any discernible patterns emerge that might justify a more strategic intervention to address particularly important causal factors. If a general criticism can be made of HR in the way that misconduct is managed, it is that often each case is treated individually, narrowly and in isolation. Making sense of the situation by trying to locate incidents of unacceptable behaviour in a wider context can be seen as an important contribution to the effective resolution of that behaviour. 'Making sense' goes beyond a simple investigation of the circumstances surrounding an incident, and involves the application of a more holistic and integrated approach, including diagnosis, interpretation and intention. Such an approach should both inform the way in which each case is handled and contribute to an outcome that is, as far as possible, fair to all parties and appropriate in the circumstances.

But the importance of choice in the management of misconduct goes beyond the question of exploratory processes and procedural regulation, and extends into the more complex world of management philosophy, values and beliefs. Consider, for example, the purpose and function of discipline in contemporary organizations. Interestingly, the use of, and need for, discipline seems at odds with developments in contemporary management thinking, with its emphasis on commitment, employee-centred HR practices, and the search for higher levels of performance and discretionary effort. This emphasis on the importance of employees as the key, if not the only, source of competitive advantage has led many writers to question some of the more traditional approaches to managing people, which include the use of sanctions and punishment to 'manage misconduct'.

Pfeffer and Varga (1999; quoted in Frost et al, 2002), for example, argue that numerous studies have demonstrated that very significant economic benefits can be gained through the implementation of high-performance or high-commitment management practices, but that there is little evidence to suggest that disciplining staff contributes to these outcomes. On the contrary, there is extensive anecdotal evidence to suggest that disciplining – particularly, but not exclusively, if this is done in a way that is perceived to be arbitrary and unfair – creates exactly the opposite effect to that which is desired.

Moreover, the growth in the knowledge economy, in which highly skilled knowledge workers are increasingly replacing manual employees as an organization's key resource, might mean that traditional approaches to discipline, as well as hierarchical control, are unlikely to be appropriate and effective managerial practices when applied to such employees. In an economic environment of sustained low unemployment, growing flexible working arrangements, and an increasing body of legislative rights and duties that protect the individual from arbitrary and unfair disciplinary action, the ability of employers to maintain traditional approaches to disciplining staff has become increasingly compromised.

While the need for an appropriate response to instances of misconduct is a necessity for many organizations, what is increasingly important is that such responses are seen as proportionate, transparent and fair, not only by those who are directly affected by them, but by their peers. A failure to deliver against these criteria not only undermines the integrity of HR, but affects the reputation of the organization, and is likely to have a detrimental effect on the attitudes and behaviour of other employees. In a somewhat perverse sense, the management of misconduct must involve a degree of consent and legitimization from those who are directly and indirectly affected by it. In the same way that applicants applying for jobs need to feel that they have been treated fairly and with 'procedural justice', so too do those subjected to disciplinary action.

Alternatives to disciplining people

This need to consider alternative ways of managing misconduct also emerges from the meanings associated with the act of discipline. Many dictionary definitions equate 'discipline' with 'punishment', seeing it as a way of exercising control, and enforcing compliance and order, along with obedience (Huberman, 1975). It is also seen in terms of a system of rules, the purpose of which is to improve and correct behaviour. Discipline is traditionally associated with 'what management does to employees' and usually involves the application, or implied use of, sanctions, ultimately ending in an individual being dismissed in cases of gross or persistent misconduct. But in less serious cases, the act of misconduct may require a less serious response: one that involves verbal or written warnings, demotion or job change. Whichever action is considered appropriate, the underlying assumption associated with the use of sanctions is that they will have the effect of dissuading the individual involved from continuing to act in unacceptable ways and will set an example to others. The analogy to the criminal justice system, under which laws, procedures and punishments are applied to reduce or eliminate unacceptable behaviour in the wider society, is difficult to avoid. So, too, is the ongoing debate between those who favour harsher and more coercive punishments, and those who believe that an interest in understanding why people engage in criminal activities is the only way to develop more effective ways of dealing with such behaviour, based on prevention and education rather than punishment.

In fact, the word 'discipline' has its roots in the word 'disciple' and implies teaching or training. From this perspective, managers and employees might view disciplinary procedures as a mechanism for solving serious behavioural problems rather than as some sort of stick with which managers can beat or punish their employees. Of course, the reality for the majority of organizations is that a dual strategy, combining elements of both approaches, is likely to be seen as the most effective approach. This approach should neither be too 'hard' nor too 'soft', although the relative weight given to each is likely to vary in ways that reflect organizational values, management philosophy and experience.

The conventional view that management needs to act firmly and fairly in dealing with acts of misconduct is one that few would argue against. Hence, the failure to respond to breaches of organizational rules and the failure to apply sanctions commensurate with the offence should be seen as a serious and unacceptable sign of managerial weakness. In other words, disciplining staff is necessary and inevitable in cases in which individuals clearly 'step out of line'. Reality is, however, often more complicated and challenging than this deceptively simple proposition suggests. Consider the following HRM Insight, which demonstrates the importance of proportionality in handling discipline.

HRM INSIGHT 5.1 The case of the Queens Medical Centre

In March 2004, the Queens Medical Centre suspended a consultant and senior lecturer in neurosurgery, who had 18 years' experience. The suspension resulted from an allegation that the individual had taken a second helping of soup in the restaurant without paying for it. In his defence, he stated that he had simply added more croutons to his soup. Three patients awaiting surgery on the day of suspension had their operations postponed. One week after his suspension, the brain surgeon was reinstated. The incident was featured in the national media throughout the week of his suspension, despite the surgeon's lack of willingness to comment.

Questions

1. Why was it considered necessary to invoke the hospital's disciplinary procedure?

2. What alternative forms of action might the HR function have taken in this example?

3. What was the overall impact of this incident likely to be in terms of the conduct and standards at the Medical Centre?

4. What recommendations might the HR function make following this incident?

5. To what degree do the likely consequences following from disciplinary action need to be considered in deciding on appropriate action?

Consequences of poor decisions in handling disciplinary matters

HRM Insight 5.1 may not have resulted in disciplinary action being taken against the consultant, but the damage done to his professional standing (he was, to all intents and purposes, accused of stealing), the stress and inconvenience caused to his patients, and the damage done to the hospital's reputation were all real. There is also a question of perceived fairness to employees of different status. The hospital, in this case, had established a precedent prior to this incident in dealing with similar situations, but with much more junior, and therefore less high-profile, employees. Without knowing the details and background to the case, it is difficult to comment on the motives and intentions of those who took the decision to suspend the consultant, but it can be seen as an example of a response that is almost preprogrammed. The stimulus, in this case, was the accusation of wrongdoing and this immediately triggered the formal response to 'invoke procedure'. This arguably excessive, and potentially dangerous, reliance on a predetermined course of action may be attractive in terms of its consistency and formal rationality, but it does raise serious questions about the exercise of managerial judgement and the role of HR in the decision-making process. Above all, it raises questions about the kind of organizational environment that elevates simple mistakes or relatively minor breaches of organizational rules to the status of major incidents.

The importance of an organization's environment to the frequency and management of both disciplinary and grievance cases cannot be overstated (Rollinson et al, 1996). Consider these two very different statements, which relate to the making of mistakes: 'If you make a mistake in this place, you get fired'; 'People should be able to work in a blame-free environment, where mistakes are both tolerated and encouraged.' Of course, these two statements, based on different student experiences of work placements, reflect two extreme points on a continuum of managerial tolerance and discretionary behaviour. The mid point would be an organizational environment that has a balanced, and arguably more sensible, approach to the making of mistakes, but choices exist as to how individual organizations decide on the general principles they use to determine the way in which they approach cases of misconduct.

Unconventional approaches to discipline at work

In Chapter 1, we referred to the case of the The Men's Warehouse, an American clothing company run by George Zimmer, which stood out from many other clothing retailers because of its distinctive philosophy of management, values and employment practices. It also represents a company that takes a rather unconventional approach to misconduct and discipline: the distinctive philosophy of its founder shapes the way in which individual acts of misconduct are interpreted and managed. O'Reilly and Pfeffer's book (2000) is concerned with how great companies achieve extraordinary results with ordinary people. They use The Men's Warehouse to illustrate the point that its success is not because of tight hierarchical and financial controls or performance management systems, but rather because of its values and philosophy.

 Signpost to Chapter 1: The Management of Human Resources, for HRM Insight about The Men's Warehouse

This commitment to creating an environment through which successful business and customer satisfaction emerges from satisfied and 'turned-on' employees means that the company puts its people first. But O'Reilly and Pfeffer found that the company drew on a pool of labour that was not always the 'best', recruited staff who had personal problems and difficulties, and those who may have had limited educational and achievement experiences. The implication is that some of the company's employees would 'break the rules', which, in most other organizations, would result in disciplinary action being taken. In The Men's Warehouse, however, an action such as stealing would not necessarily result in dismissal. The company's executive vice president for human development explains this rather surprising position:

> ... what George has seen ... are people who have never been treated particularly well, and that when you treat them well and give them a second and sometimes a third chance, even when they've ripped off a pair of socks, even when they've taken a deposit and put it into their pocket and not returned it for several days ... you try to re-educate the person ... We've looked at how to help ourselves and other people get better than most of the world thought we could ever be.
> (p 87)

The obvious question that emerges from this brief account of the attitude towards employee behaviour and discipline at the Men's Warehouse is 'why'? Why does its management accept behaviour that would lead other companies immediately towards disciplinary action? O'Reilly and Pfeffer believe that the answer lies in the way such an approach generates a strong and sustained sense of reciprocation. They argue that:

> By exceeding peoples' expectations concerning the chances they will be given, the dignity and respect with which they will be treated, and the opportunities they will have, the company builds an incredible sense of loyalty and commitment.
> (p 97)

In other words, there is a 'pay-off'. By not taking action that would be considered by others to be both legitimate and appropriate, the company's management is able to generate a powerful and sustainable response in terms of positive attitudes and performance-enhancing behaviours that would be difficult to achieve by other means. Paradoxically, choosing not to discipline someone in circumstances under which management would be entitled to do so can result in outcomes that are highly valued and, indeed, necessary for the long-term success of the organization.

Admitting mistakes – encouraging openness

Part of The Men's Warehouse mission statement refers to 'admitting our mistakes' and it is this that provides a link to our second example of unconventional approaches to misconduct and discipline. It is taken from chapter 5 of Jerry Harvey's seminal work, *The Abeline Paradox* (1988). In this chapter, Harvey tells the story of 'Captain Asoh and the Concept of Grace'; this account of motives, intent, honesty, genuine mistakes and the power of forgiveness is summarized as follows.

Captain Asoh was the pilot of a Japanese airliner that landed dead in line with the runway at San Francisco airport but, unfortunately, two-and-a-half miles short, out in the Bay. No one was injured and very little damage was done, but a serious mistake had been made and those culpable needed to be identified. At a resulting inquiry, at which all of those who were involved in the incident attended, Asoh took the stand first and was asked by the chief investigator how he had managed to land his plane in the sea, rather than at the airport. To this, he replied: 'As you Americans say, Asoh, he f*** up!'

His admission of personal responsibility, refusal to attach blame to others, and honesty were both surprising and unexpected, to the point that the investigation had little more to do than tidy up the technical details. Perhaps people are not encouraged or supposed to display such characteristics in contemporary organizations, but the question that remained to be answered was: 'What do we do with Captain Asoh?'

Harvey's reference to this story is rooted in his earlier observation that, while it is now generally recognized that organizations need people who are prepared to take risks and, in the process, possibly make mistakes (on the grounds that, if you don't make mistakes, you are unlikely to have tried anything of significance), the managers of these organizations and those who support the managers (HR) aren't actually very good at forgiving those who make genuine mistakes! As a consequence of the fear of being found out and being punished, people at all levels become very adept at concealing the truth from others, and often from themselves, to the point at which it is difficult to distinguish truth from lies. Asoh was different, because he told the truth as he saw it, he didn't try to blame someone else and he didn't lie. We know why this behaviour is not as common as it arguably should be – but why is it important at all? Harvey's argument is that the truth is important because it provides the basis for human connection. It relieves our alienation from one another and prevents us from being psychologically separated from those upon whom we lean for basic emotional support, which, he believes, is a fundamental human need and is characteristic of a healthy psychological state.

One of the interesting things about Asoh's admission that he made a mistake and his being prepared to accept personal responsibility for this is, according to Harvey, that it is an increasingly rare phenomenon. The heart of the Captain Asoh story is not only about the acceptance of personal responsibility and honesty, but also about the reactions of those who were sitting in judgement over his wrongdoing. According to Harvey, what Asoh provided was an opportunity for these people to apply something that seems to be singularly absent from many organizations today: forgiveness. This can be thought of as '*the willingness to give up resentment, and in its highest form, the extension of grace*', which is defined as '*forgiveness raised to the highest level in the form of unmerited favour*' (Harvey, 1988).

So why should Asoh have been forgiven? There are two key reasons. Firstly, because he was honest enough to admit his mistake – he was an excellent employee with an unblemished record and he never intended to cause harm or danger to anyone, so what purpose would have been served by punishing him? Secondly, the act of forgiveness is also an act of giving, and giving is a particularly human need and characteristic. The act of forgiving is, therefore, an act of altruism from which both parties gain.

The story of Captain Asoh (and it is unclear even to Harvey whether it is apocryphal or not) often produces quite diverse reaction among those who are familiar with it. For some, the references to forgiveness, the extension of grace and altruistic behaviour have little relevance to HR as it tries to shed its humanist/welfare traditions along the road towards 'a seat at the top table' and strives to increase its contribution to the 'bottom line'. Harvey, on the other hand, would consider this to be a mistake for two reasons. Altruism is an experience that is fundamentally human and good, as well as deeply satisfying to the giver, but it is also an essential requirement for survival. As Harvey puts it, '*cultures that lack the capacity for altruistic forgiveness and grace die*', or at least become dysfunctional and ineffective. But

125

there is a more pragmatic reason: that forgiving and giving creates a reciprocal reaction from those in receipt. The sense of gratitude generated when someone in authority does not exercise the right to discipline and punish, or when management decides to give someone a second chance, can be a very powerful experience for those directly involved. It can also be the basis of an enhanced sense of obligation — the desire to show that the decision was the right one — and it can result in new, and stronger, personal relationships. These are the very outcomes that are associated with a high-commitment, high-performance environment.

STUDENT ACTIVITY 5.2 Testing the hypothesis

In classroom debates over the attitude of The Men's Warehouse to mistakes and acts of misconduct, several students presented with the justification that such leniency generates a greater sense of employee responsibility and commitment rejected the argument. They claimed that such leniency would be taken as a sign of weakness and that they would subsequently be taken advantage of. Your task is to share stories about situations in which an employee has either been disciplined or given a 'second chance' and to analyse what the effects of each management action were. You should also discuss whether more or less discretion and leniency in the disciplining of employees would be likely generally to strengthen or to weaken management–employee relationships.

A more conventional approach to misconduct

Despite raising legitimate questions about the purpose, form and effectiveness of more traditional disciplinary practices, it would be unrealistic to argue against the necessity of some form of institutional framework and procedural regulation to help to manage cases of misconduct, even for the most forward-looking and employee-centred organization. The reasons for this are linked to:

- the existence of more prescriptive legislative provision in the field of employee rights, employer responsibilities and procedural requirements. This means that all organizations need to develop a reliable and defensible capability for dealing with cases of discipline and grievance;

- the constant pressure to increase performance at the individual and organizational level has led many organizations to view 'poor or unacceptable performance', linked to absence, failure to meet performance targets and general 'bloody-mindedness', as potential cases of misconduct, with the implication that more, rather than fewer, cases will need to be dealt with;

- societal changes in what is considered to be acceptable behaviour, with respect to language, attitudes and how people at work generally behave towards others, and the imposition of new standards and norms governing social interaction.

As a consequence of these influences, people's behaviour and conduct at work has become increasingly subject to more prescriptive normative frameworks and procedures that are designed to deal with breaches in these norms. For the majority of employees, and in most circumstances, such standards will be known and complied with. In other cases, in which conduct falls short of established standards, or in which action such as educational and training provision has been used in preference to formal disciplinary proceedings and has failed to produce the desired effect, the need for effective ways of dealing with misconduct becomes necessary, and it to this that we now turn (Younson, 2002).

Figure 5.1 represents a conceptual model of a generic disciplinary process.

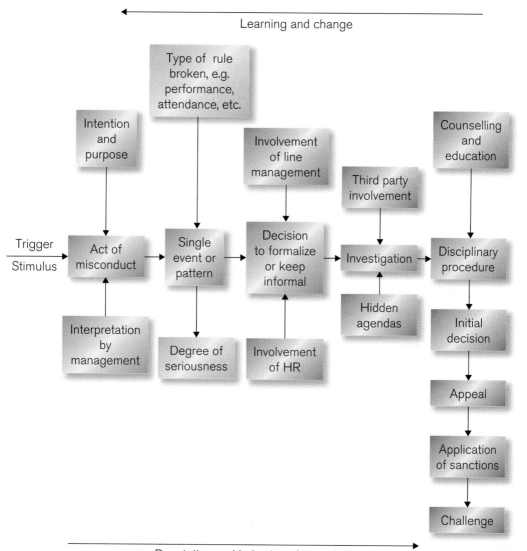

Figure 5.1 A model of the disciplinary process

STUDENT ACTIVITY 5.3

The model in Figure 5.1 helps to provide a clearer understanding of the different phases, parts, relationships and challenges associated with the management of misconduct. After reviewing the model, try to improve it, by testing it against current practice, and discuss the challenges and responsibilities that each part of the model represents.

The relationship between minor and major breaches in standards

For every major breach in standards, resulting in either dismissal or action short of dismissal, there are likely to be around ten times as many minor breaches of behavioural standards and rules. This means that the ratio of serious to less serious breaches can be 1:10. But even this representation of the number and significance of misconduct depends on information about each incident being made available to those who need to have this information, for example, HR. This does not always happen, either because those directly involved agree to contain the incident by restricting its visibility, or because they are unaware of any procedural requirement that all incidents, however minor, should be logged with HR or some other authority.

The ratio of minor breaches of rules of which management are aware to those that are unknown to them (but not necessarily to other employees) is more difficult to estimate, but is probably in the region of 1:15. The significance of these two ratios is clear: those cases of misconduct that result in formal action being taken by management represent the tip of the 'misconduct iceberg'. What is often unknown to management is the extent of behaviour that would be interpreted as unacceptable and, possibly, as misconduct if it were known to them, but which, for various reasons, is not in the public domain and may remain hidden until its seriousness escalates to the point at which it is either discovered, reported or directly observed.

There is a category of behaviours that appear to be relatively minor and for which there is some uncertainty over whether the behaviour actually represents a case of misconduct. These may be isolated incidents or may constitute regular patterns, but they are characterized by this degree of uncertainty, which must, at some point, be resolved. The longer they are allowed to continue, the more management, by its own act of omission (i.e. by doing nothing) legitimizes them. Early intervention, almost inevitably by the appropriate line manager, is important to provide guidance and interpretation of the status of the action or behaviour, and helps to resolve any uncertainties over its acceptability and seriousness.

The key to managing behaviour successfully is to address standards of compliance/non-compliance at the informal and minor level to in order to prevent any escalation in the frequency or seriousness of the problem. If an organization is over-reliant on the use of formal procedures to address conduct, this suggests that the standards and objectives of the organization are not being made clear and that the existing culture encourages non-compliance across the board. Again, we can see the importance of the organizational environment to the patterns of misconduct and to management responses to these.

The model in Figure 5.2 demonstrates the relationship between the number of major and minor breaches in rules and standards compared to the number of minor incidents, and shows the relationship between seriousness and formality of response.

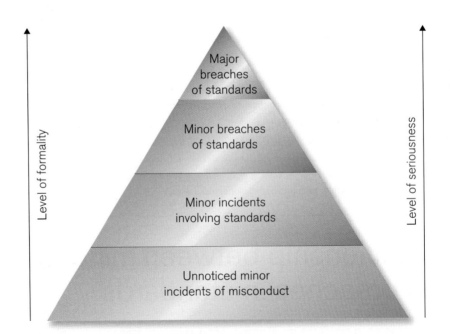

Figure 5.2 The conduct pyramid

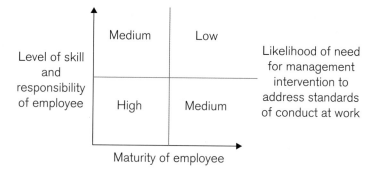

Figure 5.3 The correlation of disciplinary cases with employee skill/responsibility and maturity

As indicated earlier, the need to invoke formal disciplinary procedures can be indicative of other issues within an organization and might reflect, for example poor recruitment and selection practices, lack of training and development, ineffective pay and reward structures, or poor communications and employee relations. It may also reflect key characteristics of the labour force, such as position in the hierarchy, the type of work carried out, and the degree to which people work in what might be described as a 'factory culture'. This term is meant to cover any working environment in which employees have a more instrumental attitude to work, often involving less skilled or manually based work, and in which employees and management perceive themselves to be in an adversarial relationship. The greater the extent to which employees identify with the position of management and the wider interests of the organization, the less the likelihood of employees deliberately engaging in misconduct. As far as developing effective strategies for dealing with misconduct are concerned, this hypothesis offers a way forward that is not limited to using procedures to manage the misconduct, but includes its prevention.

The model in Figure 5.3 demonstrates how the extent to which management relies upon its formal disciplinary procedures will depend upon the make-up of an organization. Organizations employing younger employees to carry out roles requiring lower skills are likely to experience more disciplinary issues than those employing more mature and longer serving employees in jobs requiring higher levels of skill and responsibility. This means that the frequency and seriousness of disciplinary cases is likely to be strongly correlated to the demographic characteristics of the workforce, knowledge of which can help management to pre-empt patterns of misconduct and to take appropriate preventative action.

There is a risk, however, that organizations which experience infrequent cases of misconduct will be less well equipped to deal with those that do occur, particularly if they are serious, because the HR staff and line managers who need to be involved may not have the necessary experience and competencies to manage these cases effectively.

STUDENT ACTIVITY 5.4 **Developing the skills and competences needed to manage disciplinary cases**

This exercise requires students to think about what line managers need to know and be able to do in order to contribute to the effective management of misconduct, involving cases of discipline. In groups, your task is to design a two day training programme entitled 'The role of the line manager in managing misconduct'. This activity will involve establishing the knowledge and behaviours they need, and how these can be learnt. It may well involve an element of research, and should result in a PowerPoint presentation and evaluation of what is proposed.

HRM INSIGHT 5.2 The Belgian Chocolate Company

The Belgian Chocolate Company was a small confectioners employing around a hundred people to produce speciality Belgian chocolates for a major retailer. A larger manufacturer acquired it and the company was placed under the management of Townends Chocolates, a large, well-established manufacturer. Townends recruited a new plant manager for the operation, to replace the previous owner who had managed the business for twenty years before selling the company and retiring. The new plant manager was given the objective of introducing more rigorous hygiene and performance standards as already established in the main Townends factory.

Eating on the shop floor was a serious hygiene concern, which had been highlighted as one of the unhygienic practices in a recent customer audit. Following advice from the HR department at Townends, a decision was made to stamp this out completely by making it a dismissible offence under the disciplinary procedure, in the belief that, if the consequences were so severe, then the behaviour would stop immediately. The Townends management team briefed the whole workforce by attaching a notice to their wage slips – and was shocked when the first offender was caught eating in the factory only days later. In the subsequent disciplinary hearing, the reason given was that sampling product on the shop floor had been standard practice for years to ensure the quality of the product. The staff representative in attendance stated that this was no more serious than office staff failing to wash their hands on each re-entry into the factory from the office area, which was a regular occurrence.

The plant manager issued a final written warning due to the mitigating reasons given and sent a further brief, via wage slips, that eating on the shop floor for any reason and failure to wash hands on entering factory areas would constitute dismissible offences. Several days later, the plant manager witnessed the staff representative entering the factory from the office without washing her hands. She was taken into the office for an investigation and was suspended pending a disciplinary hearing. When she informed a colleague later that evening of what had taken place, a petition was signed by the majority of employees, and submitted to the plant manager, that threatened that they would 'down tools' unless their staff representative was reinstated.

Questions

1. What were the differences in culture between Townends and the Belgian Chocolate Company?

2. How might the HR function have sought to understand the issues at the newly acquired confectionery plant?

3. In the example above, what fundamental assumptions did the HR department and the new management team make?

4. What alternative measures might the HR team have recommended to identify and address the main issues facing them, given their new responsibilities?

5. How can the HR function contribute towards ensuring that the internal needs of the business are balanced with the requirements of the customer in this example?

Insights & Outcomes: visit the Online Resource Centre at www.oxfordtextbooks.co.uk/orc/banfield_kay/ to find out details about what actually happened and how this situation was handled.

Disciplinary procedures and the role of the law

The need to have disciplinary procedures in place is governed by both statutory obligations (set out by the Employment Act 2002) and guidelines established under the ACAS codes of practice, which were first introduced in the 1970s and have been updated by ACAS at regular intervals (ACAS, 2004; Incomes Data Services, 2004). Most larger organizations have established disciplinary procedures that are in line with the ACAS guidelines, which recommend, among other things, that a disciplinary procedure is made up of several stages or warnings. Under the recommendations, if an employee is involved in a minor breach of work rules, in the first instance, the employer is advised to address what is essentially a minor problem through informal conversations, but if this fails to improve standards, the formal warnings demonstrated in Table 5.1 can be used progressively.

Table 5.1 Recommended stages in a disciplinary procedure

Level	Recommended duration	Level of manager likely to implement
Verbal warning	Six months	Line manager
Written warning	Six months	Line manager
Final written warning	12 months	Senior manager
Dismissal	Permanent	Senior manager

Disciplinary stages

If the actions of an employee are serious enough, then the procedure may be entered into at the appropriate stage. For example, a major breach of the rules might lead directly to a final written warning or, in the case of serious or gross misconduct, summary dismissal (i.e. immediate dismissal without notice being either served or worked by the employee).

Statutory provisions cover certain elements of disciplinary procedures, under which there are legal requirements that must be adhered to. For example, there are clear provisions on offering employees the right to be accompanied by a work colleague or duly accredited union representative, who does not need to be employed by the organization. In these circumstances, employees can insist that disciplinary proceedings are delayed by up to five days to allow arrangements for their chosen representative to be present at the hearing. There are also requirements under statutory procedures that cover all organizations, regardless of size, applying minimum standard procedures (Employment Act (Dispute Resolution) Regulations 2004). Under these procedures, if an employer is considering dismissal or action short of dismissal (such as a demotion or suspension without pay as a disciplinary sanction), an employer must undertake the following steps.

1. Provide the employee with a written statement of the reason for the action and an invitation to a meeting.

2. Conduct a meeting after the employee has been provided with this evidence.

3. Offer the right to an appeal.

The statutory steps above do not apply to warnings and paid suspension.

Procedures can vary between organizations in all aspects, including time limits for appeals, those permitted to be present, and the levels and duration of warnings. The important thing to note in an organization is that procedures should comply with current legislation and, ideally, should closely follow at least the minimum guidelines set by ACAS if the organization has sufficient resources, i.e. it employs more than 20 people. Care should be taken to ensure that procedures, once in place, are properly communicated, including an appropriate reference in every employee's written statement of terms and conditions. It is also important in defending any potential claims for unfair dismissal to ensure that the procedures are always adhered to.

Applying disciplinary procedures fairly is a complex matter and many organizations have specific training in place for managers required to apply the procedures. These organizations will often have back-up provisions for advice from legal advisors, such as a solicitor or other appropriate professional. Many trade unions also have training for representatives and employ the services of their own legal advisors.

Gross misconduct

'Gross misconduct' is the term used to describe breaches of standards and rules that are serious and unacceptable in any circumstances. If a case of gross misconduct is identified, the likelihood is that, if the investigation provides evidence that supports the charge, the individual will face dismissal even though it may his or her first offence. Examples of offences given by ACAS that can be regarded as gross misconduct are:

- theft, fraud and deliberate falsification of records;
- fighting at work;
- sabotage and deliberate damage to company property;
- being incapable through the use of alcohol and/or drugs;
- serious negligence that could cause, or has caused, injury, loss or damage;
- serious acts of insubordination and threatening behaviour;
- unauthorized entry into computer records;
- breach of company rules governing use of the Internet.

What constitutes acts of gross misconduct can be determined by individual organizations in the light of their particular circumstances and requirements. Examples should be incorporated into employee handbooks or made known to employees in other appropriate ways. As in all cases of discipline, procedural regularity and the reasonableness of management's action will be the criteria used by an employment tribunal in the event of a subsequent claim for unfair dismissal brought by the individual concerned.

Record keeping – confidentiality and data protection

It is important that records of disciplinary meetings are kept. Often, it is the HR practitioner who is responsible for maintaining these records and, ultimately, records kept may be the evidence relied upon by a tribunal in determining whether or not a dismissal was fair. Certain records must be provided to an employee, such as the statement of grounds for pursuing disciplinary action and, if an employee has over one year's service, written reasons for dismissal. It is also advisable to document all formal warnings. Options for recording the events of formal meetings include one or other manager taking notes or the presence of an independent note taker. Employment tribunals look for detailed written records rather than minutes of meetings and will generally not accept other records, such as an electronically recorded interview. This means that, rather than summarizing the key points, a record should be kept of all points made throughout the hearing by each party. Records kept must be held securely under the Data Protection Act 1998 and employees can view information held about them, providing conditions detailed in the Act are followed, meaning that care should be taken about how information is recorded.

Witnesses – ethical and moral issues

The chances are that, if an action or behaviour that breaches formal standards or rules is occurring in an organization, then managers, particularly at more senior levels, are unlikely to be the first to know about it. It is important that an organization can trust and rely upon staff not only to do the right thing, in the sense of conforming to established norms, but to bring it the attention of their manager if they have concerns that standards are not being properly followed by a colleague.

The dilemma that may be faced by a person who witnesses something untoward is what the consequence will be to his or her self should he or she raise the issue at a more senior level. It is possible that the individual will expect confidentiality to be respected by his or her manager in such circumstances. On the other hand, anyone accused of acting inappropriately would feel that they have a right to know the identity of any person who brings such a complaint against them.

In any disciplinary investigation, it is important to consider this when taking statements from witnesses. Confidentiality should not be guaranteed unless it is possible to respect this. Anyone accused may also expect the opportunity to question a witness as part of his or her defence in a disciplinary hearing. Only if there is a risk to an individual in naming them as a witness will it be reasonable to withhold identity.

The roles of HR and line managers

The exact role of HR and line managers in carrying out disciplinary procedures varies between organizations (Rollinson et al, 1996). HR can be present in an active role, either as the party responsible for leading the investigation or the party taking the disciplinary action. In other organizations, one, or both, of these roles may be performed by two managers or by a line manager and a more senior manager, with HR taking more of an advisory role, either within the meeting or independent from the meeting. There is no correct way of doing things. It is, however, advisable to have at least two representatives present, in order to divide the roles of leading the investigation and making the disciplinary decision, so that there is a degree of impartiality in the decision-making process. Many organizations specify in their disciplinary procedures who will be in attendance, at what level and in what capacity. For example, a larger organization may wish to involve a more senior level of manager in more serious offences, for which the consequences of making an incorrect decision are wider reaching. But, ideally, the investigations should be distinct from the hearing and should involve different parties.

STUDENT ACTIVITY 5.5

1. Consider the different roles and responsibilities with which the HR professional and line manager would be associated in the management of disciplinary proceedings. Where should final responsibility lie?

2. What are the most important difficulties that both the line manager and HR specialist face in managing disciplinary cases?

3. Consider the role of an HR advisor who has an incident reported to them of a supervisor witnessing an employee clocking out another employee. This is a dismissible offence under the organization's disciplinary procedures. What mitigating factors might the employer need to consider that might lead the organization not to dismiss the employee?

Appeals

Under the statutory procedures, employees must be given the right of appeal when dismissed or if action is taken short of dismissal. In fact, failure to offer the right of appeal may result in a tribunal finding a dismissal to be automatically unfair, i.e. making such a decision regardless of the merits of the case. The ACAS guidelines recommend that the right of appeal is offered with all formal warnings. Procedures will often have a time limit and will state that the appeal must be in writing. The statutory provisions do not, however, insist on appeals being in writing and refer only to employees appealing 'without unreasonable delay'. It may consequently be sensible for employers to be flexible and accept appeals made verbally, even when time limits are not strictly adhered to. Usually organizations, for clarity, will have a clear appeal process rather than rely on their grievance procedure as the mechanism for submitting appeals. Appeals should be dealt with speedily and, wherever possible, should be heard at a meeting by a person with greater authority than whoever took the original decision. If this is not possible, the appeal should nonetheless be as impartial a meeting as possible. The purpose is to hear grounds for appeal, paying particular attention to new evidence, and if the original decision is felt to be unfair or unreasonable, it should be overturned — although it would be idealistic to suggest that the decision on appeal is not, occasionally, influenced by other considerations.

HRM INSIGHT 5.3 Sandy's Hairdressers

Sandy's is a small, privately owned hairdressing business. There are three employees – two hair-dressers and an apprentice/receptionist – and one hairdresser who works from the premises on a self-employed basis.

While the owner is on holiday, she asks the last person who leaves the premises to lock up and responsibility for the till is given to the more senior of the two employed hairdressers.

On returning from her holiday, she is informed by the senior hairdresser that the other employed hairdresser in the salon has been seen taking money from the till and that the till did not add up at the end of the day. When challenged, the person said that they had borrowed the money to get lunch and had intended to pay it back after lunch, but had forgotten. The incident happened three days ago. The owner's partner is a friend of yours and does not get involved in the business, but is registered as one of the directors. He has asked you for advice because the owner no longer trusts the person involved and does not want to continue her employment. There are no formal procedures in place due to the size of the business.

Questions

1. Consider what advice you would give.

2. What factors should the owner take into consideration and investigate?

3. What are the arguments for and against:

   i. taking a lenient line and allowing the person to continue to work, after discussing with her your concerns?

   ii. dismissing her on the grounds of stealing money from the till?

4. How should the owner handle the issue of any appeal that might follow from a decision to dismiss?

134

STUDENT ACTIVITY 5.6

Think about any disciplinary procedure with which you are familiar and consider the following questions.

1. How easy is it to read? Would employees easily understand it?

2. What impression would the procedure give if included as part of the induction material; or terms and conditions for an organization?

3. Given the ACAS guidelines on disciplinary procedures, rewrite the procedure to make appropriate improvements.

STUDENT ACTIVITY 5.7

Write a set of guidelines for managers to follow when carrying out a disciplinary investigation and hearing. These guidelines should be based on appropriate research into codes of practice and on learning from the experiences of those involved in disciplinary matters.

Grievance procedures

Grievances can be thought of as complaints made by one employee against another and, as such, they will not normally be raised by management against an employee. While having the potential to involve breaches of company rules, they do not relate to the most common causes of disciplinary action, which often involve unacceptable performance and poor attendance. In a legal sense, grievances are defined by the Employment Act 2002 (Dispute Resolution) Regulations 2004 as:

> ...a complaint by an employee about an action which his employer has taken or is contemplating taking in relation to him.

This may be considered to be too restrictive a definition in terms of the realities of employment, under which it is well known for a grievance to be raised by one employee against another, or by an employee against a manager, or by a manager against a manager. Such complaints are, in effect, claims that the behaviour of one party in relation to the other is unacceptable, in that it involves unfair and discriminatory treatment, failure to act within designated procedures or the belief that the employer has failed to meet its common law duty of care. This means that the employer must take reasonable action to protect its employees from any harmful or damaging experiences that are not an inevitable part of the occupation or environment in question. For example, a soldier accepts that injury and death are part of what being an infantry soldier involves, but being bullied during training or being denied proper psychiatric care to help him or her to come to terms with the after-effects of battle would be considered unacceptable and grounds for raising a grievance, or its equivalent, with the appropriate authorities.

As with cases of discipline, it is easy to make the mistake of seeing grievances in isolation from the social and work contexts in which they arise. Many grievances reflect what might be described as 'damaged relationships' rather than individual and isolated acts. It is well known, for example, that many employees who leave an organization often do so because of difficulties with working relationships: they don't 'leave their job', they 'leave their manager', or they leave because of the stresses of working with certain colleagues. This means that many grievances are never formally raised with management but are instead resolved by the 'aggrieved' party leaving the organization. Exit interviews can indicate whether an individual is being 'pushed out' by the inability or reluctance of management to resolve a stressful, damaging, or in some other way unacceptable situation. If HR is unaware of such situations directly or fails to use the information made available in exit interview records, the original cause of the grievance will continue to affect other relationships, with the likelihood of similar consequences.

Grievance procedures and the law

The need to have grievance procedures in place is governed both by statutory obligation (set out under the Employment Act 2002) and guidelines established under the ACAS codes of practice, which were first introduced in the 1970s and have been updated by ACAS at regular intervals.

The statutory grievance procedures lay out a two-stage process whereby, if an employee submits a grievance, this must be heard by an appropriate level of management and a written response given within set time limits. The employee then has the opportunity to appeal against any decision given. Further details of statutory procedures and guidelines can be obtained from the ACAS website (**www.acas.org**). Failure to comply with statutory procedures can result in increased awards being made if a future complaint is found to be successful in an employment tribunal.

In reality, most companies have established procedures for handling employee grievances and recognize the value of handling complaints quickly and sensitively at the earliest opportunity, and of their being handled by the closest level of management to the employee who has made the complaint.

Frequent causes of grievances

Most grievances can be linked to the following:

● unacceptable language and images, initiation rituals and other forms of informal shop/office-floor behaviour;

- harassment and bullying;
- victimization and unfair discriminatory treatment;
- unreasonable and 'unlawful' requests to take certain action that might, for example, involve breaking health and safety regulations;
- failure to honour promises or obligations, for example, over the payment of bonuses or other forms of reward.

While the basis and legitimacy of certain cases of grievance can be more readily established by looking at the 'hard' evidence, the majority are more difficult to verify simply because they involve perceptions, expectations and different views as to what is 'acceptable'.

Consider the two following scenarios.

- The captain of a Royal Navy warship is recalled from his ship because two members of his crew have lodged complaints about his 'authoritative style of management'. The remaining crew members may have shared this grievance but not formally recorded their concerns, or may have been perfectly happy with the captain's behaviour and have considered it to be within the bounds of what could be considered 'acceptable'.
- A male manager relieves a female subordinate of responsibility for one key account on the grounds that the employee has failed to meet basic performance criteria, and is subsequently accused of bullying and harassment.

Neither situation represents 'clear-cut' cases of harassment or bullying, but it is also obvious that the possibility exists for a grievance to be brought. In the second scenario, it might be argued that the female employee lodging a grievance might have done so to protect herself from possible disciplinary action and reflects the efforts of the individual to rationalize the damaging effect that the manager's decision has had on both her self-esteem and her standing within the company. The ACAS code of practice recommends that, if a grievance is raised during a disciplinary case, the latter should be suspended while the grievance is dealt with. Suffice to say that some grievances have their own 'history' and complicating factors, and cannot be taken at face value. On the other hand, many grievances are made by people who genuinely feel that they have been treated wrongly by some other member of the organization and who feel that the only way to resolve the situation, apart from leaving, is to lodge a formal grievance with the HR department.

While registering a grievance invariably implies some degree of formalization, the response from the HR department, at that early stage, may not itself be formal. Much depends on the approaches and philosophy of those involved, as well as the organization's grievance procedure, which, since the Employment Rights Act 1996, is a legal requirement for all organizations that employee at least 20 employees. Consider the situation of a female employee of an engineering company, who works in the dispatch department with several male colleagues. She complains to her supervisor about the language used by one of her male colleagues, which she finds offensive and unacceptable. On being informed of the 'grievance', which is not yet formally registered as such, the HR officer arranges an informal meeting with the two employees to establish the 'facts' of the case. During the meeting, it transpires that the offensive language complained about was also used by the female employee to her male colleague, and that the real problem is that their personal relationship has deteriorated over time. The response of the HR officer is, metaphorically, to 'bang their heads together' with a strong suggestion that they sort themselves out. Keeping the response informal not only avoids the consequences of early formalization, through which positions become entrenched, but also encourages the two parties to take responsibility for managing the problem themselves and probably results in a more satisfactory, and less damaging, outcome.

Complaints about a manager

The experience of many specialist mediators suggests that interpersonal conflict cannot always be resolved by applying formal grievance procedures, and this has led to a greater emphasis on more informal and less threatening resolution mechanisms (see the Centre for Effective Dispute Resolution at www.cedr.co.uk). But the use of an informal approach to grievance resolution depends on both parties agreeing to this and this may not always be possible to achieve, particularly if it has proved impossible to agree on a mutually acceptable agreement and if the grievance procedure reflects an adversarial, rather than a resolution, approach to the management of grievances. Interestingly, the growth in the number of grievances registered may not simply reflect an increase in incidents of interpersonal conflict, but also that organizations have failed to develop mechanisms and competences for dealing with such incidents. It may be that employers experience difficulties in managing the underlying causes of grievances because managers lack the awareness and skills to deal with conflict.

The implication of this is that organizations need to look carefully at the reasons why relationships break down and result in people leaving the organization or bringing grievances against other employees and against management. As with disciplinary cases, simply reacting to each case in isolation is unlikely to provide long-term change in the underlying causes. If left unchallenged, these will continue to generate further expressions of conflict at work.

Most larger organizations will have additional procedures to cover complaints of harassment. More details of these issues can be found in Chapter 6.

Signpost to Chapter 6: Equality in Employment, for information about harassment and bullying at work

---

KEY CONCEPT **Interpersonal conflict**

Wherever people 'work together', the potential exists for differences to emerge and, if these are left to develop, conflict to occur. Often the conflict between people is contained and does not create problems, but, under certain circumstances, it can become manifest and be expressed behaviourally, through actions and language. Interpersonal conflict exists primarily in the informal domain of day-to-day interactions, but can become formalized as it becomes manifest and difficult to ignore. The importance of interpersonal conflict lies in how it is handled. Three choices exist: 'flight', 'fight', or 'unite'. All three strategies can be adopted, but the one that offers most opportunity for long-term resolution is 'unite' (CIPD, 2007).

Summary

The vast majority of employees will not need to be disciplined by their employer because their performance and behaviour will be well within the bounds of what is considered appropriate and acceptable. The CIPD recently reported that organizations had one disciplinary case per year for every 158 employees (CIPD, 2007). The need to discipline someone should be, therefore, an unusual, and possibly exceptional, act. There will always be circumstances, however, that require an organization to take formal disciplinary measures in order to deal with a situation that is, or has become, unacceptable. The reasons why such action is considered necessary are mainly to do with poor performance, absenteeism and a failure to comply with works rules, such as those relating to safe working practices, along with dishonesty and behaviour that infringes the rights of others.

In such cases, managers may well feel justified in using formal disciplinary procedures as a way of managing the situation, but the adoption of a more informal and flexible approach as part of a more sophisticated and less prescriptive strategy is becoming more widespread. This is certainly the case when dealing with employee grievances.

The role of HR in this field is to ensure that consistency of treatment is maintained and that employee rights are protected, but it must be recognized that this role has to go beyond the implementation of procedure. The need to explore underlying causes and influences, and, wherever possible, to address these is also part of HR's role. Given what has been said about the relationship between misconduct, skill level and seniority, certain organizations who employee predominantly low-skilled workers doing mundane and repetitive work are more likely to experience the need to discipline staff than those that employ professional and higher level staff.

As far as grievances are concerned, this offers potentially more challenges to management and requires careful investigation of all aspects of each case. Often cultural and gender issues are involved, and behaviours that were acceptable in the context of a certain group of employees become less so when the demographic of the workforce changes. If grievances are individual in nature, the resolution of the complaint may be achieved more acceptably through informal processes of discussion and mediation, rather than through creating an adversarial situation by invoking formal procedure. If, however, there is a discernible pattern of grievances, e.g. from female employees who are concerned about sexist behaviour, then HR is faced with a different challenge – one of influencing attitudes and changing perceptions.

 Visit the Online Resource Centre that accompanies this book for self-test questions, weblinks, and more information on the topics covered in this chapter.
online
resource
centre
www.oxfordtextbooks.co.uk/orc/banfield_kay/

REVIEW QUESTIONS

1. What are the respective responsibilities of HR and line managers in the management of discipline and grievances?

2. What contribution might an organization's CEO make to ensure that these issues are effectively managed?

3. How does the philosophy of management affect the way in which misconduct is managed?

4. What are the features of a working organization environment that might be associated with low levels of misconduct and interpersonal conflict?

5. What are the advantages and limitations of relying on formal procedures to manage misconduct?

CASE STUDY

Unauthorized breaks at Brown Packaging

David Brown Packaging is a small, but highly efficient supplier of packaging materials to the engineering industry. David, who is both the owner and managing director of the company, set it up 18 years ago. Over the years, his business has expanded and now involves selling to national and regional customers, in addition to a growing number of overseas organizations. The company manufactures and supplies good quality products, produced to high technical specification and delivered through a just-in-time production system. This means that the company has to be highly responsive and flexible to changing customer requirements.

The culture of the company has been shaped by David and his two senior managers, Alan Davis, director of production, and Chris Wilson, who is in charge of quality and research and development (R & D). Through their emphasis on quality standards, individual responsibility and efficient organization, the company has forged a well-deserved reputation for reliability and innovation. On the employee side, considerable resources have been invested in operator training, with all shop-floor staff qualified to at least NVQ Level 2. The company's employment policies are progressive, pay is locally competitive and there is little evidence that the workforce is either dissatisfied with their conditions of employment or with how management treats them. The company has been able to create an environment in which standards of performance and commitment are high, but not at the expense of employees feeling good about their jobs. It's essentially an 'OK' place to work.

On Friday 29 May, David had been invited to play in a corporate golf day at one of the local courses and had invited one of his friends, Bob White, to join him. Bob, as well as being his golfing partner, was also an HR consultant who had helped David to develop his HR strategy some years ago and he was familiar with the set-up there. Bob arrived at the factory around 1 p.m., left his car in the car park and travelled on to the competition in David's car.

The factory was operating a two-shift system at that time and the afternoon shift ran from 2 p.m. to 10 p.m., with a 30-minute break at 6 p.m. There were, during this time, 12 people on the shop floor working on machines and dispatching products to customer orders. Each team of six operatives was led by a supervisor, who was responsible for meeting the production targets and for ensuring that the operatives knew what was expected of them. The works manager, Richard Allenby, who had overall responsibility for the shift, was not on duty that day and the two supervisors were left in charge.

At around 7 p.m., David and Bob arrived back at the factory to transfer Bob's golfing equipment into his car. On arrival, most of the shift was playing football in the car park outside of the normal break time and, despite recognizing David, continued to play. Clearly, this was both surprising and disturbing although, given the circumstances, it was difficult to know what might explain the situation. David Brown decided not to confront the situation there and then, but to raise the issue first thing on Monday morning. To say that he was angry and annoyed was something of an understatement and, as he drove away, he also expressed his disappointment with what he had experienced. Because of his professional interest, Bob asked David to let him know how the situation was handled.

Questions

1. Consider the action that David Brown should take in response to the situation.

2. Is there any form of managerial response that might be considered more effective than initiating formal disciplinary proceedings?

3. What objectives would management be seeking to achieve in the way in which the situation was handled?

4. If some form of disciplinary response were to be considered appropriate, who should be disciplined and what form should this take?

5. What are the dangers inherent to management being perceived to be acting disproportionately and unfairly?

FURTHER READING

Chartered Institute of Personnel and Development (2007) *Discipline and Grievances at Work*, CIPD factsheet, available online at www.cipd.co.uk.

Fowler, A (1998) *The Disciplinary Interview*, CIPD.

IRS Employment Review (2001) 'Managing discipline at work', 727, May, pp 5–11.

REFERENCES

Advisory Conciliation and Arbitration Service (2004) *Disciplinary and Grievance Procedures*, ACAS, available online at www.acas.org.uk.

Alleyne, R (2007) 'I was asked to wash up, says £70,000 trader', *Daily Telegraph*, Tuesday 17 April.

Chartered Institute of Personnel and Development (2007) *Managing Conflict at Work Survey*, CIPD survey report, available online at www.cipd.co.uk.

Employment Tribunals Service (2005) *Annual Report and Accounts 2004–05*, DTI, available online at www.employmenttribunals.gov.uk.

Frost, PJ, Nord, WR and Krefting, LA (2002) *HRM Reality*, 2nd edn, Prentice Hall.

Gouldner, A (1954) *The Wildcat Strike*, Antioch Press.

Harvey, J (1988) *The Abeline Paradox and Other Meditations on Management*, Jossey-Bass.

Huberman, J (1975) 'Discipline without punishment lives', *Harvard Business Review*, 53:4, Jul/Aug, pp 6–8.

Incomes Data Services (2004) *Statutory Disciplinary and Grievance Procedures*, Incomes Data Services.

O'Reilly, CA and Pfeffer, J (2000) *Hidden Value*, Harvard Business School Press, ch 4.

Rollinson, D, Hook, C, Foot, M and Handley, J (1996) ' Supervisor and manager styles in handling discipline and grievance', *Personnel Review*, 25:4, pp 38–55.

The Economist (2002) 'Enron: one year on – corporate America's woes, continued', 28 Nov, p 60.

Younson, F (2002) 'A lack of discipline', *People Management*, 8:12, 13 June, p 17.

Equality in Employment

Key Terms

Equal opportunity The process of ensuring that employment practices in an organization are fair and unbiased, and do not breach any of the legislative provisions that are in place to protect workers from unlawful discrimination.

Diversity A multifaceted approach to the management of employees, reflecting the changing social and demographic characteristics of the workforce. The approach reflects the belief that maximizing the potential and contribution of all organizational stakeholders is inextricably linked to recognizing and valuing difference, and to treating people with respect.

Discrimination Treating a person or group of people less favourably compared to another person or group of people.

Harassment Any unwelcome attention or behaviour from another that a person finds offensive or unacceptable and which results in the person feeling offended, uncomfortable or threatened, and leads to a loss of dignity or self-worth.

Bullying The abuse of power, or of physical or mental strength, by someone in a position of authority towards a person (or group of people), resulting in harmful stress and undermined self-confidence.

Learning Objectives

As a result of reading this chapter and using the Online Resource Centre, you should be able to:

- understand the legislative framework that governs equal opportunities in the UK;

- understand the nature and consequences of discrimination;

- define the range of managerial approaches to managing diversity at work;

- explain the limitations of HR strategies in managing equality issues in the workplace;

- recognize the types of behaviour that constitute harassment and bullying, and recommend organizational approaches to deal with these issues.

Introduction

Fair employment is perhaps one of the most controversial and emotive of all HR issues. It is also a theme that permeates every other aspect of HR, in the sense that the requirement for managers to act in a fair manner and to avoid unlawful discriminatory practices is not restricted to any one part of HR, but extends to them all. While we have devoted a chapter exclusively to the subject of fairness in employment, in recognition of its growing importance, the topic features in many other chapters, particularly including those dealing with recruitment and selection, rewards, grievance and discipline, and employee relations.

One reason why the focus on fairness in employment and the need to avoid certain types of discriminatory practice is growing is because employers are now required to cope with an increasingly complex and demanding raft of legislation. This legislation has been designed to protect the rights of groups of people who, historically, have been at a disadvantage in the workplace. An employer who 'gets it wrong' and fails to embrace the concepts of equal opportunities and non-discriminatory practices at work not only risks costly claims of discrimination through employment tribunals, but also loses status and respect.

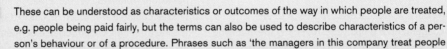

KEY CONCEPT **Fair and fairness**

These can be understood as characteristics or outcomes of the way in which people are treated, e.g. people being paid fairly, but the terms can also be used to describe characteristics of a person's behaviour or of a procedure. Phrases such as 'the managers in this company treat people fairly – there are no favourites' and 'the performance appraisal system doesn't contain bias' capture the practical importance of this concept. For the purposes of this chapter, 'fairness' encompasses a decision-making process that, when applied to employees, is based solely on merit. It is also important because of the effects of *not* treating employees fairly. As an example, research quoted in Chapter 3 shows that applicants who feel that the procedures used in recruitment assessment and selection are unfair may well decide not to continue with an application and may seek employment elsewhere (Chambers, 2002). Fair procedures in recruitment ensure that the best candidate is attracted and selected, based only on his or her individual merits, and focus on predicting the ability of prospective employees to carry out the job.

Any definition of 'fairness' normally involves some reference to equality of treatment, but another way of understanding its significance is to see fairness in the context of the distribution of benefits or obligations between two parties: in such an exchange relationship, there is – or should be – a reasonable balance between what the two parties give and receive. Fairness does not, however, necessarily mean equal treatment: unequal treatment can still be considered to be fair if it is possible to justify the different treatment experienced by an individual or group. Discriminatory treatment in the workplace is not only allowed, but actually necessary if HR is to make the contributions expected of it, but only in situations in which the criteria for treating people differently can be justified (Hyman and Brough, 1975).

Unlawful discrimination

While it is recognized that discrimination is an everyday feature of employment, it is clear that certain types of discrimination, not based on justifiable, merit-based needs of an organization, are unacceptable, offensive and potentially damaging towards those who are disadvantaged by such treatment. Furthermore, such discrimination is likely to be offensive to the majority of those employed and the community in which the organization operates, and can impair the ability of the organization to provide goods and services. Since the 1970s, a number of Acts of Parliament have defined the types of discrimination that are unlawful in the workplace and in terms of the provision of goods and services. These are summarized in Table 6.1. The legal requirements under these various Acts will be explored in more detail later in this chapter.

Table 6.1 Types of unlawful discrimination

Basis of discrimination	Applicable Act	Special provisions
Gender; marital status	Sex Discrimination Act 1975	
Race, nationality, ethnic or national origin	Race Relations Act 1976	
Disability	Disability Discrimination Act 1995	Special definition of disability and requirement to make 'reasonable adjustments'
Part-time workers	Part-Time Workers (Prevention of Less Favourable Treatment) Regulations 2002	
Gender reassignment	Addendum to Sex Discrimination Act 1999	
Religion or religious belief	Employment Equality (Religion or Belief) Regulations 2003	
Sexual orientation	Employment Equality (Sexual Orientation) Regulations 2003	
Age	Employment Equality (Age) Regulations 2006	Introduced retirement as a fair reason for dismissal and there may be an objective justification

STUDENT ACTIVITY 6.1

This exercise is designed to explore the experiences of students in relation to discriminatory and/or unfair treatment, and should be undertaken as a storytelling activity.

In groups, share personal experiences of employment or social situations in which people felt they had been discriminated against. Explore the basis of the discriminatory treatment and identify who was the discriminating party. Finally, consider which situations presented to the group might be considered to be examples of unacceptable – or legitimate – examples of discrimination.

The arguments used by those in favour of fair and equal treatment at work are based on the belief that many, historical and contemporary, employment practices have been based on personal and institutionalized ignorance and prejudice. Such characteristics have been increasingly at odds with a society in which those socially or economically disadvantaged by such practices were no longer prepared to accept them.

Signpost to Chapter 4: Managing Employee Relations, for perspectives on developments in relations between employers and employees

This led to the growth in what became known as 'equal opportunities' and also incorporated the notion of non-discriminatory treatment generally. At the heart of this movement was the strongly held conviction that people should not be treated differently on the basis of their gender, race, ethnicity, sexual orientation, age, or physical or mental impairment. This justification for not treating people differently is rooted in many of the world's great religions, but also in the humanistic philosophy that affirms the dignity and worth of all people. Such a commitment can also be found in the Treaty of Rome, signed in 1957, provisions of which have led to a Europe-wide movement to eliminate certain kinds of discriminatory employment practice (Hill, 2003).

In a somewhat simplistic, although helpful, way, the evolution from 'equal opportunities' to 'diversity', which many believe incorporates a commitment to equal opportunities, can be seen to be linked, in part, to a quite different justification. This is based on the so-called 'business', or 'pragmatic', case for treating

Table 6.2 Key drivers supporting a diversity approach in employment

Drivers for diversity	Percentage of respondents
Legal pressures	68
To recruit and retain best talent	64
Corporate responsibility	62
To be an employer of choice	62
Because it makes business sense	60
To address recruitment problems	47
Belief in social justice	46

Source: This material is taken from *Diversity in Business: How Much Progress Have Employers Made? First Findings* (CIPD) (2006), with the permission of the publisher, the Chartered Institute of Personnel and Development, London.

people fairly, with respect and, where justified, equally. Again, at the core of this argument is the belief that employee morale and performance can be undermined by managers who fail to take the questions of equal opportunities and diversity seriously. This second justification relies on the belief that treating employees in a particular way is not only about legislative compliance and the avoidance of potentially expensive and embarrassing tribunal cases, but is based on the claim that advocating diversity in employment is 'good for business' as well as being ethically sound.

This is the view of the CIPD (2006b), expressed in a recent survey on diversity in business. In the introduction to the report, the authors claim that:

> **Managing diversity involves a more proactive and inclusive agenda than minimal compliance with equal opportunities legislation. It enables employers to adopt more coherent approaches in order to add value to business by recognising all kinds of difference. By doing this, they can more easily avoid the pitfalls that can lead to backlash as a result of treating people as members of disadvantaged groups.**
>
> **(p 3)**

The reality is that, when asked to identify the key drivers for diversity within their organizations, most of the organizations surveyed identified legal pressures as the most important influence. But other drivers, such as the improvement of business performance and its moral rightness, also figured prominently in employer responses. Table 6.2 summarizes the most frequently cited reasons for adopting a diversity approach to HR.

The impact of developments in equal opportunities legislation and diversity management is not only limited to the workforce and the workplace. Customers, suppliers and the market or community in which an organization operates have increased protection and expectations as a result of a series of legislative provisions. This is particularly evident in the way in which employers operate in the labour market and in the hiring of external suppliers. For organizations such as the police, however, for which the workplace is also the community, the impact of legislative and social change governing behaviour has been profound (Macpherson, 1999).

Many employers have actively embraced the concepts of equality and diversity, and associated employment and managerial practices, recognizing that such a commitment is an expression of genuine support for these developments and of an understanding that they have been in business' best interests. For example, in the 1980s, being an 'Equal Opportunities Employer' was seen as a desirable badge that helped to attract talented applicants from a more diverse social and ethnic labour market. More recently, organizations competing in tight labour markets, particularly for knowledge workers, have recognized the importance of being perceived as an 'employer of choice' or an 'employer of first choice'. Employers who seek this status frequently emphasize the importance they attach to fair employment practices and to opportunities for all of their employees, and the value they place on diversity within their workforce. In a recent Singapore survey of entry-level graduates, looking at which employers were considered to be employers of choice and what they needed to offer to attract new graduates, the most important factor cited was good career growth and opportunities. Other factors given a high rating in the survey included corporate culture and whether the company was socially/environmentally responsible. All three factors, either directly or indirectly, relate to an organization's position on equality and diversity matters (JobsFactory, 2006; Backhaus and Tikoo, 2004).

As an example of diversity in practice, it is worth looking at the Irish economy and the influence of multinational corporations on diversity practices and management. At one level, it is simply the degree of diversity in the workforce that helps to explain the growing interest in diversity management. Microsoft, for example, attracts talented people from all over the world and about 20 per cent of its 2,000 employees are not Irish, with almost forty different nationalities represented on site. Google represents a similar story. Since opening in Ireland in 2003, it has developed to such an extent that it also employs staff from forty different countries, speaking thirty different languages. But the commitment that such companies make to diversity policies and practices might reflect the philosophy and values of the company as well as the legal requirements for equality of opportunity. In the Irish national 'Best Companies to Work for in Ireland' recognition scheme, Intel Ireland won the overall national diversity award for 'presenting new and effective ways to promote diversity in the workplace'. Speaking at a conference on women in science and technology, the head of HR development at Intel Ireland claimed that its diversity initiative was not something new, but reflected a long-established commitment to developing leadership and diversity policies, of which gender is a part. She went on to claim that such commitment is the driving factor behind her company's economic performance:

By promoting a better and more equitable environment for all its employees, Intel retains the best people and gives them the support to grow and productively use their individual insights and talents to increase our leadership across the industry worldwide.

Although organizations ignore equal opportunities at their peril, changing attitudes and behaviours to difference and diversity cannot easily be ignored, particularly because unacceptable behaviours are often culturally or institutionally embedded. Cases such as the resignation of a number of police officers from the Greater Manchester Police force, following the screening of an undercover documentary by the BBC in 2003 featuring shocking coverage of the officers' racist attitudes, reveal how, despite careful selection methods and compulsory diversity training, discriminatory practices can survive and inflict serious damage to an organization's reputation.

In summary, the trend in the UK seems to be a movement away from what can be considered the more limiting concept of 'equal opportunities' towards the more sophisticated and less prescriptive notion of 'diversity'. Given the lack of precisions in language and meaning, however, it would be unwise to see this as anything other than a generalized and, to a degree, controversial movement. In terms of what these two related ideologies represent, we have argued that:

- an equal opportunities approach is essentially about compliance and making sure that minimum standards and good practice are in place;
- a diversity approach places a greater emphasis on the economic benefits of an all-encompassing approach that looks not only to minimize the risks to the organization of claims of unlawful discrimination, but seeks to maximize the economic benefits of having a diverse workforce from many different backgrounds in order to provide a better service either to the customers or to the community that the organization serves.

If this is a useful distinction, we can also argue that diversity is the more strategic concept, seeming to be linked with competitive advantage, a more creative and productive labour force, and the leveraging of potential to support key organizational objectives. For some, these objectives may be financial; for others, the reputational benefits may be more important.

STUDENT ACTIVITY 6.2 Testing meanings and perceptions

This activity can be carried out within employing organizations, if students have access to such, or within the college/university. In groups, design a questionnaire to investigate and generate evidence on what people think about equal opportunities and diversity in relation to their meanings and values/contributions. The questionnaire does not need to be particularly long or complicated, but must address the following questions.

1. What do employees/managers think 'equal opportunities' is concerned with?

2. What do employees/managers think 'diversity' is concerned with?

3. Rather than to assume that they are a 'good thing', identify what are the advantages to different organizational stakeholders of developing HR policies and practices around both concepts.

4. What do employees/managers feel are the disadvantages and problems of organizations committing to one, or both, positions?

5. On the basis of analysis of the data collected, produce a presentation entitled 'Equal opportunities and diversity: a balanced assessment' and discuss the issues raised.

Stereotype, prejudice, and discrimination

In trying to understand what unacceptable and unjustifiable discriminatory practices are based upon, it is important to appreciate the influence on behaviour of the concepts of the 'stereotype' and 'prejudice'.

KEY CONCEPT Stereotype

A stereotype is a fixed idea or popular misconception about an individual or group of people. It can similarly be thought of as a conventional, formulaic and oversimplified opinion or image that one person has of another, which has the effect of conditioning that person's perceptions of, and attitudes towards, the other. One effect of stereotypes is that we tend to see everyone from a given group, race or category in very similar ways, with the result that we don't recognize differences.

KEY CONCEPT Prejudice

A prejudice can be thought of as a preconceived view of someone, despite knowing little or nothing about that person. Prejudices are triggered by someone reacting to superficial characteristics, such as gender, race or colour. They are formed through conscious and unconscious socialization processes, as well as through general experiences that predispose the person towards a positive or negative view of another.

As far as HR is concerned, both the influence of stereotypes and prejudices are not simply an issue for managers: they potentially affect everyone. In areas such as recruitment and selection, and promotion and career development, they can be particularly important and can help to explain how discriminatory decisions can be influenced by subjective and distorted perceptions, rather than by those based on objective and rational considerations.

146

The process of appraising employees is also an area of HR in which the potential for error, bias and prejudice is high. Coens and Jenkins (2002) talk about the tendency to categorize, i.e. the process of psychologically locating a person into a particular group that is associated with either positive or negative value judgements. This is then associated with the instinctive allocation of behavioural patterns that reflect these value judgements to individuals and groups (Coens and Jenkins, 2002, p 56).

It is, of course, human nature to evaluate a person when we meet him or her for the first time and, often, we will begin to make judgements very quickly, based on other people we have met or stereotypes that we have acquired. 'Liking' and 'disliking' may also be the product of what we might call 'chemistry', although this is not something that can be rationally explained. People will automatically make value judgements about others, often on the most limited of information, and will feel more comfortable and able to build rapport with those who they perceive to be like themselves. When meeting someone for the first time, we will often try to establish what we have in common to help to 'break the ice' and to ease the conversation. It is important then to recognize that these processes go on all the time and often at the subconscious, rather than conscious, level. The point to note is not that basic human traits and tendencies can, or should, be suspended when we enter the workplace, but rather that we all need to be aware of them and to make a conscious effort not to allow prejudice and bias to affect rational and objective decision making (Rick et al, 2000).

Approaches to fair employment

Figure 6.1 overleaf demonstrates the three different approaches that organizations can take to fair employment.

Partial or non-compliance

The first approach is described as 'partial compliance' or 'non-compliance'. This type of approach is perhaps more apparent in smaller, more stable, firms which perhaps do not feel that they have sufficient time and resources to be able to adopt all of the measures that would be regarded as 'best practice'. At risk of being controversial, many small firms operate very successfully in environments in which there are few explicit fair employment policies and often inconsistent implementation, but do not experience the level of claims that might otherwise be associated with such an approach. It may also be that organizations falling into this category come from the small to medium-sized enterprise (SME) sector, in which the pressures for survival and financial stability are such that matters of equal opportunities and diversity have less impact and importance than they might in larger, and in many public sector, organizations. Context, resources and awareness are important differentiators indicating which model organizations are likely to identify with or be capable of adopting.

Merit may not be the only basis for discriminating between employees in terms of jobs, rewards and developmental opportunities. Familial connections may have an important influence in companies that seem to adopt a more idiosyncratic approach to issues of equality and diversity. Employees who fear the consequences of challenging unfair, and possibly discriminatory, practices may be less inclined to put pressure on employers to develop more consistent, and objective, HR and employment practices. It is also possible that an unfair and subjective decision may sometimes be masked by what appears to be an objective justification, making it difficult to challenge. In other words, unfair and unlawful discriminatory treatment might be difficult to prove if the reason for a candidate failing to get a job or to be promoted is presented as a more acceptable justification, such as lack of experience and potential, rather than grounds of race or gender, or another unlawful reason.

Applicants are unlikely to challenge decisions not to appoint them if they have been treated respectfully and if the reasons for non-selection seem to be merit-based. Decisions on recruitment and promotion that are not linked to job performance criteria and evidence-based assessments may still be, in the

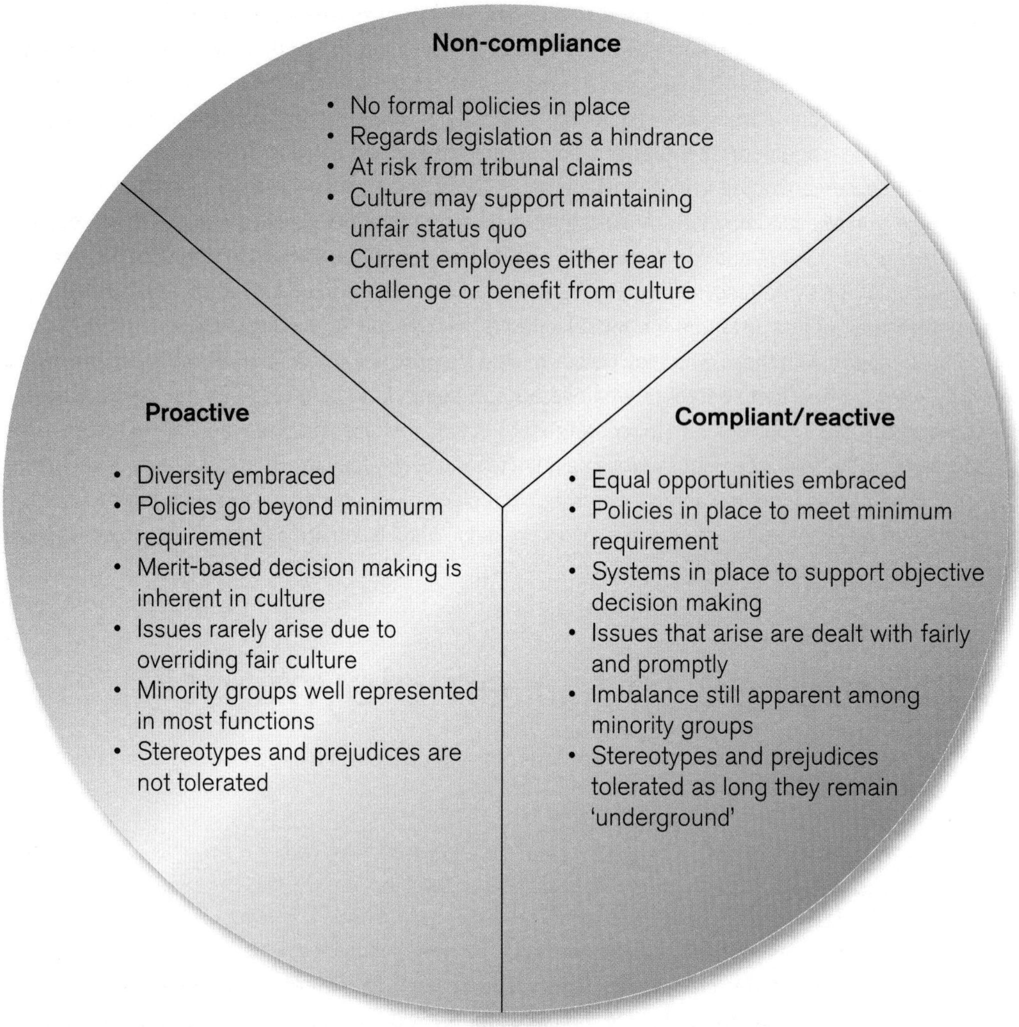

Non-compliance

- No formal policies in place
- Regards legislation as a hindrance
- At risk from tribunal claims
- Culture may support maintaining unfair status quo
- Current employees either fear to challenge or benefit from culture

Proactive

- Diversity embraced
- Policies go beyond minimurm requirement
- Merit-based decision making is inherent in culture
- Issues rarely arise due to overriding fair culture
- Minority groups well represented in most functions
- Stereotypes and prejudices are not tolerated

Compliant/reactive

- Equal opportunities embraced
- Policies in place to meet minimum requirement
- Systems in place to support objective decision making
- Issues that arise are dealt with fairly and promptly
- Imbalance still apparent among minority groups
- Stereotypes and prejudices tolerated as long they remain 'underground'

Figure 6.1 Characteristics of different organisational approaches to fair employment

minds of those who take them, rational and defendable. In other words, the person who is appointed for reasons to do with family connections and considerations of loyalty may, in the mind of the owner making the decision, be the 'best person' even though others might consider themselves better qualified using more conventional selection criteria and approaches. This kind of organizational culture survives in many owner-managed companies, particularly in countries within which family, and the importance of trust and loyalty, are held in high esteem. Rather than condemn such thinking and practices, it is important to try to understand why this type of approach still exists and is valued, even though it challenges many of the presumptions and tenets of equal opportunities and diversity.

Signpost to Chapter 8: International Human Resource Management, for more information on employing and deploying staff overseas

Compliant/reactive

The second commonly experienced approach can be described as 'reactive' or 'compliant'. This approach can be found in many successful organizations. A full set of equal opportunities and diversity policies are likely to have been developed, with a particular emphasis on assessment, recruitment and training. In organizations within which this approach has either evolved or been explicitly adopted, issues are generally dealt with promptly and effectively using established procedures, but there is likely still to be some cultural resistance to embracing fully the idea of a balanced and diverse workforce. This may be because the business case has either not been properly developed or communicated, or, if the business case has been made, has not been backed up by the predicted outcomes. In other situations, the reactive approach reflects a degree of uncertainty about how far a commitment to equal opportunities and diversity should extend. There are genuine questions raised about whether equal opportunities and diversity are ends in themselves or simply means to ends, in which case, they would need to compete with other HR and managerial strategies that might be considered more effective in meeting organizational objectives.

While managers and staff can be 'fully trained' and briefed about their obligations under both legislation and organizational policy, it is perhaps not seen as being in the interests of the organization to go beyond this minimum requirement. Prejudices and stereotypes may still be held some by managers and some staff but, due to the 'rules', everyone knows that these must not be expressed. Those in under-represented minority groups may be singled out as examples of equal opportunities good practice, but whether this can be considered fully representative is open to question. For example, 'politically correct' recruitment literature featuring female engineers, male nurses or ethnic minorities in managerial positions are impressive at one level, but the reality may be that these groups are consistently under-represented in the organization. The HR department may have all the correct policies in place but, behind the scenes, there may continue to be unchallenged biases in recruitment, training and promotional decision making.

Proactive

A 'proactive' approach is often adopted by larger organizations in ways that can be considered to be systemic or culturally embedded. A proactive approach often reflects a broad array of policies and procedures that go beyond the minimum required to be compliant with legislation and recommended good practice. For example, holiday policies that include special provisions for observance of the religious holidays of different faiths, or extended maternity, paternity and flexible working provisions, may be adopted. While the HR function can ensure the development of comprehensive, broad-reaching policy, communications and training programmes, it is the extent to which diversity is embraced at all levels of the organization and particularly by those in senior positions that distinguishes a proactive organization from one that is reactive. Diversity goes beyond simply treating everyone in the same way, recognizing instead that different groups of people have different needs and expectations of work and employment. This might be expressed in the nature and length of the working day, flexible working arrangements, the types of food offered in the cafeteria and opportunities for worship. To be a fully proactive organization, diversity issues need to inform every aspect of organizational decision making and may well extend into the field of positive action (see later in the chapter). The overriding feature of this proactive approach is a culture of tolerance that embraces the value of difference.

HRM INSIGHT 6.1 **Intel**

Intel, which is the world's leading producer of computer chips and operates globally, is a good example of a company that has embraced equal opportunities and diversity in a proactive and systemic way. In Intel, all employees are required to behave in ways that reflect its position on these matters.

As far as equality of employment opportunities are concerned, this is what the company has to say:

We respect, value, and welcome diversity in our workforce, as well as in our customers, our suppliers, and the global marketplace. Our policy is to provide equal employment opportunities for all applicants and employees.

→

We do not discriminate on the basis of race, color, religion, sex, national origin, ancestry, age, disability, veteran status, marital status, gender identity or sexual orientation. This policy applies to all aspects and stages of employment from recruitment through retirement. It prohibits harassment of any individual or group.

This commitment is supported by a genuine desire to encourage openness and a feeling among individual employees that their views and opinions are valued. The company goes on to say that:

Our long-standing Open Door guidelines encourage employees at every level, regardless of their title or role, to raise issues and to expect a timely response and resolution. We regularly conduct worldwide internal organizational surveys that include diversity aspects, and we share these survey results and their related action plans with our employees. This open exchange of ideas and concerns promotes a fair and respectful workplace for all of our employees worldwide.

(www.intel.com)

Questions

1. What advantages does this policy offer to Intel?

2. Is this an approach that might be recommended to a SME? If not, why not?

3. Is there an inconsistency between the concept of 'equality' and that of 'diversity'?

STUDENT ACTIVITY 6.3

Consider all of the types of provision made in your organization to promote diversity.

1. List as many types of provision that have not been considered as you can think of, which may support the agenda for improving diversity.

2. Compare your thoughts with those of a colleague with a different gender, age or ethnic background.

3. Consider the significance of any differences that may emerge.

Legal framework

The first elements in the legal framework for equal opportunities legislation were introduced in the 1970s, when it became unlawful to pay an employee a lower wage for doing the same job as a colleague of the opposite sex. It also became unlawful to discriminate against employees on the grounds of their gender or marital status and their race, nationality and ethnic or racial origin. In more recent years, protection has been extended to many other groups.

Direct discrimination

Direct discrimination occurs if an individual treats a person, or group of people, less favourably than he or she treats another person or group. Yet, in employment, we discriminate between people all the time: for example, managers are usually on more favourable terms and conditions than are those at more junior levels. The difference is that direct and unlawful discrimination occurs if the less favourable treatment is specifically due to one of the items in the listed in Table 6.1, which includes gender, ethnic origin or age.

Indirect discrimination

Indirect discrimination occurs if a requirement or condition, while applied equally, cannot be justified and results in less favourable treatment of a person from one group compared to others not of that group. Examples of indirect discrimination might be:

- an organization introducing a dress code that is not suitable for persons of a particular religious belief. Although that dress code would apply equally to all, it would indirectly discriminate against people of that particular religious belief;

- an organization requiring candidates to undertake a fitness test for a job, which includes lifting a 20kg weight, when the job regularly involves lifting weights of no more than 10kg. This requirement would indirectly discriminate against women, because fewer women than men would be able to meet the criteria, and it would not be justifiable given the capabilities required for carrying out the job;

- an organization deciding to advertise a senior job internally when the current ethnic or gender mix is unbalanced. This may restrict access of minority groups to more senior posts.

Genuine occupational qualification

Discrimination can be justified if there is what is known as a 'genuine occupational qualification'. For example, if an actor is required to play the part of a black person in a film, applications might justifiably be restricted to those from black people. Another example might be insisting on a particular language being spoken by a support worker or social worker employed to work specifically with people from a particular ethnic group among which spoken English tends to be limited.

'Positive action' versus 'positive discrimination'

A frequently used criticism of equal opportunities is that 'it is not fair that, for example, a black person should be offered employment rather than a white applicant who is more experienced or better qualified, just because he or she is black'. This type of 'positive discrimination' is not, however, lawful in the UK, other than for specific exceptions. In pursuing a diversity agenda, and particularly in the context of meeting targets for the employment of ethnic minorities, discriminating against non-ethnic minority applicants does occasionally occur. The following was reported in several UK newspapers in October 2006:

> **A police force has admitted breaking the law with a secret policy of 'deselecting' more than 100 potential recruits for no other reason than being white men. Gloucestershire Police said it had been trying to 'advance diversity' when it rejected the 108 men in favour of women and ethnic minority candidates, but the Chief Constable admitted that the force had acted unlawfully by rejecting the applications because of their sex and skin colour.**
> (Slack, 2006)

UK legislation allows only for 'positive action'. This means that, if an organization has a disproportionate number of people in its employment from one particular group, steps can be taken to encourage applicants from under-represented groups. It is acceptable, therefore, to state e.g. that 'applications are particularly encouraged from ethnic minorities' in a job advert, but not to select in favour of ethnic minority candidates.

Selection based on merit, however attractive this approach to discrimination is, will only result in balanced proportions of employees from different groups if merit is evenly distributed among the applicant pool or market. For example, unemployment figures are higher among non-white ethnic groups than among white ethnic groups, particularly among Pakistani, Black African and Black Caribbean ethnic groups, and GCSE figures also tend to be worse among these groups compared to other ethnic groups. It may be possible that lower academic achievement in minority groups may affect employment opportunities. Alternatively, fewer from these groups, compared to others, may be economically active and therefore be part of the available labour force.

While unemployment among Chinese British groups is higher than that of white British groups, GCSE figures among Chinese British groups are, on average, better, and there are proportionately more Chinese than white British in managerial and professional occupations (Office for National Statistics, July 2006, www.statistics.gov.uk). Clearly, this is a very complex picture with many socio-economic factors influencing employment and educational trends.

We should not assume that merit-based recruitment alone will address the imbalance in different groups in employment, partly because the accepted indicators of merit can themselves result from differences in opportunity and attainment that may be linked to other forms of discrimination and disadvantage.

Disability discrimination

What is a 'disability'?

Under the Disability Discrimination Act 1995 (DDA), 'disability' is defined as a physical or mental impairment that has a substantial and long-term adverse affect on a person's ability to carry out normal day-to-day activities. Normal day-to-day activities include a number of elements, such as mobility, manual dexterity and speech. Case law has helped to define further the types of impairment that are likely to distinguish someone as disabled and include not being able to apply make-up for a woman (*Ekpe v Commissioner of Police for the Metropolis* [2001] IRLR 605) and playing football, snooker and cycling for a 29-year-old man (*Coca-Cola Enterprises v Shergill* (2003) EAT 5-21). There are exceptions to conditions that are not classed as disabilities: people whose eyesight can be corrected by wearing spectacles, for example, and those suffering from addiction are not classed as disabled.

Table 6.3 shows the questions that are now addressed by a tribunal in making a decision about whether or not a claimant is disabled.

Table 6.3 **The questions asked by a tribunal in deciding if a claimant has a disability**

Question asked	Considerations
Does the claimant have an impairment?	Both the cause of the impairment and its effects
Does the impairment have an adverse effect on the claimant's ability to carry out day-to-day activities?	Whether any of the following are affected: ● mobility ● manual dexterity ● physical coordination ● continence ● ability to lift, carry or move everyday objects ● speech ● memory or ability to concentrate ● perception of the risk of physical danger
Is the effect of the impairment substantial?	Whether the effect is minor or trivial That effects can be cumulative Also required to deduce what the effects of the impairment would be 'but for' treatment, i.e. without treatment
Is the effect of the impairment long term?	Whether the impairment has lasted, or is likely to last, for at least 12 months

Reasonable adjustments

If a person is disabled, an employer is expected to consider making reasonable adjustments to accommodate the person's particular needs. This might include alterations to a person's working conditions, to their workplace or to access to goods, facilities and services. Adjustments might include, for example, altering someone's hours, modifying instructions or procedures, and modifying or acquiring equipment. In deciding what is reasonable, it is not only the cost that should be taken into consideration, but the effectiveness of the adjustment and the resources available to the employer, as well as the disruption to the employer.

This is a very complex area and many organizations employ specialist medical and advisory services to help to assess the extent of a person's disability and what adjustments are reasonable. In cases of disagreement, employment tribunals may be called upon to make the definitive decision. It is therefore important that medical opinions are supported by additional information, which might include details of exactly what a person can and cannot do, because medical opinion alone will be insufficient to defend a claim to a tribunal.

The types of adjustment that an employer should consider in accommodating a disabled person include:

- improving access to the premises or changing its physical features;
- reallocating duties;
- altering hours of work;
- assigning a different place of work;
- acquiring or modifying equipment;
- providing auxiliary aids;
- modifying instructions manuals or procedures;
- providing a reader or interpreter.

Facts and figures behind disability

In 2001, around one in five people of working age in private households had a long-term disability (Smith and Tworney, 2002). This is a surprisingly high number of people and encompasses a very wide number of conditions, from those more traditionally associated with disability, such as visual impairment or use of a wheelchair, to more recently defined conditions, such as dyslexia and depression.

Meager et al (1999) concluded that the most common impairments among applicants to tribunals are problems with hands or arms, problems with the back or neck, and mental impairments such as depression and anxiety. Moreover, they showed that fewer than one in ten cases involved recruitment decisions. Hurstfield et al (2004) found that less than half of the applicants to a tribunal had even considered themselves to be disabled prior to their case being submitted.

It would therefore seem that, from an employment perspective, the disability legislation is of more benefit to those in employment who lose their jobs through becoming disabled while in employment than it is to those with what might be regarded as more severe disabilities. These people may find it hard even to enter employment because the adjustments that would be required to accommodate them may be beyond that which would be considered reasonable.

HRM INSIGHT 6.2 **The extent of the requirement to make reasonable adjustments**

John has worked for a large retail outlet for four years. Two years ago, he suffered a breakdown in personal relationships outside work and he has experienced three separate spells of absence due to depression since this time. Over the two years since the breakdown, John's conduct at work has been a problem. He has received a succession of warnings for failing to follow instructions given to him by his supervisor, for taking unauthorized breaks, for smoking in an unauthorized area and has now been dismissed, following an incident in which he made an abusive hand gesture at a manager. At each stage, his employer followed disciplinary procedures that were fully compliant with ACAS guidelines on managing conduct issues.

Following his dismissal, John submitted a claim for unfair dismissal and disability discrimination. He argues that his depression is a disability and affects day-to-day activities, such as his abilities to concentrate, to be able to get out of bed in the morning and his ability to sustain normal relationships with people. He states that his depression led to his inappropriate behaviour at work, and that the company should have made reasonable adjustments and not pursued disciplinary action for minor breaches of conduct rules at work.

Questions

1. Considering Table 6.3, what arguments might the claimant and respondent in this case make in favour of and against John having a disability?

2. Consider the list of reasonable adjustments: would it be reasonable for any of these to be made for John?

3. What arguments might the respondent use to defend this case?

Age discrimination

Like disability discrimination, age discrimination legislation varies slightly from other discrimination legislation. Firstly, age is a continuum and the boundaries that distinguish one group from another can only be arbitrarily set. ACAS, in its guide for employers (2006a), recommends a series of age bands, each comprising broadly ten years, with which employers will be able to monitor numbers of employees in different age groups.

In addition to the usual aspects of the legislation, which make direct and indirect discrimination unlawful, there are specific references to elements of treatment that, until the introduction of the legislation, were common practice in many organizations.

Service-related benefits

To prevent service benefits from automatically being classed as age discriminatory, there are special provisions. Any benefit earned by having service of up to five years is exempt, i.e. a pay increment automatically earned after five years of service is more likely to be gained by an older employee, but the legislation cannot be used to challenge this. There may also be examples of non-pay benefits earned over five years, such as extra holidays, which have been put in place to reward loyalty or to increase motivation. If an employer can provide evidence that this is the case – such as an attitude survey, for example – there may be an objective justification for the practice.

Retirement provisions

The legislation also introduced 'retirement' as a fair reason for dismissal. Employers typically set their normal retirement age (NRA) at 65 year old, because it is hard to justify using a lower age. There is an obligation to inform employees between 12 and six months before this NRA of their right to request to work beyond that date. A meeting must be held to consider the request and the employer must respond in writing within given timescales. What is strange is that there is no obligation to say why a request to work beyond the NRA is refused, but it would be unfair if the reason were to relate to either age or any other unlawful discriminatory reason. Nor can the reason be any of the other fair reasons for dismissal, such as conduct, capability or redundancy, because this would mean the procedure used would be unfair. Employers are simply to state that they want the employee to retire. There are, of course, options to allow employees to continue working indefinitely or for a defined period. Unfortunately, there is a lack of clarity about this controversial situation and it will be interesting to see how this develops in case law.

Age discrimination is clearly a complex area and, as case law is established, there will be ongoing developments in this relatively new area of legislation. What is interesting is that it is not necessarily the old that discriminate in favour of the old and the young in favour of the young: Oswick and Rosenthal (2001) demonstrated that older workers are often subject to discrimination at the hands of managers of a similar age.

Equal pay

Legislation about equal pay is an extension of sex discriminaion legislation relating to the pay and benefits awarded to men and women in employment. The principle is that a man or woman engaged in 'like work', 'work of equal value' or 'work rated as equivalent' should receive the same contractual pay and benefits. For example, if a man and a woman are employed in similar jobs, but the man receives a higher salary than the woman, she can apply to an employment tribunal on the grounds that she has been unfairly discriminated against. If she is successful, the organization will be required to pay her the higher rate of pay. Awards can be backdated and comparators need not be current employees, i.e. it would be possible for a woman who is paid less than her male predecessor to bring a claim.

In order to defend an equal pay claim, an employer will need to have in place an objective job evaluation scheme that helps to justify any differences in terms of the relative value of the work. The subject of job evaluation is covered in more detail in a later chapter.

Signpost to Chapter 12: Managing Rewards, for more detail on job evaluation

The burden of proof

If an employee elects to take a complaint of discrimination to a tribunal, he or she simply has to show that there is reason to believe that he or she may have been discriminated against. It is then up to the employer to provide a 'written objective defence' against the claim, which, in effect, means that the burden of proof is upon the employer: it must demonstrate that discrimination did not take place, using whatever documentation it has available.

It is therefore important to make sure that decision making, in all aspects of employment, is fully recorded. Even if an employer has not discriminated against an employee, it will be impossible to defend a claim without such a written record. Ironically, a claim for unlawful discrimination may succeed, not because the discrimination did take place, but because the employer could not disprove it!

Recommended best practice in equal opportunities

The concept of 'best practice' has increasingly become part of the language of HR and its value, as well as its limitations, was explored in Chapter 2. In the context of equal opportunities and diversity, there is a strong prescriptive element to many of the reports and guides available to the HR practitioner (see ACAS,

2006b), and a wealth of advice is available for those seeking help in implementing equal opportunities in the workplace and wishing to embrace the concept of diversity.

The concept 'best practice' is unfortunately associated with the idea that there is only one way towards reaching a stated objective and that this is, in some way, 'better' than any other. While this is an attractive prospect, it is also simplistic and misleading. Best practice does not guarantee the outcomes that are being pursued and, indeed, what might appear to conform to best practice may result in unintended and unhelpful consequences. The Key Concepts of formal and material rationality found in Chapter 2 are helpful in understanding this point.

What is being argued here is that there is no single correct solution to ensuring equality of opportunity within an organization. Adopting a contingency perspective, the approach taken will need to be tailored to suit the needs of the particular organization, having regard for its size, resources and ability to implement whatever policy positions are agreed. It is also worth recalling that HR always needs to be aware of the importance of showing how it adds value and contributes to organizational objectives. It cannot be assumed by HR practitioners that a commitment to equal opportunities and diversity will result in universal acceptance and approval, particularly if this is perceived to be based on coercion rather than consent and if there is little concern to show how such a general commitment or specific practice is in the organization's interests.

For example, it might be argued that insisting that all applicants for jobs complete a standard application form for any vacancy is an approach to recruitment that is consistent with good practice and avoids claims that people who submit CVs are at an unfair advantage. But this policy might mean that many good applicants who do not have the time needed to fill out numerous application forms will decide only to apply to organizations that will accept their CV. Is the loss of potentially talented applicants worth more or less than recruitment policies that strenuously attempt to provide 'a level playing field'?

While the use of application forms might be recommended, this does not mean that an organization that accepts CVs has unfair recruitment practices, nor is it the case that using application forms inevitably results in a fair screening process. Having policies, training and systems in place can help promote equal opportunities, but it is the actions and decisions of managers and employees that are key to ensuring the development of a fair, diverse and merit-based culture within which all employees can thrive and contribute to their potential. The challenge is not in developing the appropriate written policies and procedures, but rather in influencing the behaviour and generating commitment of those who have to implement these (CIPD, 2006a).

What does come through from various sources (CIPD, 2005b) is the important role that senior managers, and particularly those at the head of the organization, can make in leading the organization towards a more diverse culture and fairer employment practices. But what also needs to be understood is that this involves a continuous process of change and improvement, rather than a one-off initiative. As such, its success will depend as much on the ability to implement and manage change as on the desirability and relevance of the proposed changes themselves.

But even endorsement of equal opportunities and diversity policies by the CEO and Board is likely to be ineffective if this is an action only of paying lip service to political correctness or if it is perceived to be such. Those at the top of an organization will have a greater impact by and through the standards and expectations they set in employing and managing people, and through the extent to which their own formal and informal behaviours reinforce this endorsement. It is also essential that senior management take responsibility for challenging any undesirable behaviour and for making clear, to all employees, the consequences that may follow from breaches of the organization's code of behaviour.

There are many activities that organizations can engage in to promote equality of opportunity. Figure 6.2 shows a number that can help to promote such practices and, in so doing, minimize the risk of claims for unfair and unlawful discrimination.

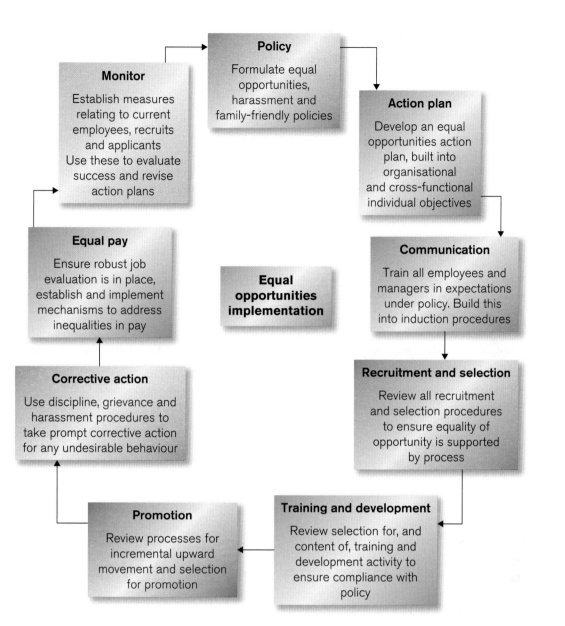

Figure 6.2 Nine recommended activities to promote equal opportunities

What should be included in an equal opportunities policy?

Equal opportunities policies should cover at least the following three areas.

● Statement of intent

This section will normally detail the organization's aim and intent to promote equal opportunities, including the commitment to a working environment with equality for all and decisions based on merit. There may also be a statement that the organization intends to have an employee base that is representative of the community from which employees originate.

● Identification of types of discrimination

This section will usually identify the areas in which discrimination is not allowable and will include all of the areas covered by the legislation described in Table 6.1, including gender, race, disability, sexual orientation, religion or belief, and age.

● Specific reference to employment practices covered

Policies will usually then give more specific details of the organization's commitment with regard to specific employment practices. Examples include ensuring that the policy is communicated to all employees; a commitment to providing a working environment that is free from harassment and an assurance that recruitment promotion, and training and development, will be based on merit. Organizations may also inform employees of their right to redress for unfair treatment through the grievance procedure and their obligation to comply with the procedure or be subject to disciplinary action.

STUDENT ACTIVITY 6.4

This activity involves looking at the equal opportunity practices currently in operation and reaching a judgement about their effectiveness. This exercise can be done in groups, but it is recommended that it is undertaken on an individual basis.

1. Identify the criteria you would use in evaluating an organization's equal opportunities policy.

2. Evaluate the equal opportunities policy of an organization with which you are familiar. (Note: you will need to collect information from within the organization to help you to complete this task.)

3. Which of the elements recommended in this chapter are included in the policy and what other commitments are also included in the policy?

Work–life balance and family-friendly legislation

Work–life balance is about recognizing the importance to employees of non-work, as well as work, commitments. A concern with getting the balance between work and non-work commitments 'right' is not only a reflection of the diverse nature and needs of the workforce, but also reflects the belief that a lack of recognition and concern on the part of management can affect productivity and motivation. Work–life balance can be understood, therefore, as being concerned with providing employees with a degree of choice in terms of how they allocate their time and energy between work and non-work commitments (DTI, 2001a,b).

The impact of poor work–life balance

A study by the CIPD (2005a) found that:

● 45 per cent of respondents indicated that working long hours had put strain on personal relationships;

● 11 per cent of respondents believed that this strain had contributed towards a divorce;

- over 60 per cent of respondents stated that working long hours had a negative impact on their work performance, including making mistakes and taking longer to complete tasks.

Such findings are also consistent with the increasing prevalence of stress in the workplace and problems of stress-related absenteeism. They reinforce one of the central themes of this book that ignoring the human dimension of employment can undermine employee productivity and contribution.

Addressing work–life balance

There is a great deal of legislation that has been introduced in support of work–life balance. Working hours, breaks and holidays are regulated by the Working Time Regulations 1998, and there are now extensive provisions for maternity and paternity leave, provisions for time off to look after a dependent in an emergency and the right for parents of small children to request flexible working. Details of these rights can be found on the ACAS website (www.acas.org.uk). Many employers will have policies that clarify how these are implemented in their organization. Others extend these policies to groups that are not covered by the legislation, offering, for example, the right to request flexible working to all staff. Some organizations also develop more extensive policies to support work–life balance, such as extended leave, i.e. allowing employees to take longer periods of unpaid holiday above normal allowances. Other polices might include career breaks, allowing longer periods away from work and compressed hours policies, allowing employees to work the same hours over fewer days (see business case studies for work–life balance at www.tuc.org.uk).

STUDENT ACTIVITY 6.5

This activity is designed to deepen your understanding of the ways in which organizations implement work–life balance policies. If undertaken in groups, the exercise allows for comparisons of organizational practices and their effects.

1. Investigate the range of work–life balance policies currently used by an organization of your choice.

2. Establish the extent to which these policies go beyond what is legislatively required and the objectives that they serve.

3. Collect information on one or more of these policies that will help you to form an opinion about whether or not they are working and reflect on whether the policies are meeting objectives.

159

Despite the attractiveness of such policies, it is important to recognize that there is a cost associated with them. While the benefits to employees of enjoying legislative rights at work are well understood, the problems that these may generate for employers, particularly those in the SME sector, also need to be recognized. Research carried out by Tenon, one of the UK's top ten accountancy firms, into the views of the owners of small firms found that over 70 per cent felt that, as a result of the growth in employment rights, their businesses were now run for the benefit of their staff instead of their staff working for them. According to Michaela Johns, director of Tenon, there is a growing frustration with employment legislation that penalizes the majority of firms who develop progressive working practices:

> My clients find it tougher to be a good employer, with the whole work–life balance drive, and also to make money, which is why they are in business in the first place.
> (*Daily Telegraph*, 2007)

Table 6.4 Examples of types of harassment

Physical	Pushing; causing physical harm; patting; being touched by another person; repeatedly or intentionally bumping into someone
Verbal	Shouting; lewd remarks; personal questions; derogatory comments; gossip; mimicking someone's accent; insults; abusive language or innuendo
Non-verbal	Rude gestures; graffiti; display of suggestive pictures; mimicking mannerisms; offensive flags or emblems; ignoring someone or 'freezing' someone out

Harassment and bullying

What is 'harassment'?

The range of behaviour that may constitute harassment ranges from extreme forms, such as physically assaulting someone, to more subtle actions, such as excluding someone from a conversation or social group. Table 6.5 comprises a list of behaviours that might constitute harassment. While some forms of harassment are a deliberate abuse of power on the part of the perpetrator, it can be the case that a person accused of harassment may be unaware of the impact of their behaviour upon another person. It is, however, the perception of the person that is subject to the harassment that should be taken into consideration when considering accusations of harassment. It should also be noted that behaviour that is considered to be acceptable by one person might be considered unwelcome by another.

The effects of harassment can be far-reaching. Left unaddressed, harassment can affect the attendance and motivation of employees, and, in extreme cases, can result in mental health problems, such as depression and anxiety. The costs to an organization can be very high if allegations of harassment are not managed swiftly and effectively. For example, in 2006, Helen Green was awarded £80,000 in compensation for the bullying she was subjected to while employed by German-owned Deutsche Bank. The harassment, which included insults such as blowing raspberries, resulted in Miss Green suffering a nervous breakdown (**www.timesonline.co.uk**).

In more serious cases of harassment, there may also be a risk of criminal charges being brought under the Protection from Harassment Act 1997.

STUDENT ACTIVITY 6.6

1. Consider which types of people, or groups of people, in an organization are most likely to be at risk from harassment and why.

2. Within your group, ask whether anyone has suffered from harassment and share your stories. Find out how the victim felt, what happened as a result of their experience and whether any action was taken to deal with the situation.

HRM INSIGHT 6.3 Discrimination in the workplace

A young male recruit of a non-white ethnic origin is recruited to work in a team led by a female team leader. Throughout the three-week probationary period, the team leader has difficulties with the new recruit, who specifically refuses to carry out what he states are menial tasks, is late back from breaks on a number of occasions and, on one occasion, uses offensive language towards the team leader. When challenged by the team leader, the new recruit accuses her of being racist and alleges that she is picking on him because of his ethnic origin.

The team leader consults her male colleague, who covered her role for two days while she was on holiday, and he tells her that he found the new recruit to be cooperative and hard working. She approaches her male line manager about the problems she is experiencing to ask for advice.

Questions

1. What information should the team leader's line manager establish as part of the discussions with the team leader and the new recruit?

2. What are the possible scenarios that might have given rise to the current situation?

3. What advice and support might the line manager give to the team leader in each of these different scenarios?

4. Should the employee be involved in the discussions and, if so, what might be communicated to him?

Insights & Outcomes: visit the Online Resource Centre at www.oxfordtextbooks.co.uk/orc/ banfield_kay/ for information about what actually happened to address this situation.

What should be contained in a harassment procedure?

Harassment and bullying policies should cover at least the following three areas.

● Statement of intent

The policy should make it clear that the organization is committed to providing a working environment that is free from any form of harassment or bullying and that such unwanted behaviour will not be tolerated.

● Definition of harassment

The policy should clarify what harassment is and what types of behaviour might class as harassment or bullying, so that all employees are clear about what behaviours are unacceptable.

● How to make a complaint

Policies will also typically give advice on how to deal with potential harassment in the workplace, including options for dealing with the problem informally and making a formal complaint. There should be a number of different channels through which employees can address their complaint. Relying solely on the grievance procedure, which might involve the line manager, may be inappropriate and unhelpful in situations in which the complaint is directed at the line manager.

STUDENT ACTIVITY 6.7

1. In working groups, write a set of operational guidelines for line managers on how to handle a complaint of harassment or bullying in the workplace.

2. Consider the relative merits of an approach to the management of harassment and bullying claims based on procedure regulation and conciliation.

HRM INSIGHT 6.4 Pawel's case

Pawel is a Polish worker who has been employed for two years within his current organization, which manufactures components for electrical equipment. Prior to his arrival, the workforce of just over a hundred employees was predominantly white British, but now employs 15 per cent ethnic minorities, mostly from other European countries, eligible to work in the UK.

161

Pawel alleges that he has been subject to harassment from co-workers for the last six months, as follows:

- six months ago, a colleague said, 'I don't know why you all come here. All you do is work for next to nothing and stop us getting pay rises';

- four months ago, the same colleague pushed past him when leaving the factory and, when challenged, said 'I thought you lot were used to being squashed – you all live ten in a house: no wonder we can't afford to buy houses round here any more';

- yesterday, the colleague shouted to colleagues, within earshot of Pawel: 'Hitler got it right putting Poland first on the list, eh lads?'

Pawel reports this to his line manager in confidence. Pawel says he has had enough of this individual. He does not want to make a big issue of things, but simply wants it to stop.

Questions

1. What are the options for dealing with Pawel's complaint?
2. What actions should Pawel's line manager consider taking?
3. What other actions might be necessary to prevent further escalation of problems?

Summary

This chapter has explored the origins and characteristics of an aspect of HR that is concerned with how people are treated at work, by managers and other employees, and the rights that all employees enjoy not to be unlawfully discriminated against. What was originally described as 'equal opportunities' has now become known as 'diversity' or 'diversity management', and is essentially concerned with how people behave at work in relation to each other and what are considered to be acceptable and unacceptable practices. Recent legislative changes have created a much stronger foundation of 'human rights' in the workplace, which mean that many previous discriminatory practices relating to gender, race and sexual orientation have now become unlawful as well as unacceptable. HR has a critical, but not exclusive, role in ensuring that, at the formal and informal levels, managers and employees know, understand and (ideally) legitimize the policies, codes and practices that serve to express the way in which each organization commits to this equality agenda.

The increasing importance given to issues of diversity represents, for some but not all, a different agenda – or at least a different emphasis. Thinking back to Chapter 2, the debate about the relationship between the two can be seen to be similar to that about the difference between Personnel Management and HRM. An interest in diversity and diversity management clearly reflects the fact of a growing demographic diversity in the labour force and the implications that this has for how people relate to each other, as well as how they are managed. The somewhat simplistic notion that diversity is 'a good thing' and that organizations should become more diverse has, however, prevented a more objective and dispassionate debate about the implications of difference in employment. Recent pronouncements by the government that too much diversity inhibits integration suggests that, certainly in the wider social context, more emphasis is now being given to what people share and have in common rather than to what separates them from each other.

From an organizational perspective, this questioning of the value of diversity has led to an interest in the so-called 'business' case, which can provide the economic rationale for investing resources in developing appropriate diversity practices. On the one hand, it is probably fair to say that not all organizations and managers are convinced about the strength of this. On the other, global companies, such as Intel, have made a commitment to equality and diversity one of the main elements of their employment and HR strategies.

Finally, the practical implementation of policies and practices that reflect an organization's approach to these issues still represents a challenging and difficult task. We have seen that, in the public sector, implementing recruitment policies that are meant to meet targets for the employment of ethnic minorities can lead to difficulties and criticisms that such policies involve positive discrimination, which is unlawful in most circumstances. The public sector is also well known for its extensive and comprehensive equal opportunities policies, written codes of practice and other expressions of its commitment not to discriminate. The approach advocated by John Harper, in Chapter 15, is quite different and, arguably, more effective. His approach is value-led and involves a very short policy statement, based on the principle that '*we do not discriminate in this organization other than on grounds of merit*'. For Harper, this is all that needs to be said and communicated: it isn't necessary to produce hundred-page policy documents.

 Signpost to Chapter 15: Case Study: Reforming the HR Function, for an example of changing a HR team hindered by complexity in its HR policies

There remain, therefore, important choices available to HR and senior managers in how they ensure that they comply with the law on discrimination. These choices extend to how they choose to go beyond this and create a working environment in which differences between people, as economic resources, are recognized and rewarded, but in which people, as human beings, are treated equally and with respect.

 Visit the Online Resource Centre that accompanies this book for self-test questions, weblinks, and more information on the topics covered in this chapter.
online resource centre **www.oxfordtextbooks.co.uk/orc/banfield_kay/**

REVIEW QUESTIONS

1. How does equal opportunity differ from diversity management? What is then the relationship between the two?

2. Does the recent emphasis on diversity imply that organizations have become more diverse in relation to their geographical coverage and recruitment patterns, and therefore that they need to develop employment policies that reflect this diversity – or do those advocating 'diversity' want organizations to become more diverse and, if so, why?

3. What bases can organizations rightfully, and necessarily, discriminate on and what kinds of discriminatory practices are now unlawful?

4. Do cultural differences justify certain types of discriminatory practice?

5. What is HR's role in establishing fair and acceptable standards of behaviour in the workplace?

163

CASE STUDY

Recruitment at Melbourne Finance

Jenny is a female manager at Melbourne Finance, a large financial organization with over 15,000 employees at more than a hundred locations throughout the UK. Part of the success of the organization is down to comprehensive training and performance management, supported by detailed assessment of key personnel and a high degree of internal promotion. The organization has clearly established equal opportunities policies and recognizes the importance of these in all aspects of its operation.

Jenny is an assistant branch manager at a larger branch. Her line manager approaches her to inform her that a promotional opportunity has arisen in another operating site. She is informed that senior →

executives in the company would like her to apply for the role because they think she would be an ideal candidate. Jenny is also informed that the position is to be advertised internally only at this stage.

Jenny then discloses to her line manager that she would be very interested in the position, but explains that she has just discovered that she is six weeks' pregnant. She asks that this information not be disclosed to any other party.

Shortly afterwards, her line manager informs Jenny that she is required to attend an interview. She then informs her line manager of her intention to disclose her pregnancy during the interview, to which her line manager responds by saying that she has already informed those on the interview panel, having felt obliged to do so.

Jenny attends the interview and, despite being the only internal candidate, she is turned down for the job and is told that the recruiting managers felt she did not have enough experience. The post is then advertised externally and an external candidate is appointed.

Towards the end of her maternity leave, another opportunity arises on a different site and Jenny is, again, approached to apply. This role is perceived to be more senior than the first. This time, her application is successful and she is offered the job on returning from maternity leave.

Jenny is convinced that the reason she did not get the first job was due to her pregnancy. Both of her interviews were conducted in a professional manner, with no reference to her pregnancy or maternity leave, so she has no direct evidence to support any claim. She contacts her line manager from her first job and shares her concerns, but the manager responds by advising her to 'let the issue go', suggesting that Jenny has secured a good promotion and it would not be wise to jeopardize her career by making an issue out of not being awarded the first post.

Questions

1. What mistakes were made by the organization in recruiting to fill the vacancy?

2. What action might Jenny have taken when turned down for the first vacancy?

3. What impact might this have in the longer term for Jenny?

4. What approach to fair employment is being taken by the organization that employs Jenny?

5. What improvements should the company make to the way in which it manages similar situations?

FURTHER READING

Clements, P and Jones, J (2005) *The Diversity Training Handbook: A Practical Guide to Understanding and Changing Attitudes*, Kogan Page.

Daniels, K and Macdonald, L (2005) *Equality, Diversity and Discrimination: A Student Text*, CIPD.

Illes, P (1995) 'Learning to work with difference', *Personnel Review*, 24:6, pp 44–60.

Storey, J (1999) 'Equal opportunity: retrospect and prospect', *Human Resource Management*, 9:1, pp 5–8.

REFERENCES

Advisory Conciliation and Arbitration Service (2006a) *Age and The Workplace: Putting the Employment Equality (Age) Regulations 2006 into Practice*, ACAS, available online at www.acas.org.uk.

Advisory Conciliation and Arbitration Service (2006b) *Tackling Discrimination and Promoting Equality: A Good Practice Guide for Employers*, ACAS, available online at www.acas.org.uk.

Backhaus, K and Tikoo, S (2004) 'Conceptualizing and researching employer branding', *Career Development International*, 9:5, pp 501–17.

Chambers, BA (2002) 'Applicant reactions and their consequences: review, advice, and recommendations for future research', *International Journal of Management Review*, 4, Dec, pp 317–33.

Chartered Institute of Personnel and Development (2005a) *Flexible Working: Impact and Implementation: An Employer Survey*, CIPD survey report, available online at www.cipd.co.uk.

Chartered Institute of Personnel and Development (2005b) *Managing Diversity: People Make the Difference At Work – But Everyone is Different*, CIPD guide, available online at www.cipd.co.uk.

Chartered Institute of Personnel and Development (2006a) *Diversity: An Overview*, CIPD factsheet, available online at www.cipd.co.uk.

Chartered Institute of Personnel and Development (2006b) *Diversity in Business: How much progress have employers made? First Findings*, CIPD survey report, available online at www.cipd.co.uk.

Coens, T and Jenkins, M (2002) *Abolishing Performance Appraisals*, Berret-Koehler.

Department of Trade and Industry (2001a) *The Essential Guide to Work–Life Balance*, DTI, available online at www.dti.gov.uk.

Department of Trade and Industry (2001b) *Work–Life Balance: The Business Case*, DTI, available online at www.dti.gov.uk.

Fresco, A (2006) '£800,000 payout for bullied City secretary', *The Times*, 1 Aug, available online at business.timesonline.co.uk.

Hill, M (2003) *Understanding Social Policy*, Blackwell, ch 6.

Hurstfield, J, Meager, N, Aston, J, Davies, J, Mann, K, Mitchell, H, O'Regan, S and Sinclair, A (2004) *Monitoring the Disability Discrimination Act 1995 Phase 3*, Disability Rights Commission Report, Department for Work and Pensions.

Hyman, R and Brough, I (1975) *Social Values and Industrial Relations: A Study of Fairness and Inequality*, Blackwell.

JobsFactory (2006) *JobsFactory Employers of Choice for Entry-Level Graduates Survey*, available online at www.careercentral.com.sg.

Macpherson, W (1999) *The Stephen Lawrence Inquiry*, HMSO.

Meagre, N, Doyle, B, Evans, C, Kersley, B, Williams, M, O'Regan, S and Tackey, N (1999) *Monitoring the Disability Discrimination Act 1995*, DfEE Research Report RR119, May, Department for Education and Employment.

Oswick, C and Rosenthal, P (2001) 'Towards a relevant theory of age discrimination in employment', in M Noon and E Ogbonna (eds) *Equality, Diversity and Disadvantage in Employment*, Palgrave, pp 156–217.

Rick, J et al (2000) 'Institutional racism: where's the prejudice in organisations?', Presentation to the British Psychological Society Occupational Psychology Conference, The Stakis Metropole Hotel, Brighton, 5–7 Jan 2000.

Slack, J (2006) 'Sorry, you can't join the police: you're a white male', *Daily Mail*, 22 Sept.

Smith, A and Twormey, B (2002) 'Labour market experiences of people with disabilities', *Labour Market Trends*, Aug, Office of National Statistics.

Tyler, R (2007) 'Employees too powerful, say employers', *Daily Telegraph*, 12 Apr.

165

Managing Health and Safety

Key Terms

Accident An unplanned event that causes, or may have caused, injury or harm to people, equipment or property.

Hazard Anything that has the potential to cause harm or injury to people, equipment or property.

Risk The likelihood that harm or injury will occur.

Contributory negligence If an injury is partly due to lack of reasonable care on behalf of the individual bringing about the claim, then the damages received may be reduced due to the claimant's own contribution towards the incident.

Due diligence Written documentary evidence that all reasonably practicable steps have been taken to ensure the health and safety of an individual or group of individuals.

Vicarious liability An employer can be liable for the acts of an employee towards another. This can arise if there is an employment relationship and if the employee commits a civil wrong during the course of their employment.

Learning Objectives

As a result of reading this chapter and using the Online Resource Centre, you should be able to:

- understand what is meant by 'health and safety' and the different approaches taken to health and safety management;

- explain the importance to organizations of health and safety measures;

- identify the key requirements of organizations under health and safety legislation;

- identify the responsibilities of managers and individuals in relation to health and safety;

- understand the role of the Health and Safety Executive (HSE);

- understand the nature of occupational health and the contribution that the function can make to an organization.

Introduction

The management of health and safety is an area that every organization needs to take very seriously. The physical and psychological consequences to an individual that result from either an injury in the workplace or work-related ill health can be traumatic and have serious long-term consequences. Employers have both legal and moral responsibilities to their employees to protect their health and safety, and to ensure that people are not injured as a result of work. The fact is that people don't expect to come to work and be injured – but human beings inevitably take risks throughout their lives. Each time we cross a road, use equipment in our kitchens at home or take part in a variety of outdoor leisure activities, there is always a degree of risk that an accident might happen. At work, the way in which we takes risks is different because a particular kind of relationship exists between employer and employee. This means that the risk is imposed through the employment relationship rather than being taken voluntarily. Employers therefore have a duty of care towards employees as a consequence of this relationship. This duty of care is recognized in law and is covered in more detail later in the chapter.

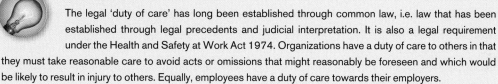

KEY CONCEPT Duty of care

The legal 'duty of care' has long been established through common law, i.e. law that has been established through legal precedents and judicial interpretation. It is also a legal requirement under the Health and Safety at Work Act 1974. Organizations have a duty of care to others in that they must take reasonable care to avoid acts or omissions that might reasonably be foreseen and which would be likely to result in injury to others. Equally, employees have a duty of care towards their employers.

In the workplace, we expect our employers to have taken steps to make sure that our working environment is safe and we expect our employers to make it clear to us what we need to do to stay safe at work. People are the most valuable resource that an organization has and it is important that they are provided with a safe environment in which to operate. This allows them to maximize their productive potential, as well as recognizing their rights, as human beings, to be treated fairly and with consideration.

Accidents

There are many solicitors now offering support on a 'no win, no fee' basis for employees who wish to make a claim for damages following accidents at work. Accidents and the legal claims that result have become a 'growth industry'. The costs of accidents in the workplace is huge and comprises:

- the monetary costs resulting from successful claims for negligence;
- the costs associated with the loss of productive time and actual production due to people being away from work;
- the costs of replacing employees absent from work due to accidents;
- additional administration costs and managerial time.

Despite the increasing costs of claims and other losses, far too many people continue to be injured at work. In 2005–06, 30 million working days were lost in the UK as a result of work-related ill health or workplace injuries. Even more shocking is the fact that, in 2005–06, 212 workers received fatal injuries and a further 146,076 injuries that resulted in three or more days off work were reported to the Health and Safety Executive (HSE, 2006).

Some workplaces are hazardous by nature, but it is not only these environments in which people are injured. Some of the most common causes of injuries are 'slips, trips and falls', which can occur in any work environment. The responsibility for health and safety is as important in less hazardous environments as it is in those, such as fishing and construction, that have traditionally been associated with dangerous and hazardous working conditions.

The legal framework that governs health and safety at work is extensive and continues to grow. There is increasing pressure to ensure that not only organizations, but those in authority are held accountable for accidents at work. The reality is that the legal environment is becoming increasingly less sympathetic towards organizations and the directors responsible for their activities, particularly if fatalities occur. Moreover, there is increasing public and political pressure to identify those responsible for breaches of health and safety regulations, and to ensure that these people are held responsible under criminal law. Successive health and safety legislation is usually complementary and builds on the existing framework, and there is extensive advice readily at hand from the Health and Safety Executive in the UK on how to meet legislative requirements (see www.hse.gov.uk).

There are, therefore, moral, economical and legal reasons for ensuring that health and safety is well managed at work. In this chapter, we will explore the legal framework and the obligations that this places on employers, and we will look at the approaches that organizations take to managing health and safety. As an example of situations likely to be faced by HR and occupational health professionals, the following introductory HRM Insight invites the reader to consider the implications and impact on organizational stakeholders of serious accidents. While this case primarily relates to customers, rather than to employees, many of the lessons to be learnt are relevant in both contexts. HR professionals can often have a responsibility to customers and the public in terms of health and safety management: a responsibility that does not exist in their other areas of accountability.

HRM INSIGHT 7.1 Clapham Junction

On 12 December 1988, 35 people died and 415 were injured when a London-bound commuter train ploughed into the back of a stationary train near Clapham Junction. The official report by Anthony Hidden QC produced 93 recommendations. The cause of the accident was a 'signal wiring defect', arising from works on the signalling system. Recommendations included improved signal testing and commissioning procedures, limits to working hours for those in safety-critical jobs and recommendations to improve the structural integrity of trains. Other safety features, such as improved luggage restraint, seating and table design, were suggested to mitigate the effects of future accidents (Hidden, 1989).

Questions

1. What were the moral and ethical implications of this accident?

2. What impact did this have on public confidence?

3. What expectations do we have as customers using public transport with regard to safety?

4. What are the differences and similarities in implications with reference to customers and the public, in comparison with employees?

The legal framework

Breaches of health and safety legislation can involve both criminal and civil liability. Unlike breaches of employment law, which are usually addressed through employment tribunals, breaches of health and safety legislation are usually addressed with a claim for damages through the civil courts (such as the county or high courts). This is a more formal system than an employment tribunal and, because organizations are required to have employer's liability insurance, claims are usually handled on behalf of organizations via their insurers. Many such claims are settled out of court. In those more exceptional cases that potentially carry criminal liability, criminal courts may impose fines or imprisonment. Table 7.1 shows the differences between the different types of legal redress that can occur in employment law and in health and safety law.

Table 7.1 The differences between the types of legal action in employment law and in health and safety law

	Civil employment law	Civil health and safety law	Criminal law
Basis of law	Employment Acts and Regulations Common law	Regulations and common law	Health and Safety at Work Act 1974 and other statutory legislation
Type of breach	Range of issues, such as unfair dismissal, discrimination, etc.	A civil wrong or 'tort'	Crime
Deciding court	Primarily employment tribunal	Civil courts, primarily county courts	Criminal courts
Potential remedies	Compensation, reinstatement or re-engagement	Compensation only	Punishment by fine or imprisonment
Parties involved	Organization v individual	Organization v individual	State v individual or organization
Standard of proof	Balance of probabilities	Balance of probabilities	Beyond reasonable doubt

KEY CONCEPT The difference between criminal and civil law

Criminal and civil law guide both employment and health and safety management. These two legal systems exist side by side in the UK and have different emphases.

Criminal law is concerned with breaches of 'criminal' legislation, under which the wrongdoing is considered serious enough to warrant police intervention. The police will investigate, and potentially detain, suspects who may then be prosecuted by the state through criminal courts. If found guilty 'beyond reasonable doubt', punishment can include fines or imprisonment.

Civil law is perhaps considered to be less serious, although financial penalties can be higher. It is concerned with wrongdoing between two parties governed by previous case rulings in a civil court or legislation, often in the form of Regulations as well as Acts of Parliament. In a civil case, the test of the 'balance of probabilities' or the showing 'reasonable belief' is less onerous to prove. If successful in a civil court or tribunal, the wronged party is usually awarded financial reparation from the other party, although reparation in employment law can include reinstatement or re-engagement.

Health and Safety at Work Act 1974 (HSWA)

The Health and Safety at Work Act 1974 (HSWA) is probably the single most important piece of legislation governing health and safety at work. The majority of subsequent legislation, including Regulations, are underpinned by the duties set out in this Act.

The Health and Safety at Work Act (HSWA) makes it a legal responsibility of every employer, so far as is reasonably practicable, to ensure the health, safety and welfare of all of its employees. What actually constitutes 'so far as is reasonably practicable' is an important test in health and safety law, and was first established in the case of *Edwards v National Coal Board* [1949] All ER 743. This case established the requirement of an employer to balance the extent of the risk with the measures necessary to avoid the risk, in terms of money, time and trouble or effort. Employers are bound by this duty to address high risks, but if the risk is very low compared to high cost, then there is no absolute duty to deal with the risk.

The HSWA also makes it the duty of every employee to take care of his or her own health and safety, and that of others at work who may be affected by the employee's acts or omissions, and to cooperate with his or her employer to enable it to meet its health and safety obligations.

Other duties under HSWA

Stranks (2006) highlights the following duties of employers under the HSWA:

- the provision of safe plant and systems;
- ensuring the absence of risk in establishing the safe use, handling, storage and transportation of substances;
- the provision of adequate training, instruction and supervision;
- the provision of safe access to, and departure from, premises;
- the provision of a safe working environment.

There are also duties assigned to employers towards others who are not workers, such as occupiers of premises and designers, manufacturers, importers and suppliers.

Framework for obligations, guidance and advice

Figure 7.1 demonstrates the different levels of legal requirements, obligations and guidance available to employers. The Health and Safety at Work Act is the umbrella under which the Regulations sit. As an Act of Parliament it is primary legislation that has been voted for in the Houses of Parliament, and there is an array of Regulations that sit beneath this. These Regulations form part of written legislation and are introduced through consultation, such as the Health & Safety (Display Screen Equipment) Regulations 1992, regarding the use of display screen equipment, and the Regulatory Reform (Fire Safety) Order 2005,

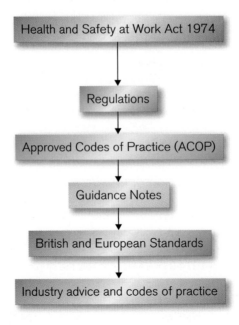

Figure 7.1 Legal obligations and guidance framework in the UK

regarding fire precautions, for example. Details of obligations under these Regulations can be found at the website of the Health and Safety Executive (www.hse.gov.uk).

Approved Codes of Practice (ACOPs) are published by the Health and Safety Commission and inform employers of what they need to do to meet their obligations under the Regulations. They can be used in a court of law to demonstrate due diligence, in that, if an employer can show that it has followed the ACOP, it can claim that it has taken all reasonably practicable steps to prevent accidents happening. While following an ACOP is not expressly required by law, the ACOP is admissible in a court of law as evidence of whether or not Regulations have been followed.

The Health and Safety Executive also issues Guidance Notes to support information available in Regulations and ACOPs. These carry less weight in a court of law and are for supplementary guidance purposes only. There is also an extensive amount of guidance and advice available from the British Standards Institute (BSI; see www.bsi-uk.com) and many employers choose to apply for the approved standard OHSAS 18001 to demonstrate their commitment to occupational health and safety. Institutes and organizations such as the Institute of Occupational Safety and Health (IOSH; see www.iosh.co.uk) also have advice and support available for employers, and there are additionally a variety of codes of practice and guidance information published by trade organizations such as EEF, the manufacturers' association (www.eef.org.uk).

HRM INSIGHT 7.2 *Herald of Free Enterprise*

On 6 March 1987, over 190 people died when P&O Ferries' roll-on, roll-off ferry *The Herald of Free Enterprise* capsized shortly after leaving Zeebrugge. Access restrictions at Zeebrugge lengthened unloading and loading times compared to other ports because there was only room for access to a single ramp to the car deck. Water had to be pumped into ballast tanks to lower the level of the ferry in the water. When the ferry left port, the ballast tanks had not been emptied and the bow doors were left open. Water flooded onto the car deck and the ferry became unstable and capsized within 90 seconds. In his report, following a public inquiry into the disaster, Lord Justice Sheen identified a 'disease of sloppiness' within the company's hierarchy and severely criticized every level within the company. The Crown Prosecution Service charged P&O Ferries and seven employees with 'corporate manslaughter', but the case collapsed because it was difficult to establish who was the 'controlling mind'. This case set the precedent for the legal admissibility of corporate manslaughter in English courts.

Questions

1. To what extent do you feel that health and safety was seen as a priority by managers and staff at P&O?

2. What type of activities and responsibilities might have been appropriate with regard to safety in this incident?

3. What challenges did staff potentially face and how might they have seen their priorities in loading and unloading cars at Zeebrugge?

4. What implications might this have had for health and safety in other areas of the business?

KEY CONCEPT Corporate manslaughter

Corporate manslaughter is a criminal offence. For a prosecution to be successful, it must be shown that there is a causal link between a fatality and a grossly negligent act or omission by a person who can be regarded as a 'controlling mind' of the company. The person, therefore, needs to be a director or senior manager of the company or someone to whom full authority is delegated. In practice, it is difficult to prove this test beyond reasonable doubt. Particularly in large companies, it is often difficult to prove that the person responsible for an act or omission is a relevant senior manager, office or director, because there is often a complex organizational structure with responsibilities spread among many people. Such links are easier to prove in smaller companies. Successful prosecutions for corporate manslaughter are still rare, given the high number of fatalities at work each year.

Understanding accidents

There are many different definitions available of the word 'accident'. For the purposes of this chapter, we will use the definition presented at its beginning: an unplanned event that causes, or may have caused, injury or harm to people, equipment or property. An accident, therefore, is something unplanned and undesirable. The fact that loss or harm may result from this event means that preventing these occurrences is a fundamental health and safety responsibility, with particular implications for management.

Accidents happen because the world in which we live is full of hazards, or things with the potential to cause harm. Accidents happen either because we fail to recognize the hazard in the first place or because we fail properly to avoid, or otherwise control, that hazard. For example, a tiger is a dangerous animal and is therefore a hazard – but we assume that it is perfectly safe to see a tiger in a zoo, because the hazard is properly controlled: the tiger is kept in a suitable enclosure from which it cannot escape and cause injury or death.

STUDENT ACTIVITY 7.1

In groups, discuss the types of hazard that may be found –

- in an office environment;

- in a factory;

- during an outdoor learning experience

and explore ways in which to make each environment safer.

The nature of accidents

There were many studies during the last century that aimed to establish the ratio between the number of major and minor accidents compared to the total number of incidents and 'near misses' in a typical workplace. One of the earliest, and perhaps most well known, of these was the work carried out by Heinrich (1931), which led to the development of the 'Heinrich accident pyramid' shown in Figure 7.2. Although the ratio can change, there are many more minor incidents than major accidents. What the model suggests, however, is that if every minor incident is fully investigated and controls are put in place to prevent any recurrence, the likelihood of a major accident can be reduced. From a strategic perspective, this might mean that concentrating resources on what might appear to be small and inconsequential accidents is a way of preventing major ones.

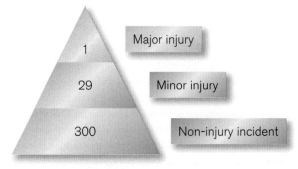

Figure 7.2 The Heinrich accident pyramid

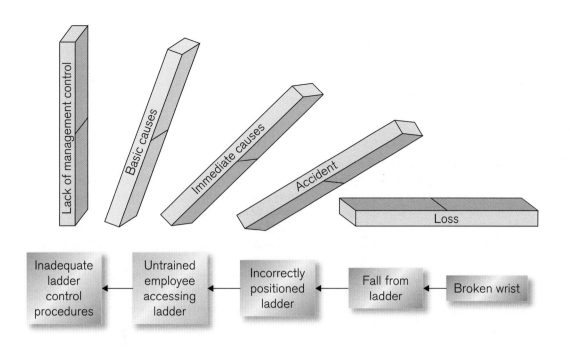

Figure 7.3 Domino theory analysis of the root cause of an accident
Source: This figure is used by permission of the copyright holder, Det Norske Veritas Inc, with all rights reserved.

What causes an accident?

Behind any accident, there will be both direct and indirect causes. For example, an employee may cut his or her hand while using an open-bladed knife to open a cardboard box at work. The *direct* cause of the accident will be the knife, but the *indirect* cause might be failure on the part of the employer to limit the use of open-bladed knives, or failure on the part of the employee to follow a safe system of work or to use appropriate protective gloves. Each of these factors might, in turn, be linked to an underlying factor, such as lack of adequate risk assessment or inadequate procedures and training.

Bird and Loftus (1976) put forward the 'domino theory' of why accidents occur. Under this theory, lack of management control leads to the basic cause of an accident, which is either a 'job factor', such as unguarded machinery, or a 'person factor', such as a lack of adequate training. This leads to the intermediate cause, which is an unsafe act or condition that, in turn, results in an accident and then a loss.

This model can be used to work backwards from any accident to identify its root cause. The example in Figure 7.3 shows how Bird and Loftus' model might be applied to an employee suffering a broken wrist through falling from a ladder. An easier way to look at this is, perhaps, to continue asking the question 'why?' until the root cause has been established. For example, if you were to ask why a person fell from a ladder, the answer might be because it was incorrectly positioned; you might then ask why it was incorrectly positioned, and so on.

Multiple cause theory

In reality, the domino theory is perhaps oversimplified: accidents usually have multiple, and often complex, combinations of factors that can be the cause of their occurrence. It is usually a combination of unsafe acts and conditions that result in an accident. For example, a person who stumbles and sprains an ankle on a staircase may have been in a hurry, carrying a heavy item or failing to hold the handrail properly.

There may also have been a damaged and worn stair or handrail that contributed to the accident. In this example, there might not be a single 'domino' or cause, but a range of causes that, in different combinations, have resulted in the accident. Nevertheless, the root cause of all accidents in the workplace can usually be attributed to ineffective management controls, because, with the benefit of hindsight, it is always easy to see how the accident might have been prevented.

HRM INSIGHT 7.3 The cause of accidents

An employee working on a construction site received a serious head injury as a result of a brick falling 20 feet from an open bucket, which was being used, along with a pulley system, to haul bricks from ground level to a second-storey window. The employee was not wearing a hard hat at the time of the accident. He subsequently submitted a claim for damages.

Due to the nature of the contract, employees were required to work very quickly to get the job done in the shortest possible time. The site manager was aware of the practice used for lifting bricks and argued that the employee was an experienced bricklayer, who had overfilled the bucket. This resulted in the brick toppling from the bucket when it swung from side to side while being lifted. The manager also argued that the employee could have worn the hard hat that he owned, but had left it in the boot of his car. The bucket did not have any means of being locked shut during the lifting process; nor did it have any mechanism that prevented it from falling if released while being lifted.

Questions

1. What might have been the basic and intermediate causes?

2. What underlying management failures might have contributed to this accident?

3. How might a similar accident be prevented in future?

4. In what ways did the company fail in its duty of care to the employee?

5. To what extent is it possible that the employee did not comply with his duty of care?

Insights & Outcomes: visit the Online Resource Centre at www.oxfordtextbooks.co.uk/orc/banfield_kay/ for an analysis of what actions should be considered to put a safe system of work in place to prevent this type of accident recurring.

Accident reporting

Certain types of accidents and occurrences of industrial diseases must, by law, be reported to the Health and Safety Executive. These include major injuries, such as fractures (other than those of toes, fingers and thumbs), injuries from electric shocks and certain eye injuries. Any accident that results in a person requiring more than three days off work must be reported. Employers must also report certain dangerous occurrences, such as incidents involving lifting machinery, and must report cases of occupational disease, such as occupational dermatitis and occupational respiratory disease. These reporting requirements are covered by the Reporting of Injuries, Diseases and Dangerous Occurrences Regulations 1995 (RIDDOR; HSE, 1995). Specific details required under these Regulations need to be gathered and recorded, and this can be done by using a standard 'accident book', available from the HSE. Alternatively, other approved forms can be used to record these details (HSE, 2003).

Many organizations go beyond these requirements by insisting that every accident and incident is recorded using the HSE accident books. These organizations may also insist on the investigation of each incident, to help to reduce the risks of similar situations in the future. If we recall the Heinrich pyramid in Figure 7.2, we will recognize that it is important to investigate all small minor occurrences because this can help prevent a major occurrence, or even a fatality, from occurring. Because it can be difficult to know how much time an employee may require off work following an injury, it is sensible to record all lost-time accidents, to ensure that adequate information is gathered in the event that the accident becomes reportable (i.e. results in more than three days' absence).

First aid provisions

If someone becomes ill, or is hurt at work, it is important that they are taken care of immediately. Employers therefore have obligations to provide first aid arrangements and equipment, and to make sure that employees are aware of these arrangements. First aid includes treating minor injuries and giving immediate attention to more serious casualties until medical help is available. This requirement does not only cover accidents at work, but also includes giving assistance to people who suddenly become ill while at work for reasons that are not work-related. The types of provision required vary, depending on the number of people employed, the nature and size of the undertaking and the location in which the employees work. Further information on first aid is available from the HSE (2006).

Accident investigation

It is extremely important to investigate accidents thoroughly if an organization is to put preventative measures in place to ensure that a similar accident does not recur. Accident investigations enable a company, firstly, to establish the cause of the accident and, secondly, to put measures in place to ensure that the accident is not repeated. It is also an important tool to enable a company to raise awareness among employees about health and safety matters, and provides an opportunity for managers to express appropriate concern for those reporting to them. Keeping accurate records of accidents is also a requirement that assists insurers in making judgements about liability and, if appropriate, about any settlement offered to the injured party should the facts point to negligence on the part of the company. Finally, without a detailed investigation, an organization cannot defend any claims for compensation in situations in which the employer does not believe it has been negligent.

Inadequately investigated accidents, therefore, have a direct financial impact upon the company in terms of the risk of further accidents and the cost of employer's liability insurance premiums, which reflect the cost of claims that cannot be defended.

A properly conducted investigation can also help to improve management systems and eliminate the indirect causes of accidents, as well as addressing direct causes. In order to achieve this, the investigation must examine root causes, and must make recommendations to examine and improve the management systems and controls that may have failed. Further advice on accident investigation is available from the HSE (2004).

Characteristics of an effective investigation

> I keep six honest serving men
> (They taught me all I knew);
> Their names are What and Why and When
> And How and Where and Who.
> (Rudyard Kipling, *The Elephant's Child*, *Just So Stories*)

Where possible, an accident investigation should:

- be carried out as quickly as possible after the accident, taking account of the need to be compassionate towards persons who may be suffering from shock or injury;

- be carried out by trained personnel;

- use appropriate photographic evidence;

- include diagrams and sketches of location and positions;

- include statements from all witnesses, who should not have had the opportunity to confer before making their statement;

- be based on the facts of what someone could actually see and hear, and not on opinion or hearsay;

- include information about behaviour, as well as about environmental conditions;

- consider relevant risk assessments and safe working practices;

- consider and record the contribution that the injured person made towards the accident, as well as other contributing people, environmental conditions and the state of equipment or facilities;

- analyse relevant data;

- identify root causes;

- make recommendations to prevent a similar accident recurring;

- include a review to ensure that corrective action is completed.

STUDENT ACTIVITY 7.2

1. In your group, design an accident investigation form to ensure that accidents are effectively investigated and that those responsible for carrying out the investigation record all of the relevant details.

2. Compare the outcome of the design exercise with those of other groups and agree on a final version.

3. Collect examples of accident investigation documentation currently being used by an organization with which you are familiar and compare your form with these.

4. Draw appropriate conclusions from a comparison between the forms.

The limitations of accident investigations

As a means of reducing accidents, a thorough investigation is a useful tool and, if carried out correctly, it can limit the number of accidents that occur in the future. Accident investigation should not, however, be relied upon as the sole means of preventing accidents and improving a company's safety record. Measuring the number of accidents is simply a measure of failure, rather than of success, and is not necessarily an effective means of preventing less frequent, but more serious, accidents occurring. Assessing the risks associated with tasks and processes is arguably a more important means of prevention, because it looks at the likelihood of an accident occurring before it takes place.

It is also important to note that not all safety issues relate to accidents. It is as important, for example, to look not only at preventing fires, but also at ways of reducing the impact should a fire occur, and of ensuring that evacuation procedures are in place and that adequate provisions are made to enable fires to be properly extinguished at the earliest opportunity. Similarly, the onset of manual injuries, such as upper limb disorders associated with repetitive tasks, can occur over a period of time and is preventable with proper health surveillance. It is important to note, in the context of prevention, that such chronic medical conditions are rarely attributable to a single accident, but are more often related to the working environment or working practices.

Risk assessment

It is a legal requirement that employers assess and manage all health and safety risks in the workplace. This involves looking at all of the risks that arise at work and then putting in place appropriate measures to ensure that these risks are properly controlled.

We have seen already that a hazard is anything with the potential to cause an accident. 'Risk' can be defined as the likelihood that harm or injury will be the result of an accident. In assessing risks, therefore, it is important to look not only at the probability of an accident happening, but at the severity of harm that might result from the accident. The Health and Safety Executive (1999a) recommends a five-step approach to assessing risks at work, as shown in Figure 7.4.

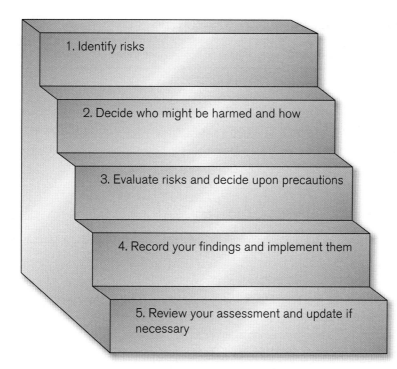

Figure 7.4 The five-step approach to assessing risks at work

Figure 7.5 shows a typical rating mechanism that managers can use to help an organization to prioritize the basis of risk, while Table 7.2 offers an example of how this might be applied. In this example, we can see how changes to the task can change the risk assessment and in so doing reduce the risk rating to an acceptable level. By following this simple methodology, the risk of receiving a cut can be reduced by training staff and using a protective glove, but can be removed almost completely by using a safety knife.

The key to risk assessment is to keep things simple and not to over focus on the rating scales. The content is more important than the actual rating. A 'competent person' should carry out assessment and training these people to the required standards is an important part of effectively managing risks. A useful staring point is to consider the 10 hazards most likely to cause serious injury or work related illness at work. These will vary from organization to organization and may include falls from ladders, dangerous driving, machinery faults, dangerous cabling, hazardous materials, such as asbestos, and so

Figure 7.5 A typical risk rating scoring system

Table 7.2 Application of a typical risk rating scoring system

Activity	Hazard	Injury	Likelihood	Severity	Risk
Untrained person using open-bladed knife to open box	The knife	Cut to hand or body	4	4	High – 16
Trained person using open-bladed knife to open box using safe system of work and protective gloves	The knife	Cut to hand or body	2	4	Medium – 8
Untrained person using safety knife to open box	The knife	Cut to hand or body	1	2	Low – 2

on. It is also helpful to involve representatives from the workforce in the assessment of risk as they will be able to help identify hazards and may be able to offer practical solutions to reduce risk levels. Industry guidance, through trade and employer organizations can also be helpful in risk identification and can provide useful examples of good risk assessment practice.

Hierarchy of risk control

Table 7.3 shows a number of strategies that an organization might use to reduce risk once an assessment is carried out. These are shown as a hierarchy that should be considered in order of preference. The first two options, 'elimination' and 'reduction', deal with the hazard itself and are therefore the most obviously effective means of reducing the risk. The second two strategies involve keeping people away from the hazard, by creating physical barriers ('enclosure') or making it difficult for a person to come into contact with the hazard ('removing person'). 'Reducing contact' is only a useful method if the risk increases with the extent of exposure to a hazard, such as noise. The final means, of 'providing personal protection', should only be used as a last resort if there is no other way of reducing risk. This is the least effective means of control, because it relies on a person's behaviour to limit the risk, i.e. the person must follow instructions in the use and maintenance of protective equipment. In this respect, the risk can only be reduced, not removed entirely.

Table 7.3 The hierarchy of risk control

Strategy	Example
Eliminate risk	A sandwich shop might stop using a meat slicer and buys its meat pre-sliced
Reduction	A cleaning company might change the types of chemical it uses in its cleaning processes to less harmful cleaning agents
Enclosure	A guard will be placed around the moving parts of a machine to prevent employees being able to touch those parts
Remove person	Overhead electrical power cables are high up to prevent people coming in to contact with them
Reduce contact	Noise reduction measures will be taken, such as building barriers or insulating walls
Provide personal protection	The use of safety goggles and gloves when handling chemicals will reduce the risk of eye splashes and contact with the skin

HRM INSIGHT 7.4 Carrying out risk assessments

A retail shop decides to extend the display area of the shop by extending the facility into a room previously used as a storage area. The two rooms are joined by a doorway that is 1.5m high and, therefore, not high enough for a significant number of customers to walk through without risking head injury. There is also a small 5cm-high step leading down into the storage area. The wall separating the two rooms is a partition wall and an adjustment to the door height would be relatively straightforward.

Questions

1. What is the hazard in this example?

2. What are the potential risks and to whom?

3. Is this an acceptable risk?

4. How might risks be controlled?

5. What steps would be regarded as reasonably practicable to control this risk?

The same shop has a cloakroom downstairs, with a similar door height. This is a door through a retaining wall and so it will be more expensive to adjust the height of the door. The room is used only occasionally, and only by staff, throughout the day.

Questions (cont'd)

6. What are the key differences in this example?

7. What control measures would be reasonable to reduce the risks in this example?

STUDENT ACTIVITY 7.3

Carry out a risk assessment for a potentially hazardous task with which you are familiar and which is performed either at work or at home. What control measures would be appropriate for the task and how might the risks be kept to a minimum?

Fire risks

The Regulatory Reform (Fire Safety) Order 2005, effective from 1 October 2006, replaced all previous legislation dealing with fire and is enforceable by regional fire authorities. Employers and building owners are responsible under the order for ensuring that a fire risk assessment is carried out and for ensuring that the necessary precautions are in place to minimize the likelihood of anyone using the premises being harmed as a result of a fire. This includes taking account of how flammable substances are stored and handled. Fire risk assessment guides have been published to give guidance to different organizations, details of which are available online at the Department for Communities and Local Government website (www.firesafetyguides.co.uk).

Role of the Health and Safety Executive (HSE)

The Health and Safety Executive (HSE) is an organization that aims to ensure that the risks to people's health and safety at work are properly controlled. As such, the HSE is the principal body responsible for the enforcement of health and safety legislation. Those employed by the HSE include inspectors, engineers, scientists, lawyers and medical professionals.

In addition to providing help, support and advice to employers on health and safety matters, and working proactively with employers to promote health and safety at work, HSE inspectors have a number of powers that they can exercise to ensure workers' health and safety. HSE inspectors can enter premises at any reasonable time or at any time, day or night, if there is reason to believe that a dangerous situation exists. In addition to regularly scheduled visits, inspectors will typically visit premises following particularly serious incidents or complaints. They have the power to seize and render harmless any substance or article that might give rise to serious injury. They have the authority to investigate accidents and complaints, and may interview individuals and take statements. They can also require that the workplace is left undisturbed pending investigation.

Outcomes from such investigations can range from verbal or written advice, to the serving of an improvement or prohibition notice. An improvement notice will require that breaches to regulations be remedied within a given timeframe. A prohibition notice may, for example, prohibit the use of a particular unsafe piece of machinery or of an unsafe substance.

HSE inspectors also have the power to prosecute employers and individuals if there is a serious breach of health and safety regulations or if there is evidence that an employer has wilfully disregarded the law, such as a failure to respond to an improvement notice.

Managing health and safety

Carrying out risk assessments is one of the main requirements under the Management of Health and Safety at Work Regulations 1999 (MHSWR). Managing health and safety is, however, about more than simply complying with the law. There are many large and successful organizations which, rather than simply reacting to accidents, requirements from insurers or demands from the HSE, recognize that proactively managing health and safety is one of the key performance indicators of their success. These companies actively strive to minimize the costs of injury at work and work-related illness, and identify and work towards goals and targets continually to improve their safety record. They also consider good health and safety to be one of their measures of commercial success (*People Management*, 2006).

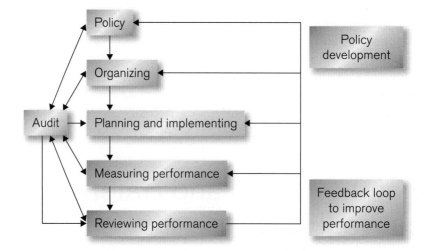

Figure 7.6 Safety management systems
© Crown Copyright/HSE.

KEY CONCEPT **Differences between work-related illness and work-related accidents**

Unlike work-related accidents, work-related illness, or work-related disease, is entirely preventable. A 'blanket' approach can control many accident risks, but work-related ill health must be considered on an individual basis.

Health and safety management systems

The HSE recommends that organizations adopt a health and safety management system that incorporates the five elements shown in Figure 7.6 (HSE, 2001).

Health and safety policy

Employers with five or more employees are required, under MHSWR to have a written health and safety policy statement. It is also a requirement to bring the policy to the attention of employees, and to review and revise the policy as necessary. The safety policy should include details of the organization's commitment to preventing accidents and the occurrence of work-related ill health, and to controlling risks, including providing safe equipment and plant, and ensuring the safe handling of substances. It should also include a commitment to providing training and to consultation.

Employers are also required to display a current certificate of their employer's liability insurance on notice boards, along with a copy of the HSE poster specifying health and safety legislation.

Organizing

It is also necessary to ensure that the organization's structure and operating procedures are in place in such a way that the policy can be put into practice. It is therefore important that everyone in the organization, from senior management down, is clear about their individual responsibilities and how they are required to contribute to the overall management of health and safety within the organization. This is important if the organization is to achieve a proactive culture, within which all employees positively contribute to a working environment free from accidents and work-related ill health, rather than a reactive culture, within which actions are taken only in response to external requirements.

Characteristics of a positive and safety-conscious culture include:

- shared ownership;
- a commitment to applying existing safety regulations and procedures;
- consultation and involvement between management and employees over strategies for implementation and improvement;
- clarity over management responsibilities.

Planning and implementing

Achieving a proactive, safety-conscious culture is not easy, of course, nor is it linked to one particular management strategy. But organizations that enjoy low accident rates share a systematic approach to the identification and elimination, or reduction, of risk. The rationale for such an approach is that, if risk assessment is adopted as an integral part of everyday operations, decisions can be made with a view to minimizing risk in all activities. For example, the design and development of new products and processes can be carried out with safety in mind more effectively if risk assessment is considered at

181

the initial conception, rather than as an afterthought once new plant has been delivered or once new products have been launched.

Many organizations also take a strategic view of health and safety, in which annual safety plans are informed by experience and new developments in the field. Such plans clarify what actions are to be implemented over the next 12 months and what resources are to be made available to meet the plan. This ensures that actions can be assigned to individuals and that these can be incorporated into objectives set through the appraisal system. For certain managers with particular health and safety responsibilities, annual performance objectives may well include specific reference to health and safety improvements.

 Signpost to Chapter 11: Managing Performance, for more information on setting performance objectives

STUDENT ACTIVITY 7.4

Consider the position of a works manager (or equivalent) who is preparing for an annual performance appraisal meeting with one of his or her factory supervisors, during which it is intended to reach agreement on certain performance objectives relating to health and safety. The task is to produce several examples of targets or objectives that might be used as a basis for discussion in that – and future – performance appraisal reviews.

Measuring performance

To ensure that plans are enacted and that safety performance is improved, it is important to measure the effectiveness of accident improvement initiatives. This might involve regular measures, such as tracking accident statistics or claims history, or might involve a combined measure, agreed through a predetermined audit mechanism. It is also important to monitor and measure the delivery of safety improvement plans, to ensure that all actions identified under the plan are completed in line with the timescales set. Each step in the management system needs to be regularly reviewed to ensure that policies, responsibilities, plans and activities remain relevant, and to make any necessary changes. This review represents an important feedback loop that helps to ensure future developments and plans are informed by relevant data and information.

 Signpost to Chapter 9: HR Planning and Measurement, for more information on measuring performance in HR

Auditing

Carrying out an audit of health and safety is a useful way of determining the extent to which health and safety measures and controls are being properly applied in the workplace. An audit also provides a useful means of giving feedback to employees and managers about areas in which they are meeting their responsibilities and areas in which improvement is required. Effective audits are carried out at frequent intervals and should be undertaken by competent persons, properly trained in auditing. Some organizations have in-house audit systems that have been designed to support their health and safety management system. Other organizations use external bodies, such as trade associations or the British Standards Institute, both for carrying out auditing and for providing an auditing framework. The route taken will depend on factors such as the availability of in-house expertise, the relative costs of different options and the degree of risk in the workplace.

Consultation requirements

Employers are required to consult with their employees over matters regarding health and safety. If there is a recognized trade union, with a union-appointed safety representative, employers must consult with that representative on matters affecting the employees he or she represents. If there is no recognized union, employers can consult either directly with employees or through an elected representative. It is also a requirement to bring these consultation arrangements to the attention of employees. Used properly, consultation can be a very effective way of ensuring that arrangements put in place to manage health and safety are appropriate and as successful as possible. It also allows those directly engaged in operational activities to offer useful suggestions to help improve health and safety. Further information on consultation requirements can also be obtained from the HSE.

 Signpost Chapter 4: Managing Employee Relations, for general information about employer obligations to consult with employees

 STUDENT ACTIVITY 7.5

Often, the first opportunity to engage with new employees on health and safety matters is during the induction process. Working in groups, you should address the following.

1. Decide upon an organization and type of employee known to the group – a supermarket, for example – and produce an induction checklist to cover the main health and safety issues, and the requirements affecting the organization/employees chosen.
2. What will the contribution of line managers need to be to reinforce the health and safety message once the formal induction training has been completed?

183

Behavioural approach

The HSE estimate that at least 80 per cent of accidents can be attributed, at least in part, to the actions or omissions of people (HSE, 1999b). It is therefore not sufficient, when considering ways of preventing accidents, to consider only technical aspects, such as installing guards and barriers or issuing personal protective equipment.

Many organizations adopt what is known as a 'behavioural' approach to health and safety, in addition to other measures, and benefit from extremely successful health and safety records as a result. This approach enables the organization to influence its employees' behaviour and encourages an organizational culture that takes health and safety into consideration as part of its everyday operation. In the context of accidents and accident prevention, it would be an oversimplification to think that these were caused by carelessness on the part of those directly involved. Accidents can happen to the most conscientious of workers and human error can result from many sources. For example, an employee may not have been aware that his or her behaviour was unsafe or may have misunderstood instructions. It might also be the case that risks have been taken with the best of intentions, due to pressures to meet other targets, or it might simply be the case that actions taken have become customary practice in the area, despite contravening safe systems or written rules.

Because it is not always possible to eliminate all of the hazards and risks experienced at work, despite the existence of comprehensive health and safety policies, an approach to directly influencing behaviour, based on a different and complementary methodology, may be needed. The first stage in such a methodology is trying to understand why people behave as they do.

There are many human factors that influence the way in which we behave. People have different personalities and our attitudes vary, depending upon experiences and circumstances. Individual behaviour and behavioural patterns are also a function of the social environment in which people live and work, and this helps to explain the importance of group pressures and group behaviours, which group members are expected to accept and to which they are expected to conform. If a person moves from a job in an organization with a strong safety culture to one in an organization with a less proactive approach, it is possible that, over a period of time, the person will begin to adopt new and unsafe practices that are typical of the new organization. Changing the safety culture is a challenge that must be driven by management if it is to influence behaviour successfully and improve the health and safety record of the organization. Using the 'ABC model' of behaviour and performance can be a useful tool in helping managers to influence employee behaviour in the required direction.

The ABC model

Krause (1997) described what he called the 'ABC' approach to understanding behaviour relating to safety. The basis of the ABC approach is that all behaviour ('B') has an antecedent ('A'), or a set of circumstances that precede and help to determine the behaviour, along with a consequence ('C'). For example, in 2006, it became a legal requirement in the UK that all children of either up to the age of 12 or 135cm in height have a properly fitted child seat when a passenger in a car. Prior to the introduction of this rule, some parents did not use car seats. This behaviour is analysed in Table 7.3.

It can be seen that there are a number of antecedents, or reasons why a parent may have decided not to use a car seat. Behaviour is more likely to be influenced by immediate consequences and so, in the example shown, the potential consequences may not influence behaviour as strongly as the immediate consequences. In this example, a parent may therefore take a risk because of the convenience and the benefit of saving time and money.

In some cases, behaviour was influenced by increased awareness of the risks. Manufacturers of car seats, other parents and information from health visitors, for example, have encouraged more widespread use of car seats. These are all examples of antecedents that have influenced behaviour. Now that legislation has been introduced, there is also the consequence of being prosecuted for failure to use the correct

Table 7.4 Example of the use of the ABC model

Antecedent	Behaviour	Consequence
• Ignorance of risk • Reluctance to spend money on a car seat • Speed and ease of getting children into the car • Inconvenience of having to swap car seats • Public awareness campaigns • Peer pressure • Manufacturer information • Media reports • Awareness of risks and new legislation	Unwanted behaviour: • not using a correct car seat for a child of either under 12 years old or under 135cm in height Desired behaviour: • using a correct car seat for children either under 12 years old or under 135cm in height	Immediate: • saves money • saves time Potential: • high risk of serious injury or fatality, but unlikely occurrence of accident • risk of prosecution • reduced risk in the event of an accident • free from prosecution

type of seat. To influence behaviour effectively, the consequences will need to be immediate, and this means that enforcement agencies need to monitor the situation and take swift action if parents do not comply with the law.

It can therefore be seen that, by changing the antecedents and the consequences, we can influence behaviour. Consequences are usually more influential than antecedents, so it is important in the workplace to ensure that unwanted behaviour is dealt with using appropriate corrective action, such as training, counselling or disciplinary action, and that this is taken as promptly after the undesired behaviour as possible to increase its impact and effect. It is equally important to use positive reinforcements, such as rewards, recognition and praise, if behaviour is consistent with, and supportive of, health and safety requirements. Regular auditing represents a form of reinforcement, in the sense that it can highlight positive behaviours and provide employees with appropriate feedback that encourages safe behaviour and promotes a safety culture within the organization.

The model is particularly useful in helping to modify unsafe behaviour. Analysing the role of antecedents and consequences – there may well be none – can help to identify appropriate corrective action, based on changing antecedents and building in either negative or positive consequences, resulting in behavioural change.

HRM INSIGHT 7.5 The ABC model in practice

An electrical firm was contracted to install a new intruder alarm system at a college. The cabling for the system had to be installed along service ducts, the access to which was via manholes along one of the main corridors in the building. To limit disruption to the college, the installation was scheduled to take place during the holiday period, during which fewer people would be using the building. There would, however, still be a number of members of staff in the building, preparing coursework and carrying out administration duties.

The contractors lifted two manhole covers along the corridor and, during the installation, there were times at which the contractor's staff were off-site while working in the duct. The contractors did not erect any form of barrier around the manhole while the covers were lifted. As a result, an employee leaving her office and carrying a number of papers fell 1.5m down one of the open access points, fracturing her leg in two places and badly cutting her head, which required stitches. She had no idea that there were contractors working in the building and, while she had heard voices outside her office, she was unaware of the manhole covers being lifted or of maintenance work taking place.

Questions

1. What was the unsafe behaviour in this example?

2. Using Table 7.4 as a framework, identify the antecedents, behaviours and consequences in this example.

3. What antecedents and consequences might the manager of the contractors have employed to promote safe behaviour?

STUDENT ACTIVITY 7.6

Identify a persistent unsafe behaviour in an organization with which you are familiar.

1. List the antecedents and consequences that encourage the unsafe behaviour.

2. Design a set of antecedents and consequences that will help to eliminate the unsafe behaviour.

3. Explain how you would monitor the effects of the changes you decide upon.

The role of occupational health

Accidents cannot be entirely prevented in the workplace. No matter how carefully we manage risks, while a risk exists, there remains a possibility that an accident will occur. Work-related disease, on the other hand, is entirely preventable. People do not suddenly become ill as a result of work: work-related illness develops over a period of time, either as a result of exposure to something that can cause illness, such as asbestos, or from exposure to conditions that can cause ill health. For example, an employee may be exposed to a reagent, such as flour, through working in a food business and may, over a period of time, become sensitized to the reagent and go on to develop industrial asthma as a result. Not all employees will react to this type of reagent in the same way and, therefore, an approach to controlling risks of this type will need to be carried out on an individual basis.

There is now an increasing emphasis on preventing work-related diseases and insurers are particularly concerned about this area of health and safety. Due to the time that can elapse between exposure to the condition and the diagnosis of the illness, a failure to take appropriate remedial action or poor control mechanisms can result in a large volume of unanticipated and expensive claims.

Occupational health management is about managing the relationship between work and health. It is about assessing each individual to establish whether or not he or she is fit to carry out the tasks required, and it is about controlling the tasks and working environment to ensure that they do not have a long-term adverse effect on the health of the employee.

Occupational health practitioners also have an important role to play in advising and supporting first aid provisions in the workplace, and can have a positive impact by supporting health promotion activities.

The role of the Employment Medical Advisory Service (EMAS)

The Employment Medical Advisory Service (EMAS) is the medical advisory division of the HSE and its focus is on the prevention of work-related illness. EMAS, like the rest of the HSE, employ people in different capacities, such as nurses and doctors. EMAS doctors (medical inspectors) have the same powers as HSE inspectors. Their role is to investigate complaints, investigate ill health reported under RIDDOR requirements, and to provide advice to employers, employees and trade unions, as well as to professionals employed in occupational health.

Work-related ill health

Examples of work-related ill health might include musculoskeletal problems, such as back pain, vibration white finger (caused by the long-term use of vibrating equipment) and work-related upper limb disorders (WRULD), which can be caused by prolonged repeated movements of hands, wrists and arms. Prolonged exposure to sensitizing reagents can result in occupational respiratory disease and the handling of certain substances can result in occupational dermatitis.

Prolonged exposure to noise can cause loss of hearing and there are therefore specific Regulations relating to noise at work: the Control of Noise at Work Regulations 2005 (the Noise Regulations). We do not propose to explore these risks and Regulations in detail in this chapter, but more information is available from the HSE.

Work-related stress

Work-related stress is another area of increasing importance and many people suffer ill health as a result of stress in the workplace. It is important that organizations identify the stress risks in the workplace and adopt policies and measures to control stress, as they do other hazards. Because stress is a health-related issue, risk assessment should also take into consideration the differing capabilities of individuals for working in stressful situations. While the onset of feeling stressed as a result of work is not always predictable, early intervention is necessary to prevent any long-term harm to the employee, who might otherwise suffer from work-related stress.

It is important to distinguish here between acceptable levels of stress, including manageable stressful events or periods at work, and the medical harm of long-term exposure to unacceptable levels of stress. Employees should be aware of how to go about approaching their employer if they feel that their health is being adversely affected by stress at work (CIPD, 2006).

Health surveillance

To prevent work-related ill health, it is important that a competent person is designated to carry out appropriate health surveillance prior to employment and to establish that potential employees are fit to carry out the job for which they have applied. This responsibility also extends to establishing whether the job needs to be adapted in any way to limit risks to health. A pre-employment health assessment can also identify whether or not reasonable adjustments must be considered under the Disability Discrimination Act 1995.

 Signpost to Chapter 6: Equality in Employment, for details of employers' obligations under the DDA

The base-line health assessment recorded at this stage is an important record that forms the basis for comparison to future assessments, establishing whether or not there is any evidence of an employee's health deteriorating as a result of work.

The frequency and nature of ongoing health surveillance will vary depending on the nature of the job and the individual. For example, employees working in dustier environments will require more frequent respiratory function testing.

Summary

Management of health and safety is an area of significant importance that needs to be well managed and taken seriously by all organizations. The requirement to reduce accidents is no longer the main emphasis in health and safety: risk management is now the dominant area of employer responsibility in meeting their 'duty of care' towards their employees.

The consequences of failing adequately to manage risk can involve many adverse affects and can result in companies being prosecuted under both civil and criminal law, with penalties of increasing severity.

The Health and Safety Executive has an important role to play in health and safety, and has significant powers, both advisory and investigative, to ensure that health and safety is properly managed in all organizations.

Organizations need to adopt a holistic approach to health and safety management, encompassing not only policy and how they organize themselves, but also the details of planning and implementing controls, and of measuring, reviewing and auditing their health and safety performance.

Management activity should also consider the impact of health upon an employee's ability to carry out his or her job and the impact of work on that employee's health. Occupational health professionals, supported by EMAS, the medical advisory arm of the Health and Safety Executive, have an important part to play in preventing occupational illness.

 ## REVIEW QUESTIONS

1. Who should be involved in assessing risk and why?

2. What do the terms 'hazard' and 'risk' mean, and why is the distinction important?

3. Investigating accidents and putting preventative measures in place does not prevent further accidents occurring – but what does?

4. Why is work-related disease entirely preventable?

5. What are the potential costs to an organization of poorly managed health and safety?

6. How can the behavioural approach to safety reduce accidents and when is it appropriate to adopt this approach?

CASE STUDY
Netherton Cat Shelter

Netherton Cat Shelter is a recently established voluntary organization with charitable status. It was initially set up with a substantial legacy left by a very wealthy cat lover, who did not have any family to whom she could leave her estate. The shelter takes in stray and unwanted cats, and cares for them, with the aim of rehoming as many cats as possible. It continues to be funded through donations, fund raising activity and legacies left to the shelter. A voluntary committee, comprising eight volunteers, has been established to govern the activity of the cat shelter. Two full-time managers are employed to run the shelter on a day-to-day basis and there are two part-time cleaners employed, who cover in the absence of the managers. All of the other work of the shelter is carried out by an extensive body of volunteers, who are involved with activities ranging from cleaning the building, cats' bedding, litter trays and other equipment used, through to fund-raising events and helping with open days, on which members of the public come to see and choose a cat.

The two managers have joint responsibility for health and safety, but because the shelter is newly established, very little is set up. There is a health and safety policy in place and the shelter has appropriate insurance. The managers are both relatively new to the job and had little handover with the previous managers, so systems have slipped. The formal system for recording accidents has not been properly implemented and there are no risk assessments in place. The committee has, to date, not really taken its obligations very seriously because it has been unclear about the extent to which legislation applies, given the charitable status of the shelter. The shelter is regarded as a 'nice, safe place to work' and, because there have never really been any accidents, no one has ever really bothered to put any time into establishing correct management procedures.

Last week, a volunteer was asked to clean out the floors. Standard procedure involves household-type bleach being diluted in a bucket for floor cleaning and mops are used. While emptying the bleach into the bucket, the volunteer splashed her eye with bleach. It didn't really irritate at the time so, once his eye had stopped watering, he carried on with the task. Later in the evening, his eye became very sore, so he decided to go to hospital. He telephoned the shelter the next day, saying that his family were encouraging him to go and see a 'no win, no fee' solicitor and put in a claim. He doesn't want to do this because it will take money from the shelter, but he thought he should mention it in case anyone else has an accident when cleaning the floors.

Word has now been spread around the shelter and several of the volunteers have complained that the shelter keeps running out of rubber gloves. Two of the volunteers have complained that they have developed skin rashes as a result of having to clean without gloves. These volunteers have stated that they really think the committee should be better organized and that it is taking advantage of all of their unpaid hard work.

Questions

1. What activities would you recommend that the managers plan to audit health and safety at the shelter?

2. What would you regard to be the most urgent actions in respect of the incidents reported over the last week?

3. How would you go about helping the shelter to identify the main risks that need the quick establishment of risk assessment?

4. What options might be available to the shelter to get some support in getting basic systems set up?

5. What are the potential implications to the shelter if it continues to ignore its health and safety obligations?

FURTHER READING

Duncan, M, Cahill, F and Heighway, P (2006) *Health and Safety at Work Essentials*, 5th edn, Law Pack.

Health and Safety Executive (2006) *The Essentials of Health and Safety at Work*, 4th edn, HSE Books.

REFERENCES

Bird, FE and Loftus, RG (1976) *Loss Control Management*, Institute Press.

Chartered Institute of Personnel and Development (2006) *Stress at Work*, CIPD factsheet, available online at www.cipd.co.uk.

Health and Safety Commission (2006) Health and Safety Statistics, Office for National Statistics.

Health and Safety Executive (1995) *A Guide to the Reporting of Injuries, Diseases and Dangerous Occurrences Regulations (L73)*, HSE Books.

Health and Safety Executive (1999a) *An Introduction to Health and Safety (INDG259)*, HSE Books.

Health and Safety Executive (1999b) *Reducing Error and Influencing Behaviour (HSG48)*, HSE Books.

Health and Safety Executive (2001) *A Guide to Measuring Health and Safety Performance (HSG65)*, HSE Books.

Health and Safety Executive (2003) *Accident Book (BI510)*, HSE Books.

Health and Safety Executive (2004) *Investigating Accidents and Incidents: A Workbook for Employers, Unions, Safety Representatives and Safety Professionals (HSG245)*, HSE Books.

Health and Safety Executive (2006) *Basic Advice on First Aid at Work (INDG347)*, HSE Books.

Heinrich, HW (1931) *Industrial Accident Prevention*, McGraw-Hill.

Hidden, A (1989) *Investigation into the Clapham Junction Railway Accident*, HMSO.

Krause, T (1997) *The Behaviour-Based Safety Process: Managing Involvement for an Injury-Free Culture*, 2nd edn, John Wiley and Sons.

People Management (2006) 'Tesco staff put their backs into HSE push', 26 October, p 14.

Stranks, J (2006) *The Manager's Guide to Health and Safety at Work*, 8th edn, Kogan Page.

8 International Human Resource Management

Introduction

International HRM (IHRM) is a field of growing importance in the human resources arena, and there is a growing number of UK organizations that operate in more than one country. The emphasis on maximizing performance by treating resources as global, rather than country-specific, applies increasingly to human resources, and this perspective informs how they are employed and managed. With the onset of more cost-effective transport systems and swifter, more effective, methods of communication, organizations that previously operated in a number of countries, but with each country being responsible only for local sourcing and the supply of products and services to markets in its own country, are now seeing the benefits of global sourcing and supply. Equally, economic expansion, particularly in China and India, and the forecast for higher growth rates overseas has led many organizations to the conclusion that they need to have the organizational capability to operate in these countries and across national borders, in order to benefit from this predicted growth.

To be a truly global organization, it is not sufficient simply to operate in a number of countries. The global organization has the capability of operating and managing at a level at which service to its customers is not restricted by local geographies. Products and services can be sourced from the optimum location, and price and quality, rather than national identity, become critical business criteria. The search for raw materials to fuel world economic growth, and the search for markets for goods and services as this growth creates new wealth and greater demand, are having a profound effect on the way in which senior executives think about business. Success in this global arena is a function of a number of key factors, but the ability to generate and sustain the organizational capability to operate in these markets is absolutely critical. The human resource is an integral component of the competitive organizational capability that global companies need to maintain their international presence (Hira and Hira, 2005).

Few, if any, HR practitioners are now immune from the effects of globalization and the internationalization of business, and the aim of this chapter is to explain what are the implications of this inexorable trend for those with specific responsibilities for managing people. But, before we outline those areas of HR that have been influenced either directly or indirectly by the opening up of borders and the increasingly free movement of goods, services and people, it is worth remembering that this is not a new, or indeed recent, phenomenon. The pace of change has undeniably increased over the past twenty years – but remember our reference in Chapter 1 to the building of the Pyramids: it is unlikely that many of the workers used in their construction came from outside the borders of Egypt, but for certain of the more skilled trades, workers may well have been brought from other parts of the Middle East. This is a view that accords with the research of David (1997), who, based on the evidence of ancient artefacts in the building area, argued that:

> **The workforce at the town may therefore have included elements from a number of countries, as well as native-born Egyptians.**
> (p 249)

The construction of Britain's canal and rail networks in the eighteenth and nineteenth centuries certainly depended heavily on 'foreign' labour, in the form of Irish 'navvies'. Before this, the forced migration of the French Huguenots into England in the sixteenth and seventeenth centuries represented a major source of skilled labour, expertise and know-how that transformed the country's cloth industry. More recently, in the nineteenth century, the expansion of the British Empire was dependent on engineers, traders and others living and working overseas. In the twentieth century, immigrants from the West Indies and the Asian subcontinent provided a much-needed source of labour for the UK's textile and steel industries. The point is that flows of labour into the UK, doing business abroad, and the employment of UK technical experts and managers on overseas contracts, are not new ideas; what *is* new is the scale and complexity of these developments, and their implications for the HR practitioner.

In the context of an introductory text, it is not practical to try to cover all aspects of IHRM and, for the purposes of this chapter, the following are the areas to which we will pay particular attention:

- the employment of overseas workers in the UK;
- the use of UK expatriate staff to work on overseas projects;
- the cultural issues related to establishing overseas businesses and outsourcing the production of goods and services;
- employing and managing a diverse workforce;
- competences of the IHRM manager.

International HRM

International HRM, as an area of academic study, followed the emergence of HRM, but shares the same strategic focus and emphasis on vertical and horizontal integration. Its antecedents lay in the comparative study of industrial relations, which focused on national differences in employment and managerial practices, the collective organization of labour and conflict resolution mechanisms (Ferner and Hyman, 1998). It has, however, evolved into a distinctive, and increasingly recognized, subject in its own right, as the implications of globalization and international business have impacted on the use of human resources and the role of the HR professional (Scullion and Linehan, 2005; Edwards and Rees, 2006).

As far as IHRM is concerned, academics have tended to adopt one of two approaches.

- It is seen as essentially HRM 'writ large', and associated with a domestic and national agenda transferred and relocated into an international arena.

  A definition that fits this approach is given by Scullion (1995), who claimed that IHRM could be understood as:

  > ... the HRM strategies, policies and practices which firms pursue in response to the internationalization of business.

  This approach gives particular emphasis to the international context and transnational requirements associated with such activities as:

  - recruitment and selection;
  - performance and reward strategies;
  - the management and control of diverse workforces.

- It is viewed in a more strategic sense, in ways that mirror the HRM/SHRM debate, and highlights the importance of leveraging maximum contributions from an organization's global human resources in the pursuit of competitive advantage. Seen in this way, IHRM encompasses the above three sets of activities, but additionally involves:

  - facilitating organizational learning and knowledge management across borders and between internationally dispersed operating units (Glaister et al, 2003);
  - the internationalization of management throughout the organization, reflecting its global presence and operations;
  - the internationalization of organizational culture to reflect multiple dimensions of diversity.

From the perspective of the HR practitioner, the internationalization of business has had the effect of adding new responsibilities to those previously restricted to a regional and national perspective, such as the employment and management of expatriate workers and 'foreign' nationals. It has also created new levels of complexity and challenge, resulting from organizations extending their operations internationally and, as a consequence, having to come to terms with the implications of different cultures, business environments and legal systems.

Harris et al (2001), in their study of the implications of globalization on HR, capture the essence of these challenges when they argue that:

Whilst managers in organisations working in a single-country environment are still subject to the twists and turns of external events, the manager working in an international environment must try to assess the impact of multi-country, regional and global trends. Hardly surprising, choices in this context become complex and ambiguous.

They suggest that a domestically based company developing an international dimension will need to think carefully about:

● the kind of HR strategy that will facilitate the transition and operation as an international organization;

● the implications of such a transition for the kind of managers the organization requires and the competences they will need to be effective in a different context;

● whether it will be appropriate to develop a standardized set of employment policies and practices, or to allow flexibility and variability to reflect local and regional differences;

● strategies for resourcing, rewarding and managing the performance of employees;

● employee recognition and representational issues.

The first HRM Insight in this chapter offers a view of the complications and difficulties that companies can face as a result of 'going international' – difficulties the HR practitioner is likely to have to resolve.

HRM INSIGHT 8.1 TNN International

TNN International is a UK-based global manufacturer and supplier of air-conditioning systems. Due to predicted expansion in overseas markets, TNN would like to appoint a sales manager to manage South American operations and to coordinate the activities of a potentially growing team of sales representatives based in Mexico. This position has been advertised internally. Applicants include an expatriate British sales representative, who is employed on a considerably more generous package than are the other candidates due to his expatriate status and who was involved in the start-up of the South American operation because of personal contacts with local agents. There are two Mexican applicants, both of whom joined the operation from a competitor, and both have had a significant influence in growing sales. Finally, there is a female sales representative, currently based in South Africa, who has been extremely successful in developing this market and, for family reasons, is looking to move to Mexico.

The successful candidate will be responsible for managing the remaining team members who have, to date, reported to the international business manager in the UK. You have heard unofficially from other international sales agents that the expatriate British worker is adamant that he will not work for a Mexican because this will affect his credibility with his customers. You have also independently heard that the two Mexican male candidates have expressed a determination to not work for a woman for 'cultural' reasons, stating that the Mexican customers will not accept working with a female manager. The UK business has a clear fair employment policy that it extends to all of its international businesses.

Questions

1. How should the informal complaints of the expatriate British worker and the two Mexican workers be addressed prior to the selection process?

2. What selection methods might be used to establish a fair basis for making the recruitment decision?

3. What action might need to be taken after the conclusion of the selection process?

But international companies, particularly those that are relatively new and are in the fast-moving IT sector, face a much wider range of HR challenges that go well beyond those associated with overseas recruitment. Many have relatively undeveloped HR functions and little in the way of strategies that address the kind of questions that Harris et al (2001) suggest are associated with the 'road to internationalization', which is often driven by the attractiveness of favourable tax environments, and of educated and skilled labour forces.

Such companies often experience rapid growth, linked to technological advantages and market demand, but sometimes in the absence of anything other than the most basic HR activities, such as recruitment and selection, and payroll. The need to develop a more effective HR function, linking its operation explicitly to an HR strategy for the business, is likely to be recognized, at some point, as a necessary development in building the organization's capability to sustain its growth and expansion.

Interestingly, many of the HR challenges and problems that these companies face when they become 'international' and seek to build for future expansion are similar to those faced by organizations operating only in a domestic context. There are, however, important differences to do with managing change, creating consistency and uniformity of practice, and challenging entrenched perceptions about gender, culture and contribution. HRM Insight 8.2 tells the story of the difficulties that one HR professional encountered in introducing an HR department into an environment that had previously operated without one.

HRM INSIGHT 8.2 Developing the HR function in an international company

The following case study illustrates the challenges, and some of the key issues, facing the HR manager in a French-owned electronics company operating in Ireland. The case concentrates on the experiences of establishing HR in an environment that had not previously had a centralized HR function and the difficulties of implementing agreed HR policy in the face of managerial inertia and resistance.

Jean LeFebre, an innovative entrepreneur who understood the fast-changing electronics industry and recognized the potential that leading-edge technologies offered in the rapidly growing telecommunications sector, established International Electronics in France in 1986. Despite some initial problems, the company grew from a €20m company in 1995 to a company with a turnover of €350m ten years later.

As the company increased its production and turnover, the strategic decision was taken to establish a manufacturing plant in Ireland; its Cork factory was established in 1995. Because of its success and the favourable economic environment in Ireland, Cork became the predominant manufacturing site for the company's complete product range. The company does, however, have distribution and research and development (R & D) facilities, along with software engineering sites, in Germany, Sweden, Hong Kong and Japan. It recently opened a manufacturing site in China, but this only supplies the local Asian market. In terms of its general HR approach, the company has slightly different policies to reflect differences in local legislation but, overall, has a set of corporate policies and practices to which it expects all of its subunits to adhere.

From its inception, the company coped with its rapid growth, an ever-changing environment, and the difficulties associated with managing the company on a global basis without an HR function, but in 1995, the decision was taken that things had to change and an HR director was appointed. The HR director was based in France, where the head office was located, with a brief to introduce formalized systems and procedures into the company. As a result of her appointment, Catherine Dupre oversaw the recruitment of several key managerial personnel, one being the head of human resources in Cork. The appointee, Ciara O'Sullivan, who qualified as an accountant before moving into HR, began work in January 2006 when the headcount stood at 180.

As the only female in the eight-strong management team, Ciara was faced with a number of important questions: where to start; what to do first; how to begin the contribution of the HR function to the company's operational and strategic objectives. It soon became apparent that her first priorities were to find out what policies were in place, who was responsible for what and whether any procedures had been established to support these practices.

One of her first tasks was to conduct an audit of the organization from a HR perspective. This involved one-to-one meetings with colleagues on the senior management team to establish their levels of need in areas such as recruitment and selection, induction, the socialization of new employees, contracts of employment and general administration, training and development methods and records, and, finally, performance management and appraisal.

As it transpired, this was only the tip of the iceberg. As well as dealing with all of the above, Ciara experienced a significant degree of negativity towards the HR function that was, in certain respects, more difficult to deal with than some of the more straightforward matters. As she remarked:

While most would see this function as necessary and indeed useful, some find it the complete opposite: literally a thorn in the side of progress.

In trying to introduce change, she was constantly confronted with the phrase 'but this is the way it's always been done', and began to wonder what it was about change and the introduction of new processes that upset a small minority of individuals. One explanation was that they felt threatened by the introduction of some form of control or that they would have to conform to the same standards as the rest of the employees. Whatever the case, their initial reaction was a defence of the status quo.

One event that captured the difficulties facing Ciara was the need to shed a small number of temporary workers, due to a short-term downturn in business predicted to last four weeks. The management team had agreed the need for this and the situation was not unusual for those workers who were employed on a contingent basis. The key decision, however, was which employees should be let go? Although not, in itself, a difficult question to answer, it led to a great deal of discussion and disagreement.

One suggestion was that the LIFO ('last in, first out') method should be used because it was a practice that had been used in the past, although not very successfully. The problem was complicated because Ciara had, in the preceding period, implemented an intensive recruitment drive to find suitable, flexible and adaptable employees for one particular area of the factory. Having heavily invested in this process, and having spent valuable resources on medical examinations and training, she felt that the application of the LIFO criteria was not in the best interest of the company. She preferred to use the criterion of functionality, which meant that employees would be chosen on the basis of their role and value to the company.

One part of the plant was chronically overstaffed and had a surplus of staff working on contingent contracts. It seemed obvious to Ciara that the small number who needed to be let go could be selected from this group, but this suggestion was immediately rejected by the relevant manager, who told Ciara (politely) to mind her own business and 'stop interfering in things [she knew] nothing about'.

The manager in question, in defence of the LIFO approach, argued:

> This is the way it's always been done. Why fix it, if it isn't broken?

Tensions arose between Ciara and several of the management team over the way in which to handle the situation and, the longer the impasse continued, the more the company was haemorrhaging valuable resources in the form of higher wage costs and unproductive workers. She decided to pick up the phone and talk to the managing director about the problem and, if necessary, involve the HR director. Politically, however, this was not without its problems because, while the group HR director had overall responsibility for employment matters, she left the Cork site very much in the hands of Ciara.

Questions

1. Why is Ireland such a popular location for international manufacturing companies? What are the distinctive features of the Irish labour market that attract overseas investments?

2. Why did the company feel it was necessary to establish a centralized HR function in 1995 and what challenges did the HR director face in establishing the function?

3. What support might Ciara have expected from the HR director and managing director in her efforts to get HR embedded in the Cork plant?

4. What action might Ciara have taken to overcome the resistance to change generally and the employment problem specifically?

5. Should she have involved senior managers from headquarters? If yes, in what capacity and what might the consequences have been?

Insights & Outcomes: visit the Online Resource Centre at www.oxfordtextbooks.co.uk/ orc/banfield_kay/ for an explanation of how the issues confronting the HR manager were resolved.

Globalization

The internationalization of management has, for some, become an expression of what has become known as 'globalization' (Edwards and Rees, 2006). Accepting that there is an ongoing debate about what this actually means, Edwards and Rees believe that, as far as IHRM is concerned, the most important aspects of globalization are:

- *global production*, meaning that transnational corporations produce, distribute, and sell goods and services around the world;

- *global organizations*, for which the ability to resource and manage global production systems impacts directly on HR and management, both of which have to come to terms with social and cultural differences.

Each of these is facilitated by the growth in global financial systems and the expansion of global communications networks.

Globalization is also associated with the rapid, and relatively recent, development of a 'global economy'. What this means is that national economic and social identities and differences are becoming less distinctive, and arguably more irrelevant, as market forces and free trade move national economies and economic organizations towards a more convergent and universalistic state (Edwards and Rees, 2006, p 6). While the effects of globalization are clearly accelerating, including the ideas of systems of finance, production and trade that are 'without boundary', care must be taken not to overstate the effects that this has on national employment systems, and on the social and cultural differences that not only exist between national economies, but within them.

Thinking about the debate on globalization and the impact that this is having on HR, what does it actually mean for the HR practitioner in terms of his or her work? Without representing an exhaustive list, the following represent situations that are related to the growth of transnational corporations and a converging global economic system.

- More people are working for transnationals in an HR capacity. Increasing numbers of newly qualified and experienced HR practitioners are employed by 'global' enterprises, such as Gazprom (the Russian gas supplier), or work for overseas companies that set up UK or Irish subsidiaries. These new employment contexts raise interesting questions about the way in which social and cultural differences are managed within the workplace and the status that HR enjoys within these organizations. A particularly important issue here relates to gender and the extent to which females working for overseas companies face problems of acceptance and discrimination (Wirth, 2002).

> Signpost to Chapter 6: Equality in Employment, for examples of discriminatory employment practices

- UK-based organizations are, because of inward migration and a more diverse indigenous workforce, employing more people from diverse social, cultural and religious backgrounds. Managing diversity has become less of an aspiration for those organizations seeking to adjust to demographic change and more of a reality. The CIPD reports that one in three UK employers are actively recruiting migrant workers to work in such diverse industries as the NHS, agriculture, food processing and hospitality, and the implications for recruitment and selection, and induction practices, as well as for communications, welfare and training, are obvious.

- Increasingly, HR practitioners, particularly more senior ones, have to undertake overseas assignments or secondments, or are responsible for organizing the expatriation and repatriation of other managers.

- HR professionals are developing new approaches to individual and organizational learning, and generating knowledge-sharing networks that connect to the different parts of the transnational/global organization.

- HR professionals in global organizations are also developing ways of communicating with people in different parts of the world, and building the capability to track and monitor employment numbers, costs, and the outcome of management development programmes across national boundaries.

Figure 8.1 presents the different challenges and responsibilities facing the international HR manager at the strategic level.

International transactions and administration

- Pay and conditions
- Legal issues
- Recruitment and selection
- Induction
- Database maintenance
- Managing expatriation and repatriation

Building capability and resource development

- Fast-tracking and developing managers
- Career and succession planning
- Developing knowledge management systems
- IT-driven learning

Business-driven activities

- Reorganization
- Efficiency drives
- Supporting overseas start-ups, e.g. new factories etc.
- Outsourcing, e.g. overseas call centres

Developing and implementing strategy

- Strategic HR planning
- Performance and reward management
- Managing closures, acquisitions and mergers
- Culture building

Figure 8.1 The four dimensions of the international HR manager's role and contribution

The international HR manager and culture

KEY CONCEPT Culture

Culture, as a force and a phenomenon, exists within professions, religions, organizations and geographical regions. Our interest is primarily in national cultures. 'Culture' can be understood as the shared beliefs, values and understandings that define and distinguish one group from another. It is what Hofstede and Hofstede (2004) call 'the collective programming of the mind'. The culture with which people identify influences and shapes their behaviour in relation to their environment. Cultural clashes exist if people are exposed to different belief and value systems, but fail to learn to adapt to such differences. From an IHRM perspective, the inability to understand and manage culture and cultural differences is often the reason why expatriate assignments fail, and why some immigrants and migrant workers in the UK find difficulty in assimilating into the British way of life.

Despite the feeling that globalization and the convergence of economic systems is reducing national differences, it would be wrong to ignore the continued existence of cultural differences between nations – differences that impact both directly and indirectly on the employment and management of people. At one level, such differences manifest themselves in restrictions: for example, on the employment of women and the types of work they are allowed to do. While the emancipation of women in Western societies has resulted in very high labour market participation rates and increasing female representation across occupational boundaries, in other societies, there remain significant cultural and legal restrictions on what women are allowed to do and be.

Less obvious cultural differences restrict, or make it socially unacceptable to engage in, certain behaviours that might be taken for granted in other cultures. For example, in certain countries/organizations, the status and position of people in the organizational hierarchy carries far more formal importance than it would in other national contexts, creating a strong sense of deference from those of lower status and in subordinate positions. In itself, the reluctance on the part of those lower down the hierarchy to question those in more senior positions may not be a problem, but it will affect the ability of the organization to introduce more egalitarian and democratic practices, such as 360-degree appraisal systems and open discussion forums. Cultural sensitivity and the ability to manage in situations of cultural difference, and indeed of cultural conflict, consequently becomes an important requirement for the manager with international HR responsibilities.

National cultures are important because they help people to understand:

- what they are and how they fit into society;
- how they relate to each other;
- what social conventions are important and why;
- how they perceive work and what it means in the broader context of their lives;
- the importance of time and the significance of space in relation to personal and professional relationships.

Successfully working across cultural boundaries is often associated with the person moving into, and feeling comfortable within, a different cultural environment. This inevitably involves being prepared to learn new social and business conventions, and to adjust psychologically to different values and cultural norms. The corollary of this is equally valid: the inability to cope with cultural difference is associated with ineffective performance and failed overseas assignments, secondments and postings. As Hofstede (2004) points out:

> **Culture is more often a source of conflict than of synergy. Cultural differences are a nuisance at best and often a disaster.**
> (See www.geert-hofstede.com.)

Hofstede's work has been particularly influential in identifying national cultural identities and the differences in the ways in which people behave and organizations function. As a result of his research, he found that nationality affected many cultural assumptions and business practices, with the key cultural differences being explained by the following five variables.

- Power distance

  This refers to the degree to which members of a society or organization accept and expect that power is distributed unequally. This dimension also represents the degree of inequality that exists within social institutions and, while all societies reflect differences in the distribution of power and the resulting pattern of inequality, some are more unequal than others.

- Individualism

  This represents the degree to which people identify themselves as individuals or as members of a social group (or 'collectivity'). In certain Western societies, social ties are loose and the interests of the individual are given primacy; in other societies, such as that of Japan, there is a strong collectivist ethic and group identity. This might mean, as a generalization, that effective team/group working is more difficult to achieve in the USA than it is in Japan, or at least in Japanese companies that reflect Japanese cultural work practices. Equally, Japanese culture might inhibit individuality and creativity.

- Masculinity/femininity

  This concept refers to the distribution of roles and relationships between genders. In different cultures, men are characterized, to varying degrees, by a tendency to be assertive and competitive, while women are regarded as caring and modest. Women working in cultures that are closer to the masculinity pole have a tendency to 'behave like men', i.e. they become competitive and assertive, believing that becoming 'more like men' is necessary to achieve personal and professional recognition and success.

● Uncertainty avoidance

Uncertainty avoidance represents the extent to which a society exhibits a tolerance for uncertainty and ambiguity. On an individual level, it helps to predict how well a person from a culture that has a low tolerance of uncertainty and ambiguity would cope if, for example, he or she were to work in an organization within which uncertainty and ambiguity were frequently experienced. Uncertainty-avoiding cultures try to minimize the possibility of the 'unknown' by developing strict laws and rules, and by adhering to philosophical and religious teachings that produce a greater number of social 'absolutes'. People who live and work in uncertainty accepting cultures are more tolerant of different opinions, rely on fewer rules, and adopt a more questioning and relativist approach.

● Long-term versus short-term orientation

This describes the 'time horizon' of a society or organization, or the importance that it attaches to the future as compared to the past and present. From the point of view of working and doing business in different cultures, knowing where they score in this dimension can be very important because it can help managers to appreciate the time needed to build relationships, to become accepted and to be trusted. Eastern nations tend to score especially high on this dimension, while Western nations score low and developing nations very low (high, in this sense, meaning a long time horizon).

STUDENT ACTIVITY 8.1 Reflecting on cultural experiences

This is an exercise that can be done in seminar groups and can result in a presentation, or more informally and based on individual reflection. Each approach will depend on an ability to reflect on experiences of cultural difference and to make sense of these.

1. Share stories of overseas travel or working that has involved experiencing different cultural situations.
2. Think of the most powerful or difficult problem that you have experienced or had to deal with while overseas and share this with the group.
3. Explain what effect this had on you and how you dealt with it.
4. As a group, discuss the implications of these cultural experiences in relation to working abroad and the support that HR professionals might need to provide for those working in different cultural environments.

Culture shock

'Culture shock' is a term used to describe the anxiety and feelings of surprise, disorientation and confusion felt when people have to operate within a different culture or social environment. It is often the outcome of the negative experience of moving from a familiar culture to one that is unfamiliar. But it is not simply the effect of the new that is potentially destabilizing: it is also linked to the shock and discomfort of being separated from family, friends and the other things that matter in a person's life, such as church, social club, pub and local shops.

For many people, the experience of moving to a different cultural environment, without the benefit of any acculturation experiences, can be expressed in terms of four stages. Not everyone passes through all of the phases, of course; much depends on the individual, their duration in the new location and whether the move involves an individual or group.

1. The 'honeymoon' phase

This is not always experienced and depends on the nature of the new location, but when everything new seems to be 'different and better', those affected may experience a temporary sense of pleasure.

2. **The 'distress' phase**

At this point, which may occur after a few days, weeks or even months, new things are seen in a different light and begin to be compared unfavourably with those 'at home'. Small irritations become exaggerated, and feelings of loss and loneliness can develop.

3. **The 'autonomy and independence' phase**

After a period of time, people become more confident in, and familiar with, their 'new' environment. They have, either consciously or subconsciously, engaged in a social learning process, which changes their perceptions of their new environment from being different to being normal. Entering this phase also implies a degree of social integration, as opposed to social and psychological isolation.

4. **The 'reverse culture shock' phase**

Perhaps the most well-known example of this phase is that of soldiers coming home after time spent in a war zone: coming to terms with the very different conditions and relationships in a peacetime environment can produce very serious and lasting psychological effects. Although not as intense as those of soldiers, the experiences of expatriates and their families returning to the UK after a two- or three-year secondment or assignment abroad can involve similar psychological stresses and difficulties of adjustment (Gunn, 2003).

For a detailed analysis of the issues and of the challenges involved in the repatriation of managers returning to their country of origin after an overseas assignment, see Scullion and Linehan (2005).

HRM Insight 8.3 illustrates the problems associated with overseas secondment, for which family considerations need to be taken into account, and is a good example of the challenges facing those in HR.

HRM INSIGHT 8.3 Virginia Power Tools

Virginia Power Tools is a large multinational company quoted on the New York Stock Exchange. It manufactures and sells high-precision power tools to the automotive industry worldwide. The resignation of the managing director of the UK arm of the business, who has been headhunted by a competitor company, has prompted Virginia to place the executive immediately on garden leave for the duration of his notice, pending negotiations over his departure, because Virginia is concerned about conflicting interests. Virginia estimates that it may take up to 12 months to select and recruit a replacement, and the company has therefore decided to second an existing US employee, Bob Homer, vice president of a similar-sized operation in the USA, to the UK. He will both run operations and lead the recruitment of a replacement.

While it is anticipated that this secondment will initially last for 12 months, there is a possibility that the company's commitment to acquire businesses overseas as part of its global expansion programme may result in further UK-based assignments for Bob. Bob is married with two children, aged three and six years.

Questions

1. What alternatives, in terms of benefits and support, might form part of the package to encourage Bob to move to the UK?

2. What arrangements might need to be considered to support Bob's family?

3. What arrangements will the UK HR team need to put in place to enable Bob to be employed in the UK?

4. Is there a case to use external specialist companies to provide support for Bob and his family? If so, what might this involve?

International workers

Increasing numbers of HR practitioners and non-specialist managers in companies that 'do business overseas' have responsibilities for employees who are located abroad or who are expected to make frequent trips abroad. Such workers may be categorized as follows:

- international commuters;
- contract expatriates;
- employees used on long-term business trips;
- assignees on short-term or medium-term business trips;
- cadres of global managers;
- international transferees (from one subsidiary to another);
- 'self-initiated movers' (SIMs), who live and work away from their home country;
- mobile and project-based workers;
- domestically based employees dealing with international suppliers and/or clients;
- immigrants attracted to the UK labour market;
- temporary migrant workers employed on seasonal and fixed-term contracts;
- illegal immigrants, who are not working legally or officially, but are economically active in the 'black economy'.

International management competences

Understanding the cultural and business environments in which international managers have to operate and the potential difficulties associated with the repatriation process helps HR staff in the decisions they have to make in the recruitment, selection and development of these managers. Key to the successful management of these processes is the ability to identify the key skills and competences that those working overseas need to possess. The case study at the end of the chapter provides insights into what these might be, but this is only one person's account of what major overseas assignments involve and it is important to look carefully at what research tells us about these competences. Moreover, how are these skills and competences actually acquired? Are the 'real' challenges of HR in the areas of assessment and selection, or in designing learning experiences that build on what these managers already know and can do?

One of the most interesting findings from recent research into the recruitment and selection of international managers, and one that confirms a view expressed elsewhere in this book, is provided by Paul Sparrow (2006). As a result of his work, commissioned by the CIPD, he found that:

> **The majority of expatriate skills are learnt through experience – they learn how to manage across cultures in most instances without education in cross-cultural skills.**
> **(p 7)**

This suggests that the key HR decision is taken at the assessment and selection stage, at which point evidence of the ability to learn from experience and to be able to cope with potentially stressful environments becomes an important differentiator.

The report identified the following characteristics as being associated with the successful expatriate manager.

● Professional and technical competence, and experience on the job

This area also included general maturity, knowledge of the company and experience of performing the job in the 'home' organization.

● Personality traits and relational abilities

Included under this head are also important communication skills, but not only those involving language ability. The category also relates to personal maturity, tolerance, respect for the host country and adaptability.

● Perceptual dimensions and life strategies

This area relates to, among other things, the ability to learn from experiences, and the avoidance of being judgemental and evaluative in relation to different social values and social conventions. In other words, it relates to avoiding an ethnocentric stance.

● Self-maintenance factors

These characteristics relate to the ability to function independently, to cope with stress and pressure, and to exhibit confidence in carrying out specific tasks.

● Leadership and motivational factors

This final area of competency relates to the development of relationships, the use of initiative and the ability to take appropriate action, and a general interest in working overseas.

The outcome of Sparrow's research into relevant managerial competences is certainly consistent with the personal account of Chris Atkin, and with other individuals' 'stories' of what working overseas involves and the demands such work makes of managers who have to carry out important duties in an often unusual and demanding environment. Based on his work, Sparrow offers an interesting and useful competency framework, which rests on the three fundamental attributes that those working overseas need to have: emotional stability; confidence and relationship building; openness to different experiences. This framework is presented in Figure 8.2.

STUDENT ACTIVITY 8.2 **Designing an assessment centre for managers working on international assignments**

This is a demanding activity that requires careful planning and preparation. It is also one that needs to be done collaboratively. Groups can set their own parameters on the scale and level of sophistication of the exercise, and can add detail to the context. To give the exercise extra realism, your tutor might play the role of the managing director and give you feedback on your proposals.

You are a team of HR practitioners working for a global engineering company, with manufacturing and distribution centres in India, China and Japan. Currently, these centres are managed by local staff, who report directly to the UK-based head of overseas production. Because of continuing expansion of the centres and the building of an additional unit in Malaysia, the managing director has decided that the current reporting lines are no longer appropriate. He has decided to create the new position of managing director for Asia, with executive responsibilities for all of the company's business in that region. The appointee would report directly to the UK-based MD. Your job is to provide the MD with a shortlist of three candidates from which he will make the final choice.

He wants to be kept informed of developments on this new appointment and wants you to report back to him with answers to the following questions.

1. What is your recruitment strategy?

2. What is your person specification?

3. What activities will you use in the assessment centre? He also wants to know how this will operate.

4. What will be the main criteria for deciding on who is to be included in the final shortlist?

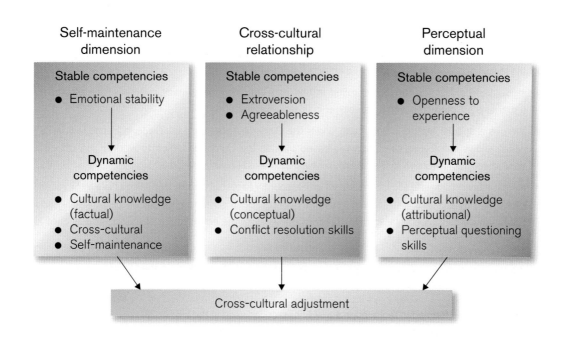

Figure 8.2 A competency model for overseas working

Source: This material is taken from *International Recruitment, Selection and Assessment* (PR Sparrow) (2006), with the permission of the publisher, the Chartered Institute of Personnel and Development, London.

Working legally in the UK

203

Increasingly, IHRM is as much about employing overseas workers as it is about preparing, rewarding and developing UK managers who work abroad, and recent evidence suggests that the number of overseas workers in the UK is increasing. According to *People Management*, nearly half of employers in London now rely on migrant workers to plug skills gaps that exist in the indigenous workforce, with 48 per cent of employers surveyed stating that they are reliant on staff from other EU countries and 37 per cent dependent on non-EU workers (*People Management*, 2006).

With the opening up of borders and more liberal government policies on immigration and migrant workers, international HRM is increasingly being experienced as part of the domestic HR context; it is definitely not something that only exists outside the UK. This means that, in addition to taking responsibility for facilitating people working outside of the UK, HR is facing growing demands associated with the employment of 'foreign' labour at home. Many of the issues relating to the recruitment and employment of overseas workers involve establishing the legal and employment status of non-UK workers. Failure to conform to the ever-changing laws and regulations that determine who can and who cannot work in the UK can result in criminal prosecutions if employers are found to be employing people who do not have the right to be in the country or to work here.

Anyone holding an EU passport has the right to work in the UK and anywhere else in the EU, unless there are specific country restrictions that affect new member States. Most people who are not EU passport holders need a work permit to work legally. The six forms of work permits currently available relate to situations in which:

- business and commercial considerations are such that an employer in this country is unable to fill a vacancy by recruiting a 'resident worker' and therefore applies for a permit to appoint a candidate who originates from a non-EU country, who is not otherwise eligible to work in the UK;

- overseas workers join a specific training and work experience scheme, which relates to a professional or specialist qualification, or period of work experience;

- those involved work in the sports and entertainment industries;

- students from outside the EU, enrolled in first or higher degree courses overseas, are allowed to undertake an internship with an employer in this country;

- there is a special arrangement, made under the General Agreement on Trade in Services (GATS), which allows employees of companies based outside the European Union to work in the UK on a service contract awarded to their employer by a UK-based organization;

- a sector-based scheme allows employers in this country to recruit people from elsewhere to fill vacancies that they are unable to fill with 'resident workers'. Such schemes operate in the hospitality and food manufacturing sectors, and would, for example, allow the employment of a Bangladeshi chef to work in an 'Indian' restaurant.

There are also many situations in which overseas workers can legally work in the UK without having to possess a work permit. Examples include:

- those receiving training in techniques and work practices used in the UK;

- those coming to the UK to set up a new business, or to take over or join an existing business as a partner or director, or as a sole trader;

- ministers of religion, missionaries and members of religious orders;

- seasonal workers at agricultural camps under approved schemes;

- doctors, dentists and general practitioners in postgraduate training.

What complicates matters further is that some people who seem to meet one of the above criteria may still need a work permit and/or a visa, and that, because these schemes are subject to change, it is important to check with official sources of information to be absolutely clear about what is, or is not, needed for any particular person to work legally in the UK (see www.workingintheuk.gov.uk).

In addition to the employment of EU passport holders and non-EU citizens under one of the six work permit schemes, UK companies can employ overseas workers on the basis of what is called the Highly Skilled Migrant Programme (HSMP). This is a scheme that allows people to migrate into the UK to look for work or self-employment opportunities, and is based on a points system using the following criteria:

- educational qualifications;

- work experience;

- past earnings;

- achievement in the chosen field;

- achievements of spouse or partner.

For a detailed description of the regulations and procedures associated with overseas workers being employed in the UK, see also www.workpermit.com.

Of importance to HR professionals involved in employing overseas workers is the view, held by a leading expert on the employment of migrant workers, that recruiting non-UK staff is more complicated and demanding than employing UK workers, and needs careful thought if costly mistakes are to be avoided and if the potential gains from such employment are to be realized (Davison, 2005). Davison recommends that employers need to undertake the following.

- Understand the candidate

  This means being sensitive to his or her reasons for wishing to work in the UK, his or her expectations in terms of the job and pay, and his or her cultural background.

- Select the recruitment agency with care

  If an employer is not recruiting directly – and this is probably the situation that many are in – it is important to ensure that agencies providing workers are reputable, have established networks in the sourcing country and have built a positive reputation for standards and reliability.

- Provide support

  Managerial and professional support is necessary for all workers, but it is particularly important for migrant workers. Support may extend to helping the worker to find accommodation, and helping the worker to adjust to new working environments and relationships.

- Be sure about the legal basis of employment

  As explained above, the need to establish the legal entitlement to work in the UK is vital, as is the completion of all supportive documentation and procedural regulation, to ensure complete conformity with UK rules and requirements.

- Consider the language issue

  If language competency is important in performing the job successfully (for example, if migrant workers are in regular contact with customers or if they need to read and understand health and safety information), employers may need to consider the provision of language training. Employers must at least identify language problems and take appropriate action to resolve them.

- Remember to think about their existing employees

  Failing to recognize the genuine concerns of existing staff, while appearing only to be interested in the well being of migrant workers, will be considered to be a serious managerial failing – one, moreover, that can have serious consequences for the organization overall. Whether valid or not, worries over job security and pay levels are often expressed by the existing workforce when their employer begins to recruit people from low wage economies, and these concerns need to be addressed by management. The quality of existing employee–management relationships and the frequency of communications between the two parties are likely to be important factors in influencing how effectively concerns expressed by existing workers are dealt with.

205

Summary

Diversity in employment is not only being driven by the ethnic, age and gender differences within UK society, but by globalization, the internationalization of the labour force and economic migration. All of these are trends that are likely to continue. In Chapter 2, we explored the different historical influences that shaped the development of the specialized management function that become known as Personnel Management and then Human Resource Management, and identified the key influences of social and religious values, management theory, trade unionism and industrial conflict. Today, we can add further seminal influences on what HR is becoming and its agenda: internationalization and globalization. Workforce diversity is only one manifestation of this; others include managing expatriate workers and supporting their families, developing new management strategies for recruiting and developing in a global labour market, coping with cultural differences and complying with different employment regulations and traditions. At the same time, HR continues to be tasked with delivering administrative efficiency and providing operational support to managers, while not forgetting the importance of maintaining effective communications with staff, gaining employee commitment and providing a positive working environment.

The implications for HR of these challenges are profound, and are unlikely to be met unless organizations develop the 'right' level of HR capacity and capability to equip them to operate in this new, and more demanding, context. This may not involve employing more HR staff: interestingly, some of the organizations that have been in the forefront of developing new models of HR have employed outsourcing,

IT-enabled HR services and service flexibility to generate their status as truly international and global (examples being the Royal Bank of Scotland and Diageo).

It is not only the shape of the HR 'architecture' that changes: perhaps as significant are the implications for the HR professional. New, business-related skills are becoming increasing critical, both for personal and professional credibility, and for the function's standing with other stakeholders. New competences linked to operating and managing in an international context will be crucial in the development of new HR tools and interventions, such as those needed to facilitate learning and knowledge sharing within the international organization. And, as always, the ability to develop and relate HR strategies to operational performance will continue to be valued and expected from those in HR. Not only is HR being shaped by the forces of internationalization and globalization, so too is the profile of those who work in the function.

 Visit the Online Resource Centre that accompanies this book for self-test questions, weblinks, and more information on the topics covered in this chapter.
www.oxfordtextbooks.co.uk/orc/banfield_kay/

REVIEW QUESTIONS

1. How do cultural differences affect HR and the management of people?

2. Why do individuals and organizations have to become less ethnocentric and more polycentric when operating in an international context?

3. What key attributes and competences does the HR professional working for an international company need?

4. What is the link between diversity and internationalization?

CASE STUDY
Chris Atkin's story

The following is based on an interview with the subject.

Chris Atkin can be reliably described as an 'international manager', with over 39 years' experience of travelling and 'doing business', in Europe initially, then in the Middle and Far East, in South Africa and in Australasia. He might best be described as an 'international commuter', because his job as sales director for Dormer Tools meant that he was frequently away for up to four weeks at a time. Dormer Tools was a world-class producer of engineering cutting tools, used in almost all metal manufacturing processes. It sold a range of high-quality products through a network of international distributors and agents. Starting out as a management trainee, he spent the first five years with Dormer in manufacturing, and then moved into sales and marketing, after the managing director suggested that his outgoing personality might make him well suited to that function.

Early experiences of working in the Middle and Far East created an element of culture shock, when he was exposed to very different traditions, values and ways of working. It became clear to him that becoming culturally aware and sensitive was a precondition of building trust and mutual understanding with potential business partners and clients. Using Saudi Arabia as an example, it was clear that it was very much a 'man's world', certainly during the time he worked there, and there would be no contact or socialization with female family members. Of course, times change and, at the recent wedding of the daughter of one of his business associates in Dubai, around a hundred people attended, and although males and females dined separately, they all came together afterwards.

Reflecting on 'doing business abroad', Chris thought that the following were important points to remember.

● Don't make promises that can't be kept – people have long memories and, if you let them down, they will remember and refuse to do business with you again.

● Be aware of how business is conducted in different parts of the world – Saudis, for example, like to barter before agreeing a deal and the need for them to feel that they have achieved a good deal means that negotiating skills, and the ability to keep something in reserve as a concession, are important.

● Preserving a strong ethical stance in business dealings is important – realistically, in certain countries, potential customers will seek additional commissions or will link a sale directly to an 'illegal payment'. It is important, when negotiating contracts, to remember the long-term benefits to one's personal reputation and the safety of avoiding questionable business dealings.

One of the points that came over clearly in the interview was the need for UK managers working abroad to have certain competences, the most important for Chris being as follows.

● **The ability to work alone, along with personal endurance and resilience**

In the early period of his international role, there was little backup from the home company and telecommunications were far less developed than they are now. The ability to make business decisions in relative isolation was an important requirement.

● **Understanding the implications of 'getting business'**

This means thinking about whether the manufacturing plant's capacity to produce and deliver products in the quantities agreed and on time was an important requirement.

● **Problem solving and problem preventing**

This involves seeing beyond 'the deal' and taking a longer term, more holistic, perspective, as well as being able to resolve difficulties that might be preventing a deal from being concluded.

● **The ability to help customers to solve technical problems**

This means not only selling the cutting tools, but offering advice on the machines that will use them, helping with maintenance issues and advising on operative training.

● **Language and cultural understanding**

Learning the basics of Arabic, for example, was very helpful for the business side of his work, but also facilitated social interaction and personal acceptance.

Talking about the support he received from what was called 'personnel' in those days, Chris accepted that, in the 1970s and 1980s, the function in his company was not as developed and influential as it is now. Even so, he admitted that he never really understood what it was about! The people who worked in it always seemed busy, but were not business-orientated and lacked a real identity, although this changed under the influence of developments in HRM, with the HR manager now sitting in on commercial discussions with other senior managers. Chris' main recollections of his 'own HR people', however, was that they were 'a race apart', physically isolated from other management functions in the same building and only visible during a strike or the threat of industrial action.

The main 'HR' interventions with Chris were conducted by the managing director, rather than by HR staff, and involved annual appraisals, the setting of performance targets and the development of strategies for developing new markets. His advice to HR is to spend more time with the people who are working abroad, discover what they need to know and the support they require, and find out where they are going, so that intelligence can be gathered about these countries to help the managers to prepare for their assignments, particularly if families are also involved.

Finally, one particular experience that Chris had is worth recounting. Invited by an Saudi sheik to a traditional Bedouin feast, he was presented with a dish of rice that contained sheep's eyes – a delicacy in ➜

certain parts of Saudi Arabia. Knowing that, when offered one, he could not refuse to accept it because to do so would be construed as an insult to his hosts, he accepted it and a second when this, too, was offered. The experience wasn't particularly pleasant, but on the basis of understanding the importance of social etiquette, he built up a lifelong friendship with his host, who later presented him with a complete set of traditional Arabian clothing as a token of his respect, something that Chris experienced as a very humbling occasion.

Questions

1. With international secondments and overseas business travel now much more frequent than they used to be, what is the role of HR in supporting this?

2. What competences do HR staff need to have to be effective in preparing and supporting expatriates?

3. What can be done to avoid or limit the effect of culture shock?

4. Consider HR's role in developing an ethical code of practice for managers working and doing business abroad.

FURTHER READING

Chartered Institute of Personnel and Development (2005) *International Organisations: Assessing the Effectiveness of Their HR Function*, CIPD practical tool, available online to CIPD members at www.cipd.co.uk.

Hofstede, G (2001) *Culture's Consequences: Comparing Values, Behaviors, Institutions, and Organizations Across Nations*, Sage.

Ozbilgin, M (2005) *International Human Resource Management*, Palgrave MacMillan.

Perkins, SJ (2006) *International Reward and Recognition*, CIPD research report, summary available online at www.cipd.co.uk.

Trompenaars, F and Hampden Turner, C (1997) *Riding the Waves of Culture: Understanding Cultural Diversity in Business*, 2nd edn, Nicholas Brealey Publishing Ltd.

REFERENCES

David, R (1997) *The Pyramid Builders of Ancient Egypt: A Modern Investigation of Pharaoh's Workforce*, Routledge.

Davison, L (2005) 'How to recruit migrant workers', *People Management*, 1 September, p 50.

Edwards, T and Rees, C (2006) *International Human Resource Management*, FT/Prentice Hall.

Ferner, A and Hyman, R (1998) *Changing Industrial Relations in Europe*, Blackwell.

Glaister, KW, Husan, R and Buckley, PJ (2003) 'Learning to manage international joint ventures', *International Business Review*, 12:1, pp 83–108.

Gunn, N (2003) 'Repatriation the right way', *Expatica HR*, available online at www.expatica.com.

Harris, H, Brewster, C and Sparrow, P (2001) *Globalisation and HR*, CIPD.

Hira, R and Hira, J (2005) *Outsourcing America: What's Behind Our National Crisis and How We Can Reclaim American Jobs*, AMACOM.

Hosftede, G and Hofstede, GJ (2004) *Cultures and Organizations: Software of the Mind*, McGraw Hill.

People Management (2006) 'Migrants plug city skills gaps', 28 December, p 9.

Scullion, H (1995) 'International Human Resource Management', in J Storey (ed) *Human Resource Management: A Critical Text*, Routledge.

Scullion, H and Linehan, M (2005) *International Human Resource Management*, Palgrave, ch 7.

Sparrow, P (2006) *International Recruitment, Selection and Assessment*, CIPD research report, summary available online at www.cipd.co.uk.

Wirth, R (2002) *Breaking Through the Glass Ceiling: Women in Management*, Presentation at the First ILO International Conference on 'Pay Equity Between Women and Men: Myth or Reality'.

HRM Processes

3

HR Planning and Measurement

9

Key Terms

Planning Can be understood as a set of techniques, an approach and a mindset, all of which relate to achieving specified objectives. It should be understood as a process, rather than a time-constrained event.

Human resource planning (HRP) Originally known as 'manpower planning', this is concerned with planning and controlling the quantity and quality of labour available to an organization.

Metrics Relates to what and how something is measured. HR metrics focus on key aspects of the labour force, its behaviours, and its costs and contributions. The use of measures is increasingly associated with important features of the HR function, as part of the process of evaluating its efficiency and effectiveness.

Balanced scorecard A specific model for measuring business outcomes, devised by management theorists Kaplan and Norton, that allows managers to balance the financial perspective with those of the customer, internal processes, and innovation and learning. The model has been adapted and applied for use within the HR function.

Bradford absence index This technique calculates the impact on business of an individual's absence pattern based on the frequency and number of days lost.

Learning Objectives

As a result of reading this chapter and using the Online Resource Centre, you should be able to:

- understand the importance of human resource planning (HRP) and measurement;
- recognize the different approaches to HR planning that can be adopted;
- identify the range of metrics that can be used to measure HR management;
- understand the limitations and problems associated with the use of metrics in HR.

Introduction

Think again about the building of the Egyptian Pyramids and other great monuments to human civilization: where did all of those workers come from? How many were required and what skills did they need at each stage of construction? Who decided when their employment was over and how did they know how many might need replacing, as a result of death, illness and absence, during the period over which the particular project lasted?

If there had been any HR professionals around at that time, these would have been the kinds of challenges and issues that they would have been faced with:

- how many people do we need?
- when do we need them?
- what skills and competences do they need to have?
- where can we find them?
- what is it going to cost us to employ them?
- how can we ensure that we have neither too many nor too few in relation to construction or production requirements?
- how can we reduce our labour force in ways that reflect social and legal norms, and maintain our reputation as an employer, ensure that labour costs stay within budget, but also maintain the organization's commitment to the welfare of its employees?

These are deceptively straightforward questions that are as relevant today as they were in the past. Successful organizations are successful, in part, precisely because they have been able to provide consistently effective answers to these questions, even though their internal and external environments are constantly changing and evolving in response to economic and social forces. The HR professional, working with line managers, has a key role to play in ensuring that an optimum balance is struck between the number and quality of people employed, the associated employment costs, the organization's requirements for productive capacity and associated budgetary constraints.

Although the economic and financial imperatives vary between the public and private sectors – and most commentators would argue that, historically, these are much more influential in the private sector – people are rarely employed for any reason other than that they are an economic resource necessary for the creation of goods and services. This means that human resource planning (HRP) is not simply about meeting the demand for labour, but also involves understanding and managing the costs associated with employing any given number of people. As has been seen recently, the NHS has found that successfully recruiting the required numbers of doctors and nurses to meet establishment numbers is not the whole story. Budgetary constraints have led to situations in which many hospital posts have been axed and staff redeployed, temporary contracts not renewed, the use of agency staff reduced or curtailed and, in extreme circumstances, staff made redundant. HRP is about getting the right number of people with the required skills and competences in post at the right time, but this has to be achieved within changing budgetary constraints and has to reflect the organization's ability to pay the costs of employment (Royal College of Nursing, 2007).

From an economic perspective, employees represent a cost as well as a source of added value and while the costs of employing someone are relatively easy to calculate, the value they bring is not. This is key to understanding that HRP is not simply about the production of 'manpower plans' and futuristic scenario planning, but needs to be seen as an important dimension of almost all aspects of HR. In particular, it connects to the implementation and effectiveness of an organization's recruitment strategies, its labour reduction strategies, the continual search for improvements in productivity and the consequences that follow from this in relation to changes in the demand for labour. Going back to the example of the Egyptian Pyramids, if they were being built today, what would be the essential differences in the employment and use of labour? There would be fewer people employed, all would have a greater range and depth of skills, they would be more flexible and productive, and the strategies for employing and managing them would be more sophisticated. All of these changes relate to improvements in the planning and control of the labour resource: a requirement that, in the context of tight labour markets and high labour costs, is increasingly important for the vast majority of organizations.

The long-term trend in Western economies is for organizations to operate effectively with fewer employees – a fact that reflects increasing labour productivity and the increased use of technology. This does not mean, however, that fewer people are economically active or that there are fewer jobs available. But managing a gradual reduction in the labour force is not always easily achieved. Organizations can face unpredictable changes in competitive and financial conditions, such as cheap imports, unfavourable movements in exchange rates, increased costs of employing people and tightening budgetary constraints. As a result, they can quickly find that they are employing too much labour at too high a cost and quickly need to reduce either employment numbers or overall employment costs. Given the relative inflexibility of wage rates and salaries, which means that it is difficult to force through pay reductions, by reducing supply levels, either in terms of hours or people employed, HRP strategies need to be developed that allow organizations to respond quickly to changing demand conditions.

The following situation represents the kinds of environmental change that impact directly on employer's costs.

In response to proposed increases in the number of statutory holidays from 20 days to 28 days, Bob Cotton the chief executive of the British Hospitality Association commented that the change represented an additional 3.5 per cent on payroll costs. Whatever the social case for such changes, the impact on employment costs cannot be avoided:

> **If you start pushing up the wage bill too high you start shedding labour to pay for those left in work.**
> (*Daily Telegraph*, 2006)

His comment captures the pressures and dilemmas with which employers have to work in deciding on their employment strategies.

On the other hand, a numerical shortage of labour or qualitative imbalances can have a serious effect on the organization's ability to meet demand for its goods and services. This can result in reduced revenues, lost orders and dissatisfied customers: having too few employees of the right quality can have equally serious financial consequences as having too many employees! The challenge of HRP is to reconcile changes in the supply and demand for labour, and to produce, as far as possible, a labour force that can be flexed in terms of numbers and quality in response to changes in demand. To achieve this while avoiding the creation of damaging conflict with the employees and their representative institutions is, it might be argued, the 'holy grail' of HRP. The fact that few organizations seem to have been able to achieve this goal is testimony to the difficulties and challenges facing the HR professional in this aspect of their work.

Competing interests

Despite the frequently used aphorism that 'people are an organization's most important asset', the harsh reality is that employees are both an asset and a cost. If an organization experiences financial change, economic downturn and budgetary pressure, it is inevitable that, sooner or later, reductions in the cost and numbers of employees will have to be made. As Holbeche (2002) argues, in the context of the primacy of stakeholder interests and the ability to maintain employment levels:

> **Even in this age of information, when the value of intellectual capital should be becoming more apparent, business priorities, shareholder returns and bottom-line considerations take precedence over employee concerns.**
> (Holbeche, p 3, 2002)

It is the human resource planning function within HR that is most closely associated with the need to find, and keep, the right balance between the changing demand for labour and a reliable source of supply.

Ultimately, those charged with managing organizations give priority to the survival and financial stability of the organization in question. This does not necessarily preclude making a genuine commitment to considering the needs and interests of the employees wherever possible, but if decisions have to be made to cut jobs and to reduce employee numbers to preserve the long-term employment prospects of others, there is little to be gained from delaying or avoiding the issue. There is, however, a degree of choice in the way in which job cuts and employment losses are implemented, and making the right choice can minimize the consequences of job losses, preserve the reputation of the employer and maintain good employee relations. HRM Insight 9.1 offers an insight into how HR planning decisions are influenced by changing product market conditions and the way in which the welfare of those employees affected by job losses can be considered in the implementation of such changes.

Signpost to Chapter 4: Managing Employee Relations

HRM INSIGHT 9.1 The Czech manufacturing company

A Czech manufacturing company employed approximately 250 people and was located in a provincial town in the east of the country. Its main product line involved the manufacturing of highly sophisticated and complex computer control systems, used in process manufacturing industries. Each cost around £1m (at today's prices), and these were sold mainly in the American and European markets. The company's managing director explained that changes in demand for the product had major implications for the company in relation to income, profits and the ability to maintain stable levels of employment. An average of 15 of these control systems were sold annually.

When asked how he responded to the failure to meet projected sales targets, he made it clear that, while part of his company's philosophy was to ensure stable employment, it was not always possible to do this while maintaining the financial stability of the company. Losing even one order meant that a certain number of manufacturing operatives had to be released, but the really important point was that these people were re-employed when demand picked up. On a tour around the factory, he pointed out many members of staff who had lost their jobs and had been re-employed on more than one occasion. The company kept in contact with staff who had been made redundant and, while some found alternative jobs, some experienced short-term unemployment. Many of those that had found other work, as well as those who remained unemployed, were prepared to return to the company despite knowing that future employment could not be guaranteed.

When demand for the company's products exceeded capacity, the company could call upon such experienced workers to return and take up their old jobs. Supply strategies for the longer term included close liaison with the local technical college, involving student visits to the factory and managers giving pre-graduation talks to the students. An intensive programme of training also ensured that existing employees, through constant reskilling, became more productive and flexible, and one of the defining features of the management's employment strategy was investment in its employees.

The ability to attract new staff and those who had experienced the loss of their jobs was not the outcome of any technical planning process, but reflected a much more holistic approach to employing and managing people. The distinctive features of this approach are:

- a system of communication and consultation that involved all employees and ensured that staff knew the reasons behind employment decisions;

- a united senior management team, which realized that securing the long-term interests of the company and the majority of its employees sometimes involved difficult decisions that necessitated job reductions;

- a unionized workforce that, while engaged in negotiations over wages and conditions, realized that its own interests and those of the management were essentially the same in relation to the long-term future of the company;

- a workforce that trusted the managing director and his senior management team to act in its long-term best interests;

- a distinctive philosophy of management that saw employees as central to the success and future of the company, and which required managers to reflect this commitment as far as possible in the way in which employees were treated.

Questions

1. Where does this kind of management philosophy come from and why is it important?

2. What other responses to falling demand for labour might UK companies make to minimize the effects of job losses?

3. What labour supply strategies might UK companies make in response to increases and decreases in demand for labour?

4. What advantages would management expect to experience as a result of offering secure employment prospects within realistic limits?

The planning process

Planning, generally, is integral to any organized activity. It often is not only an option, but a necessity, and most organizations, particularly larger ones, engage in some form of planning as part of the process of strategic and operational management. Given that people are a critical organizational resource and source of significant cost, it is logical that managers need to plan for meeting the organization's human resource requirements. This is particularly the case if labour markets are tight and if the time taken to train people in the required skills, e.g. as doctors, can take a number of years.

Planning, however, is a process that has been associated with spectacular failures and white elephants. In the 1960s, the Labour Government under Harold Wilson produced a 'National Plan', which claimed to be a blueprint for managing the whole economy – but its use and value, and indeed relevance, were soon questioned, as the economic environment on which it based its assumptions and forecasts changed. The eventual failure of Communism can be linked to the inefficiencies and defects of its centralized economic planning system, under which resources, production targets and markets were determined centrally, with little regard for what people wanted and needed.

The assumptions that both of these centralized planning models were based upon quickly lost their validity as social, political and economic forces changed the environments to which the economic plans related. A plan, as with a strategy, is only as good and as useful as the assumptions about the future internal and external environment on which it is based are accurate. Understanding the limitations and fragility of planning and plans is as important to the HR planner as is the potential value that the planning process and the resultant HR plans offer. Given the rapidly changing environments in which most organizations operate, human resource plans must be flexible, i.e. they must be adapted constantly to reflect changes in the environment if they are to retain their potential utility. Planning that is seen more as discrete events and mechanistic activity than as an ongoing and adaptive process is unlikely to contribute much of value to organizational effectiveness.

HRP, if based on poor data, limited forecasting models and an inability to see the wider HR and business picture, can result in inaccurate and misleading estimates of supply and demand numbers, resulting in either a costly surplus or shortage of employees. As John Bramham (p 62, 1994), one of the most influential writers on HRP states:

> In preparing 'plans' the need for flexibility is stressed. No plan in any fixed sense will be relevant for long. The success of planning in an organization will be judged by how well the organization can anticipate or adapt to the unforeseen.

This is a view supported by Bratton and Gold (p 192, 1999), who state that:

> The domination of equations, which mechanistically provide for solutions for problems based on the behaviour of people, may actually become divorced from the real world and have a good chance of missing the real problems. Hence the poor reputation of manpower planning.

We are in an era in which almost all organizations are struggling to cope with an unprecedented level of change and it would too simplistic to see planning as being able to 'see' or predict at any point in time. The prevalent approach to planning an organization's human resources in the 1970s and 1980s is seen, in retrospect, as having been overly prescriptive and inflexible (bin Idris and Eldridge, 1998).

This view was echoed in an earlier Institute for Employment Studies (IES) report that concluded:

> When it concerns human resources, there are the more specific criticisms that it is over-quantitative and neglects the qualitative aspects of contribution. The issue has become not how many people should be employed, but ensuring that all members of staff are making an effective contribution.
> (Reilly, 1996)

The importance of this statement lies in the recognition that numbers, in themselves, are less important than what people contribute, the behaviours they exhibit and the potential they possess. The HR planner, and the whole approach to planning, now need to reflect the importance of distinguishing between:

> ... the numbers of people in employment from what they actually do and are capable of doing at work.

Many of the problems associated with what was known, in the 1980s and early 1990s, as 'manpower planning' were linked to the following:

- the planning process was more a series of activities than an ongoing process, meaning that information from the internal and external environments was often outdated and irrelevant;
- the idea that a plan, in the form of a single document, once written, was complete was attractive but misguided. The danger is that people come to believe that the contents of the plan and what it forecasts are fixed in time rather than contingent and provisional;
- it focused too heavily on the quantitative aspect of employment and neglected issues of variability in contribution and performance;
- the lack of flexibility and ability frequently to change planning scenarios and forecasts meant that many plans quickly became out of date;
- forecasting and predicting future economic conditions and attempts to reconcile these with the organization's workforce requirements were often carried out in an isolated and detached way.

More recent attempts to explain and justify the role of HRP emphasize the need not to try to predict the future, but to use planning to challenge assumptions about the future and to engage in more sophisticated 'scenario planning' activities. HRP is now much more about finding ways to achieve a better internal integration of HR activities in order to be clearer about what the workforce requirements will be in the future, in terms of skill and competency requirements, and how these needs can be met. Quality, potential and 'fit', rather than simply numbers, of employees required is seen as a particularly important dimension of the planning process and its outcomes.

Table 9.1 provides a summary of the essential features of the HR planning process, and the actions needed to ensure that each key feature can be effectively managed and add value to the organization.

 Signpost to Chapter 13: HR and the New Opening

Table 9.1 Features of effective HR planning

Essential feature	Essential actions
Based on organization's objectives	The HR plan should grow out of the organization's objectives and strategic aims. For example, expansion plans may require a greater focus on recruitment, while upgrading skills may be necessary if technological advancement is required.
Flexible	The HR plan may need to change in order to ensure that organizational objectives are met in the event of unseen demands or change. These might be market changes, such as a recession resulting in job losses to save costs, or internal unexpected change, such as the resignation of unexpected numbers of key personnel, leading to refocused efforts in recruitment and retention.
Built-in contingencies	There may be aspects of the plan that allow for resource to be diverted elsewhere in the event of unplanned events. For example, temporary or interim staff may be required to cover unexpected absence.
Defined value-added outcomes	All activity should be carefully scrutinized to examine whether or not it truly adds value. For example, an increased number of staff committee meetings with the intention of improving communications may actually escalate the number of complaints and encourage more time away from productive work.
Regularly reviewed	Objectives set early in the year may no longer be relevant as the year progresses. For example, there may have been plans for a programme of management training, which might be cancelled in the event of a decision to make a layer of management redundant.
Overall strategic direction	All aspects of the plan should directly or indirectly contribute towards the overall strategic direction of the business. For example, improved induction procedures may enhance productivity, despite more time away from direct work in the initial weeks, because of enhanced long-term retention of staff.
Timelines identified	Plans should include a timeframe over which activity will be completed. For example, succession planning may be an annual activity, reviewed at a set time each year.
Priorities identified	There may be some aspects of the HR plan that are more important than others and activity may be prioritized, particularly if there are seasonal demands. A retail chain may be more focused on recruiting, rather than training, new staff during the lead-up to Christmas and may focus on training for development during the quieter times of the year.
Resource identified	Different levels of HR support may be required for different aspects of the plan and the plan should take account of the availability of staff to support activity.
Acknowledges reactive requirements	Remember that allowing time for the day-to-day reactive issues is just as important and often more valued. A prompt reaction to an unexpected challenge can stop problems from quickly escalating further; effective plans acknowledge this valuable role.

HRM INSIGHT 9.2 Recruitment of nurses in Ireland

As with many Western European countries, Ireland has experienced significant shortages of qualified nurses as its fast-growing economy creates more employment opportunities, both at home and abroad, for young people who might otherwise have entered the nursing profession. In 2005, a potentially serious shortage of nurses was identified. The problem was not only exacerbated by the movement to four-year degree courses as opposed to the traditional three-year diploma course, but also by changes in the work–life balance of many Irish nurses, who began to value and expect more flexible employment contracts. This led to a move to increased job-sharing and part-time employment in circumstances in which these suited the nurses' personal circumstances. This meant that, while the numbers of nurses might increase or remain stable depending on the effectiveness of recruitment strategies, the actual supply of nurses, expressed in terms of 'nursing time', actually fell.

➡

One of the Irish Health Board regions that had responsibility for the recruitment of nurses engaged in a planning exercise that embraced a three-year planning cycle. The HR team involved was particularly interested in analysing the data on the following:

- wastage rates of nurses;
- the number of nurses who had left, but who might be expected to return to, the profession;
- changes in recruitment patterns;
- changes in the frequency of nurses wanting career breaks;
- the incidence and duration of maternity leave;
- projected changes in the demand for nurses as the demands on the healthcare sector in Ireland grew over time.

The planning team was not only interested in overall supply and demand figures, but needed to break the numbers down into different nursing specialisms and for each hospital within the region. The conclusion that the team reached was that the projected shortfall in nurses over the next three years could not be met from the indigenous Irish labour force. The team recommended that an overseas recruitment campaign would be needed to meet predicted nursing shortages. In addition to recruiting overseas nurses, the strategy adopted also involved working to increase the recruitment of Irish nurses. This supply strategy involved:

- promoting nursing as a career for young people;
- encouraging nurses who had left the profession, because of career breaks, family commitments or job changes, to return to nursing;
- looking carefully at the reasons why nurses were leaving their profession and developing more effective retention strategies.

It was agreed that the Board would meet the projected shortage by recruiting from overseas, concentrating its efforts in the Philippines and India because of the quality of the nurse training procedures and use of English in those countries. The initial target was set at 370 nurses, some of whom would be offered jobs in other Health Boards. They were to be offered two-year contracts, with the possibility of a further two-year renewal period.

Questions

1. What selection criteria would you use in deciding which overseas applicants should be offered jobs?

2. What pre-employment and acculturation activities would you offer for those selected and what would be the objectives of this?

3. Would you consider a trial period, after which the contract would be either confirmed or ended? Give reasons for your decision on this and, if one was considered appropriate, explain how it would operate.

4. What criteria would you use for evaluating the overall success of the overseas recruitment strategy?

Insights & Outcomes: visit the Online Resource Centre at www.oxfordtextbooks.co.uk/orc/banfield_kay/ for further information on the outcome of the overseas recruitment strategy.

STUDENT ACTIVITY 9.1

1. Working in groups, prepare a brochure, or similar document, for distribution to schools, colleges and universities, outlining the reasons why young people should consider nursing as a career, the opportunities it would offer them and how they might find out more about jobs in nursing.

2. Research the reasons why nurses leave their jobs/the profession and consider what hospitals/nurse managers might do to reduce wastage rates, spelling out the implications associated with your recommendations.

STUDENT ACTIVITY 9.2 **Researching the relationship between more flexible working arrangements and changes in productivity**

As has already been pointed out, productivity (an economic relationship between inputs and outputs) is of particular importance to managers. It measures what an individual unit of labour, or the entire workforce, produces in terms of value or volume, and links this to the numbers of employees and their cost. With the growth in flexible-working employment contracts, and HR policies that support and regulate these, a question has arisen as to the economic or productivity consequences associated with such practices. The critical question that managers need to know the answer to is: 'Are employees who enjoy job-sharing and home-working opportunities more or less productive because of these different working arrangements?'

Your task is to research the evidence on flexible-working and 'family-friendly' employment practices and answer the following questions. Your answers can be presented in the form of a PowerPoint presentation or in a group briefing paper. Note that the evidence available can be found in reports and journal articles, from appropriate websites, and by surveying employees and managers in organizations that have committed to such practices.

1. More organizations are prepared to offer part-time and job-sharing contracts to their employees – but what are the advantages and disadvantages of such contracts?

2. Does the available evidence suggest that employees who are offered these contracts become more or less productive, and, if the former, why?

3. What are the implications for the HR department and line managers of managing staff on such contracts?

4. On balance, does the evidence suggest that such contracts and working arrangements benefit the employee more than the organization?

KEY CONCEPT **Whole-time equivalents (WTEs)**

This is a quantitative measurement of the number of staff available to or in the establishment that allows for staff on different employment contracts to be reflected in the 'head count'. A simple system of weighting operates, under which a full-time employee working a nominal 35 hours – or whatever is the company/industry standard working week – is allocated a weighting of 1. A part-time worker who works half the standard hours is weighted 0.5; one who works two days each week is weighted at 0.4. As organizations, particularly the NHS, move to more employee-friendly and flexible contracts, the actual numbers of nurses and doctors, for example, can increase while the WTE figure falls. Expanding the output of medical schools can, paradoxically, be associated with a fall in general practitioner WTEs because more GPs work on a part-time basis.

221

Several references have already been made in this chapter to the choices available to organizations faced with shortages, or surpluses, of labour. Table 9.2 offers an indication of the most frequently used strategies, some of which can be thought of in operational terms, while others have a more strategic dimension. In considering these options, think carefully about the costs and benefits each involves and the consequences to employee relations, on both an individual and a collective basis, of adopting each one.

Manpower planning or HRP?

As was made clear in Chapter 2, human resource management is associated with a degree of terminological complexity and confusion that is rarely found in other management functions, with the result that both students and practitioners are often confused about the meaning(s) of commonly used terms and

Table 9.2 Management strategies related to changes in the demand and supply for labour

A **short-term fall** in the demand for labour can involve:	A **long-term fall** in the demand for labour can involve:
• reducing or eliminating overtime working	• moving some employees from full-time to part-time contracts
• postponing the recruitment of workers to replace those who have left	• introducing short-time working
• freezing establishment numbers	• introducing voluntary or compulsory redundancy
• ceasing the use of agency staff	
A **short-term rise** in the demand for labour can involve:	A **long-term shortage** of labour can involve:
• increasing advertising spend and improving its effectiveness	• developing alternative labour markets, e.g. overseas recruitment
• increasing the use of temporary staff and short-term contract workers	• substituting technology for labour
• using 'golden hellos' to attract new recruits	• increasing the degree of functional flexibility through changes in training strategies
• increasing overtime	• introducing flexible working strategies
	• improving the perceived value of the reward package

expressions. In the context of this chapter, the central question is whether the term 'manpower planning' carries essentially the same meaning as 'human resource planning' (HRP).

At the conceptual and philosophical level, these two terms and their meanings can be seen to be analogous to those of 'Personnel Management' and 'Human Resource Management', and result in a similar debate about the relationship between the two. To add to the terminological confusion, the equivalent term used in the USA is 'workforce planning', but as far as this chapter is concerned, that term will be seen as equivalent to HRP (Watson, 2002).

According to Bramham (1994):

> There is a big difference between human resource planning and manpower planning ... in terms of process and purpose.
>
> (p 155)

He argues that HRP is concerned with motivating people and involves processes in which costs, numbers, control and systems interact, whereas manpower planning is concerned with the numerical requirements of forecasting. Despite this, he accepts that there are important areas of overlap and interconnection (see Bennison and Casson, 1984).

It might be argued that Bramham's position on this issue has, to a degree, been superseded by a simple change in definition, driven by the need to avoid the use of discriminatory language, and by the incorporation of the more restrictive forecasting function into the wider and more encompassing human resource planning activity. If there is a meaningful and useful distinction to be made, it is probably based on the differences between strategic and operational requirements and focus; if this is a defensible point of view, it justifies Bramham's position and allows HRP to be defined as:

> ... involving the strategic alignment of an organization's human capital with its business direction, and employing the use of methodical processes in analysing the current workforce, determining future workforce needs, identifying the gap between the present and future, and implementing solutions so the organization can accomplish its mission, goals, and objectives.

Manpower planning, meanwhile, is:

> ...part of the wider HRP function, but having a more operational focus and purpose that involves identifying the numbers of people required at appropriate skill levels across a given shift or production pattern in order to meet production or work requirements.

In summary, HRP has evolved from what was originally a process involving forecasting changes in the demand and supply for labour into a more sophisticated and integral part of HR. While an ability to predict changes in the external environment is still valued as a contribution to effective decision making in the employment of people, the limitations and uncertainties of 'knowing' what the external environment will look like at any point in time are better understood today than they perhaps used to be (Bennison, 1980). What has also changed and become increasingly important influences on what HRP represents can be expressed in terms of:

- the importance of the organization's internal environment, particularly the impact on its labour requirements of such activities as succession planning, competency development, retention levels, productivity and efficiency initiatives;

- a movement away from the notion that organizations can always be proactive when it comes to planning human resources, based on the unsustainable belief that future environmental conditions can be accurately predicted;

- a greater recognition that HRP is increasingly associated with both strategic and operational dimensions;

- the importance of flexibility in HR plans;

- the critical need for management thinking and organizations to be able to adapt quickly to environmental changes;

- the need for HR practitioners to develop appropriate planning tools and provide managers with a range of options in terms of known and 'predicted' environmental conditions.

From a senior management perspective, the perceived effectiveness and value of HR's contribution to the planning and management of human resources is less to do with whether those involved are reactive or proactive, or whether they have a 'manpower plan' or not, but more to do with whether they are effective in meeting the organization's labour requirements, within existing budgetary constraints. They must also provide 'solutions' that fit the strategic and operational requirements of the organization. The general criticisms levelled against the HR department outlined in Chapter 2, in terms of the relevance of its priorities and activities, can be revisited in the context of HRP. The HR department is likely to be criticized because of its inability to distinguish between the HR plan and an HR plan for the organization, and because it is slow to respond to changing resource requirements. Such criticism is likely to be compounded by a perception that its contribution to HRP is marginal and ineffective, at least as far as delivering against the organization's capacity and capability requirements is concerned. This may well mean that it is as legitimate and appropriate for HR to concentrate energy on actions that help to overcome unexpected problems in meeting quantity and quality targets as it is for HR to engage in pre-planned and proactive activities, such as forecasting future demand and supply conditions. HRP has a short-term relevance and value as well as a long-term dimension and, as was pointed out recently to one of the authors, the long term is getting shorter!

Despite the recognition that making effective contributions in the field of HRP sometimes involves the HR practitioner reacting to unforeseen events, constructing some sort of HR plan, the key features of which reflect a detailed understanding of the organization's internal and external environments, is still considered to be an important tool for the management of employment numbers, employment costs and the quality of an organization's human resources. Its construction and format are likely to differ depending

Table 9.3 Constructing the HR plan – key questions and sources of information

Key question	Useful sources of information
What are the purpose, strategy and objectives of the HRP function?	• Organizational objectives • Department objectives • Job descriptions
What are the strengths and weaknesses of the current labour force?	• SWOT analysis • Customer service survey
How do we classify positions and grades?	• Manpower plan • Grading structure • Job evaluation scheme • Job descriptions
What are the external labour market changes?	• Market data • Jobcentre Plus statistics
What are the age, skill, gender and ethnicity profiles?	• Personal records • Training files
What forthcoming legislation may affect us?	• Consultation Papers • Recently reported case law • New Regulations
What is our current demographic and ethnic spread compared to the community?	• Equal opportunities monitoring data demographics analysis • Data from Commission for Racial Equality and Equal Opportunities Commission
How do we retain specialist skills?	• Turnover data • Skills audit • Appraisal data
Do we have the right organizational structure for future demands?	• Organizational structures • Organization's strategic aims and objectives
What skills will we need in future?	• New product development strategy • Organization's strategic aims and objectives

on the requirements of different organizations, but as a guide to the key issues against which the plan needs to deliver, Table 9.3 provides a useful summary.

HRP measurement and metrics

Historically, measurement in HR was very much associated with HRP and involved the production of estimates or 'precise' measures covering:

• changes in the existing supply of labour as a result of:
   – people leaving the organization, often described as 'labour wastage', or 'labour turnover' if losses are replaced by the recruitment of new employees;

- people being absent from work because of illness or other reasons;
- the loss of productive time resulting from wasteful working practices and lower-than-acceptable performance levels;

● changes in the demand for labour, which can only meaningfully result from an assessment of changes in:

- production levels and work requirements;
- establishment numbers;
- changes in employment budgets;
- the expansion or contraction of productive capacity;
- changes in labour productivity and working methods;
- the application of new technology.

Developing reliable demand forecasting models has always been more difficult to achieve than measuring changes in the supply of labour, for the simple reason that variations in the demand for an organization's products or services can never be predicted with a sufficient degree of certainty. Consider, for example, the loss of jobs resulting from mergers, which can be both significant and sudden, as the (at the time of writing) proposed link between Barclays and ABN Amro illustrates (*Daily Telegraph*, 2007). Difficulties of accurate demand forecasting are particularly acute in the private sector, but even in the public sector, in which product markets are less volatile, changes in funding and budgetary pressures can also affect the ability to make long-term predictions about demand requirements.

Changes in demand can often be linked to known changes in labour supply, e.g. a known level of wastage, and can be used to establish demand requirements, in terms of replacing people who leave. Knowledge of wastage levels is also an important factor in making decisions about demand requirements over the longer term. On the one hand, if an organization is expanding, simply replacing labour that is lost will not deliver the numbers and quality of employees required, leading to the need for additional recruitment. On the other hand, an organization that needs to make reductions in its labour force as a result, for example, of a decision to outsource may be able to avoid or limit the need for compulsory redundancies by not replacing the numbers of people who are predicted to leave over a given period.

Before we move on to consider some of the most commonly used measurement techniques, it is important to make the point that the results of these calculations do not, in themselves, represent anything other than a contribution to subsequent decisions about how organizations manage situations of labour surplus or shortage. Depending on expectations of future requirements, managers may choose to accept a short-term surplus in the knowledge that demand will increase in the medium term and that the cost of a short-term reduction strategy, followed by the costs of hiring new staff, would be more than the costs associated with running a short to medium-term surplus. Much depends on the organization's ability to live with short-term surpluses, and on its philosophy towards its employees and their welfare.

Equally, shortages of labour do not necessarily result in new recruitment. There are other ways to meet demand requirements, through, for example, the use of overtime working, reorganizing working methods and introducing new contractual arrangements for existing staff. There is no single 'correct' strategy for managing surpluses or shortages for all organizations; rather, it is a matter of choosing the one that best fits, or a combination of several that fit, the particular circumstances of each individual organization in ways that minimize costs, maximize productivity and, as far as possible, reflect the interests of employees. As shown in HRM Insight 9.3, the situations faced by managers in responding to changes in their workforce, even though the numbers involved might be relatively few, can be complicated and challenging.

225

HRM INSIGHT 9.3 The case of Sunside Leisure

Sunside Leisure is a privately owned business, which operates a number of leisure facilities. These range from hotels, leisure centres, sports facilities, gyms and swimming pools, and the organization employs around 500 staff in total. The HR team consists of an HR director, an HR manager and two administrators. In three months' time, the HR manager is due to start maternity leave and will therefore be out of the business for between six and 12 months. She has indicated that she will probably take only six months off and, after this time, intends to return on a full-time basis. Additionally, one of the HR administrators is due to go on maternity leave in six weeks' time. She has indicated that she will probably be on leave for 12 months and may wish to return part time, for two or three days each week.

The team is committed to the following activities in addition to the normal day-to-day recruitment, administration, induction, performance management and communications activity:

● delivery of equal opportunities training to fifty managers and team leaders (consisting of five one-day workshops, which were originally going to be delivered by the HR manager in four months' time);

● wage negotiations covering fifty staff who transferred under TUPE from facilities that were originally managed by the local council, but which negotiations are likely to be sensitive due to a disparity in rates between the different facilities;

● restructuring of the catering teams, including outsourcing to third-party caterers of ten employees and potentially reducing the requirement for a team leader;

● a recruitment campaign to increase headcount at two leisure centres for the increased summer demand and to provide 'out-of-school' summer sports clubs for 5–12 year olds in the area.

Questions

1. What options might the HR director consider for covering the periods of maternity leave in the department?

2. What additional resources might be required and where might they be found?

3. How might the HR plans be affected by the current situation and how can these effects be minimized?

Absence

Absence through sickness or other reasons represents a significant cost to most organizations, with sickness absence alone estimated to cost UK businesses over £13.4bn each year (CBI, 2007). While it is inevitable that the majority of employees will be unable to attend work from time to time due to ill health, it is a fact that some employees will take more time off than others. Employers tend to expect that employees will only take time off when they are genuinely unable to work, but there will always be occasions on which employees take time off, claiming ill health, when they might have come to work, known euphemistically as 'taking a sickie'.

Absence rates vary between different organizations and between different types of job. It might be argued that it is easy to manage with minor illness if the working environment is warm and comfortable, compared to more physically demanding environments, and that more motivated employees with a greater degree of responsibility will be less inclined to take time off when they are ill. The propensity to take time off may also be linked to the extent to which the psychological environment is positive and supportive. The significance of work-related stress in relation to absenteeism has already been highlighted in Chapter 7 and absence from work may, in certain cases, represent a way of escaping from a stressful environment.

➔ Signpost to Chapter 7: Managing Health and Safety

Whatever the reason for absence, there is no doubt that it impacts on the organization's ability to meet its objectives and puts pressure on those who have to cover the extra workload. According to ACAS (2006), the effects of high absence levels are wide-ranging and affect everyone in the organization;

managers and employees, together with their representatives, need to work to keep absence under control and to minimize its costs.

The costs of unacceptably high levels of absence are normally expressed financially, and are based on calculating the value of lost production and sick payments. These financial measures also include:

- the costs of additional staffing levels and overtime working to cover anticipated absences;
- the cost of replacement labour;
- costs associated with delayed production and disruptions to planning schedules;
- costs associated with loss of quality or service levels;
- costs resulting from low morale and dissatisfaction.

Monitoring absence rates forms a key element of absence management and most organizations track absenteeism on a weekly, or monthly, basis to monitor the effectiveness of absence management strategies. This often involves calculating absence using a formula and comparing the resultant figure with an internal or external benchmark standard.

The *absence rate* is usually calculated as follows:

$$\frac{\text{Number of days' absence within team}}{\text{Number of working days available}} \times 100\%$$

For example, a team of five people who each work five days a week, less bank holidays, can work a total of (365−104−8) 253 days each, making a team total of 1,265 potential working days. If 50 days were to be lost through absence, the team's absence rate would be:

$$\frac{50 \times 100\%}{1,265} = 3.95\%$$

A calculation for the whole organization is similarly based on the time lost as a result of absence. The formula usually used for calculating the *lost time rate* is:

$$\frac{\text{Total absence in days/hours over a given period}}{\text{Total time in days/hours available over the period}} \times 100$$

In the case of a hotel, for example, we can work out total hours available per month by multiplying each employee's monthly contracted time (remembering that this figure will reflect different employment contracts) and adding the individual totals together. This assumes, of course, that the hotel actually monitors and records absences, aggregates the time lost through absence, expressed preferably in hours, and calculates the lost time rate. By using the same calculation on a departmental basis, it is possible to develop a more detailed pattern of absences that will be useful in deciding on what corrective action to take.

One of the limitations of the lost time rate calculation is that it cannot distinguish the pattern of absence in terms of whether few employees are taking long periods of absence or whether many employees have infrequent bouts of absence. Consequently, the calculation of what is known as the *frequency rate* is often preferred to, or used in conjunction with, the lost time rate. The formula for this is:

$$\frac{\text{Number of spells of absence over a given period}}{\text{Number of workers employed over the period}} \times 100$$

A similar calculation can also be used to establish the individual frequency rate, expressed in terms of:

$$\frac{\text{Number of employees with one or more spells of absence over a given period}}{\text{Number of workers employed over the period}} \times 100$$

The Bradford absence index is useful because it gives weighting to the frequency of absences, reflecting the belief that many frequent spells of absence are more disruptive and costly than fewer, longer absences, which can be more easily managed because it is easier to make contingency plans. The index is calculated by using the formula:

Index = S × S × H

Where:

S = the number of recorded absences;

H = the total number of hours absent.

The formula can be applied to each individual and to the organization as a whole.

As an example, consider two hotel employees, one a porter and the second a chef. If the porter were to be absent on five separate days during a month, totalling 40 hours, his or her absence index would be:

Index = 5 × 5 × 40 = 1,000

The index for the chef, who was absent only once during the month for one week, would be:

Index = 1 × 1 × 40 = 40

The problem with this method of calculating absence, as with the others, is that it cannot show the actual costs of any given level or individual pattern of absence. It might be argued that, although the index for the chef is much lower, his or her absence in the month might be more of a problem than that of the porter simply because of the chef's more valuable contribution and the revenue lost in the restaurant because of his or her absence. Not all employees have the same value in terms of their contribution to the organization and the costs of absence will vary in relation to the value of work that is lost. This point is developed in more detail later in the chapter.

HRM INSIGHT 9.4 Sickness absence in the public sector

A belief that recorded sickness absence in the public sector is higher that in the private sector and represents a huge cost to the taxpayer is supported by research carried out by the government, using results from two other contemporary surveys into sickness absence (CBI in association with AXA, 2004; CIPD, 2004 – see Table 9.4).

Of particular interest here is the cost of sickness absence. Figures presented in the report suggest that, at an annual average of ten days per person, sickness absence among the 523,000 civil servants costs over £375m and, in local authorities, up to £900m per year. With a target reduction of 30 per cent in civil service sickness absence rates alone, it is estimated that approximately 1.7 million working days would be saved, equivalent to more than 7,000 additional employees. Expressed in a different way, reducing the absence rate by this amount means that the current level of work undertaken by civil servants could be achieved, broadly speaking, with 7,000 fewer employees.

Questions

1. How might the differences in sickness absence between the two sectors be explained?

2. What short-term actions might the managers with responsibility for reducing sickness absence rates by 30 per cent take that might contribute to achieving this target?

3. What actions could the HR practitioners take over the longer term to complement the short-term measures?

Table 9.4 Summary of 2004 absence surveys – average recorded days absence per employee per year in public and private sectors

	2003–04	2002–03	2001–02	2000–01
CBI (all)		7.2	6.8	7.0 (estimate)
CBI (public sector)		8.9	8.9	10.1
CBI (private sector)		6.9	6.5	6.7
CIPD (all)	9.1	9.0		
CIPD (public sector)	10.7	10.6		
CIPD (private sector)	7.8	7.0		

© Crown Copyright/CBI

Turnover

'Turnover' differs from 'wastage' only in the sense that the use of the former term relates to those who leave an organization and are replaced, while the latter relates only to the number of those who leave. For practical purposes, both relate to the loss of people and the terms can be used interchangeably.

According to the latest CIPD survey (CIPD, 2007), overall employee annual turnover rate for the UK is 18.1 per cent. The report found that annual turnover levels vary considerably from industry to industry, with the highest average rates (22.6 per cent) found in private sector organizations and, within this sector, the hotels, catering and leisure industry reports rates of turnover at 10 per cent higher than the average for the sector (32.6 per cent). The public sector has an average turnover rate of 13.7 per cent. While there are situations in which high wastage rates may actually help an organization to resolve a situation of labour surplus, persistently high rates outside of the organization or industry benchmark range are usually a cause for concern: when skilled and experienced employees decide to leave, it usually represents a significant loss and a cost to the organization. Finding suitable candidates to replace leavers takes time and resources in terms of recruitment and training (remember the estimates of recruitment costs explored in Chapter 3).

It is inevitable, however, that, from time to time, employees will choose to leave and either pursue careers elsewhere, retire, take a career break or return to education. These are examples of what is known as 'voluntary quits'. In addition to employees who choose to leave, there is a number who are dismissed or who are performance managed out of the organization. High turnover rates create particular pressures for the HR department, which is primarily responsible for replacing those who leave, but also for line managers who face disruption to production and service standards. This is the necessary result of having to induct and train new employees, who are usually less experienced and productive compared to those they replace: it takes time before new recruits perform at their optimum levels. The result is a reduced ability to meet objectives, reduced levels of productivity and higher unit costs. It is therefore important for managers to measure labour turnover, monitor its impact and take appropriate action to minimize its effects. As far as the latter is concerned, this should at least involve operating efficient and effective replacement procedures, but the effective management of turnover also involves understanding and dealing with its underlying causes.

Measuring turnover

Turnover is typically measured over a 12-month period to smooth out seasonal differences, but can be tracked weekly or monthly to provide a more detailed and contemporary understanding of what is happening.

Turnover is calculated as follows:

$$\frac{\text{Number of leavers over a given period}}{\text{Number employed at the period end}} \times 100\%$$

For example, if 25 people left over the last 12 months and the current number of employees is 275, turnover would be calculated as:

$$\frac{25}{275} \times 100\% = 9.09\%$$

Variations on this method involve taking the average number employed during the period. For example, in an organization employing 235 people at the start of the period and 275 at the end, with 25 leavers, the calculation would be:

$$\frac{25 \times 100}{(235 + 275)/2} = 9.8\%$$

Figure 9.1 shows how annual turnover can be tracked on a monthly basis to show trends. In the graph, annual labour turnover within this organization is showing a downward trend throughout 2006.

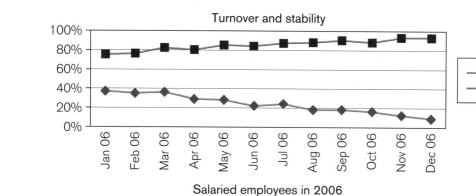

Figure 9.1 Annual labour turnover and stability tracked monthly as a percentage through 2006

Stability

'Stability' is a useful measure to accompany turnover and can give a better reflection of the retention of employees than can turnover. If turnover is high, it is difficult to establish which employees are those that are leaving without carrying out more in-depth analysis. It may be that new employees are poorly inducted and often leave within the first few weeks, and that longer serving staff tend to stay. Or it might be the case that a large portion of longer serving employees is nearing retirement and that the increase in turnover is due to a demographic 'surge'.

Stability is a measure of the percentage of employees with more than a stipulated amount of service. For example, it may be useful to know what percentage of staff has over one year's service and can therefore be assumed to have become experienced and qualified. Stability can be calculated as follows:

$$\frac{\text{Number of staff with over one year's service over a given period}}{\text{Number of staff employed at period end}} \times 100\%$$

For example, if the organization of 275 employees in the turnover example were to have 259 employees with over one year's service, stability would be calculated as follows:

$$\frac{259}{275} \times 100\% = 94.18\%$$

This information is particularly useful to establish the kind of problem from which the organization is suffering. For example, if annual turnover is 45 per cent and stability is 90 per cent, then it can be seen that it is mostly shorter serving employees who are leaving and that retention seems to be better among longer serving employees. It is also important to assess both turnover and stability against the overall change in numbers employed. For example, stability figures will fall during expansion, due to the number of new positions created, and turnover may be very high, along with very high stability, if an organization reduces in size resulting in little recruitment and large numbers of redundancies. Figure 9.1 also shows an organization with increasing stability among its workforce throughout 2006.

Vitality

Some organizations, particularly larger ones with a variety of more senior positions, may have policies that encourage and promote the development of staff, and which try to balance external recruitment to more senior positions with internal promotions. 'Vitality' is a method of measuring the balance of internal promotion versus external recruitment or loss of employees. Although much less commonly measured than turnover, it can be a useful measure of career development and employee satisfaction.

Recruitment vitality is measured as follows:

$$\frac{\text{Number of roles filled by internal promotion} - \text{number of roles filled externally}}{\text{Number of positions filled}} \times 100\%$$

High negative scores indicate a preference for external recruitment, suggesting that it there is little opportunity for internal promotion and that it is likely that internal potential is not being tapped. High positive scores indicate that most posts are being filled internally and that external markets are not being fully exploited to bring in new ideas, skills and methods of working.

A similar calculation can made for *turnover vitality*:

$$\frac{\text{Number of roles vacated due to internal promotion} - \text{number of roles vacated due to departure}}{\text{Number of roles becoming vacant}} \times 100\%$$

High negative scores indicate that employees are leaving to advance their careers, while high positive scores indicate that employees rarely leave to pursue careers externally and benefit from internal promotion as a preference.

→ Signpost to Chapter 3: Recruitment and Selection

HRM INSIGHT 9.5 The case of Lincester Passenger Transport Executive

Lincester Passenger Transport Executive is responsible for providing the majority of local passenger transport for the town of Lincester. One hundred and fifty drivers are employed across a variety of shifts, providing a bus service seven days a week to the general public. The organization also employs ten maintenance, and twenty administration and managerial, staff. Turnover has risen among drivers over the last five years, from 10 to 25 per cent. Driving staff are expensive to recruit and train. In addition, 25 per cent of the drivers will be eligible for retirement in the next five years.

Questions

1. List as many reasons as you can think of that might contribute to the high levels of labour turnover among driving staff. How might you establish the 'real' reasons for the turnover of drivers?

2. What range of HR activities might the Lincester Passenger Transport Executive consider over the next 12 months to help to improve retention?

3. What HR metrics should the organization track and how might information be gathered to monitor any improvement in employee retention that might be achieved?

4. What strategies might managers consider to deal with the retirement problem?

Measurement in HR – the wider debate

One of the central objectives of this book is not only to provide insights into what skills and knowledge HR practitioners and line managers need to manage employees effectively, and how these activities might be carried out, but also to explain why these activities are important and the consequences that might follow from doing them, not doing them well or not doing them at all, as the case may be. This approach is particularly important as far as measurement and the use of metrics in HR is concerned, and the issues surrounding the development of wider and more sophisticated approaches to measurement now need to be considered.

To put this issue into a wider context, it is necessary to recognize that the increasing use of metrics to monitor organizational performance is not restricted to HR. The public sector, in particular, has been subject to the development and application of many different performance measures and targets, and there is an extensive literature on the experiences and effects of performance measurement strategies (Propper and Wilson, 2003).

In the USA, the work of writers such as Jac Fitz-Enz (2000) and Wayne Cascio (1991), in measuring the economic value of employee performance and producing measures that allow the financial costs of employee behaviour to be calculated, has been instrumental in bringing the debate about measurement in HR to centre stage. In the UK, the contributions of Kearns (2000), Mooney (2001) and Mayo (2001) are increasingly influencing the approach to the priorities and agenda of HR professionals.

Mooney (2001), in particular, provides a powerful argument in support of the use of measurement in HR. He starts off his chapter on 'HR Metrics' by quoting W Edwards Deming, who said:

You don't have to do this – survival isn't compulsory.

This is Mooney's way of stressing the importance he attaches to the extensive use of measurement in HR. He is particularly critical of the HR community because of its reluctance to understand why measurement is important and the value it can provide. He claims that, while almost every other facet of business has committed to measuring its contribution and effectiveness, HR has been reluctant to go down this route, and argues that this is directly linked to the lack of status and respect from which many in HR suffer.

> **The absence of quantification forces HR departments to remain on the periphery of strategic decision making, rather than occupying the central role which the importance of the function requires.**
> (p 93)

With this comment, Mooney reinforces the importance of the distinction that Ulrich (1996) makes between HR activities and HR outcomes, under which what HR 'does' is less important to its organizational standing and reputation among other stakeholders than is what it achieves, or its outcomes. Measurement of these 'deliverables' and the added value they represent is now seen as a critical part of what managing the HR function involves.

Part of the problem with measurement in HR is the belief that the economic value or effectiveness of people and HR activities cannot be calculated, and Fitz-Enz (2000) accepts that there are difficulties associated with measuring the economic effectiveness of people, particularly in service and professional work, although less so in manufacturing. He, like Mooney, is a strong believer in the importance of incorporating rigorous measurement systems into the HR function, arguing that:

> **The bottom line is that although it is not easy to evaluate staff work in quantitative terms, it can be and is being done.**
> (p 21)

This strategic approach to measurement has significantly different implications for HR practitioners than the measurements associated with HRP and its association with absence and turnover rates. Mooney argues that it is the management and effective reduction of absence and turnover that has the potential for reducing the financial costs of employment, not the measurement of the rates alone.

➡ Signpost to Chapter 15: Reforming the HR Function

Training is another key HR activity, representing, according to Mooney (2001), up to 6 per cent of many organizations' payroll costs. In a worst-case scenario, training can be wasteful, disconnected from an organization's HR and business strategy, and a net consumer of resources, rather than a net contributor. In such circumstances, the logical course of action would be to overhaul the training function radically, to outsource it, or simply to stop those training courses for which there is little, or no, evidence of the actual delivery of added value, in terms of new or enhanced competences and improved performance levels.

Expressing the contribution of training in terms of total spend, training days delivered or numbers of employees 'trained' is no longer considered by those critical of HR's approach to measurement to be particularly useful. Such measures say little about outcomes or the value of training. The costs of training, both direct and indirect, need to be known so that the allocation of physical and financial resources can be accurately correlated with the value of the benefits associated with each training activity. Training needs to be seen as an investment, rather than as a consumer of resources, and to this end, being able to calculate or estimate the value of the returns is as important as knowing what the costs of training are.

STUDENT ACTIVITY 9.3 Calculating the costs and benefits of training

1. In groups, discuss the different types of costs associated with training employees. You can choose any type of training with which you are familiar, including:

- induction training;
- skills training;
- management development.

The objective is to produce a formula that incorporates all of the costs associated with the type of training you have chosen.

2. Estimate the financial values of each type of cost, and use your formula to produce an overall cost and a cost per trainee, making your own assumptions about the structure of the chosen course and numbers involved.

3. Devise a formula for estimating the value of the benefits or outcomes associated with the type of training chosen. These do not necessarily have to be expressed in financial terms. This is likely to be more difficult, but is nevertheless a worthwhile exercise.

233

Mayo (2001) is another influential writer who believes in the importance of quantification in HR. He is committed to the principle that everything can be quantified, and in ways that facilitate management and change. He claims that:

> Whether we are talking about the capability or potential of people, the culture in which they work ... measures for these can be found and tracked.
> (p 9)

Mayo's main contribution is in his work on measuring the asset value of employees, rather than on measuring absence or turnover levels. His more sophisticated approach involves measuring:

- people's human capital, which varies between employees, can rise as a result of personal and competency growth, and collectively represents the totality of human capital human available to the organization;
- aspects of the working environment, such as leadership, the level of practical support, the extent of team and cooperative working, the extent of learning and development, and the effective use of rewards and recognition;
- the financial and non-financial value to the organization generated by each/all employees.

He argues that, while employees do represent a cost in terms of their wages/salaries and other benefits, they are also an asset, in the sense that they create and add value. He is also clear that some employees represent a net cost, in the sense that the value of their contribution is less than the costs of employing them. Some employees are, or become, 'liabilities' and it is important that managers are able, through appropriate measurement activities, to identify these employees, as well as those who represent a high positive asset value.

The ability to calculate each person's *human asset worth* (HAW), and give it a numerical value that can be tracked over time and which can be compared with that of other employees, is based on the following formula:

$$\frac{HAW = EC \times IAM}{1000}$$

Where:

HAW = human asset worth;

EC = employment costs;

IAM = individual asset multiplier.

Essentially, Mayo's model is based on knowing what it costs to employ a person, and this is not only their wage or salary, but a more complete understanding of the costs associated with employment and the value of those factors, such as capability, potential, contribution and what he terms 'alignment to organizational values', that collectively express the person's gross asset worth or value (see further Mayo, 2001, pp 82 and 83).

There are, of course, questions that can be asked about the methodology and assumptions that underlie Mayo's model, but his concern with finding ways of measuring, and thereby distinguishing, individual asset values is understandable when so little is known about this area.

Measurement in HR – some important reservations

Despite the enthusiasm for measurement, the debate about its relevance, value and consequences is by no means one-sided. The purpose of this part of the chapter is to address some of the concerns associated with the increasing use of measurement and its extension to different areas of the HR function.

The first point to make relates to the collection of data that allows measurements to be made of the chosen parameter or variable. Without appropriate monitoring and recording systems, and without the accumulation of reliable data, managers can often find that they are presented with 'snapshots' rather than meaningful trends. Actions based on partial, flawed, unreliable or misleading data will undermine, rather than advance, the ability of measurement to improve HR's contribution to organizational performance: they might result in the wrong decisions being taken. Mooney (2001, p 95) suggests that managers need to consider the following criteria in deciding on their strategy on measurement.

- The relevance of the chosen measure to the overall business performance

    If the data relates to an aspect of employment or HR that is of no, or limited, value (defined by the appropriate stakeholders), little is gained from expending energy and resources in measuring it. Becker et al (2001), in their work on measurement in HR, make a similar point when they question how well existing HR measures capture the 'strategic HR drivers'. They go on to claim that there is often experienced:

    > ...a disconnect between what is measured and what is important.
    > (p 2)

- The amount of control that the HR function has over a particular measure

    The phenomenon or behaviour that is of interest to managers – for example, employee satisfaction with organizational leadership – is a result of a wide range of experiences outside the control of HR. The question arises: 'Is this something that the HR department should measure if it can't do much to influence these experiences?'

- The ease and reliability of data collection

    This raises questions about whether decisions on what to measure are unduly influenced by the ease with which data can be collected and analysed, rather than driven by the value and importance of the phenomena to which the data relates.

- Data quality

  This point relates to the reliability and integrity of the data, and the way in which it is analysed and interpreted. The key question is: 'What does the data actually show and can it be relied upon?'

Pfeffer and Sutton (2000) are two writers who, while accepting the potential value that appropriate and reliable measures can bring, are concerned to highlight the pitfalls and problems that managers face when the measurement process 'goes wrong'. They begin their chapter, 'When Measurement Obstructs Good Judgement', by claiming that:

> **Measures and the measurement process, especially badly designed or unnecessarily complex measures, are amongst the biggest barriers to turning knowledge into action.**
> (p 139)

They are particularly concerned about the many examples of measurement processes that fuel destructive behaviour, rather than helping managers dealing with it. They also claim that, even when such destructive measurement practices are identified, little is done to correct things.

Perhaps the most well-known, but nevertheless important, observation that they make is that measures focus particular attention on what is measured, often at the expense of other equally – or perhaps more – important behaviours. They point out that measures affect what people do, as well as what they notice and ignore, arguing that, as a consequence:

> **…everyone knows that what gets measured gets done, and that what is not measured gets ignored.**
> (p 140)

In addressing the potential and actual problems that managers experience with measurement, Pfeffer and Sutton offer the following suggestions:

- effective measurement systems that drive behaviour need to be simple enough to focus attention on key elements and fair enough that employees believe in, and support, them;

- measurements need to guide and direct behaviour, but not be so powerful and coercive that they become substitutes for judgement and wisdom. Managers need to interpret and ascribe meanings to what the measures are producing. The meaning may not be immediately apparent and managers may be unwilling to accept the 'correct' interpretation if this seems to reflect badly upon their actions;

- managers should avoid the overuse of 'end-of-process' measures, which can provide insights into how well or badly something has gone – but, because these are 'end' measures, it is often too late to correct a problem. Consider the use of evaluation questionnaires that ask students what they feel about a module after they have completed it. 'In-process' measures instead allow for the correction of mistakes and for more effective control in time to make a difference.

 STUDENT ACTIVITY 9.4

Read the case 'The best laid incentive plans' in the *Harvard Busines Review* (2003) 81:1, pp 27–37.

1. Explain what the case has to say about the relationship between data and actual behaviour.

2. In groups, discuss the examples of employees responding in unexpected and undesirable ways to the measures to which they were subject, and, in particular, try to explain their motivations and objectives.

3. Explore the underlying assumptions made by Hiram Phillips and his consultants about the use of the measures and the behaviour of employees.

4. Evaluate the choice of the performance measures imposed on the company and its employees, and consider alternative, and more effective, ones.

5. Given the original objectives, present your own ideas on the use of measures to improve performance.

Summary

HR professionals are increasingly required to take a more strategic role within their organizations, but the ability to operate strategically and the invitation to do so are heavily dependent on their ability to show clearly and consistently how their contribution can add value and contribute to organizational perform-ance. Understanding how employees create value and measuring the value creation processes is the challenge that the HR professional faces. Organizations, because they are unique, need to develop differ-ent approaches to the measurement of the things that are important to them and which help them create value, either through the reduction of costs (for example, those of sickness absence) or through increas-ing the asset value of their employees. One of the most important things that HR needs to know about are the consequences of its actions and policies, and whether these are positive, neutral or negative.

Workforce planning is an obvious aspect of HR that requires reliable and useful measurement tools and approaches, but there are many others that seem to be increasingly subject to measurement and evaluation. In considering what to measure and how, two things stand out. Firstly, measures are not ends in themselves, but means to ends. In other words, they contribute to the achievement of objectives and outcomes that matter to organizational stakeholders; if they don't, they fail the functionality test. Secondly, as the case study that ends the chapter shows, getting it wrong can have serious con-sequences. What many managers often fail to realize is that the introduction of HR measures does not simply represent a technical innovation or initiative. For those affected by measures and targets, their significance and impact is likely to be perceived and experienced in a rather different way: measures and targets can become instruments of coercion and punishment, and, because employees react to this perception, they can distort behaviour. The notion of unintended consequences considered in Chapter 2 is particularly relevant in such cases.

 Visit the Online Resource Centre that accompanies this book for self-test questions, weblinks, and more information on the topics covered in this chapter.
www.oxfordtextbooks.co.uk/orc/banfield_kay/

online resource centre

REVIEW QUESTIONS

1. How is human resource (or workforce) planning (HRP/WP) different from what used to be known as 'manpower planning'?

2. What the quantitative and qualitative aspects of HRP/WP?

3. What is the link between HRP and flexible employment patterns?

4. Why can the use of targets and measurements of performance distort behaviour and lead to the manipulation of figures, and how can this consequence be avoided?

5. What are the key contributions to effective HRP that HR professionals and line managers must make?

Northwood Council employs over 13,000 employees and is the largest employer in its local area, which has a population of 200,000 people. A brief overview of its workforce characteristics is as follows:

- 51 per cent work on a part-time basis;
- 32 per cent are male;
- over 50 per cent are aged 40+;
- 90 per cent are classified as white British;
- less than 1 per cent consider themselves to have a disability;
- over 30 per cent have worked at Northwood for over ten years.

Compared to the overall national average of eight days' absence per employee per year, Northwood continues to have a high level of absence. Over the past few years, managing absence has become a strategic priority for the Council, and it has invested considerable amounts of time and resources to try to reduce absence levels.

The average number of days' absence per employee for each of the last few years is as follows:

- *2001–02*: 10.66 days;
- *2002–03*: 11.31 days;
- *2003–04*: 15.7 days;
- *2004–05*: 13.21 days;
- *2005–06*: 12.29 days.

It can be seen that there was a significant reduction in absence between 2003–04 and 2004–05, and this can be attributed to some of the absence management interventions that were put into place. This included providing absence data to managers, the introduction of new absence management policy and procedures, and the provision of training for managers.

The absence management policy is a comprehensive document, which details the responsibilities of all parties when managing absence and also shows all of the procedures that have been followed. This includes the requirement that managers carry out a return-to-work interview after every absence. Northwood has also identified a set of 'trigger points', which means that, after a specified number of days or occasions of absence, a counselling interview will take place between the manager and the employee. Associated absence management practices include an emphasis on accurate recording and monitoring of absence data, and the use of departmental targets. Northwood has also tried to demonstrate its commitment to improving the well being of its staff by promoting a series of health-based events, such as routes for lunchtime walks and basic health checks during the working day.

The organization has been making steady progress in reducing its absence levels and has also set some ambitious future targets for the average number of days' absence per employee over each of the coming four years, as follow.

- *2007–08*: 11.25 days;
- *2008–09*: 10.75 days;
- *2009–10*: 10.25 days;
- *2010–11*: 9.9 days.

There is confidence that the absence levels can be reduced further because of the commitment of the organization to achieving this. Senior managers have this as one of their strategic priorities, and this has been communicated to managers and employees throughout all layers of the organization. Northwood →

has also looked to address some of the associated HR areas, such as work–life balance, general employee satisfaction and the content of job roles.

Questions

1. How might you explain the huge rise in absence levels between 2001–02 and 2003–04?

2. Why do you think that the interventions used to reduce absence between 2003–04 and 2004–05 managed to reduce absence so significantly?

3. Does the demographic profile of the organization have an impact on absence?

4. Are there any absence management interventions that the organization has not covered?

5. How do you think the trade unions have viewed the organization's growing focus on absence management?

FURTHER READING

Chartered Institute of Personnel and Development (2007) *New Directions in Managing Employee Absence*, CIPD research report.

House of Commons Health Committee (2007) *Fourth Report on Workforce Planning*, available online at www.publications.parliament.uk.

IRS Employment Review (2006) 'Recruitment and Retention', Issue 839, available online at www.irser.co.uk.

Liff, S (2000) 'Manpower or human resource planning: what's in a name?', in S Bach and K Sisson (eds) *Personnel Management: A Comprehensive Guide to Personnel Management*, 3rd edn, Blackwell.

Mintzberg, H (1994) *The Rise and Fall of Strategic Planning*, Prentice Hall.

Turner, P (2002) *HR Forecasting and Planning*, CIPD.

REFERENCES

Advisory Conciliation and Arbitration Service (2006) *Managing Attendence and Employee Turnover*, ACAS advisory booklet, available online at www.acas.org.uk.

Becker, BE, Huselid, MA and Ulrich, D (2001) *The HR Scorecard*, Harvard Business School Press.

Bennison, M (1980) *The IMS Approach to Manpower Planning*, IMS, ch 1.

Bennison, M and Casson, J (1984) *Manpower Planning Handbook*, IMS.

bin Idris, AR and Eldridge, D (1998) 'Reconceptualising human resource planning in response to institutional change', *International Journal of Manpower*, 19:5, pp 343–57.

Bramham, J (1994) *Human Resource Planning*, IPD.

Bratton, J and Gold, J (1999) *Human Resource Management*, 2nd edn, MacMillan Business.

Cascio, WF (1991) *Costing Human Resources: The Financial Impact of Behaviour in Organizations*, PWS-Kent.

Chartered Institute of Personnel and Development (2004) *Employee Absence: A Survey of Management Policy and Practice*, CIPD survey report, available online at www.cipd.co.uk.

Chartered Institute of Personnel and Development (2007) *Recruitment, Retention and Turnover*, CIPD survey report, available online at www.cipd.co.uk.

Confederation of British Industry (2004), *Workplace Absence Rises Amid Concerns Over Long-Term Sickness: CBI/AXA Survey*, CBI press release, available online at www.cbi.org.uk.

Dey, I and Power, H (2007) 'Bloodbath at ABN in London', *Daily Telegraph*, 1 April, p 7.

Fitz-Enz, J (2000) *The ROI of Human Capital*, AMACOM.

Health and Safety Executive (2004) *Managing Sickness Absence in the Public Sector – A Joint Review by the Ministerial Task Force for Health, Safety and Productivity and the Cabinet Office*, available online at **www.hse.gov.uk.**

Holbeche, L (2002) *Aligning Human Resources and Business Strategy*, Butterworth-Heinemann.

Kearns, P (2000) *Measuring and Managing Employee Performance*, FT/Prentice Hall.

Kerr, S (2003) 'The best laid incentive plans', *Harvard Business Review.* 81:1, pp 27–37.

Mayo, A (2001) *The Human Value of the Enterprise*, Nicholas Brealey Publishing.

Mooney, P (2001) *Turbo-Charging the HR Function*, CIPD.

Pfeffer, J and Sutton, RI (2000) *The Knowing–Doing Gap*, Harvard Business School Press.

Propper, C and Wilson, D (2003) 'The use and usefulness of performance measures in the public sector', *Oxford Review of Economic Policy*, 19:2, pp 250–67.

Reilly, P (1996) *Human Resource Planning: An Introduction*, IES Report No 312. See the summary of the report online at www.employment-studies.co.uk/.

Royal College of Nursing (2007) *Our NHS – Today and Tomorrow*, available online at **www.rcn.org.uk.**

Ulrich, D (1996) *Human Resource Champions*, Harvard Business School Press.

Wallop, H (2006) 'Bank holidays time off law "will penalise firms"', *Daily Telegraph*, 28 August.

Watson, TJ (2002) *Organising and Managing Work*, FT/Prentice Hall.

10 Learning and Development

Key Terms

Learning A fundamental and natural human process involving growth and change. Learning is about behavioural modification. It cannot be seen, but is inferred from differences in what we know, believe, and can do. Learning is the way in which we can improve and be different from that which we were. Learning needs to be understood as both a process and an outcome.

Training Can best be understood as planned, structured, and often formalized learning experiences that seek to develop specific skills and knowledge needed for effective job performance. Historically, employees have learnt many of the competencies they need to perform effectively by being trained.

Development A term often used to describe changes in the whole person and what they can do. It reflects the belief that all people have the potential to be more and do more, and that this potential needs to be developed as well as utilized. People can develop to a limited degree through training, but development implies the employment of a much wider range of learning experiences and methods, such as coaching and mentoring, not all of which are necessarily connected to the working environment.

Competence The combination of skills, knowledge, and experience that results in a person's ability to carry out specific tasks and procedures to a required standard. Can be equated to 'know-how' (Gladstone, 2000). A specific competency can also be understood as an underlying characteristic of a person, i.e. a trait, a belief, an ability or an attitude, that distinguishes one person from another and explains differences in job performance (Rothwell, 2004).

Human resource development This term came into usage in the late 1980s and early 1990s, and is used by many writers, but fewer practitioners, in preference to training. Its relationship to training is similar to that between Human Resource Management and Personnel Management, in that it represents a more holistic and strategic approach to learning than does training (Walton, 1999).

Learning Objectives

As a result of reading this chapter and using the Online Resource Centre, you should be able to:

- understand how people learn and recognize that training represents only one way in which people can learn at work;

- understand and explain why training and development are important to an organization and to its employees;

- identify different approaches to delivering learning;

- understand the importance of evaluating training and other approaches to work-based learning.

Introduction

Humans are designed to learn: people who don't learn rarely survive or prosper. While we are born with different levels of inherited capabilities and potential, we are all programmed to learn and, through learning, grow as individuals. But some people seem to learn more than others, learn more quickly and attain higher levels of performance. Learning is a common characteristic, but also one that distinguishes one person from another in that some people seem to be 'better learners'.

From the day on which we are born, we embark on a lifelong journey of learning. We are the most versatile of all animals and are able to adapt to the widest variety of environments, because of our capacity to learn the skills, knowledge and best approach to be successful in the environment in which we find ourselves. The make-up of the human brain is much the same whether we choose to live and work in a fast-paced city environment or to adopt a subsistence lifestyle in a remote area with very low population density. The capabilities we must acquire to survive and succeed in these different environments are, however, themselves vastly different and we require very different learning experiences to enable us to develop the necessary skills to survive and do well in each.

Most people will thrive when exposed to positive learning experiences and will continue to enjoy learning throughout their lives, but it is important to recognize that people can also be damaged by negative experiences of learning, particularly as children. This can have a lasting effect on their motivation to learn later in life, as adults. Nevertheless, learning new skills and acquiring knowledge, and therefore becoming better equipped to survive and succeed, are important to everyone because these connect to a person's sense of achievement and self-esteem.

STUDENT ACTIVITY 10.1

The following appeared in a CIPD examination paper in 2006:

Reading about what looked like an interesting website that invited people to write in with 'their most dangerous idea', you checked it out and found that the head of learning at an American university claimed that schools were bad for children and should be closed. His argument was based on the belief that learning in schools involves children being spoon-fed information and repeatedly tested to see if they can regurgitate it. This creates stressed-out children and adults who avoid all learning because it reminds them of their school experiences. He concluded his entry by saying that 'we need to produce adults who love learning and can think for themselves'.

1. In the context of your own experience of learning, what were the things that you enjoyed about learning and what didn't you like?

2. Think about the learning achievements that have been particularly important to you. Why were they important and how did you develop as a result of these experiences?

3. How can we make learning enjoyable and meaningful for adults, particularly those who have experienced learning failures?

We can learn in many different ways, not all of which produce the kinds of outcomes to which either the individual or the training professional is committed. Learning at work, and for work, involves particular difficulties and challenges. Training, as a way of learning, is, from a managerial perspective, usually seen in instrumental terms. This means that learning is linked to the acquisition of new or increased competencies and capabilities, which are used in the production of goods or services. These competencies and capabilities are only needed because they help to create value and wealth for the company. Quite simply, people and their capabilities are used by those who employ and manage them to generate goods and services that have a social or financial value.

People are employed not only for what they already know and can do, but also for what they may subsequently learn to do. Because of the dynamic nature of the working environment, employees are constantly expected to update their knowledge, learn new skills and acquire new capabilities. There is a presumption, therefore, that all employees will not only work, but will also continue to learn. To be effective and to continue to make a positive contribution to the employing organization, employees need to be active learners. But it is also important to recognize that, if an employee believes that the only beneficiary from his or her improved competence is the employer, learning through training will inevitably be seen as something he or she is required, rather than wants, to do. The positive motivation to learn cannot be taken for granted and must be nurtured, so that employees see learning as important for themselves as well as for the organization.

KEY CONCEPT Motivation

This is about the drives and needs within each person that direct and influence their behaviours. People are constantly interpreting their environment by reference to their own and others' interests, and act accordingly. Unless employees *want* to learn, they will try to avoid it. Coercing people to learn rarely works and is often counterproductive. If they are forced to participate in training, the most that will happen is that they will 'be there'. The reality is that the desired learning will not take place because those attending the activity lack the motivation to learn from it.

HRM INSIGHT 10.1 Occupational health training at Southfield College

Southfield College decided to close one of its main sites, situated at the edge of the city, in which the college was located. On completion of the new arts block, located within the city centre campus, staff were moved into the new building during the summer break. At the beginning of the new academic term, all staff in the new building received an email from the head of the college's health and safety department, informing them that they were required to attend a health and safety training event. The purpose of this event was to inform staff about fire regulations and procedures in the new building. This was scheduled at a particularly busy period in the academic year and there was little enthusiasm for attending the training among the staff.

Because it clashed with another commitment, one of the lecturers informed the HR department that he would be unable to attend. Shortly afterwards, he and everyone else who worked in the new building were informed by letter that failure to attend the training event would be considered a disciplinary offence.

Questions

1. How might the effectiveness of the planned training be affected by the way in which staff were notified of the event and why?

2. What might have been done differently to create a positive attitude towards the planned training?

3. What effect do you think the intervention from HR had on staff attitudes to HR and their motivation to participate in future training events?

'Learning' was 'training'

Think again about our reference, in Chapter 1, to the people building the Egyptian Pyramids and the British railway/canal networks: how did the workers acquire the knowledge and skills that they needed to carry out all of the tasks and operations they were required to perform? They learnt primarily by 'doing', which means that they learnt from the experience of working, but also, as operations became more complex and challenging, they would have learned by being trained. Obviously experience played its part, as it still does today, but increasingly more focused and directed learning, which involved people being taught and instructed by others who already possessed the required knowledge and skills, would have been the way in which more and more employees acquired the behavioural capabilities they needed to do their jobs.

Over time, learning became increasingly structured, planned and formalized. Training was seen as the means by which people could learn what they needed to know and do. Training itself became a profession. As Davis and Davis (1998) conclude:

> Training, with great impetus from the exigencies of two world wars became a function within organizations, and its processes became formalised. Like other work, training itself became work and was assigned to the people who performed it. This became the basis assumption about the place of training in organizations for almost half a century and is still the basic concept that governs how learning takes place in most organizations.

Why train employees?

Consider for a moment how training and development fits into HR and the strategic organizational agenda. In Chapter 1, the development of the human resource was explained as a key objective of organizations that, in order to remain competitive and efficient, need constantly to refresh the skills and competencies of their employees. Developing the resource is one of the fundamental objectives of people management, because it is through employees' growth and development that they increase their asset value and acquire new, or higher, capabilities that organizations need and managers can utilize.

But training can also be seen to be in the interests of employees who, through planned and structured learning, can acquire new competencies and capabilities, which they own. It adds to the value of their human capital. This not only increases their value to the employer, but increases their attractiveness to other employers: it enhances their employability and value in the labour market. In practical terms, this can result in increases in pay (skill and qualification-based pay are part of many organizations' reward strategy) or lead to offers of more rewarding jobs elsewhere.

KEY CONCEPT Human capital

The knowledge, skills, abilities and capacity to develop and innovate that is possessed by people in an organization (CIPD, 2006).

As well as supporting both employee and managerial interests, training is important because of the way in which it has the potential for facilitating:

- organizational change;
- functional flexibility;
- attitudinal change;
- statutory compliance.

Using a mechanical metaphor, training, as part of a strategy for learning and personal development, is arguably the most powerful 'lever' that managers can use to achieve these important objectives.

It is rare for major new organizational initiatives not to be linked to training of some sort or another, but there is a danger that training can be overloaded with expectation and used inappropriately or unrealistically. Training can be ineffective as well as effective – much depends on whether training is the 'right' lever to pull and, of course, on who is pulling it (Boydell and Leary, 1996).

Training can also be an expensive activity and the resources needed to equip a specialized function do not come cheaply. Off-the-job training will incur the cost of either purchasing the professional training support or of providing a skilled person in the organization to design and deliver the training. Often both will be involved. On top of this, there is the cost of releasing employees and covering their work for the period during which they are undergoing training. Additionally, there will be cost involved with expenses that are incurred by trainers and trainees, including facilities and materials. So why do organizations bother with all of this expense? Why not simply recruit someone who is fully trained already?

More often than not, it is not possible to recruit the ideal person with the exact skills needed for the job. Even when good candidates are available, they will still need to learn the unique systems, processes and procedures operating within the organization. In addition, change is a feature of most organizations and, as a consequence, so is the need to learn the new skills necessary for adapting to changing products, technologies and markets. Technology, in particular, is constantly being improved and updated; new working arrangements are frequently introduced as a result of reorganization and attempts to re-engineer operating processes and procedures, and all of these require the employee to learn new things.

Training, for many, is therefore an essential part of surviving change and maintaining the currency of what they know and what they can do.

Table 10.1 summarizes the potential power that training possesses.

Table 10.1 The six 'Es' of training – why organizations train employees

Engage	Effective training provides the opportunity for employees to connect with the organization, and with its policies and methods of working. It helps to ensure that employees 'buy into', or engage with, the organization's culture. It helps to make employees feel valued and develop working relationships with their colleagues.
Educate	Training can help to educate or increase the knowledge and awareness of individuals and teams.
Enhance	Training can help to enhance or improve the skills and competence of individuals and teams within an organization.
Empower	By properly training employees, an organization can increase the accountability of teams and individuals, and can ensure that faster, better quality decisions can be made, while avoiding the need to pass decision making unnecessarily up the organizational chain.
Energize	Participation in training can help to energize, motivate and inspire employees. It provides an opportunity to take a step back and allows people to consider how they can best contribute towards the effectiveness of the organization.
Enlighten	Training can also be an effective means of helping individuals to see things in a different way. It can help employees reach an often sudden conclusion that there is a better, more effective, way of doing something and can help to unlock previously untapped potential.

HRM INSIGHT 10.2 Taylor's Laundry Services

Taylor's is a medium-sized, privately owned business, employing around 200 people. It supplies industrial clothing to a variety of private and public sector customers, and provides a regular laundry service for those customers who require it. Most employees work in the laundry, ensuring that garments are properly washed, dried and sorted for return to customers within a short timeframe. Most jobs have relatively low skill requirements and new recruits are regarded as being able to pick up the work very quickly on the job. They are therefore put straight on the job on their first day in the business, having been shown where the fire exits are and how to operate the washing and drying machinery.

Time off the job for training is seen as costly and so people pick up the job by asking more experienced staff what to do. Staff turnover is high, with even relatively new employees passing on skills to new recruits.

Questions

1. What kind of training would this organization benefit from?

2. What cost is the company incurring as a result of the lack of effective training provision?

3. How is the lack of a training function impacting on other HR issues?

4. How would you design a realistic training intervention(s) that would address the above problems?

Criticisms of training

While the theoretical case for training is undeniable, the reality is often disappointing. There is a sense that training – or, perhaps more accurately, those with training responsibilities – have too often failed to deliver what has been promised and expected, to the point at which the credibility of the training function has been compromised. Criticisms of the effectiveness of training are not new (Megginson et al, 1993), but, worryingly, persist. Davis and Davis (1998, ch 2) suggest that one explanation for training's credibility problem is because '*learning got left out* '.

They, at least, would agree that, if not left out, learning must either have been neglected or that the central role of learning in training has not been fully understood or articulated. They offer two reasons for this worrying neglect.

- Training, frequently seen as a response to a performance problem, has become routinized and, under pressure to provide a response, trainers have failed to reflect on the reasons for its successes and failures.

  Particular factors that have a bearing on whether training 'works' are:

  – trainee motivation;

  – the importance of practice and application;

  – the critical role of the line manager in supporting trainees.

- Trainers themselves often lack sufficient understanding of learning theories and, while they may be knowledgeable about the technique, subject matter or procedure, many are not professional trainers. This is an important point because it suggests that, whatever the inherent limitations of training are, the key to its success or failure are the personal and professional qualities of those who train, and the extent to which they can effectively manage the whole training process.

Writing more recently, Sloman and Webster (2005) offer an interesting insight into the problems of training. Partly, they argue, these are due to changes in the nature of work and the kind of employees on which organizations increasingly depend for their long-term success, i.e. those they describe as 'knowledge workers'. They claim that traditional classroom-based training courses are likely to be of limited value to the learning and development of this category of employee. While this is a realistic and sensible conclusion, their hypothesis that '*a shift is taking place from training to learning*' is not quite as straightforward as it seems.

They are not, however, alone in emphasizing the limitations of training and the need to focus on generating learning through more effective methods and approaches. The *IRS Management Review* also emphasizes the trend away from training to learning. Describing training as a reactive activity designed to resolve short-term operational deficiencies rather than being connected to the long-term needs of the individual or the business, the point is made that:

> **...organisations have recognised that the traditional ad hoc approach to training is incompatible with the need to adapt quickly to changing business circumstances.**
> **(IRS, 1998)**

This distinction between training and learning was explored in an earlier article by Sloman (2004), who reflected on the limitations of course-based training and its emphasis on content, instruction and the passive involvement of trainees, leading to prescribed behavioural change. He concluded that learning was the way forward, generated by:

- motivated participants;
- self-direction;
- work-based processes and locations.

In addition to uncertainties over whether learning is, or can be, generated through training, there is the added problem of line managers failing to understand their responsibilities with regard to the use of training. According to Cosgrove and Speed (1995, cited by Rothwell, 1996), senior managers often fail to specify what they expect from the training function and training professionals, in an attempt to please everyone and gain support for their work, raise unrealistic expectations of what training can deliver. They fail to understand the importance of integrating it with corporate strategy.

HRM INSIGHT 10.3 Paul Kearns' story of an unhelpful director

Many years ago, when I had only been in my new job as head of training for a couple of weeks, our technical director came into my office and asked me if I could organise some presentation skills training for his team of engineers. I have to admit that I did not particularly like the way he just expected me to deal with his requests immediately, without any prior discussion. So my first reaction was, 'can we sit down and talk about exactly what you want?' This was not the reaction he had been used to from my predecessor. He seemed impatient and more or less intimated, 'what is there to talk about?' As far as he was concerned it was a simple matter of sending his engineers on a course.

(This material is taken from *Evaluating the ROI from Learning*, by Kearns, P., 2005, with the permission of the publisher, the Chartered Institute of Personnel and Development, London.)

Questions

1. What did Kearns want to talk to the director about and why?

2. If Kearns had simply done what he had been asked and organized presentation skills training for the engineers, what might the outcome have been?

3. What strategy might Kearns adopt to try to change the attitude of the director towards training and the role of training experts?

Rothwell (1996) shares with Ulrich (1998) the view that, historically, training has been focused too much on activities, such as organizing and delivering courses, rather than on hard results and valued outcomes. Moreover, Rothwell believes that many customers of training mistakenly believe that high-profile training activity automatically means results and that offering more training inevitably improves performance. Both assumptions are questionable. In his critique of traditional approaches to training, he argues that the main problems that need to be overcome in any attempt to 'reframe' training are as follows.

● **Its lack of focus**

There are too many terms in the field – education, development etc. – and different job titles within the training community create confusion about what people actually do and what training actually means.

● **Its lack of management support**

Senior executives and line management often express concerns over training's importance, costs, credibility and effectiveness, and fail to understand their own responsibilities.

● **It is not conducted and managed systematically**

Poorly carried out training needs analysis fails to identify the nature of the performance problem; training methods and materials are not carefully matched with training requirements and little is done to ensure that transfer of learning takes place.

● **It is not linked to other organizational initiatives**

Training is often undertaken in isolation from other HR practices and management initiatives, and, however effective it might have been, quickly loses its impact because of this 'lack of connectivity'. Training becomes something that is 'bolted on' rather than integrated and embedded.

● **It can be used unrealistically to try to achieve attitudinal change, which is rarely, if at all, achievable through conventional training interventions**

In such areas as diversity, equal opportunities and racial awareness, deeply rooted prejudices, beliefs and behaviours are unlikely to be touched and changed through instruction or course-based training.

Training can, if properly designed and managed, help employees to acquire knowledge and skills; it is much more difficult to believe that it can change the way in which they think and see the world.

STUDENT ACTIVITY 10.2 'Fixing the problem'

Look carefully at Figure 10.1, which represents a model of what might be described as a 'flawed approach to training', and answer the following questions.

1. Taking each stage in turn, identify what changes and improvements should be made.
2. How might the trainees contribute to each stage of the model?
3. What might line managers contribute?

As a result of answering the above questions, design your own improved model of the training process. You can carry this out as a group activity, and present your results for discussion and evaluation.

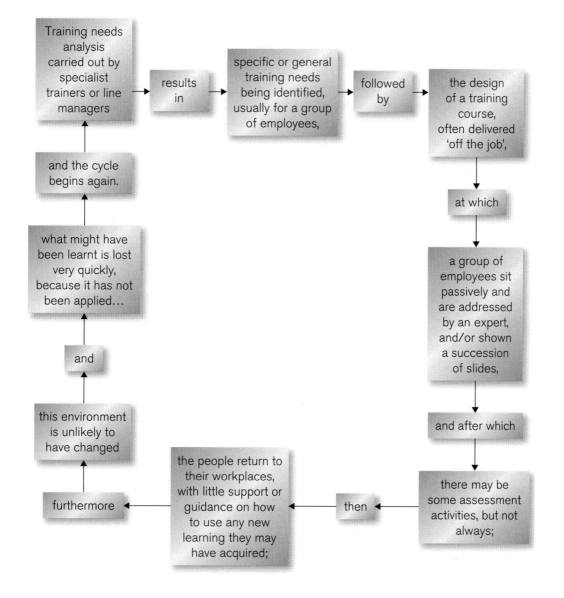

Figure 10.1 A flawed model of the training cycle

If the employee's experience of training reflects even parts of the approach to training illustrated in Figure 10.1, the probability of any positive and lasting outcomes being created is likely to be low or non-existent. In fact, it might even be negative, because employees may be deterred from any further participation in training by the negative experiences of a flawed process. The specific weaknesses and problems associated with this model are not difficult to identify and include:

- the lack of direct involvement and ownership of trainees;
- the assumption that other people – line managers and trainers – know what employees need to learn and that reliable processes exist to identify learning requirements;
- the practice of subjecting employees, who may have quite different interests, skills, knowledge and motivation, to the same training programmes;
- the belief that taking employees 'off the job' and out of their working environment facilitates learning;
- the belief that the transfer and application of any new learning that might occur is not problematical;
- the failure to recognize that employees learn as much, if not more, from informal processes and interactions than they do from planned and formalized interventions;
- the idea that training can be wholly managed and controlled by others and still be effective.

On a more optimistic note

A combination of budgetary pressures and the need for training to re-establish its credibility as a 'value-adding' activity has resulted in an improved understanding of what training can and cannot achieve, and a more effective use of training interventions. According to Peter Cresswell (in Hope, 2005), general manager for consultancy services at Siemens:

> Over the years training has improved considerably. We are now looking at how effective the training has actually been. It is important that organizations know what they want out of training and are able to measure it, to prove that they have achieved their objectives.

Evidence from recent research, into the way in which many organizations have redefined and aligned their training and development functions, shows that traditional models and thinking about training have been replaced with more effective and valued approaches, based in part on a closer integration between training and business strategy. Of particular interest is the way in which the 'business partner' model of HR is driving training in a more strategic and focused direction (see Hirsh and Tamkin, 2005a, b; Smethurst, 2006a).

Signpost to Chapter 2: HRM: An Academic and Professional Perspective, for insights into the value of the HR function

Many organizations are reporting major new training and development initiatives (see Warren, 2006; Smethurst, 2006a). Research carried out by the Adult Learning Inspectorate and published in its 2004–05 report (Scott, 2005) provides evidence of more widespread improvements in training. It found that 75 per cent of providers of learning at work had passed inspections in the previous 12 months, compared to only 40 per cent four years before.

What emerges from many of these examples of new thinking and practices in training is the importance of the following (Hope, 2005):

- employees who want to participate actively in their own learning;
- close working relationships between trainers and line managers that result in agreement on training plans, skill and competency needs, and line support for learners;
- accurate diagnosis of training and development needs;
- opportunities for the reinforcement of learning through practice;

- designing bespoke training solutions rather than offering 'courses for all';
- a connection between the delivery of training, its evaluation, and the planning and design of future training interventions, i.e. a cycle of learning and application;
- a strong relationship between the required learning outcomes and the learning methods employed.

Different perceptions of the value of training

In addition to the debate about whether, and under what circumstances, training delivers the required learning outcomes, significant differences have been expressed over the economic status of training (Kearns, 2005).

Training as a cost

As argued earlier in the chapter, there are direct and indirect costs involved in training employees that have to be paid for, either from a central training budget or from budgets devolved to line managers. Training can also be perceived as an overhead, i.e. a charge on all income-generating departments irrespective of whether they actually benefit from any centralized training provision. Seen as a cost, training is likely to be limited in scope and intensity: costs, generally, are something to be reduced. It might be thought that organizations that employ low-skilled workers are more likely to see the costs of training in a negative way, believing that adequate supplies of labour in the external labour market can meet all of their skill requirements. Surprisingly, however, the perception that training is a cost to be minimized is not restricted to such companies. Pfeffer (1998) provides evidence of national differences in the amount of training provided among motor manufacturing plants. He presents data that shows Japanese plants providing 364 hours of training in the first six months for new employees, while the respective figures for European and Australian plants are 178 days and 40 days respectively. One can speculate that, in the latter two examples, training is seen more as a cost to be controlled rather than as an investment.

In their study of human resource practices in UK companies, Truss et al (1997) provide similar evidence of minimal levels of training being provided. In one large retailing and distribution company, it was found that less than half of the employees received any training in the year prior to the research. In only two of the other seven organizations studied did more than half of the respondents indicate that they had received the training they needed to do their jobs.

Training as an investment

Seen from this perspective, training represents a key instrument in developing capacity and capability to support organizational objectives. As Kearns (2005) states:

We should think of it as an important lever through which we can gain competitive advantage.
(p 13)

This means, however, that the contribution which training makes needs to be systematically evaluated and that some attempt must be made to calculate the returns on investment in training. Pfeffer (1998) again provides interesting examples of organizations that spend heavily on training and relate this spend to changes in key performance indicators. He cites the Men's Warehouse, whose sustained growth in revenues and net earnings is linked to its investment in training. According to Pfeffer:

The key to its success has been how it treats its people and particularly the emphasis it has placed on training, an approach that separates it from many of its competitors.
(p 88)

Interestingly, while claiming that training is an investment, Pfeffer accepts that return on investment calculations are difficult, if not impossible, and that successful firms who invest heavily in training:

... do so almost as a matter of faith and because of their belief in the connection between people and profits.
(p 89)

HRM Insight 10.3 illustrates that, while the financial quantification of the worth of training is (for most practical purposes) not an option, a belief in its value and relevance shapes many organizations' support for it.

HRM INSIGHT 10.4 **The German engineering company**

Some years ago, one of the authors was part of a group of staff and students on a visit to West Germany. The purpose of the visit was broadly educational, and involved visiting different organizations to learn about management and how businesses in Germany were run. One of the companies visited was a medium-sized engineering company that manufactured a range of products used in the construction industry. At that time, and as with other European economies, West Germany was in the grip of a recession and demand for the company's products was falling. Similar businesses in the UK were shedding labour and cutting back on their training programmes, particularly those for craft apprentices. Training resources tend to be plentiful when companies are doing well, but in periods of economic difficulty, they tend to be the first to be cut. It is a cost that can easily be identified and from which, consequently, savings can be made.

Talking to the training manager in the German company, I asked him whether his company was planning a similar cost-reduction strategy. His answer was, in many ways, surprising because it represented a more forward-thinking and strategic approach to training. He said that the company was definitely not planning to cut the number of apprentices it employed, nor the training they received. When asked why, he asserted that these apprentices were the future of the company and that, when business picked up, they would be fully skilled and able to meet the expected increase in demand for the company's products. He also made the point that, within reason, employees not engaged full time on production might use their time in developing new skills that would increase their functional flexibility and value to the company.

Questions

1. What are the implications for training of an organization's shedding of labour and cutting back on training when demand falls?

2. How can underutilized resources be used to provide training?

3. The German company's approach to training reflected part of a wider management philosophy: how might this be characterized?

STUDENT ACTIVITY 10.3

The costs of training cannot easily be ignored, particularly if there is uncertainty over the value of the training delivered. This activity is designed to generate a genuine understanding of training costs and how they can be reduced without cutting back on the training provided.

1. What are the costs associated with training? How can these be reduced without compromising the learning experience?

2. What are the advantages and disadvantages of spending a fixed proportion of turnover on training and requiring everyone to spend a minimum number of days being trained?

3. How can training be evaluated and how might the return on investment be calculated?

4. Is there a case for employees paying part of the costs of their own training and, if so, what is it?

Types of training

Training differs widely in terms of its purpose and focus. The following categories represent the most familiar contexts in which training is used.

1. Induction training

This type of training is used to facilitate the entry, participation and socialization of new recruits into the job and organization. This form of training primarily provides knowledge about key aspects of the employment contract, HR procedures, health and safety issues, and the social organization of work.

 Signpost to Chapter 13: Case Study: HR and the New Opening, for an example of the importance of induction training in a new hotel

2. Job-specific operational procedures

Employees whose work involves performing manual or administrative tasks that define the work they do need to be competent in each of the tasks or elements that constitute their jobs. Each task or element has a knowledge and skill level that, once attained, means that the employee is qualified or competent to do the job. Training, often based on a mixture of on-the-job and classroom-based instruction followed by practice and testing, has been the conventional way of generating what can be described as job 'know-how'.

3. Technology training

An increasing number of employees use technology as part of their jobs and job performance is often critically linked to the ability to use software applications. Learning the intricacies of software functionalities through trial and error, watching others or by any other informal method would probably take longer, involve more mistakes and cost more than a training-based approach. Training will involve an element of instruction, structured practice and feedback from the trainer, and testing against established performance standards.

4. Mandatory training

This is training that the organization must perform in order to comply with its own, or externally imposed, rules and regulations. Much of this is driven by health and safety regulations, and involves a mixture of knowledge and some operational skills. Training tends to be the preferred way of generating the required learning, with a mixture of training methods used under the control of 'experts'.

5. Improvement training

Improvement training is focused on developing competencies that are additional to core job competencies, and which are designed to improve the effectiveness and efficiency of job performance. The areas that are covered might include problem solving, selling techniques, customer service, the giving of feedback, interviewing methods, change management, and so on. Training, in the form of planned and structured knowledge-exchange sessions, is usually employed for these purposes, at least in part, to provide the necessary knowledge base. This type of training does, however, lend itself to more experiential learning, with videos, exercises, role playing and reflection being used in addition to more traditional methods.

6. Attitudinal training

Training has been increasingly used to influence not only what employees know and can do, but what they believe, how they think and how they behave towards others. The growth in the use of training in areas such as equal opportunities, diversity and race relations reflects the growing importance of such matters socially and the importance they are given by many HR professionals, particularly in the public sector. This type of training relies heavily on the role of experts, classroom instruction, and the transference of language, beliefs and procedures in highly formalized settings. As suggested earlier, such methods have not always proved successful, and more powerful and effective learning experiences may need to be employed if changes in attitudes and behaviour are to be achieved. One of the difficulties of using training to change attitudes is that is difficult to establish what has actually been achieved. Success is more likely to be expressed in terms of participation rates and budgetary expenditure, rather than in terms of the value of any improvements in job performance.

→ Signpost to Chapter 6: Equality in Employment, for insights into equal opportunities training and its effectiveness

STUDENT ACTIVITY 10.4

Choose any one, or more, of these six types of training and design an actual training event or activity that would deliver specified learning outcomes. Make any realistic assumptions you want to, and think creatively about what you need to do and how to achieve the objective of generating the required learning. Present your ideas for discussion and evaluation.

Developments in workplace learning

The debate referred to earlier in this chapter about training and learning involved two key issues.

Firstly, questions were raised about the limitations of training, particularly with regards to over-reliance on training courses and the role of the trainer as 'expert', and whether such criticisms undermined the credibility of training as a planned and structured source of learning. We concluded that training continues to have a role to play, but only if the responsible parties respond to criticisms from participants and line managers, and begin to develop practices that are grounded in appropriate theories and principles of learning, which also reflect actual business requirements.

Secondly, the trend away from 'training' towards 'learning' suggests that non-course-based approaches and practices need to be developed to reflect developments in the nature of work and of workers. This means that structured learning, i.e. learning that is planned and is associated with specific outcomes, should be more individualized and learner-centred rather than 'imposed from above', and must be embedded in the working environment.

This recognition that the workplace, rather than the training room, should be the primary context in which learning is located is a theme shared by many of the writers to whom we have already referred. 'Workplace learning', or 'work-based learning', is associated with the following contemporary beliefs:

- that the workplace, in terms of its physical and social environments, is a site for learning and offers a range of learning opportunities;
- that many of these opportunities are informal and opportunistic rather than formal and planned;
- that the workplace needs to be understood as a learning, as well as a working, environment;
- that working and learning are inextricably linked.

According to Stern and Sommerlad (1999), these beliefs translate into the following representations of the relationship between learning and work.

1. In the first instance, learning and working are spatially separated: they exist at different times, with forms of structured learning activities (training) occurring off the job. This usually involves in-company training, using dedicated training rooms and expert instructors, with opportunities for experiential learning and practice.

2. In the second instance, the workplace is itself conceptualized as an environment for learning. The emphasis on on-the-job learning methods encompasses those that are highly structured and those that are located at the informal end of the spectrum. According to Stern and Sommerlad (1999, p 2),

learning is primarily intentional and planned, and is aimed at training employees '*by supporting, structuring and monitoring their learning*'.

The two main forms of on-the-job training that emerge from this conception are:

- experience-led learning opportunities, through such means as job rotation, job enlargement, the sequencing of the learner's activities, and increasing the variety and complexity of tasks;
- training on the job, through coaching, mentoring, work shadowing, supervision, instruction and feedback.

A third form of learning is associated with the concept of 'continuous learning' (Zuboff, 1998). Learning, from this perspective, is seen as an everyday part of the job and the working experience. Employees become learners and teachers, with knowledge and ideas being shared among what Lave and Wenger (1991) call 'communities of practice', within which learning emerges out of the social interactions between co-workers and customers/clients. Contemporary thinking about HRD is also concerned with the characteristics and learning implications of the workplace. Clark (2005), for example, claims that:

> ...**developing a supportive learning climate has come to the fore of the human resource development literature.**

Interestingly, he argues that the environment is not simply a source of learning opportunities and practices, but that certain aspects of the environment are likely to influence the learning of individuals and groups. These aspects include:

- culture;
- HR policies;
- interpersonal dynamics;
- work practices;
- line manager capabilities and orientations.

What emerges from this brief reference to the learning environment is the importance of context. Whether learning emerges from the ongoing social interaction at the place of work or as a result of more planned and structured training interventions, the influence on these experiences of a wider set of factors cannot be ignored. If HR professionals are genuinely interested in increasing the effectiveness of workplace learning, it will be necessary to address barriers to learning that may exist in the workplace itself, in addition to developing more effective learning interventions.

STUDENT ACTIVITY 10.5 **Designing a learning environment**

This is a group exercise and requires access to a working environment, which can be the university or college if you are full-time students. The objective is to discover people's views about the extent to which their working environment facilitates learning.

1. Design a questionnaire that seeks to measure the extent to which the working environment affects learning. The questions should focus on key influences, practices and behaviours that are linked to learning, as well as barriers to learning, and should be completed by a representative sample of employees/students.

2. Present the findings of the survey and discuss the results.

3. Establish what are the main barriers, or obstacles, to learning.

4. Discuss changes that might be made to the learning environment that would increase the amount of learning created or which would remove the blockages to learning.

The growth of e-learning

Martyn Sloman's influential book on e-learning (2001) places this new approach to learning in a wider context. He argues that this development it is not simply about the use of technology, claiming that:

Today's training professionals are operating at the beginning of a revolution. Importantly, it is about much more than the arrival of a new platform for the delivery of training. The context in which the trainer operates, internal and external relationships and the role itself can be expected to undergo profound changes.

KEY CONCEPT e-learning

This can be understood as learning that is delivered, enabled or mediated using electronic technology for the explicit purpose of training in organizations (CIPD, 2007a).

As with most new developments in HR, the emergence of e-learning has not been without controversy, central to which has been the role of technology. Elliott Masie (**www.masie.com**), for example, not only argues that e-learning is not about computers and computing, but that the 'e' should be an abbreviation for 'experience', not 'electronic'. The point being made is that there is real danger in concentrating on systems, portals, and technology-driven 'learning solutions', and in seeing them as ends rather than means. As Sloman says:

There is a danger of becoming seduced by the functionality of the technology rather than concentrating on its use.

(p 42)

Forms of e-learning

- Web-based training

  In corporate training, technology is used primarily to deliver content to the end user without significant interaction with (or support from) training professionals, peers or managers.

- Interactive online learning

  Particularly used in further and higher education, but also in organizations with their own intranet, the emphasis here is on the delivery of courses and support material online. Platforms such as 'Blackboard' also provide opportunities for exchanges of information, interaction with tutors, collaborative activities, and, depending on the nature of the course, assessment and online feedback. There has also been a very significant growth in the private sector, with specialist companies offering a range of generic and bespoke e-learning solutions (Alcock, 2005).

- Informal e-learning

  Beyond these 'course-based' approaches to e-learning are the growing opportunities for technology to support informal learning in the workplace. In many knowledge-intensive organizations, technology is linked with knowledge management strategies and developing intranet capabilities to facilitate knowledge exchange linked to 'communities of practice'.

- Standalone e-learning materials

  These take the form of CD ROM-based learning. In this case, there is no support provision or interaction outside of the CD ROM-based material.

The case for e-learning

The following arguments have been put forward in support of e-learning.

- It frees people from the spatial and physical restrictions associated with classroom-based learning. This means that people can, theoretically, learn at times and in locations suitable to them and their lifestyles.
- It creates the ability to offer flexibility in the way in which people learn. A person can learn at his or her own pace and can choose a learning package that is suitable for his or her own learning style.
- E-learning has the potential to reduce significantly the cost of training. Despite the high initial investment in e-learning packages, these have the ability to support the learning of large numbers of people both on, and off, site.
- E-learning helps to create the 'independent learner', who is able to take control of his or her own learning.
- It facilitates the tracking of progress and achievements.
- It is critical for connecting people and databases, and for facilitating collaborative working and learning.

But what is the reality of adopting an e-learning strategy? Are the claims made in its support justified by the experiences of both trainers and employees who are using e-learning methods? Evidence from the CIPD (2007b) suggests a growing trend towards the use of e-learning. It found that:

- 48 per cent of respondents reported that they used e-learning;
- over two-thirds (67 per cent) expected its use to increase.

These findings confirmed the results of an online poll conducted by the CIPD in 2004, which concluded that, despite issues over implementation, e-learning had become an accepted part of training provision (CIPD, 2005).

The evidence from individual organizations that have invested heavily in an e-learning strategy suggests that e-learning is not a solution in itself, but can make an important contribution to workplace learning and training (see **www.cipd.co.uk** for case studies in this field). The experience of Hilton International may be indicative of the limitations of e-learning. Commenting on the organization's experience, Hilton's director of international learning and development said that:

> ... e-learning will never replace any other learning method. Certain areas can be learnt only up to a point with e-learning.
> (Smethurst, 2006b)

The message seems to be that developing and implementing an e-learning strategy takes time, commitment and considerable resources. Those companies that see this as an evolving and improving process, based on a realistic understanding of its limitations, are those that are likely to reap the promised benefits. On the other hand, those that have unrealistic expectations, apply it to types of learning for which it is unsuited, and fail to provide effective learner support and feedback mechanisms, are likely to express disappointment with the experience.

Understanding and managing the learning process

So far, this chapter has focused on *what* people at work need to learn and why, and the different *methods* that can be made available for them to learn. What has only been indirectly alluded to – the actual way in which learning takes place – must now be addressed.

Learning, as a process, has several important characteristics:

- you cannot see it happening – it is essentially a cognitive process;

- you can only see that learning has taken place through changes in the way people think, behave and work;

- people may well have learnt something new or already possess a valued competency, but may choose not to use and display it;

- 'real' learning relates to knowledge, skills and attitudes that are embedded within the individual. Some learning can be described as temporary and superficial, which can be easily lost;

- no one can learn for you. HR professionals and line managers can help others to learn, provide 'learning-rich' learning environments and support learning with a wide range of resources, but learning is only something that individuals can do, i.e. learning lies within the domain of the individual;

- we may choose not to engage in certain kinds of learning because of being apprehensive about what we might learn about ourselves or about others, or because we cannot see its relevance. This means that employees need to feel positive about the outcomes of the learning process before they make a commitment to learn.

STUDENT ACTIVITY 10.6 How people learn

Consider the following set of statements about the relative effectiveness of different learning experiences.

People remember (learn):

- 10 per cent of what they read;

- 20 per cent of what they hear;

- 30 per cent of what they see;

- 50 per cent of what they see and hear;

- 70 per cent of what they talk over with others;

- 80 per cent of what they use in real life;

- 95 per cent of what they teach someone.
  (Glasser, 1986)

1. What explains the differences in the learning associated with these seven ways of learning?

2. Which of these ways of generating learning are associated with your own experiences at university or in the workplace?

3. Is there any relationship between the way in which you are required to learn and how effective learning experiences are?

4. What are the implications of your conclusions for the design of learning interventions?

The Kolb learning cycle

Perhaps the best-known representation of how learning is created was presented by David Kolb (1984). His 'learning cycle' offers important insights into the different ways in which people can learn, and into the choices and preferences that exist in our own learning.

The theory is based on the fact that our learning experiences are not discrete experiences, but form part of the constantly evolving view that we develop of the world around us. It is a model that reflects the importance of learning from the consequences of our own, and others', actions. This enables us to

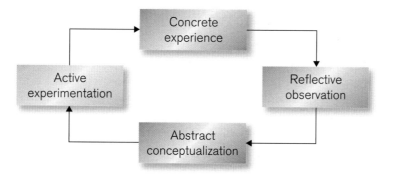

Figure 10.2 Kolb's experiential learning cycle

Source: Kolb, David A, *Experiential Learning: Experience as a Source of Learning*, © 1984, p 42, Fig 3.1. Adapted with the permission of Pearson Education Inc, Upper Saddle River, NJ.

understand, interact with and manipulate our environment to our advantage. For example, children initially learn to eat with their fingers and to associate eating with pleasure, not only because of the taste, but also because it removes the discomfort of being hungry. They then learn to use a spoon, so that they can eat food that cannot be eaten easily with their hands and, eventually, they learn to use cutlery to enable them to eat without making a mess. Each of these learning experiences builds on the last and becomes part of an increasingly complex pattern of behaviour, including social skills and rules used at mealtimes. This learning process is cyclical and each part of the learning builds upon the last.

Kolb defined how people learn from their experiences by going through the four following steps.

● Concrete experience

This is the stage in learning during which the learner carries out an action that has observable consequences. Kolb used the example of a child touching a hot stove. In a work context, it might be easier to imagine selecting a computer icon that you have not previously used and the function of which you do not understand.

● Reflective observation

This is the stage in learning during which the learner reflects upon their action and the outcome of that action. In Kolb's action, the child realizes that the stove burned his hand and that this hurts. In our work context example, you might reflect upon the fact that the icon in a word processing package created a large indented dot on the page.

● Abstract conceptualization

This is the stage in learning during which the learner develops a theory that can be applied to similar scenarios. In Kolb's example, the child theorizes and draws the conclusion that touching a hot surface will hurt. In our example about learning to use a computer, the learner may draw the conclusion that the icon can be used to create a bullet point in a piece of text.

● Active experimentation

This is the stage in learning during which the learner tests the theory out to see if the correct conclusion has been drawn. In Kolb's example, the child may put his hand near the stove to see if it feels hot. In our word processing example, the learner may type text and select the icon again to see if, in fact, this icon does enable the learner to create bullet points within a document.

In turn, this cycle can lead to further experience. For example, Kolb's child might begin to learn about other items that are hot; our computer learner may go on to explore other icons, such as numbered bullet points, and so on. Hence the learning process is ongoing and cyclical.

257

Experiential learning at work

What relevance, then, does this have in a workplace? It is important to understand that to 'grow' individual and group capability, and therefore increase or change the supply of labour to the organization, employees need to be engaged in some kind of planned and structured learning. Failure to recognize this will inevitably result in a less qualified and less productive workforce than that which might be achieved using workplace learning. Unplanned and unstructured (informal) learning will almost inevitably take place, but, depending on the nature of the experience, it may not be what is required from a managerial perspective. For example, bad habits and negative attitudes may develop as part of an ongoing socialization process.

We can also help people to learn by helping them through the learning cycle. The job of a driving instructor is to take the learner driver through a series of learning experiences in a safe and structured manner, to ensure that the full set of driving skills and knowledge needed to pass a driving test are learnt; the workplace is no different. By helping to shape not only the actual experiences, but also the reflection, conceptualization and experimentation stages of learning, managers can facilitate the required learning outcomes and permanent learning.

If the objective is to help an employee to learn about a new computer system, effective learning will require the individual to be given the opportunity to experience every aspect of the system. Reflection should be structured to help the learner to draw conclusions, such as 'this really isn't that difficult' rather than 'I don't like this new system'. Conceptualization may include helping the learner to draw conclusions such as 'I can use the manual to work out quite a lot about how to write reports, without needing too much assistance', rather than 'this new system is useless'. Ideally, the learner will then feel comfortable with experimenting with the new system. For example, the learner might be able to make enquiries and enter more complex data, in the knowledge that they can do so within parameters acceptable to the organization. Although associated with the way in which children learn, 'playing' with the new system – almost seeing it as a toy or puzzle – is a powerful form of experimentation that is equally appropriate to certain kinds of adult learning.

258

Learning styles

Honey and Mumford developed Kolb's model of learning further. They expressed the view that the learning cycle can be entered at any stage and that the preferred entry point to the learning cycle is determined by the individual's preferred learning style. They described four learning styles, which relate to entering the learning cycle at different points, as shown in Figure 10.3.

● Activists

   People with this learning style like to learn by doing. They like new experiences and opportunities to learn. They like to be involved and prefer to learn by doing, rather than by sitting and listening. They are the learners who are regarded as those who will read the instructions only if all else fails!

● Reflectors

   Those with this learning style like to think, observe and reflect before actually trying something. They enjoy reviewing what has happened and what they have learnt, and will prefer to reach conclusions in their own time.

● Theorists

   Those with this style will prefer to think problems through in a step-by-step, logical way and to ask questions. They tend to be detached and analytical, and to prefer models and systems. A theorist is, perhaps, more likely to pick up the instructions first.

● Pragmatists

   Individuals with this learning style like practical solutions and enjoy testing their ideas. They like to experiment and try out their ideas. They act quickly and confidently, and have a down-to-earth approach, responding to problems as a challenge.

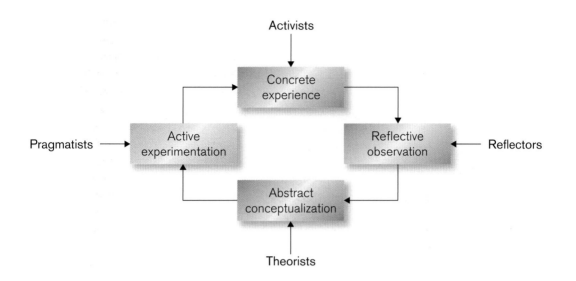

Figure 10.3 Honey and Mumford's learning styles in relation to Kolb's learning cycle

Source: Adapted from Kolb, David A, *Experiential Learning: Experience as a Source of Learning*, and Honey, P and Mumford, A 2006 *The Learning Styles Questionnaire.*

The relevance of learning styles to the provision of training

Learners will have different preferred learning styles and it is important to take these into consideration when designing a learning intervention, whether or not this involves one-to-one training, group training or learning through involvement in new activities.

In a one-to-one training session, it might be helpful to identify the learner's preferred style and enter the learning cycle at this point. For example, if we consider our earlier example about learning how to use a new computer system, the activists and pragmatists may prefer to switch it on and start pressing buttons, reflecting upon this later. Theorists and reflectors, however, may prefer an overview or a presentation about the new system, why it is being introduced and what processes they will be required to learn. In addition, learners may need additional support and encouragement to move outside their own preferred learning style, and to become familiar with those they are less inclined to adopt. Hence, an activist may need to be encouraged to reflect on their learning, whereas a reflector may need more encouragement to carry out activities. Kolb's conceptualization of learning suggests that all four of the approaches to learning, when combined, represent the more powerful and effective experience.

STUDENT ACTIVITY 10.7

Write down a list of new skills or knowledge that you have acquired recently. Next to each item, write down how you went about learning these skills. Use this information to identify your preferred learning style. Share your thoughts with a friend or colleague. Consider your own development needs and how you might best address these, given your preferred learning style.

Steps in learning

Learning is not always an easy process. Despite the sense of achievement that can be attained, sometimes it can be a difficult and uncomfortable process, particularly when the learner is developing unfamiliar skills or learning about more difficult concepts. We have seen how Kolb described learning as a cycle of experience, through to experimentation, but this model does not address the emotional experience

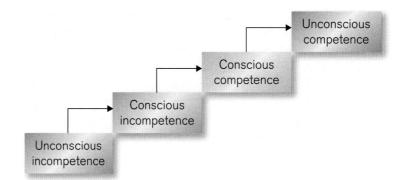

Figure 10.4 The conscious competence model
Source: www.businessballs.com

that we can go through when struggling to learn something new. Learning is usually not a surprise experience that 'pops up' at random and helps us to realize that the world operates in a particular way. More often than not, we go through a deliberate process of acquiring skills. Once mastered, it is difficult to understand what we found about learning that skill to be such a challenging experience. A useful way of understanding how learning progresses from one stage to another is presented in Figure 10.4. This model is useful in that it highlights the different stages through which the learner progresses until full competence is attained.

Within the 'conscious competence' model, the learner starts from a position of being unaware of the nature of the learning need. For example, before you start to learn to drive, it looks a bit tricky, but you know that it is something to do with pedals and a steering wheel. This is referred to as being in a state of 'unconscious incompetence' (Stage 1), i.e. the learner is unaware of his or her lack of competence. The first step in learning is to become aware of that shortfall and to move to a state of 'conscious incompetence' (Stage 2). Our learner driver, at this point, is struggling to master the basic manoeuvres in his or her car and may well frequently stall or crunch gears, and will need to be told exactly what to do by the instructor. As skills are acquired, the learner climbs another step, into 'conscious competence' (Stage 3). At this point, our learner may pass his or her test, but is still conscious of each of the actions that contribute towards driving, such as changing gear or the observation and signalling routine 'mirror, signal, manoeuvre'. Eventually, once the skills become very familiar, the learner is no longer conscious of each of the individual actions that make up the new skill. This is described as 'unconscious competence' (Stage 4) and, for our driver, will represent the point at which driving becomes automatic, i.e. the driver is no longer conscious of observations and actions that have become 'second nature'. This state of unconscious competence is similar to that described by the term 'tacit knowledge'. At this point, knowledge and know-how have become embedded within the individual to the point at which the ability to carry out a series of operations, such as driving, fitting a boiler or operating a piece of machinery, have become 'second nature'.

KEY CONCEPT Tacit knowledge

A term used to describe knowledge of, or about, things that has been gained from various sources and which is internalized by an individual, through the process of 'doing' and practice (Little et al, 2002).

Trainers can mistakenly assume trainees to be at Stage 2 and focus effort towards achieving Stage 3, when often trainees are only at Stage 1. The trainer assumes that the trainee is aware of, and understands the importance of meeting, a skill or competency deficiency and of the benefits from learning. This is not the case if trainees are still at the stage of unconscious incompetence: they will not be able to address achieving conscious competence until they've become consciously and fully aware of their own *in*competence. This is a fundamental reason for the failure of many training activities, and emphasizes the importance of trainers not making unfounded assumptions about trainee awareness and motivation. If the awareness of skill and deficiency is low or non-existent – i.e. if the learner is at the unconscious incompetence stage – the trainee or learner will simply not see the need for learning. It is essential to establish *awareness* of a weakness or training need prior to attempting the training needed to move trainees from Stage 2 to Stage 3.

Applications of the conscious competence model

It is important, in the context of the working environment, to understand that each of the above stages has to be mastered before moving on to the next stage. A learner will not be able to learn unless he or she becomes aware of what it is that he or she is not doing effectively. It can be very disconcerting, particularly for an employee who has carried out their duties in a particular way for a long time, to discover that this is no longer regarded as being the most effective method of doing things. It is therefore important to be sensitive and empathic as a trainer, and to structure training so that skills can be learnt in easily achievable steps that will allow the learner quickly to develop conscious competence. This will ensure that the learner has the satisfaction of having mastered one skill before attempting to move on to the next item. A music student, for example, will first learn to master relatively easy short tunes before moving on to more complex pieces of music; in the working/learning environment, it is important to give consideration to what can be successfully achieved by which methods to maintain employee satisfaction.

If a learner becomes overwhelmed by the magnitude of what is not known and by the scale of what needs to be learnt, there is a probability that he or she will become defensive and uncooperative. This might result in loss of motivation, denial about his or her shortcomings and negative attitudes towards the training. It is important, therefore, that a 'safe' psychological learning environment is created, in which shortcomings can be openly addressed without unnecessary concern on the part of the learner. In more challenging training about personal styles or attitudes, the organization may prefer to consider using an external independent trainer and may consider including the trainee on a programme with people with whom the employee is unlikely to work with on a daily basis, to encourage openness and participation.

261

HRM INSIGHT 10.5 Mountainside Training Centre

Mountainside Training Centre was asked to run a week-long Outward Bound-style training course for managers of Henry Associates Finance and Investments (HAFI). HAFI wanted to get the most from investing in this expensive training, so training consisted of long days, starting at 8.30 a.m. and continuing into the evenings, and included an overnight exercise during which participants were required to continue throughout the night by splitting into two shifts. Participants were also expected to network in the evenings by socializing together, leaving little time for rest and personal reflection.

The training centre recommended that the groups follow the Kolb learning cycle by doing an activity, receiving feedback, and producing guidelines and action plans as a team for the next exercise. The training therefore consisted mainly of outdoor activities, followed by discussions about what had gone wrong in order to learn from mistakes made and to improve team performance in the next exercise. The exercises throughout the week were of increasing duration and complexity, and trainees were encouraged to develop weaknesses by having a go at roles they wouldn't normally play. Feedback included detailed comments about personal style from the trainers and from other group members. People who were not natural leaders were expected to lead the group; people naturally good at problem solving were expected to let others try out their ideas and be more considerate to team members, and so on.

To make the most of this expensive training, underpinning theory, on subjects including management, team working, motivation and communication, was given to trainees as documents and books, which were to →

be read outside of the structured activity (managers were expected to be capable of studying this in their own time).

Questions

1. Consider Kolb's experiential learning model: how was reflection interpreted? Was true reflection time given?

2. Which learning styles were not catered for by this training course?

3. Which learning styles would not respond well to this training programme?

4. With reference to the conscious competence model, which steps were missed out?

5. What recommendations would you make to improve the quality of the training provided?

Insights & Outcomes: visit the Online Resource Centre at www.oxfordtextbooks.co.uk/orc/ banfield_kay/ for an insight into the outcomes of this training course

---

STUDENT ACTIVITY 10.8

Consider learning or training situations in which you have been involved recently. Identify an experience that you thought was effective and one that was ineffective. Using the models described above and/or other models of the learning process, explain why the two experiences produced different outcomes. Reflecting on this explanation, produce a set of guidelines that trainers can follow to ensure the effectiveness of any structured learning experience.

Moving forward – the power of accelerated learning

A consistent theme in this chapter is that looking at, and correcting, deficiencies in how people learn and how they are trained can improve the value and effectiveness of training. We would argue that, through understanding how these two processes can be improved, both employees and managers will benefit. What 'accelerated learning' offers is a set of principles, values and practices that represent an alternative to conventional approaches to learning, particularly the use of course-based training, which have the potential of generating enjoyable and productive learning experiences. Proponents of accelerated learning reject learning based on mechanization, standardization, external control, 'one size fits all', behaviouristic conditioning and an emphasis on instruction and passive listening, suggesting instead a very different, but more effective, approach (Meier, 2000).

Meier compares what he calls 'traditional learning' with 'accelerated learning', using the dimensions shown in Table 10.2.

Table 10.2 A comparison of traditional and accelerated learning

Traditional learning	Accelerated learning
Rigid	Flexible
Sombre and serious	Enjoyable
Single-pathed	Multi-pathed
Competitive	Collaborative
Behaviouristic	Humanistic
Verbal	Multi-sensory
Controlling	Nurturing
Cognitive	Cognitive, emotional and physical
Means-centred	Results-based

Meier argues that any approach to, or philosophy of, learning is underpinned by a set of assumptions about what people need in order to optimize their learning. As far as accelerated learning is concerned, these assumptions are as follows.

● A positive learning environment

People learn best when their social, physical and emotional environments are positive, supportive and stimulating.

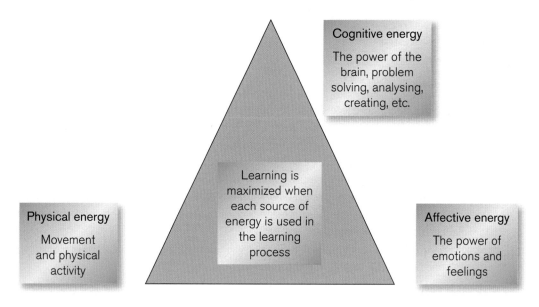 Signpost to Chapter 1: The Management of Human Resources, for insights into the importance of a learning environment to employees

● Total learner involvement

Active involvement and responsibility are key to effective and sustained learning. Meier points out that learning is not a spectator sport, but participatory.

● Collaboration among learners

People generally learn best in an environment characterized by working together with others. Learning can, and often does, happen through what a person does on his or her own, but effective and deeper learning is often associated with groups and teams engaging in a shared learning experience.

● Variety that appeals to all learning preferences and styles

Learning becomes 'accelerated' and more effective when the full range of people's senses and energies are engaged and used in learning (see Figure 10.5).

● Contextual learning

Again, the importance of context is emphasized. Learning 'out of context' and in isolation from the working environment is harder to absorb, and can easily be lost. Meier believes that:

> ...the best learning comes from doing the work itself in a continual process of 'real world' immersion, feedback, reflection, evaluation and re-immersion.
> (2000, p xviii)

Based on the characteristics and assumptions of accelerated learning, Meier offers what he describes as a 'universalistic' model of learning (2000, p 53). This features four phases, or components, all of which

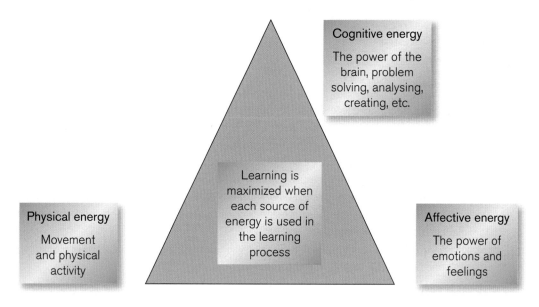

Cognitive energy

The power of the brain, problem solving, analysing, creating, etc.

Learning is maximized when each source of energy is used in the learning process

Physical energy

Movement and physical activity

Affective energy

The power of emotions and feelings

Figure 10.5 The energy triangle

must be present in one form or another, or, according to Meier, no real learning occurs. The four phases or components are:

- *preparation* – the arousal of interest;
- *presentation* – the initial encounter and involvement with new areas of knowledge or skill;
- *practice* – the integration and embedding of the new knowledge or skill;
- *performance* – applying the knowledge or skill to the job.

Finally, and to continue the thinking behind the ideas associated with accelerated learning, we want to offer an interesting and challenging hypothesis: that enjoyment and learning outcomes are positively correlated to the amount and variety of energy consumed in the learning experience. Consider, as an example, being involved in business simulation or skills development exercises, as opposed to sitting in a lecture theatre listening to a PowerPoint presentation. Which learning experience consumes most energy and which is likely to be the most productive of learning? The concept of the 'energy triangle' presented in Figure 10.5 describes the three types of energy that need to be utilized in learning and what they involve.

STUDENT ACTIVITY 10.9 Testing the hypothesis

1. Think of two learning situations, one of which was enjoyable and productive, and one that wasn't. Rate both on a scale of 1–10, with 10 the most enjoyable and productive.

2. On a scale of 1–10, rate each of the two experiences in relation to the three types of energy generated. Add the three values together.

3. Compare the ratings from task 1 to the aggregate energy score in task 2 and establish whether the hypothesis has validity.

Summary

One of the aims of this chapter has been to clarify the often-experienced confusion between training and learning. It is a mistake to think of these as separate and independent activities. Training is a way of generating learning, based on the use of certain techniques and methods. Magee and Thayer (1961) explained this relationship when they said:

> **The central process in training is learning.**

Training has, however, been subject to sustained criticism precisely because it is felt that it does not represent a powerful and reliable means of generating the learning that managers and employees require. The problem that people such as Martyn Sloman (2001) have with training is twofold. Firstly, it is often badly designed and delivered, or based on a faulty diagnosis of training needs; secondly, it is considered an inappropriate way of meeting certain learning requirements for which other, more individualized, learning methods, such as coaching and mentoring, are likely to produce the required results. While the purpose of training is to generate learning, whether it does so and whether it meets the expectations of different stakeholders is problematical and uncertain.

Tom Boydell (2003) summarized the position of many who feel that HR professionals have placed too much emphasis and reliance on training when he asserted:

> I think most learning does not arise as a result of training. If you ask yourself, or a group of people, to identify 4 or 5 or whatever really important things you or they have learned in the past year/2 years/life so far, I would be surprised if many came as the result of training – ie of

someone else telling or showing you, deciding for you, what the right answer is, the best way to do things, the correct way to be.

The critical question then becomes: 'Can training be reformulated and reframed, so that it can overcome many of its limitations and deliver valued contributions to the development of employees?' Perhaps one way in which this can be achieved is for those responsible for the management of training to incorporate principles and practices associated with the theory of accelerated learning. It seems to us that the shift within the training profession from an emphasis on training to one of learning is, in one sense, absolutely appropriate and justified. Learning is the key to change, improved performance and personal growth. The central question is: 'How can we achieve this in the most effective and efficient ways possible?'

It also must be recognized that, in the same way that '*learning got left out* [of training]' (Davis and Davis, 1998), we might also conclude that 'people have been left out of learning'. Perhaps there is even a link between these two statements. Certainly, we would argue that understanding the human dimension of learning is critical to any efforts to make training more effective: if training is seen only in terms of models, procedures, budgets, activities and roles, it will continue to disappoint and fail to deliver. The human dimension has to be at the heart of the training experience. As learning becomes less an option and more a necessity, the failure to create learning is increasingly unacceptable and costly to employees and organizations. The problem is not one of not knowing how to meet this challenge, but of learning how to use what we know about what works and what doesn't, and understanding why.

Visit the Online Resource Centre that accompanies this book for self-test questions, weblinks, and more information on the topics covered in this chapter.
online resource centre www.oxfordtextbooks.co.uk/orc/banfield_kay/

REVIEW QUESTIONS

265

1. What does 'from training to learning' mean and why has this shift in emphasis come about?

2. What changes need to be made in the assumptions upon which current approaches to training are based?

3. What does an employee-centred approach to learning involve and what are its implications for trainers?

4. What are the respective roles of the HR professional and the line manager in generating learning at work?

5. Why is the motivational state of learners important to the outcome of learning interventions?

6. How can HR demonstrate the economic and business case for learning and development activities?

CASE STUDY

Training at Central Hotels

Central Hotels owned and managed 25 mid-range hotels in the UK, offering residential, conferencing and leisure facilities to a wide range of customers. In a competitive environment, quality of service was a factor in the company retaining its reputation as providing a reliable and professional service to its customers. With a mixture of permanent and temporary/casual workers, the training of new staff and helping those who needed to develop improved competences was an ongoing, and important, activity.

The head of the company's training function realized that course-based training, with trainers instructing staff in various skills, simply was not working and couldn't deliver real changes in attitudes and behaviours, particularly in the area of customer service. With the help of outside consultants, she devised a new training package, which was called 'rainbow training'. This reflected the fact that there were seven ➔

modules or elements, each reflecting a key set of competencies. For example, one covered 'supporting your colleagues', while another related to 'enhancing the customer experience'. The interesting thing about the package was that it was only prescriptive in the objectives that were laid down for each of the modules; each hotel was responsible for devising how the objectives would be met. There were suggestions about using certain types of activity and, particularly, using a collaborative approach, but the staff, led by each hotel's operations manager, were left to create their own solutions, which needed to include all staff.

In the Nottingham hotel, David Wilson had the challenge of meeting the objectives of the rainbow training package. Most of his staff were interested in the new approach to training, and were glad they weren't being forced to sit in a classroom and be 'lectured' at. There were, however, one or two members of staff with whom he knew he would have problems. One was the hotel's head barman, Ken Barnes. Ken had worked at the hotel for over seven years and, in all that time, hadn't really changed much. He had a view of what his job involved and, basically, 'did it his way'. In a job that involved frequent interaction with customers, he wasn't what might be described as customer focused and never went out of his way to help others. He did his job and that was it.

David felt sure that, unless he could overcome Ken's attitude problem, his involvement in rainbow training would be limited and not particularly enthusiastic. David decided to take the risky decision of asking Ken to lead the group developing ideas for enhancing the customer experience. He explained to Ken what he wanted, and that it was Ken's responsibility to set an example to the other team members in working collaboratively and cooperatively. The training ideas with which Ken's team came up would then be used to train staff in other departments in customer care.

To David's surprise and relief, Ken's team worked well together and came up with some creative and interesting proposals. These were then delivered over a six-month period throughout the hotel. The effects of this training on levels of customer satisfaction was quickly noticed through changes in the monthly customer satisfaction index, but David noticed another, quite different, outcome: Ken Barnes had changed. He became more sociable and flexible in his attitude to work; he was confident and developed a range of important social skills that he had never had before. He became a valued member of the hotel's staff and seemed to have acquired more self-esteem. Was he the same person, but a different worker – or a different person and a better worker?

David now realized that training could be enjoyable and stimulating, and deliver 'bottom-line' results. He also began to realize the power that the rainbow training approach possessed and the way in which it could not only generate important work-related competencies, but, in important ways, change people.

Questions

1. It might be argued that what was seen in this case study was an example of what is described as the 'Hawthorne Effect'. This can be understood as an increase in worker motivation and productivity, produced by the psychological stimulus of being singled out and made to feel important. What are the origins of this phenomenon and how can it be used to support structured learning?

2. Why are ownership and responsibility important in the design and delivery of training?

3. Are there any training situations in which the principles and practices of accelerated learning cannot be applied? If so, why?

4. In the example above, consider the barriers to learning and how these were overcome.

5. Consider the six 'E's of training described earlier in this chapter: what was the reason in this case study for the training and was this requirement ultimately met?

FURTHER READING

Beard, C and Wilson, JP (2002) *The Power of Experiential Learning*, Kogan Page.

Bramley, P (1996) *Evaluating Training*, CIPD.

Corely, A and Eades, E (2004) 'Becoming critically reflective practitioners: academics' and students' reflections on the issues involved', *HRD International*, 7:1, pp 137–44.

Cotton, J (1995) *The Theory of Learning*, Kogan Page.

Le Deist, FD and Winterton, J (2005) 'What is competence?', *HRD International*, 8:1, pp 27–46.

Macpherson, A, Elliot, M, Harris, I and Homan, G (2004) 'E-learning: reflections and evaluation of corporate programmes', *HRD International*, 7:3, pp 295–313.

Quinones, MA and Ehrenstein, A (1997) *Training for a Rapidly Changing Workforce*, American Psychological Association.

Slotte, V, Tynjälä, P and Hytönen, T (2004) 'How do practitioners describe learning at work?', *HRD International*, 7:4, pp 481–99.

REFERENCES

Alcock, M (2005) 'Time for e-learning to be handed back to the trainers?', available online at www.trainingreference.co.uk.

Boydell, T (2003) 'Difference between training and learning', comment available online at www.trainingzone.co.uk.

Boydell, T and Leary, M (1996) *Identifying Training Needs*, CIPD.

Chartered Institute of Personnel and Development (2005) *E-Learning Survey Results Report*, CIPD survey report, available online at www.cipd.co.uk.

Chartered Institute of Personnel and Development (2006) *Human Capital*, CIPD factsheet, available online at www.cipd.co.uk.

Chartered Institute of Personnel and Development (2007a) *E-learning: Progress and Prospects*, CIPD factsheet, available online at www.cipd.co.uk.

Chartered Institute of Personnel and Development (2007b) *Training and Development*, CIPD survey report, available online at www.cipd.co.uk.

Clark, N (2005) 'Workplace learning environments and its relationship with learning outcomes in healthcare organizations', *HRD International*, 8:2, pp 185–205.

Davis, JR and Davis, AB (1998) *Effective Training Strategies*, Berrett-Koehler.

Gladstone, B (2000) *From Know-How to Knowledge*, Spiro Press.

Glasser, W (1986) *Choice Theory in the Classroom*, HarperCollins Publishers Inc.

Hirsh, W and Tamkin, P (2005a) 'Piece by piece', *People Management*, 8 Dec, pp 32–4.

Hirsh, W and Tamkin, P (2005b) *Planning Training for Your Business*, IES Report 422.

Honey, P and Mumford, A (2006) *The Learning Styles Questionnaire*, 80-item version, Peter Honey Publications.

Hope, K (2006) 'Class act', *People Management*, 15 September, p 16.

IRS (1998) 'Using human resources to achieve strategic objectives: learning strategies review', *IRS Management Review*, Issue 8.

Kearns, P (2005) *Evaluating the ROI from Learning*, CIPD.

Kolb, DA (1984) *Experiential Learning: Experience as a Source of Learning*, Pearson Education.

Lave, J and Wenger, E (1991) *Situated Learning: Legitimate Peripheral Participation*, Cambridge University Press.

Little, S, Quintas, P and Ray, T (2002) *Managing Knowledge*, Sage, ch 3.

McGhee, W and Thayer, P (1961) *Training in Business and Industry*, John Wiley and Sons.

Megginson, D, Banfield, P and Joy-Matthews, J (1993) *Human Resource Development*, Kogan Page.

Meier, D (2000) *The Accelerated Learning Handbook*, McGraw-Hill.

Pfeffer, J (1998) *Hidden Equation*, HBS Press, ch 3.

Rothwell, WJ (1996) *Beyond Training and Development: State-of-the-Art Strategies for Enhancing Human Performance*, AMACOM/American Management Association.

Rothwell, WJ (2004) *Beyond Training and Development: The Groundbreaking Classic on Human Performance Enhancement*, AMACOM/American Management Association.

Scott, A (2005) 'Quality of work-based training improves', *PM online*, 7 December, available online to CIPD members at www.peoplemanagement.co.uk.

Sloman, M (2001) *The e-Learning Revolution*, CIPD.

Sloman, M (2004) 'Learner drivers', *People Management*, 2 Sept, p 36.

Sloman, M and Webster, L (2005) 'Training to learning', *Training and Development*, 59:9, pp 58–63.

Smethurst, S (2006a) 'Course of treatment', *People Management*, 9 March, pp 34–6.

Smethurst, S (2006b) 'Staying power', *People Management*, 6 April, p 34.

Stern, E and Sommerlad, E (1999) *Workplace Learning, Culture and Performance: Issues in People Management*, CIPD.

Truss, C, Gratton, L, Hope, V, McGovern, P and Stiles, P (1997) 'Soft and hard models of Human Resource Management: a reappraisal', *Journal of Management Studies*, 34:1, pp 53–73.

Ulrich, D (1998) 'A new mandate for human resources', *Harvard Business Review*, 76:1, pp 125–34.

Walton, J (1999) *Strategic Human Resource Development*, Pearson Education, ch 3.

Warren, C (2006) 'University challenge', *People Management*, 9 March, p 30–3.

Zuboff, S (1998) *In the Age of the Smart Machine*, Basic Books.

Managing Performance

11

Learning Objectives

As a result of reading this chapter and using the Online Resource Centre, you should be able to:

- understand what managing performance involves and how performance can be conceptualised;

- understand and appreciate the different approaches to modelling performance;

- recognize the importance of measurement in performance management, and appreciate the arguments for and against the use of targets and objectives;

- debate constructively the arguments for and against the use of the appraisal process in managing performance;

- critically evaluate different performance enhancement strategies.

Introduction

One of the difficulties in trying to make sense of what performance management 'is' and what it might mean for managers and employees, is that, as Armstrong and Baron (1998) state:

> **...performance management is a fairly imprecise term, and performance management processes manifest themselves in many different forms. There is no one right way of managing performance.**
>
> **(p 7)**

What can be said with some certainty is that performance management is not synonymous with the appraisal process, which is one technique (or instrument) used by many organizations to 'manage' performance. Unfortunately, appraisal techniques often constitute the only method of managing performance. A much more sophisticated and useful conceptualization is provided by Lockett (1992), who emphasizes the need to see performance management in an ecological way, within which the different elements of a living system interact and influence each other, rather than as a series of unrelated functions.

In Chapter 1, we identified employee utilization as one of the fundament objectives of management; in contemporary organizations, performance management is that aspect of management that is associated with delivering this objective. Simply having a performance management system in place does not, however, guarantee higher levels of performance than would otherwise have existed without the 'benefit' of the system features. As with many other aspects of HR, formal and material rationality are not necessarily synonymous.

The search for higher levels of individual and team performance is important to all organizations, and ways must be found to ensure that performance levels are sustained and enhanced. Despite improvements in equipment, materials and processes, organizational performance is still linked to the quality of people that an organization employs and what they do at work. You can have the best equipment and systems in your sector, and the most up-to-date processes, but if you don't have the right number and quality of people doing what is needed, the organization will not function properly. 'Managing performance' fundamentally means that employees know what is expected of them and act in ways that contribute to the best interests of the organization, but what this means and how it is delivered for each individual organization will inevitably differ, because each faces a unique set of circumstances and challenges. There are no universal solutions to performance management problems and each organization must, through a process of diagnosis, action, evaluation and learning, develop its own strategy and practices.

According to Mabey et al (1998), performance management refers to a set of techniques and procedures that serve to:

- provide information on the contribution of human resources to the strategic objectives of the organization;
- form a framework of techniques to secure the maximum output for any given level of inputs;
- provide a means of inspecting how well individual performance-enhancing processes actually deliver performance in relation to targets and objectives.

They define performance management as:

> **A framework in which performance by individuals can be directed, monitored, motivated and refined.**

There are, then, a number of common principles that are useful in understanding what needs to be done.

Basic requirements of managing performance

- **Everyone should know what to, and what not to, do**

  Performance management is not something that will be successful if it is 'done' once a year: it is more of a process than an event. These ongoing processes need to be connected not only to each other, but to every aspect of the organization's activities. (This is a practical example of the concepts of vertical and horizontal integration discussed in Chapter 2.) Moreover, it is as important to establish what *not* to do as well as what *is* to be done: doing 'more' is not particularly helpful or sensible if this involves doing more of the wrong thing! Simply asking the individual to undertake more activities, without first establishing if there any that are no longer required or which should be replaced with a more efficient activity, can be both detrimental to the organization and demotivating to employees, who may struggle with a seemingly ever-increasing workload.

- **Everyone contributes**

  It is important for employees, as well as managers, to contribute to the effective management of performance. Line managers do not know everything, nor should they be seen as the only stakeholder capable of contributing to improving performance. The position adopted here is that employees are fundamentally responsible for their own performance, in the same way that they are responsible for their own learning and development, and excluding them from any initiatives to improve performance makes no sense and will almost certainly result in failure. Even if such initiatives involve only annual objective setting, employee involvement in the process is likely to contribute to higher individual motivation, legitimation of the process and increased commitment. Contemporary thinking about improving employee performance has moved away from simply communicating what needs to be done, towards achieving the employee's active support and engagement in the process.

- **Everyone develops the necessary skills**

  For an organization to maximize its performance, every employee should be encouraged to grow by acquiring new skills and competences that will enhance their effectiveness. Development need not be restricted to HR-organized training courses, but can include a range of formal and informal learning experiences, including secondments, coaching and project work.

  → Signpost to Chapter 10: Learning and Development, for further information on training and development

- **Managers must have the necessary skills**

  Ask a group of managers if they are effective in managing the performance of their teams and most, if not all, will probably say that they are. But if you were to ask those that they manage the same question, a different picture might emerge. The existence of this 'perception gap' suggests that there are important issues around what is known by managers, and how this is interpreted and valued. For example, employees might feel that they are working hard and trying to do their best, but, for differing reasons, some of which will be to do with the quality of interpersonal relationships, this endeavour is not recognized. What is critical to the effective management of performance is the contribution of line managers to the engagement of their staff in the delivery of performance. To be effective in this role, managers need a range of technical and process skills, without which their ability to influence employee performance will inevitably be compromised. It might be argued, therefore, that employee performance is as much a function of the quality of managers as it is of the skills and competences of employees.

- **Managers measure and monitor**

  We have already emphasized that effective performance management cannot be 'done' once a year. The process is ongoing and, to be effective, managers need to measure performance on an ongoing basis, to ensure that it remains on track and that employees continuously develop their skills. Distinguishing performance management as a process, rather than an event, helps to identify the nature of the management engagement process and avoids situations developing in which it is 'the time' to do something, such as 'the time' to carry out annual staff appraisals.

The performance management cycle

Figure 11.1 presents the key activities and areas of responsibility associated with an integrated and holistic performance management system. The fundamental importance given to evaluating the effectiveness of the individual and the cumulative effects of these activities is consistent with Ulrich's emphasis on the outcomes of HR interventions rather than on activities per se (Ulrich, 1998).

Performance management should not be seen as a once-a-year task, but as an ongoing process or cycle. The model in Figure 11.1 shows that the first step in this cycle is for the organization to define its long-term strategy and strategic intentions. The objectives of the organization define the goals and targets over a shorter period and will need to be regularly assessed to establish their alignment with the strategy. For example, these might express the levels of service to be provided, or the level of sales or profitability, or the activities planned in the near future.

In order to be able to measure success at regular intervals, the key measures, or metrics (see Chapter 9), need to be established. Unless an organization defines what is important and how this will be measured, it will be difficult to assign the necessary resource to ensure that the objectives are, as far as possible, achieved. Once this is agreed, it is easier to decide which team will be responsible for each element that goes towards the overall objectives. The organizational objectives can then be translated into departmental and team goals, and then into individual goals and objectives. The individual objectives

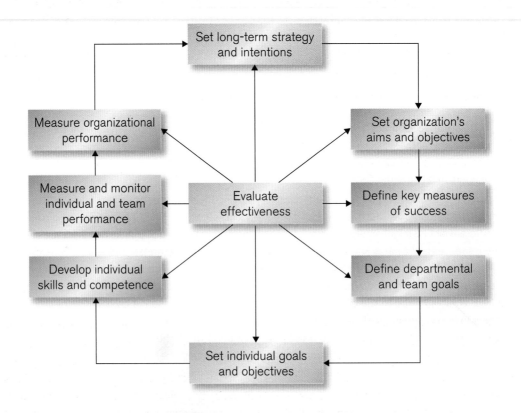

Figure 11.1 Activities associated with performance management

are often agreed and finalized during an appraisal interview, which will be explored in greater detail later in the chapter.

The next step in the process is to develop the skills and abilities of the individuals and teams, to ensure that they are able to maximize their efforts in achieving their objectives. The performance of individuals and teams is then measured, and the results can be pooled to establish a regular measure of the organization's performance. Increasingly, key performance outcomes are a function of teams rather than of individuals, although the relative importance of one or the other depends on the nature of the work being undertaken and the social organization of work.

Making sense of performance

'Performance' is a term used frequently in HR, but it has no precise or agreed meaning: it can mean different things to different stakeholders and this can create problems in 'what' is managed. Just let your mind wander and think of what you associate the word 'performance' with. You may think of actors who 'perform' on the stage or cinema set, who entertain an audience. Those who have delivered an outstanding performance can then be nominated for awards, with those considered to have performed better than any of the other nominated persons receiving the highest award – perhaps an Oscar. You may also associate performance with sport and athletes, who constantly strive to reduce the time they take to run a set distance, increase the weights they can lift or the height they can jump. Such initial associations confirm that 'performance' is not something that is restricted to the world of employment and work, and there may be much that we can learn from these other contexts in which improved performance is an important objective.

But performance is also of vital importance to the way in which organizations are managed and to what people do at work. How well businesses perform often determines their status, financial value and survivability, and the performance of each employee and how well they work together as teams is an enduring managerial concern.

Whatever the industry, the level at which people function or the jobs being performed, managers are faced with four fundamental questions:

- what are the key determinants of organizational performance?
- how well are my staff currently performing in their jobs?
- how can their performance be improved?
- what are the causes of underperformance?

Employ only talented people?

Pfeffer and O'Reilly's book, *Hidden Value* (2000), provides a useful starting point to the analysis of organizational performance. They begin by asking the question:

What's the most important factor for success in today's knowledge-based economy?

In other words, what will make some organizations more successful, and therefore more likely to survive and prosper, than others? Pfeffer and O'Reilly quote from the McKinsey report, *The War for Talent* (McKinsey Co, 2000), to present the 'conventional' answer to these questions – that superior organizational performance will come from the superior performance of talented people. The implication of this view is, therefore, that the performance 'problem' is solved by employing only the most talented people, who, it is assumed, will naturally perform to their capability and deliver the high levels of performance that organizations require. If it were only that simple!

One important drawback to adopting this performance management strategy is that there are a finite number of exceptionally talented people around and, if all organizations are trying to employ them, the following might happen:

- because demand will exceed supply, the cost of employing such talent will increase to the point at which their productivity will fall;

- because they can command high prices, these people are much more likely to change employers more frequently than other employees, which means that what they can give to an organization is transitory;

- undue emphasis on potentially high performers may well result in 'ordinary' performers becoming disillusioned, and less committed to their work and organization, which can result in reduced performance;

- there is no guarantee that even the most talented staff will always perform to their potential – capability has to be engaged and harnessed, and this cannot be taken for granted.

There is, of course, persuasive anecdotal evidence that those with exceptional talent are often crucial to organizations becoming, and remaining, successful and the importance of recruiting the best possible employees or of refusing to employ those that don't meet a minimum specification is undeniable. So, too, is the need to retain talented staff, so that their capability and potential has a chance of being realized.

But the real challenge facing organizations in understanding what the 'secret' of high performance is, according to Pfeffer and O'Reilly (2000), is that of creating cultures and systems in which talented staff can actually use their talents. They go beyond this, however, and emphasize that the key to long-term organizational success is to ensure that management practices are in place that ensure extraordinary results from almost everybody (Pfeffer and O'Reilly, 2000, p 2). Their emphasis on the environment in which people work and perform, which can liberate the potential of all employees, is an important step forward in understanding the limitations of concentrating a performance management strategy on individuals without having any regard for the quality and characteristics of the social and psychological environment in which they work.

Having made the point that organizational success comes from driving the performance of all employees, rather than simply recruiting highly talented people, the McKinsey report (McKinsey Co, 2000) offers insights into what companies should do to become successful that suggest that recruiting high performers is only part of set of requirements that drive performance of both people and the organization.

STUDENT ACTIVITY 11.1

Working either individually or in groups, and using the links on the Online Resource Centre to access the McKinsey report (2000), undertake the following tasks.

1. Summarize the seven key points made in the report.

2. Taking each one in turn, consider the implications for HR of trying to implement each requirement.

3. Consider the risks and benefits associated with each requirement.

4. Consider what is left out or underemphasized in the report.

We will be returning to the ideas and contributions of O'Reilly and Pfeffer (2000) later, particularly in the search for evidence that links managerial strategies and practices to employee performance. Before we do that, however, we need to continue to search for clarity over the meaning of the term 'performance' and how this relates to similar terms.

The search for conceptual clarity – what does 'performance' actually mean?

One of the difficulties that students and managers face is the confusion that can exist when we talk about performance and how it can be managed. The following concepts are sometimes used interchangeably and are related, but each has its own distinctive meaning and significance.

● Productivity

This is a concept that links the inputs to a production process to its outputs, expressed in quantitative or financial terms. Applied to the individual, it can thought of as being close to performance, but is much more precise and is subject to quantitative measurement. In engineering and manufacturing contexts, in which it is easier to measure labour inputs and outputs, productivity has traditionally been the preferred concept that managers use and measure.

● Effectiveness

This can be understood as the relationship between targets or objectives set and what is actually achieved. If the targets or objectives are not particularly stretching or are impossible to meet, however, whether an employee is considered effective or not is more a function of the target or objective-setting process than of anything that the employee might do.

● Effort

This is difficult concept that is often linked to the intensity of work, i.e. how hard an employee works, but not necessarily linked to outcomes. People who have a strong work ethic are, however, likely to put a great deal more effort into their work compared to those who are less strongly motivated, and are also likely to be committed and high-performing employees.

● The effort bargain

This is a powerful concept that captures the often imprecise relationship between what employees 'do' at work and the rewards that they receive.

● Discretionary effort

This term captures the belief that employees only give a part of what they are capable of and that moving to higher levels of performance, effort or contribution is at their discretion, rather than subject to management control.

● Contribution

This is a broader concept than performance. Contribution is seen as what employees can do in addition to doing their jobs. This is particularly important if jobs actually limit what people are allowed to do, with job descriptions representing barriers to what people are allowed to do.

Fundamentally, performance is about achievement, but reflecting the definition offered at the beginning of the chapter, it combines achievement with capability – what people are capable of achieving. Two important consequences follow from this definition.

● Not all employees are capable of the same levels of performance. All organizations contain people who have different existing capabilities and differences in potential. Employees, in other words, are different in terms of their innate capabilities and in terms of what they want to, and can, achieve. Using a sporting analogy, however hard most footballers try, the majority will never perform at the level of David Beckham or Wayne Rooney, or others who are exceptionally talented and driven. While effort is important, it is not the same as inherent or acquired talent or capability. 'Trying hard', if this effort is focused and directed to desired outcomes, is clearly an important element in performance, but effort alone is rarely sufficient to explain high-performing employees. In observing changes in management thinking and philosophy, driven by the ideas of such writers as Charles Handy and Tom Peters, John Lockett (1992) argues that one key feature of this shift in thinking is the emphasis from effort towards performance:

There is an urgent need for people at work to achieve results – results which meet the company's performance requirements. Scoring 'A' for effort is no longer relevant, unless that effort is harnessed towards those requirements.

● Simply achieving set objectives is not necessarily an indication of high performance if the targets or objectives set are too low and do not realistically stretch an individual or reflect his or her capability. This means that, while one individual might achieve more than another, they might actually be seen as a lower performer because, while one achieved all that they were capable of, the other did not. Using objectives to manage performance, while an attractive proposition, can therefore be difficult and fraught with dangers, particularly if objectives change and if they are expressed in qualitative, rather than quantitative, ways.

If performance can be conceptualized as the relationship between what people are capable of achieving and what is actually achieved, how does this differ from 'effectiveness'? Quite simply, someone who is 'effective' is someone who meets expectations or achieves the objectives set for them. Critical to understanding the significance of this distinction is the recognition that, while both performance and effectiveness are related to achieving standards and meeting expectations, an employee can be effective and not a high performer because the standards and expectations against which their performance is being measured were pitched at too low a level. The key point here is that maximum performance is achieved when employees use their capabilities to the fullest, drawing on all of their physical, intellectual or emotional energies, and when they are set targets and objectives that stretch the individual (or team) to the highest sustainable level of performance.

Productivity and performance

So how does productivity fit into to this conceptual framework and why is it important to be clear about how it differs from performance? 'Productivity' describes the relationship between inputs and outputs, and the efficient use of productive resources. As far as labour productivity is concerned, several measures are in current usage, with an emphasis on either the cost of labour inputs, related to the value of outputs produced, or the quantity or volume of inputs, related to the numbers of units produced.

Examples from the manufacturing sector would be the number of person hours needed to produce a car, calculated by taking all input labour hours and dividing this figure by the total number of cars produced over a given time period. In an educational context, the productivity of lecturers might be calculated by dividing the total number of lecturing staff by the total number of students taught. More useful are input and output measures that focus on financial values and changes in these. In this way, the cost of labour, rather than the numbers or total hours employed, would be related to the value, rather than the volume, of output. Returning to the manufacturing example, labour productivity might be expressed as the cost of labour inputs divided by the value of products or services produced. Productivity is more useful and relevant if accurate measures of the two variables can be made. It is therefore less appropriate to the management of performance in the service or professional sectors.

The productivity of a labour force generally, or of an individual employee, is not the same as its, or his or her, performance. Productivity can be increased by improved performance – i.e. by workers becoming more skilled, through enhanced motivation or giving greater effort – but increases in labour productivity can also result from reduced costs, increased prices and automation. While most organizations are committed to productivity improvements that are based on increased individual performance, other parallel strategies linked to cost reductions, price changes and new technology make it very difficult to isolate the impact of different contributions, particularly that of improved performance to changes in productivity.

But why are these distinctions important? One reason is to do with the need for conceptual clarity. Meanings that become blurred and confused often undermine management's ability to analyse situations, and to understand fully the significance of desired organizational outcomes and the contribution employees might make to these. Arguably, even more important than the need for clear thinking on these matters are the practical implications and challenges of managing what employees do in, and achieve through, their jobs and their wider organizational contributions. Perhaps the best way to demonstrate what these challenges might involve is to consider the relationship between employee performance, effectiveness and productivity to employee pay. Although the use of performance-related pay is dealt with in more detail later in this chapter and in Chapter 12, it is important to be clear about what managers are trying to influence and achieve when they use pay to affect employee behaviour. Many schemes that reward employees and managers for 'something additional' to their normal level of performance fail, and fall into disrepute, simply because the link between the extra pay and what employees or managers achieve is unclear, and difficult to measure with any degree of consistency and reliability.

→ Signpost to Chapter 12: Managing Rewards, for perspectives on linking rewards to performance

Yet the use of additional payments to influence employee behaviour and performance has long been a part of mainstream management thinking and practice (Taylor, 1998). Essentially, this involves rewarding employees for achieving a level of performance that exceeds the 'norm' or an established standard. Take, for example, a bricklayer. He or she might be given, or agree to, a daily rate of laying e.g. 1,500 bricks, which would be linked to basic pay. If the bricklayer were to fail to lay the 1,500 bricks in a day, basic pay might still be paid unless the employment contract were to be based on variable pay, under which each brick paid would carry with it a financial value, meaning that the more laid from a zero base, the more the bricklayer would be paid. In most examples of performance-related pay, however, increased, or variable, pay is paid above an agreed base line of performance: in this case, a base line of 1,500 bricks. Performance in excess of that standard results in additional payments, determined by collective agreements or individual arrangements.

In such situations, performance can easily be made operational and hence measured, and high performers, either because of their extra effort or skills, will be paid more than low performers. Higher levels of performance can then be seen as directly linked to the use of additional payments – but consider the appropriateness of linking additional pay to effectiveness. If performance is difficult to operationalize and measure, which is often the case for many managerial, administrative and professional workers, achieving annual objectives is often used as a basis for 'performance-related pay'. The obvious problem here is that, unless the objectives used to establish effectiveness actually deliver increased performance, which means performance that is significantly in excess of the 'norm', not only will the additional payment be unjustified, but productivity will fall because the cost of the labour inputs will have increased without any change in the value of the product or service delivered by the employee. This is the basis of the claim that the use of financial incentives to manage what people do at work, unless they are tightly managed and linked to real improvements in the value of what employees achieve, result in a long-term decline in productivity, even though measures of effectiveness or performance might rise. The case study presented at the end of this chapter illustrates well the pitfalls that HR faces in trying to manage performance and productivity.

Understanding what influences performance

Earlier in this chapter, we suggested that one of the important questions to which managers need to know the answer is what explains low performance and how can this problem be addressed? The use of a sporting analogy, to which some readers will be directly able to relate, helps to identify explanations for low and unsatisfactory performance problems.

An experienced golfer with a handicap of 15 regularly performs to this standard at the club of which he is a member. On a golfing holiday with some friends, he plays three of the top links courses in Scotland

and returned scores well in excess of his handicap; in other words, he performed badly. Consider the possible explanations for this.

- It might be that the three courses were more difficult than his own, and that his poor performance was simply a function of the newness and level of difficulty of the courses. He played as well as he normally did, but because the courses were harder than he was used to, his performance fell relative to the challenge he faced.

- The playing conditions might have played a part in his poor performance. The wind might have been blowing and it might have been raining. In other words, the physical environment might have been a factor.

- Although appropriate to his own course, his clubs might not have been right for the different challenge he faced. In other words, he might have lacked the right equipment to play well.

- He might also have lacked the level and range of skills to perform well in a more challenging environment. Limitations in his ability to perform might have been a factor.

- There might have been something about him on those days that affected his performance: he might not have been in the right frame of mind, or he might have been nervous or a little overawed by the occasion. He might have been physically below par and have not had the energy to deliver a sustained performance over all 54 holes or he might have lacked sufficient motivation to go out and play well. Collectively, these factors relate to the person's state of mind, and his psychological and physical well being.

- Finally, he might have been missing help from his club professional or coach, who would normally give him tips on what he was doing wrong and offer constructive advice on what to do differently to improve his performance. In other words, he lacked some of the necessary support to help his performance.

The use of this sporting analogy is useful because it suggests that we can draw upon our own experiences of performance, many of which may lie outside the world of work, to help us to understand human behaviour and the factors that influence our performance at work.

In addition to the possible explanations offered above for performance problems, WE Deming, cited in Rothwell (1996, p 12), provides a further insight into where the most frequently experienced performance problems are to be found. As does the French consultant cited a little later in this chapter, Deming holds the view that what workers do or do not do is not the main reason why organizations experience these problems. He argues:

The workers are handicapped by the system, and the system belongs to management.

Rothwell (1996), in supporting this emphasis on managerial responsibility, claims that:

As little as 20% of all human performance problems is attributable to individual employees; as much as 80% of all such problems is attributable to the work environments or systems in which employees work.

Explanations are closely linked to 'solutions' and, as far as the effective management of performance is concerned, accurately diagnosing underlying causes is the basis for the 'right' solutions. Get the diagnosis wrong and any attempt to manage a performance problem is unlikely to have any significant impact; it might even worsen the situation. The following situations are often linked to performance problems, but the appropriate managerial responses are quite different.

Understanding different performance situations

Managers are faced with a wide range of situations that create very different kinds of performance problems and it is necessary to consider these in more detail.

● People absent from work

If people are not at work, they cannot perform and their absence will also result in falls in productivity levels. Sick pay and fixed employment costs mean that, even though people are absent from work, the costs of employing them largely remain the same, while their added-value contributions become zero. The higher the level of absence and the longer the time for which people are away from work, the bigger the performance loss becomes. The challenge for management then becomes one of finding effective ways of reducing absenteeism.

Signpost to Chapter 9: HR Planning and Measurement, for information on measuring and managing absenteeism

● People at work who don't perform

Given the need to become as competitive and efficient as possible, pressures to increase performance are found in most organizations. Employees who are physically absent from work represent one kind of problem, but those who just turn up to 'do their jobs' and no more present a different challenge to management. If people don't want to perform at any level other than that with which they are comfortable, then there can be a serious underutilization of labour that, sooner or later, affects the performance of the organization itself. Examples of employees who do as little as possible are more likely to be found in parts of the public sector that are protected from financial and competitive pressures. In serious cases, a culture of underperforming can develop, which can be more difficult to change than cases of individual underperformance. How can these problems be managed? Consider the approach adopted by an internationally renowned CEO in HRM Insight 11.1.

HRM INSIGHT 11.1 The case of the GE 'people factory'

In his book about his experiences as the CEO of GE (General Electric), one of the most successful USA-based global businesses listed on the New York Stock Exchange, Jack Welch (Welch and Byrne, 2003) describes the mechanism used throughout GE to manage performance. In this approach, an employee's performance is described in terms of their performance against last year's objectives with 'A performers' being in the top 20 per cent, 'B performers' being in the middle 70 per cent in terms of performance and 'C performers' defined as the bottom 10 per cent. Under this model, the company insisted that every manager identify the lowest performing 10 per cent. Failure to do so would result in the manager being categorized as a 'C' performer. In Welch's words, '*the underperformers generally had to go*', presumably meaning that, in most cases, those identified as the lowest performing 10 per cent would generally lose their job or be encouraged to leave. Welch also expresses the view that anyone in this category should not have received any pay rise.

Questions

1. What advantages might be achieved by an organization in implementing this model?

2. What might the disadvantages be to the organization and what impact might this approach have on the employees of the organization?

3. Consider the above model from the point of view of a manager of a team of ten people. What dilemmas might a manager face if asked to rate his or her team against this model?

4. What are the legal, moral and ethical implications of using this system to identify the poorest performing 10 per cent of the salaried workforce, given the intention to terminate the employment of employees in this group under the strategy described?

5. How might the top 20 per cent of performers be positively and negatively affected by this policy?

● Legitimizing low standards

Although not obviously a problem, the existence of high performers who coexist with those who are satisfied with, or are allowed to deliver, lower levels of performance does create certain challenges and difficulties. If there are no negative consequences for being a low performer, why should a low performer want to improve? Moreover, what message does this send to high performers, if it doesn't matter? Not addressing the problem of low performance can, paradoxically, result in its legitimization, making subsequent attempts to address the problem more difficult than they would otherwise have been.

● Raising performance expectations and standards

How can managers stimulate people to raise their 'average' level of performance to sustainably higher levels? This is not about raising performance on a temporary basis, although this can be important under crisis circumstances, but about leveraging up everyone's performance to a new and higher level that becomes the new performance base line. The Hay Group (Jirasinghe and Houldsworth, 2006) has found that many organizations adopt a performance enhancement strategy that combines elements from two broad approaches. Some give an emphasis to improving performance through the development of employees (a 'soft' approach), while others prefer one based on measurement (a 'hard' approach). The conclusion reached is that the most successful companies adopt a balanced and rounded approach, combining elements of both, including measures on teamwork, long-term thinking, building human capital, developing and managing talent, and maintaining of customer loyalty.

● Removing the barriers to higher performance

The final situation that has to be managed is fundamentally different to the other four. If management feels that there are performance problems, the often-implicit assumption is that employees need to be encouraged, induced or paid for additional effort or performance, and an effective mix of antecedents and consequences are designed to impact on employee behaviour. In many cases in which job performance and wider contribution linked to the exercise of discretionary effort give cause for concern, the problem is less to do with lack of ability or motivation and more to do with the existence of 'organizational blockages'. Quite simply, this means that there are influences that originate in the culture, working environment or management behaviour that act to suppress employees' natural desire to 'give more'. The challenge is, therefore, to clear the blockages that are preventing people from improving their performance.

STUDENT ACTIVITY 11.2

This activity relates to the situation in which management is attempting to build performance to permanently higher levels. According to the Hay Group's research (Jirasinghe and Houldsworth, 2006) into what companies actually do to achieve this, there are two quite distinctive approaches: developing performance and measuring. Your task is to construct a matrix for each strategy, in which the theoretical advantages and disadvantages of each approach are listed. You should also record your views on the roles of HR professionals and line managers in supporting both strategies.

Signpost to Chapter 9: HR Planning and Measurement, for information on linking performance and reward

The role of the manager in performance management

Several years ago, one of the authors was attending an international conference on Human Resource Management in Beirut. One of the speakers was a Frenchman, who had worked for more than twenty years as a senior HR executive for American Express and who, after leaving, had built up his own performance management consultancy. During a conversation about his work as a consultant, he made an interesting comment about his thinking on where most performance problems lie:

Whenever I am asked by the CEO of a business to try to sort out their performance problems, I always say that I will only agree to work for them on the basis that I will not be recommending any of the employees are made redundant as a way of solving the problem. Almost all problems of organizational underperformance are not due to what employees do or don't do – they are generally because of deficiencies in management.

The point of the story is that, while individual performance is an important factor in explaining organizational success, it rarely explains organizational failure. People can be working hard and achieving performance targets, but a business can still fail. As an example, consider the case of MG Rover and think about the reasons for which this company went into receivership (Holweg and Olive, 2005).

The need to ensure that each employee is performing close to his or her potential is, however, one of the most important objectives in any performance management system and, arguably, the most frequently used single instrument for managing individual performance is the appraisal process.

The performance appraisal process

A performance appraisal is a process that is commonly used throughout many organizations to evaluate or appraise employees' performance in the past and to consider how to maximize the employee's future contribution. The timescale under consideration is often a year, but performance may be appraised over a shorter period, from as little as a few weeks for a newly hired employee.

Signpost to Chapter 13: Case Study: HR and the New Opening, for examples of the importance of measuring performance of newly hired employees

The process usually includes a preparation stage, completed by both the employee and the manager. This may involve filling in either a pre-appraisal form or a draft copy of the appraisal form, so that these can be brought together for discussion during an appraisal meeting. To avoid favouritism and to ensure that a consistent approach is adopted across the organization, there may be some input in the preparation stage from the manager's manager. Often appraisals will cascade through an organization and the appraisals are completed in order of seniority to ensure that objectives are passed down through each level of employee.

The appraisal then typically takes place at a meeting between the employee and his or her manager, and discussions take place covering each of the elements of the employee's job that the manager and employee wish to consider. Table 11.1 overleaf gives some examples of the elements that are often included in an appraisal process.

A final record is then made of what was discussed and agreed at the meeting, including performance in the past, objectives for the future and development plans to support the employee to achieve these targets. This document is then copied for each of the parties and forms the basis of ongoing assessment against the objectives set. The whole process is shown in Figure 11.2 on p 283.

STUDENT ACTIVITY 11.3

1. Working in groups, design and produce an appraisal form for use with members of your seminar group, or a group of employees with which you are familiar. This form must record all relevant information on an individual's performance over a given period and should have a section outlining future objectives to improve performance.

2. Write a set of guidance notes to help you and your lecturer, or other employees and their manager, to prepare for and complete the appraisal effectively.

3. Reflect on what you learnt by engaging in this activity.

Table 11.1 Items that might be covered in an annual performance appraisal

Item	Details	Why might this be included?
Personal information	Name; department; service details; date commenced in role; date of appraisal meeting	A record of personal information and dates to give context of the appraisal
Last year's objectives	Details of objectives set at last year's appraisal	To clarify what level of performance was required for the preceding year
Performance against last year's objectives	Details of the extent to which objectives were met	To assess the extent to which performance last year reached the expected standard
Performance rating	A grade or score relating to overall performance	To give a score relative others in the organization – often linked to performance-related pay
Additional achievements	Other achievements during the previous year	To establish additional contribution during year that was not anticipated as part of objectives initially set
Summary of last year's development activity	Details of training and development activities last year and the benefits of these	To assess the effectiveness of development activity over the previous year
Employee's strengths	Manager's view about what an employee is good at	To praise and recognize the employee's best qualities
Employee's weaknesses	Manager's view about areas in which performance could be improved	To identify areas of skill, knowledge or attitude that might be improved
Planned training	Training activity and courses scheduled for forthcoming year	To identify training courses to address training needs identified
Other planned development activity	Other development activity, such as projects, coaching or secondment	To identify other planned activities to help to address weaknesses or to build skills and knowledge that will be required in the near future
Next year's objectives	Details of objectives for the forthcoming year, including measures and constraints	To agree the standards expected of the employee over the coming 12 months
Manager's summary	A summary of the manager's overall view of performance during the year	To record the manager's overall view of the employee
Senior managers' comments	A summary of the next level of management's view of the employee's performance	To provide an opportunity for the next level of management to ratify the process and provide feedback
Employee's comments	An opportunity for the employee to make his or her own comments	To provide an opportunity for the employee to comment, including on areas of agreement or disagreement
Signatures	Signatures and dates of acceptance of the record of meeting	Ensures all interested parties acknowledge receipt of the formal record

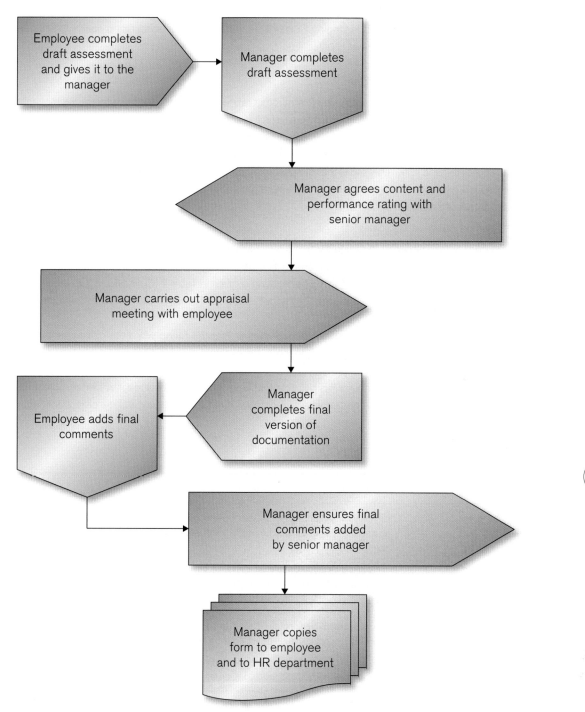

Figure 11.2 The performance appraisal process

Rating performance

Many appraisals require the manager to rate the performance of each employee in order to compare performance among colleagues. Rating systems can also be used to link performance to pay. Rating systems can be a useful indication to an employee of the extent to which the company recognizes their contribution; a lower score can be an effective way of alerting an employee that there is need for them to improve their work performance (Coens and Jenkins, 2000).

283

Signpost to Chapter 12: Managing Rewards, for more details of using rating scales to link performance and reward

- **Manager-allocated rating scales**

  Rating scales vary in complexity. A simple method of rating performance might be to ask the manager to chose a rating using a scale, an example of which is shown in Table 11.2. In this example, the manager chooses the rating that is felt to be most appropriate for the employee, given the manager's knowledge of that employee's overall performance since the last appraisal. While this system is easy to implement and relatively simple, the rating is highly subjective and will be susceptible to a manager making a judgement based upon his or her overall perception of the employee, rather than on hard indicators of actual performance.

- **Objective-based rating scales**

  One way of trying to avoid the subjectivity of a rating scale is for the manager to assess an employee's performance against the objectives set and to allocate a rating based upon the extent to which these objectives are met. An example of this type of rating is given in Table 11.3. Providing that the objectives were set in such a way that the required target level of performance was clearly defined, then the rating allocated can reflect this.

  The advantage of linking the rating to objectives is that the rating will more closely reflect the employee's actual performance. You will notice, in the example in Table 11.3, we have referred to the level of support and supervision provided to an employee, which may exceed that normally expected for any given level of performance. It is possible that an employee has only reached certain objectives as a result of levels of support and supervision that should not be necessary, and the organization may

Table 11.2 Example of a performance rating scale

Rating	Description
Outstanding	Employee demonstrates a level of performance that substantially exceeds that expected. Demonstrates an outstanding ability to meet all challenges within current role
Above standard	Employee has demonstrated a level of performance above that expected and has met challenges with a high degree of proficiency
Satisfactory	Employee's performance is at a standard that is satisfactory and acceptable
Needs some improvement	Some areas of performance need to be improved to reach a satisfactory level; more than a typical level of supervision required to meet objectives
Poor	Performance falls below the expected standard and unsatisfactory performance needs to be addressed, with considerable input required from supervision

Table 11.3 Example of an objective-based rating scale

Rating	Description
Exceeds	Employee measurably exceeds all objectives in every respect
Fulfils	Employee has met all agreed objectives to a standard that is fully satisfactory
Developing	Employee is relatively new to role and has met objectives to a satisfactory level, given level of experience and training
Below standard	Some areas of objectives not met, and employee requires more support and supervision than should be necessary to achieve objectives

wish to take this into account in rating performance. Ratings such as these are often then linked to the pay award given to an employee.

- Points-based rating scales

  There are also a variety of systems for rating job performance that allocate points to different aspects of the job that employees perform. To be effective, points-based appraisal rating systems require comprehensive, reliable and consistent information on performance against each job element or objective. Unless it is possible to meet these criteria, these systems are unlikely to possess the necessary credibility to be accepted and legitimized.

The value of rating performance

In general, the more objective a system is, the more value there is to rating performance because the rating given will actually relate to job performance. In reality, there are many jobs in which it is relatively easy to measure and rate performance, such as the sales levels achieved by a sales representative or the number of calls answered per hour by a telephone enquiry receptionist. Even in these examples, however, outside factors, such as the demand for these services, will influence performance levels.

The more complex a system is, the more effort and time needs to go into designing, maintaining and implementing it. HR professionals, often seen as the guardians of the appraisal process, must have regard for the time spent by managers in carrying out appraisals and completing the associated paperwork or online forms. A degree of sensitivity and awareness of the loopholes and 'short cuts' that can develop is also required, otherwise the appraisal process can become increasingly detached and ineffective as a positive contribution to improved performance. The criticisms levelled at performance appraisal by Coens and Jenkins (2000), which were highlighted in Chapter 2 and particularly in relation to rating errors, illustrate many of the pitfalls and deficiencies that organizations have experienced in implementing and maintaining such approaches to performance management.

→ Signpost to Chapter 2: HRM: An Academic and Professional Perspective, for details of Coens and Jenkins' criticisms of performance appraisals

Setting objectives

A key factor in the success of any organization is its ability to ensure that everyone clearly understands what they are required to do to contribute to its success. Everyone has a part to play in achieving the organization objectives, and setting objectives for individual and teams is an important part of any performance management process.

SMART is an acronym used to describe key characteristics of appraisal objectives. Each of the letters stands for the following:

S specific (one end result is clearly described);

M measurable outcome (the outcome can be measured);

A agreed (manager and report agree the outcome);

R realistic (i.e. 'what is the maximum we can realistically achieve including target and stretch?');

T timely (i.e. 'by when will it be achieved?').

It is also important to remember that objectives can become outdated as circumstances change, and management must respond quickly to new situations and demands.

Tracking progress and amending objectives to reflect new conditions and priorities is an essential part of 'managing objectives' if employees are to stay focused on what's important, rather than on what was originally agreed. Whatever objectives are agreed and possibly changed should limit employee performance, in that they prevent or inhibit employees from responding to other needs or engaging in other value-added activities that are not incorporated in an employee's formal objectives.

Direct objectives

Most organizations will have a financial budget to which it must adhere. Some sections of the organization will be responsible for bringing money in through bidding for funding, achieving sales or raising funds. Other teams will require resources that have a cost attached to them and the team may be responsible for securing the most effective resource possible within the predetermined cost. If an individual or team is responsible for a section of this budget, this might be expressed as a direct objective as follows:

Achieve sales of £500,000 in lingerie by the end of December 2008.

Many objectives that can be quantified, either by using financial values, percentage changes or physical quantities and expressed in these ways, represent a stronger motivational influence on employee behaviour because progress towards the agreed objectives can be monitored and displayed. If this is not possible, an alternative approach to agreeing objectives is required, possibly expressing these in a qualitative way. The problem with this approach, however, is that it becomes more difficult to agree on measures that accurately express progress and achievement.

Indirect objectives

- Key performance indicators (KPIs)

  It may also be possible to have a measure in place the achievement of which, although not referred to directly in the organization's central objectives, contributes to these objectives being met. Such objectives become supportive or secondary, rather than primary. It is therefore important to adopt these measures and set targets, which are often referred to as 'key performance indicators', or 'KPIs'. An example might be:

  Attract an average of 5,000 visitors per month to Mayfield Hall Museum throughout the summer season in 2008.

  In this example, the 'KPI' is visitor numbers and this directly correlates to revenue generated from ticket sales.

- Project measures

  If objectives cannot easily be expressed in terms of numbers that are directly or indirectly related to the organization's main aims and objectives, then targets might also be expressed in terms of delivery of a project that, if completed successfully, will contribute towards the organization achieving its strategic objectives. An example might be:

  Retender the combined schools catering contract for the Stokehampton district, incorporating government guidelines on healthy eating and maintaining current overall costs for the three years commencing on 1 April 2009.

The drawbacks of setting objectives

It should be noted that some jobs lend themselves more readily to objective setting than do others. For example, a sales representative with a clearly defined sales target is perhaps in a role better suited to objectives than an administrator, who may need to respond flexibly to manage a variable, and at times unpredictable, workload.

Setting objectives presumes that required actions or outputs can be predicted and sometimes this simply is not the case. Many jobs consist of complex patterns of decision making and long-term strategic planning, and the flexibility and creativity needed to deliver success in these roles can be stifled by rigid objectives. Many employees will have the self-motivation and capability to add value to an organization, identifying what needs to be done and how best to contribute to this in the absence of, or regardless of, what objectives are set. Furthermore, this creative capability can be further stifled if the attainment of prescribed objectives is related to future pay awards.

Giving effective feedback

Employees and managers generally benefit from honest, objective feedback about how things are going. A constant exchange of information, often generated through what might be described as 'performance conversation', helps everyone to stay on track and the organization to stay competitive. Problems come to the surface before they get out of hand, information that can improve performance gets to the right people before it's too late and people build stronger working relationships because of feedback.

Effective feedback helps an employee to understand how others perceive their behaviour and performance. It may not always be welcome if it contains implied or explicit criticisms, but it is an essential part of any performance management system. The purpose of giving feedback is not to change employees and try to mould them into what their manager would like them to be, but is about furnishing them with information about their behaviour and performance. Helping employees to understand how they are perceived at work, and not only by their line manager, gives them the opportunity to learn about themselves and to decide whether they need to change in some way or another.

Effective feedback, then, offers people information about themselves in a way that leaves them with a choice about how to act. The objective of giving feedback is to clarify and not judge. To be effective, the receiver needs to feels empowered and motivated to change and this can be achieved if the feedback is delivered in ways that do not damage the employee's self-esteem. Any negative feedback needs to be balanced by feedback that is positive and encouraging, so that the overall effect of the experience works to improve the employee's sense of worth and value, and motivates them to do better.

287

STUDENT ACTIVITY 11.4 **Giving constructive feedback**

Consider the following statements:

'We all think you could answer the phone more politely. You are always upsetting people on the phone.'

'I usually find you to be very helpful, but I think you might be more effective when you are explaining technical problems if you were to use diagrams and check that people understand as you go.'

'You are too aggressive when you are trying to get patients to explain why they need an urgent appointment.'

'You are efficient with all the administration and I feel you could use this to build a better rapport with your colleagues, when under pressure, if you were more sympathetic when they aren't as quick as you. For example, when Mary was busy last week, she might have appreciated an offer of help with understanding the system.'

'Good effort. Well done with the Samuels contract.'

'I am delighted with how you handled the Johnson case. The customer particularly valued the level of detail and layout in your report and summary. I think we will see a real benefit if we take this approach with our other accounts when you get the opportunity.'

1. Decide whether or not you think the feedback statements given are constructive or not constructive and consider what aspects of the statement make it more or less constructive.

2. Research the literature on giving constructive feedback and give a presentation to your group on what are considered to be essential features of the process.

3. After seminar presentations, practise giving constructive feedback and ask those receiving it what impact your comments had.

360° feedback

One of the more recent developments in the use of appraisals to manage performance, is 360-degree (360°) feedback. This involves seeking contributions about what a person achieves and how he or she operates not only from the line manager, but from others who are in contact with the person and are in a position to offer such feedback. Using this process, an employee, but more often a manager, can receive structured feedback from a variety of sources to assist him or her in improving performance. Typically, a questionnaire is sent to a selection of colleagues, subordinates and, possibly, external contacts. The completed questionnaires are returned anonymously to an independent third party. The same questionnaire is also completed by the employee and by his or her manager, and the responses are compared between each group.

To be effective, feedback to the employee of the results should ideally be undertaken by a trained facilitator, who can help the employee to understand his or her own strengths and weaknesses, and can use the information to produce a development plan. While this tool can be extremely effective in helping an employee to understand exactly how he or she is perceived, the process must be properly managed. The employee is unlikely to benefit unless he or she remains open-minded and willing to participate in the process. Without a reasonable degree of trust, the process of seeking feedback at different levels might be detrimental to working relationships. Other staff may be reluctant to comment, and may need to be encouraged to be open and honest, and reassured that responses are anonymous. The feedback will also be more meaningful if any scores and responses are supported by examples and written comments to aid clarification. The design of the questionnaire is also crucial. While generic, 'off-the-shelf' questionnaires are available, organizations may benefit from designing their own process relevant to the skill sets they deem to be important to their own managers and teams (Coomber, 2006).

Development plans

A development plan is an important tool to help an individual plan how he or she can best maximize his or her skills and knowledge. This can form a part of an appraisal process, but a more detailed development plan can help to enhance the development of any individual. For example, an organization may wish to use development plans to fast-track employees who are identified as having high potential (Stringer and Cheloha, 2003). Typically, development plans will list all structured activity that is designed to address specific development needs. This might be to help build upon weaker areas, to develop existing skills and knowledge, or to develop new skills and expertise in readiness for future challenges. An effective development plan will encompass a broad range of developmental activity and will have only a small element of development reliant on attendance of training courses. Other activities may involve coaching or mentoring, participation in project work, secondment to another role or department, and opportunities to carry out new tasks or be exposed to new situations and challenges in the workplace.

Managing problem performance

Earlier, we made reference to a situation with which managers are often confronted – that of performance that is consistently below what is reasonable and acceptable. In a worst-case scenario, managers will ignore the problem or rationalize it away, interpreting it as less of a problem than it really is. But pretending they don't exist rarely solves problems of underperformance and the effective management of performance not only involves developing systems and procedures, but engaging with those employees whose behaviour is unacceptable.

In serious cases involving managerial staff, this may involve managing people out of the organization through the use of what are referred to as 'compromise agreements'. These are forms of contracts that end the employment relationship by mutual agreement and involve the employee giving up his or her employment protection rights in exchange for a financial payment, and often a favourable reference. In cases in which the problem is considered irretrievable, often involving a breakdown in the relationship between employee and management, rather than invoke disciplinary procedure leading to dismissal, management may wish to consider a solution to the problem that is less damaging for both parties.

In less serious situations, management can consider the mechanisms that normally lie outside an existing appraisal process.

- An informal performance review

  This involves a meeting between a manager and an employee to highlight areas of concern with the employee's current performance, to discuss and set targets for improvement, and, if appropriate, to arrange support and training to achieve these targets.

- A formal performance review

  This is a meeting between a manager, often with an HR practitioner or another manager present, and the employee, who should be informed of the right to be accompanied by a representative. At a formal meeting, concerns about performance can be discussed, targets set for improvement and consequences of failure to improve can be highlighted, which may ultimately include demotion, transfer or termination of employment. A timescale for improvement, training and support can also be agreed.

Both types of review are, or should be, based on the principles that employees need to be given the opportunity to improve their performance before further action is taken and that raising concerns informally first is preferable to invoking formal procedure or action. Both types of meeting are, however, likely to cover the same content, including:

- discussing areas of concern;
- setting targets and timescales for improvement;
- agreeing appropriate training and support.

289

> **STUDENT ACTIVITY 11.5**
>
> 1. As a group, develop a manager's guide to effective appraisal interviewing.
> 2. Design and, if possible, pilot a training session for first-line supervisors on 'effective performance appraisal interviewing'.
> 3. Survey a group of employees who have experienced performance appraisals, and present and discuss your findings with the group.

Summary

Managing employee performance is rarely not an option in contemporary organizations, simply because of the pressure that managers are under to remain competitive and to deliver productivity improvements. One way in which these can be achieved is by getting employees to perform at sustainably higher levels. This can be achieved through increasing effort levels, by accessing effort that is discretionary and under the control of the employee, through working more efficiently, or through reducing the amount of unproductive time due to absence and wasteful activities.

At a more strategic level, management can remove relatively low performers and replace them with new recruits, who either can perform at higher levels or have the potential to do so. This kind of strategy is associated with a high-performance culture in which high standards of effort and commitment are expected from all employees; in this type of culture, low performance is simply not acceptable from either employees or managers. The culture of an organization and the expectations held by its senior management are critical factors that influence what people do at work and what they want to do. Often employees want to do more, but are inhibited from doing so because, paradoxically, high performance from a few employees, compared to the majority, focuses attention on an endemic problem that some managers prefer to remain hidden. In such situations, the problem of low performance has little to do with the skills and capabilities of employees, and is rather a symptom of weak and ineffective management.

The ability of performance appraisal schemes to drive performance upwards remains a highly debatable question. Authors such as Coens and Jenkins (2000) argue that their research suggests that the majority of such schemes not only do not improve individual performance levels, but actually undermine them (Grint, 1993). This is to do with the undermining effects of managers sitting in judgement on their subordinates and the biases that inevitably intrude into the assessment not only of an employee's performance, but of the person.

The belief that higher levels of performance can be achieved by offering incentives or other inducements is historically associated with certain industries, such as construction and engineering. In such industries, there is an often explicitly accepted assumption, held by both managers and workers, that there are two levels of performance: one linked to the basic wage and a higher one, up to 33 per cent higher, that is associated with additional incentives. Employee performance in these conditions does not exceed the norm unless financial incentives are provided through some form of performance-related pay scheme. The problem with such schemes, as explained in more detail in Chapter 12, is that it costs to access higher levels of performance and this can often contribute to falls in labour productivity. To avoid this, organizations are looking to improve productivity by creating a working environment that encourages employees to use their potential to the full, rewards them for this (but not necessarily in a financial way), and generates higher levels of employee engagement with the organization and its objectives.

Visit the Online Resource Centre that accompanies this book for self-test questions, weblinks, and more information on the topics covered in this chapter.
online resource centre **www.oxfordtextbooks.co.uk/orc/banfield_kay/**

REVIEW QUESTIONS

1. What are the key features of the working environment that have an impact on an employee's level of performance?

2. How does 'performance' differ from 'productivity' and what is the relationship between the two?

3. What kind of appraiser biases might be found in the performance appraisal process and how might these be managed?

4. What are the features of 'high-performance work practices'?

5. What does the concept 'discretionary effort' mean and why is this important in managing performance?

6. Strategically, what are the advantages of developing the performance capabilities of existing staff compared to recruiting high-performing people?

In situations in which managers are under pressure to increase pay in a way that does not increase wage costs, which might decrease labour productivity, agreements with groups of employees to link increases to changes in employee behaviour can result in improvements in productivity. In other words, agreements can generate added value or reduced cost, with either the savings or increased output values becoming the source of increased payments. Employees, through greater utilization of their intellectual and physical labour, effectively pay for their own pay increases. The management of United Steels, within which the light machine shop (LMS) was located, was faced with a similar situation. The shop stewards representing the fifty workers employed in the LMS had submitted a pay claim, but after discussions with Peter Wilson, employment relations manager for United Steels, had agreed to consider a proposal for a productivity agreement.

The LMS was one small department in a complex of steel-producing and heavy engineering facilities, and was physically on the perimeter of the complex, well away from where most of the senior managers were located. It was essentially a fabrication shop, in which products such as steel frames, tables and panels were made.

Peter discussed the options with his team and it was decided that a scheme should be designed that would generate increased revenue, which could be shared between the company and the employees covered by the scheme. He asked George Black, one of the employee relations officers, to come up with an idea that might deliver the required objectives. George looked at the current system of working and payment, and found the following.

- All of the employees were paid an hourly rate based on their skill level. This was known as the 'consolidated time rate' and was paid irrespective of the amount of work each individual completed. There was an unspoken understanding within the shop of the level of output that was needed before management began to show a concern about performance levels.

- Each job allocated by the shop foreman to an individual worker had a time allowance attached to it. This allowed time figure was the result of a time study, under which the foreman would apply time study practices to arrive at a time that was neither too easy nor too difficult to meet. All new jobs had to be timed by the foreman and an allowed time determined. Existing jobs were often subject to retiming as design changes changed the 'amount of work' that was involved.

- Workers were able to increase their weekly wages by completing jobs that had an aggregate allowed time in excess of 40 hours (a 40-hour week was in place). If, for example, an individual completed jobs having an allowed time of 47 hours, he would receive 47 times his hourly rate.

- Individual performance could only effectively be increased by workers increasing their focused effort, i.e. by working harder and smarter, and by using their skills to full effect.

- Current management attitudes and practices meant that the decisions on performance levels were largely in the hands of the workers.

- The shop foreman was only in contact with his line manager infrequently and the HR representatives were rarely seen on the shop floor. He spent most of his time with the workers he was managing and was particularly influenced by the strong trade union presence, manifested by two experienced shop stewards who had worked in the shop for many years. He didn't want any trouble that might involve senior management and he was very much interested in a 'negotiated order'.

George was relatively inexperienced in designing 'productivity' schemes, but, after discussing the best approach to take with a colleague, he came up with the following proposal.

- The scheme would be based on the ability of workers to earn a non-consolidated bonus by increasing their weekly output of steel components.

- The principle underpinning the scheme would be the relationship between allowed times and actual times. The time the workers *actually* took to complete each time job or part of a job would be recorded, along with the *allowed* time, on each job card issued by the shop foreman.

- All job cards for the previous six months would be collected and the aggregate allowed times calculated. The aggregate actual times would also be calculated and compared to the allowed times using the formula:

$$\frac{\text{Allowed times}}{\text{Actual times}} \times 100 = \text{productivity index}$$

The data collected produced the following base-line index:

$$\frac{57,850}{52,000} \times 100 = 111$$

- A 13-week moving average would be used to iron out weekly fluctuations in output, with the first bonus payment being paid in Week 13.

- Bonus payments would be paid to each worker pro rata to his or her skill grade, with skilled workers receiving 100 per cent bonus, semi-skilled workers receiving 90 per cent and those designated as unskilled, 80 per cent.

- Actual payments, at 100 per cent, would be £3 per week for every percentage point by which the productivity index exceeded its base line.

Questions

1. What were management's objectives in designing this scheme?

2. Was the scheme about performance or productivity?

3. If the index were to increase from its base line, what might the explanations for this be?

4. Are there any potential flaws in the scheme?

5. How do you think the behaviour of the workers in the LMS would have changed as a result of the scheme being implemented? Would their behaviour have reflected what the HR staff expected?

 Insights & Outcomes: visit the Online Resource Centre at www.oxfordtextbooks.co.uk/orc/banfield_kay/ for an account of why the bonus scheme failed and the lessons that were learnt.

FURTHER READING

Boice, DF and Kleiner, BH (1997) 'Designing effective performance appraisal systems', *Work Study*, 46:6, pp 197–201.

Fisher, CM (1994) 'The difference between appraisal schemes: variations and acceptability part II', *Personnel Review*, 24:1, pp 51–66.

Incomes Data Services (2003) *Performance Management*, IDS Study.

IRS (2003) 'Performance management: policy and practices', *IRS Employment Review*, Issue 781, pp 12–19.

Soltani, A, Van der Meer, R and Williams, T (2005) 'A contrast of HRM and TQM approaches to performance management', *British Journal of Management*, 16:6, pp 403–17.

REFERENCES

Armstrong, M and Baron, A (1998) *A Performance Management: The New Realities*, IPD.

Coens, T and Jenkins, M (2000) *Abolishing Performance Appraisals*, Berrett Koehler.

Coomber, J (2006) *360 Feedback*, CIPD factsheet, available online at **www.cipd.co.uk**.

Grint, K (1993) 'What's wrong with performance appraisals? A critique and a suggestion', *Human Resource Management*, 3:3, pp 61–77.

Holweg, M and Olive, N (2005) *Who Killed MG Rover?*, Cambridge-MIT Institute Centre for Competitiveness and Innovation at Cambridge University, available online at **www.innovation.jims.cam.ac.uk**.

Jirasinghe, D and Houldsworth, E (2006) *Managing and Measuring Employee Performance: Henley Management College & Hay Group*, Kogan Page.

Lockett, J (1992) *Effective Performance Management: A Strategic Guide to Getting the Best from People*, Kogan Page.

Mabey, C, Salaman, G and Story, J (1998) *Human Resource Management: A Strategic Introduction*, Blackwell.

McKinsey Co (2000) 'War for talent II – seven ways to win', *Fast Company*, Issue 42, p 98, available online at **www.fastcompany.com**.

Morhman JR and Morhman, S (1995) 'Performance management is running the business', *Compensation and Benefits Review*, 27:4, pp 69–76.

Pfeffer, J and O'Reilly, CA (2000) *Hidden Value*, Harvard Business School Press.

Rothwell, W (1996) *Beyond Training and Developing*, AMACOM.

Stringer, RA and Cheloha, RS (2003) 'The power of a development plan', *Human Resource Planning*, 26:4, pp 10–17.

Taylor, FW (1998) *The Principles of Scientific Management*, Dover Publications Inc.

Ulrich, D (1998) 'A new mandate for Human Resources', *Harvard Business Review*, 76:1, pp 124–34.

Welch, J and Byrne, JA (2003) *Straight from the Gut*, Warner Books.

12 Managing Rewards

Learning Objectives

As a result of reading this chapter and using the Online Resource Centre, you should be able to.

- understand that rewards can take different forms and serve different purposes;

- understand the principles that underpin different types of payment system and how these systems work;

- understand how to link the use and management of rewards to employee behaviour, particularly that which relates to job performance;

- contribute to the processes involved in changing reward structures and making them more effective;

- identify the factors that influence an organization's use of reward practices.

Introduction

Putting rewards in context

According to the CIPD (Arkin, 2005), there has never been a better time to become a specialist in reward management. This view is based on evidence generated by the Institute's 2005 annual reward survey (CIPD, 2005), which found that demand for such expertise is growing, with more organizations taking on specialist reward practitioners. Interesting as this trend might be for those wishing to develop a career in this field, the real significance of the report lies in the way in which it casts light on the forces and pressures influencing reward practices, and the challenges facing managers in the way in which they respond to these pressures.

But why are rewards, and the way in which they are managed and experienced at work, such an important part of human resource management? A useful starting point is recognizing that rewards are a basic element of the employment relationship, and have a critical influence on the satisfaction and commitment of employees. Organizations that fail to understand this fundamental relationship are likely to be less competitive and successful than those that do, and which deliver consistently effective reward policies and practices. Quite simply, employees who are frustrated and dissatisfied with the rewards they receive will express this through how they behave and perform in their jobs; in ways that are unlikely to be in the interests of the organization. Organizations that make mistakes in the way in which they manage rewards are almost certainly going to experience damaging consequences, in the forms of low productivity, higher turnover and a general lack of employee engagement. The bigger the mistakes, the higher the costs that the organization will experience.

It is similarly important to recognize that the way in which rewards are managed will also, either directly or indirectly, impact on other aspects of HR. For example, a sense of unfairness and dissatisfaction with pay will probably have an effect on the form and level of industrial conflict, and the preparedness of employees to participate with management in a more collaborative approach to employee relations. As Paul Bissell (in Arkin, 2005) observed:

> **Organizations are realizing what a powerful lever reward is and how it needs to complement their other business strategies, whereas historically people have tended to view it in glorious isolation.**

What this means is that reward management is not simply about the basic issues of paying people fairly in relation to market rates, the job they do and how well they perform in the job, but extends to the impact of reward decisions on recruitment, retention, training, flexibility and performance, in addition to their effect on morale and commitment. It is self-evident that, without satisfactory rewards, the organization will not be able either to attract or retain the calibre of employee it requires, with the right skills and competencies to deliver the contributions that the organization needs in order to be successful and competitive. In fact, it would not be an exaggeration to suggest that rewards have a significance that pervades almost every aspect of employment and work. It is not surprising, therefore, that interest in reward management is growing.

KEY CONCEPT **Fairness**

There are issues relating to pay and rewards generally that generate subjective feelings of what is, and what is not, 'fair'. This often involves employees looking to other employees, and comparing what they do and what they get paid in relation to these 'comparator' employees. If there is a perception of unfairness, there is great potential for disharmony and the impact upon motivation can be significant. Judgements about what is fair and what is not fair are also found in relation to the rewards experiences of male and female employees doing the same or similar work, and if differences in pay or benefits exist that cannot be justified by differences in the value of jobs, the feeling of unfairness that often follows can ultimately involve the aggrieved party challenging the employer through an equal pay claim.

But while the issue of pay and reward is fundamental to the behaviour and performance of employees, it is arguably one of the most contentious and difficult areas of HR to manage. It is perhaps for this reason that the remuneration packages of reward specialists tend to be significantly greater than those enjoyed by the majority of HR generalists (CIPD, 2005). This level of recognition of the important role and contribution played by reward specialists is partly due to the scale and range of reward matters. From managing the payroll, pensions and other contractual benefits, those involved also have to make critical decisions on wage and salary levels, pay increases, and sort out the never-ending disputes and disagreements over bonus payments. The costs of the pay and of the total reward packages represent, for most organizations, a significant proportion of their total budget and these costs need to be managed effectively to ensure that they remain within acceptable limits. Reward specialists not only have to ensure that employees are fairly and adequately paid (both highly subjective), but must also avoid significant overpayment, in the context of what the organization can afford to pay to remain competitive and in business.

Managing rewards can also involve large-scale, sector-based pay modernization projects, which seek to replace ageing and ineffective pay policies with common pay structures, based on national job evaluation frameworks and harmonized conditions of employment. The NHS' Agenda for Change project is a good example of a major reward management initiative and, in this case, links the development of a new national competency framework to a simplified structure of jobs and payment levels (Department of Health, 2004).

The challenging nature of reward management is also the result of the increasingly complicated nature of the 'reward package'. Rewards are far from being solely about pay. According to Thompson (2002):

> . . . the era in which reward was just about cash and benefits is gone forever; increasingly the emphasis in leading organizations is on a total reward approach, including more intangible rewards like the work environment and quality of life considerations, the opportunity for advancement and recognition, and flexible working.

Moreover, as reward systems are integrated with other areas of HR, and have to respond to external pressures and legislative change, it becomes increasingly difficult to envisage a situation in which managers have, in some finite sense, 'solved the problem'. It is much more sensible to conceptualize reward management as an ongoing engagement – an attempt to reconcile the interests and expectations of different organizational stakeholders – that is undertaken in the knowledge that these different interests and expectations can never be fully met or reconciled. As Daniels (2000) alleges:

> Few organizations are satisfied with their reward and recognition systems. Furthermore, every change in these systems results in someone else becoming unhappy. Most often, management becomes cynical, because no matter what they try, nobody is satisfied.

Differences over what constitutes 'fair' and 'effective' reward systems, and uncertainties about the behavioural impact of particular rewards and reward practices, makes the job of the HR practitioner working in this field particularly problematical and challenging. There are no simple or universalistic answers and prescriptions that are guaranteed to work. What emerges from the different academic contributions, research findings and individual experiences is that there is no consensus on how organizations should be rewarding their employees, nor is there any certainty that the use of particular rewards will actually generate the behaviours and outcomes desired by managers. Furthermore, not all commentators hold the same views as to the effects on behaviour of particular types of reward.

A good example of the polarization of opinion over the use of rewards can be seen in the arguments relating to the use of rewards to encourage higher levels of individual performance, i.e. those relating to performance-related pay. Many managers and employees genuinely believe that rewards used in this way do have a positive impact on employee motivation and, used appropriately, can increase individual performance levels. This is often described as the 'incentivized' level of performance. On the other hand, writers such as Herzberg (2003) and Kohn (1993a) have consistently taken the view that such rewards not only fail to deliver the intended outcomes, but actually distort behaviour and have a long-term detrimental effect on productivity. Kohn even equates these additional payments with bribes and argues that they should not be used, despite the fact that many managers and employees believe that people will do a better job if they have been promised some kind of reward or incentive.

The difficulties faced by managers in determining the most appropriate and effective reward strategy for their organizations are not only highlighted in the academic literature, but also in the realities of organizational life. The dilemma they face is that, while employees value rewards and generally would like more of them, rewards can be very costly for the organization and if pay is the predominant form of reward, overpaying employees can be an expensive mistake – remember that it is much easier to give rewards than it is to take them away! At the same time, it is natural to expect that employees will want to maximize their remuneration and reward levels, to reflect their views about their value and the contribution that they believe they make to the organization. This tension between what employees feel they are worth and what managers consider it is economically prudent to pay is often at the heart of disagreements and conflict between the two parties, particularly if financial rewards are involved.

It is quite easy to establish the existence of tensions and disagreements over pay. If an organization were to seek the opinions of its employees on this subject, it would be far more likely to find that employees consider themselves underpaid rather than overpaid. Whether they would consider themselves to be under- rather than over-rewarded is a separate question, but given that pay is the most visible and, arguably, the most important reward provided by employment, the tendency for employees to believe that they are paid less than they feel they deserve helps to explain why pay is often the cause of many outbreaks of industrial conflict.

Student Activity 12.1 is designed to provide insights into the complexities and apparent paradoxes associated with the use and perception of rewards.

STUDENT ACTIVITY 12.1

Consider in what situations the following paradoxes might arise and why:

- a reward can be seen as a punishment;
- a reward can become a bribe;
- the award of an annual bonus can result in disappointment and a sense of rejection;
- the offer of a pay increase is rejected by union officials as 'insulting';
- a pay increase is also perceived as a pay decrease.

What do we mean by rewards?

We should not take it for granted that all of the main organizational stakeholders share the same views about what constitutes a reward and the value that any particular reward represents. For too long, rewards have only been equated with pay and this perception needs to be challenged. As Thompson (2002) argues:

> . . . we need to re-think what is and what is not a reward.

Rewards can, in one sense, represent instruments for controlling behaviour. Consider their use, first of all, in a non-employment context. Anyone who has visited Disney SeaWorld theme parks will almost certainly have observed the use of rewards to reinforce desired behaviour in animals. When a seal, dolphin or killer whale performs an act correctly, the trainers pat it, praise it and feed it fish as a reward for doing the right thing. This is what is known as 'instrumental conditioning', under which desired behaviours are immediately followed by a reward. The animal quickly begins to associate certain behaviours with particular consequences, i.e. the reward, and because the reward is desired, it quickly learns to associate one with the other.

Children similarly learn through the use of various kinds of reward. Being well behaved can become associated with sweets and chocolate, extra TV time and special rights. Interestingly, however, while the use of rewards to train animals seems to work most of the time, the same can't be said for children, who don't seem to play to the same set of rules as animals!

So what if rewards are withheld? Does this constitute a form of punishment? It is important to remember that, just as rewards have the potential to give pleasure and satisfy a fundamental need if they are given, withholding or withdrawing rewards has the potential to hurt. From a behavioural perspective, managers need to try to predict the reactions that follow from using rewards in different ways.

Kohn (1993a) argues that rewards and punishment are not really opposites, but different sides of the same coin. He suggests that the giving and the withholding of a reward each represent strategies that amount to manipulating the behaviour of an animal, child and an employee. In this sense, a reward represents an extrinsic – that is, an externally located – source of motivation that, according to Kohn, does not alter a person's emotional or cognitive commitment, which are the keys to understanding and influencing behaviour.

But managers are not dealing with animals or children, and the questions they are particularly interested in are:

- can rewards be used to condition the behaviour of employees and, if so, in what circumstances?
- what types of reward have the greatest impact on employee behaviour?
- is the distinction between extrinsic and intrinsic rewards a useful one, and, if so, why?
- are there any problems and costs associated with the inappropriate use of rewards?

Failing to reward in circumstances in which the employee honestly believes that the reward is deserved and rightful can have interesting consequences, HRM Insight 12.1 illustrates.

HRM INSIGHT 12.1 The case of the disaffected consultant

Alex Wilkinson was a senior manager in a public utility, who had made the transition to the consultancy sector after taking an early retirement package. As a corporate strategist with many years' experience of project management, he became a valued member of his new company, which specialized in designing and project managing international development contracts. He also became involved in the delivery of prestigious programmes for corporate clients, and was seen as one of the few consultants who had personal and professional credibility with corporate and governmental clients.

For some time, Alex had been working with a senior colleague on a joint EU/UK government-funded project to introduce new management practices into the electronics sector of an emerging Eastern European country. As a result of the senior project manager being relocated, Alex was asked to take over and to manage the project's pilot phase, which involved him in frequent visits to Eastern Europe, to help build the necessary infrastructure and establish a resource base. Seen as dynamic and successful, he was asked if he would be prepared to take over as project director, based in Sofia, on a two-year contract, after which he would return to his consultancy post.

He had several meetings with his managing director to discuss the situation and made it clear that he was keen to take up the offer. On the other hand, the MD was concerned at the prospect of losing such a valued member of the company and began to express thoughts about whether the funding level provided for in the existing contract was really high enough to justify remaining involved after completion of the pilot phase. After discussions with Alex, the UK government department responsible for coordinating the project on behalf of the EU made the MD an offer. If he would be prepared to second Alex for a two-year period, they would not only meet his current reward package, but would also pay the consultancy twice his salary in compensation for his temporary absence. Alex saw this as an important opportunity for his personal and professional development, and a reward for all of the effort and hard work he had put into the project over the previous 12 months. He anticipated that an agreement would be reached on the basis of the deal offered.

It came as an unpleasant surprise when the MD told him that he would not approve the secondment and that, moreover, they would not be seeking further involvement in the project beyond phase one. Four weeks later, Alex tendered his resignation, joined a rival consultancy and began negotiating with the government on phase two, which was the rollout of the piloted programme to the remaining parts of the electronics sector. Three months later, Alex moved to Sofia to take over as project director.

Questions

1. Was Alex being unreasonable in expecting the consultancy to reward him by allowing him to take the secondment?

2. What was the rationale behind the MD's decision to refuse Alex's request for a secondment? On what grounds, if any, might this be justified?

3. Estimate the losses and gains to the consultancy resulting from its decision and Alex's move.

4. Might the MD have handled the situation differently?

HRM Insight 12.1 suggests that employees are not simply interested in material rewards and that, if organizations are seeking to strengthen employees' commitment through the management of rewards, paying them more is unlikely to achieve this. Most people would not reject an increase in their pay, but only when the wage or salary becomes seriously out of line with expectations or long-established comparators does pay, in the sense that the level is perceived to be too low, begin to have a significant impact on employee behaviour. As HRM Insight 12.1 indicates, the absence or withholding of opportunities, a lack of recognition for achievement or a feeling that the organization doesn't value its employees all have the potential to create dissatisfaction and disagreement with management's behaviour and decisions. Some, like Alex, will resign and move to other employment; others will, through different circumstances, stay, but do less; those who feel particularly strongly may openly challenge management from within.

Characteristics of rewards

We would argue that, whatever form it takes, a reward must have the following characteristics.

- It must have a value in itself or because of what it represents. In other words, its value is linked to the fulfilment of a basic human need or one that is socially acquired.

- It must be relevant and important to the individual. A company car, for example, is not important to the employee who either cannot drive or has no need of a car, and free membership of a fitness club is unlikely to be attractive to someone who has no interest in physical activity.

- It must be associated with, or serve, a purpose. A reward is something that can be used to achieve an outcome that is desired by one party or the other.

- A reward needs to have a behavioural effect on the person receiving the reward, although the actual effect may not be that which was intended.

- There must conscious recognition on the part of the receiver and giver that an act of rewarding has taken place.

Whatever the intention of the 'giver', it is the receiver who effectively gives meaning to an exchange or transaction, and managers must be at least aware of the possibility that their motivation and intentions may be misinterpreted or misconstrued by the receiver. Although the nature of a reward is often seen as unproblematical, this is far from reality and this is not only a question of conceptual clarity. Managers' reward strategies are, in part, based on their own views about what employees' value, the assumptions they make about the behavioural impact that might follow from the use of particular kinds of rewards, and the operation of the reward and payment systems that they use. If their assumptions are flawed, it is likely that the objectives associated with a particular reward scheme will not be achieved.

Rewards categories

Rewards are usually placed in the following categories.

- **Monetary rewards**
  - Basic pay
  - Bonuses
  - Commission payments
  - Overtime
  - Condition payments

- **Benefits associated with working for the organization**
  - Pensions
  - Health care
  - Subsidized meals, loans, etc.
  - Membership of health and fitness clubs
  - Company cars or petrol allowances
  - Flexible working arrangements

- **Psychological rewards**

  The source of these is embedded in the work that people do and the environment in which they work.
  - Recognition
  - Praise
  - Being valued
  - Being part of a social community
  - Achievement
  - Recognizing that work is important and has an intrinsic value
  - Fun and enjoyment

- **Personal rewards**
  - Promotion
  - Advancement and development
  - Acquisition of new competencies
  - Increased employability

The recently developed concept of 'total rewards' is important because it provides managers today with the opportunity to identify, and use, a much wider range and variety of rewards than was perhaps available or understood by earlier generations. Many of these are non-materialistic, relate to the psychological well being of employees and exist in the working environment. Recognizing the importance of these types of reward, Pfeffer (1998) argues that:

> Creating a fun, challenging and empowered work environment in which individuals are able to use their abilities to do meaningful jobs for which they are shown appreciation is likely to be a more certain way to enhance motivation and performance – even though creating such an environment may be more difficult and take more time than merely turning the award lever.

This view that pay may have far less of an impact on employees' day-to-day behaviour than other forms of reward is supported by research undertaken by Sanders and Sidney, the HR consultancy. Quoting from their findings that employees value work friendships as much as pay, Deeks (2000) reported that:

Of the 313 employees surveyed, 80 per cent claimed that they enjoyed going to work mainly because of the people they worked with. Two-thirds indicated that the workplace community influenced whether they stayed with an organization. A further 62 per cent said that the workplace community had alleviated other areas of dissatisfaction, such as pay.

The idea that managers can manipulate employee behaviour by having control over different reward levers is as dangerous as it is attractive, but the belief that certain kinds of rewards, particularly monetary incentives, can deliver significant improvements in performance is shared by many managers and employers. This belief was brought to the fore by the experiences and writings of FW Taylor (1998). Taylor believed that workers who placed a high value on money and were not of high intelligence would respond positively to the prospect of earning more through increasing their performance. Such circumstances as Taylor describes are not fundamentally different to those we thought about earlier in relation to animals performing at SeaWorld centres, where careful training regimes linked to performance standards were reinforced by rewards that the animals valued.

Despite challenges from writers such as Kohn (1993) and Herzberg (2003), the influence of the Taylorist belief in the use and effectiveness of financial incentives is still pervasive, and not only among managers: many employees in sales, construction and engineering would probably hold similar views. What unites both managers and employees is the notion that there are, in fact, two levels of employee performance. One can be described as the 'normal' level, which corresponds to employees providing effort and output levels reflecting what they consider to be fair and appropriate in relation to the contractually based reward package. This is often expressed in the phrase:

A fair day's work for a fair day's pay.

But over and above this exists what is thought of as the 'incentivized' level of effort and performance, which can only be accessed through additional monetary payments, in the form of incentives. Those who adopt this view also tend to believe that the incentivized level of effort and performance can only be accessed through additional financial payments that are between 25 to 33 per cent of pay.

The case that individual performance levels can move significantly between different performance levels is not, in itself, the central question; crucial is whether increased performance can only be delivered through the use of financial incentives and whether the use of such payments, under certain circumstances, can actually be dysfunctional. These are the questions that those critical of the use of financial incentives are asking and, in so doing, these critics are beginning to point to other, more effective, forms of reward that can be used to improve employee performance.

The cases for and against incentive-based rewards

One of the most consistent critics of the use of incentives and incentive-based payment systems is Alfie Kohn (1993a,b; 1995). The starting point for Konh's critique is the acceptance that, as in the UK, many US managers, and those that advise them:

... believe in the redemptive power of rewards.

But his research – based on numerous articles, studies and experiments, not all of which are industry-based – indicates that rewards:

... typically undermine the very processes they are intended to enhance.

These problems appear to go beyond the design and implementation of incentive-based pay systems. Kohn argues that:

>...the failure of any given incentive programme is due less to a glitch in that program than to the inadequacy of the psychological assumptions that ground all such plans.

Kohn suggests that incentives, in their many different forms, not only achieve (at best) temporary compliance or short-term behavioural changes that may be manifested in improved performance, but do not alter the attitudes that underlie behaviour. This is a very similar view to that expressed by Herzberg (2003) in his famous article on employee motivation, in which he distinguished 'movement' from 'motivation'. Herzberg saw incentives as having the capacity to 'move' people, with further movement only being achieved by more incentives. Motivation, on the other hand, was based on an inner force, under which behaviour comes primarily from a person wanting to do something rather than from external stimulation, which he describes as being equivalent to bribes.

What, then, are the reasons why rewards, in the form of incentives, fail? Kohn suggests the following factors.

- Pay is not a motivator

   This is not meant to imply that money is unimportant or that paying less than is considered fair is acceptable, but rather that paying people more will not encourage them to do better or more work over the long term.

- Rewards punish

   This is about feeling controlled and manipulated by managers, if the rewards that employees expect or hope to receive are withheld or withdrawn.

- Rewards rupture relationships

   The pursuit of personal rewards has the effect of reducing cooperation and fracturing relationships: rewards individualize work.

- Rewards ignore reasons

   The use of incentives is often an easier way of trying to address problems of behaviour and performance than exploring and understanding the underlying causes of the problems.

- Rewards discourage risk taking

   Because employee behaviour is increasingly focused on trying to achieve the incentive, behaviour that is not seen to be relevant to this is downgraded, even though it still might be important to the organization.

- Rewards undermine interest

   This is about the way in which the use of extrinsic controls and influences are thought to undermine employee commitment and interest in their work, because they reduce interest in anything else.

Kohn's article and criticisms of using rewards to generate commitment and improved performance produced a predictable response from many managers, consultants and other academics, whose views were also published in the *Harvard Business Review* (Bennett Stewart et al, 1993). In the article, the contributors argued that:

- rewards should not be confused with incentives and people should be rewarded for a job well done. Companies should not stop paying for performance, but should avoid using incentives;

- while much of what Kohn says about the limits of behaviourist psychology and the instrumental use of incentives has a degree of validity, integrating the use of incentives and gain-sharing, as part of wider strategy of work reorganization and participative working, can achieve very significant results;

- incentive schemes have a limited time during which they can be effective and, within this timeframe, they can be important elements of a wider reward package;

- many rewards are not perceived as bribes, but as equitable outcomes that reflect the contributions that people have made;

- while the negative aspects of using of piece rates and merit pay to reinforce task-orientated behaviour are understood, appropriate rewards for improved performance make sense intuitively and practically, and they are neither wrong nor intrinsically demotivating.

It is possible to reconcile the differences between Kohn's position and those who, while accepting some of his arguments, believe that he has gone too far in appearing to reject any positive outcomes from using rewards to influence employee behaviour. Both are, to a certain extent, 'right' and, while incentive-based rewards may have a part to play in influencing employee performance, over-reliance on such rewards is dangerous. Metaphorically, in rejecting the possible beneficial effects of incentives, we might be 'throwing the baby out with the bathwater'!

KEY CONCEPT Expectation

This is one of the most powerful and important concepts in the field of reward management. It focuses attention on the behavioural impact of different 'reward experiences' and on whether the amount or form of any given reward creates a positive or negative response. The more people expect, whether this is considered reasonable or not, is not the point; what is the point is that expectations, if not met, will result in disappointment and behaviours that reflect this emotional state. Conversely, the less an employee expects, the lower the likelihood of disappointment with what he or she receives.

HRM Insight 12.2 looks into the 'power of expectation'.

HRM INSIGHT 12.2 The American Shoe Corporation

The American Shoe Corporation (ASC) is a long-established and family-owned business, with manufacturing plants in West Virginia and Pennsylvania. It has some 250 employees, many of whom are from the same families and have worked for the company for many years. In recent years, the industry generally had been damaged by overseas competition from low-cost producers and several other US shoe producers had either outsourced their manufacturing operations, laid off part of their workforce or, in some cases, gone out of business.

On the day before the company was due to announce its results for the preceding financial year, employees received letters asking them to attend a meeting on the following Monday morning with the works manager of the two respective factories. The reaction to this letter was predictable. Many anticipated bad news and expected that some would be told their jobs had to go, and, by the time of the meeting, there was an air of pessimistic apprehension among the two groups of workers.

Both works managers began the meeting by sharing the same message with their staff. The head of the company, in the light of a reasonable set of results and to reflect his gratitude and appreciation for the commitment and loyalty showed by his staff, was awarding each man and woman $1,000 for each complete year of service, with a pro rata payment for those with less than one year's service. For some, this meant payments of over $20,000 and for those whose husband or wife worked there, this meant a combined amount of even more.

The reaction of many employees was a mixture of surprise, disbelief and a deep sense of appreciation, with some reduced to tears. They knew that this would be unlikely to be repeated, but they also knew that the payments genuinely reflected the beliefs and philosophy of the company's owner, who did try to treat his employees as part of a wider family.

Questions

1. What might the motives of the company's owner have been in deciding to reward his staff in this way?

2. What effect do you think the decision had on the behaviour of his staff?

3. Would the same effects on employee behaviour have been achieved by giving the same overall amount paid as an increase in base pay over the next three years or as improvements in the benefit package, rather than in the form of a 'loyalty reward'?

4. Are there any negative consequences that might follow from this act?

5. Think of other examples of circumstances in which discretionary rewards might be used to positive effect.

The status of rewards

Our earlier reference to the use of rewards in training animals and conditioning the behaviour of children is useful in the sense that it draws attention both to the use of rewards as an expression of power and to their functionality. Rewards have also been categorized in relation to the form they take. We need now to consider the conceptual basis of rewards and how rewards that are seen in quite different ways affect behaviour.

Rewards as rights

Rewards become rights largely through the process of managers offering employment, and through the prospective employee agreeing to accept the terms and conditions embodied in the contract of employment. Many of the expressed terms of the contract refer to what the employer is contracted to provide to the employee, in the form of a set wage or salary, holidays, pension, sick pay entitlements, and so on. These represent what the Americans call forms of 'compensation for having to work', and the benefits that employers provide over and above the financial package. These rewards, or forms of compensation, need to be understood as a set of rights associated with being employed by a particular organization, which continue to be provided for as long as the contract remains in place.

Consider the weekly or monthly pay cheque. When employees open their pay slips, do they see what they have been paid as a reward or as something to which they have a right because they have earned it? Here, again, we see evidence to support the argument that rewards need to be seen in the context of reciprocation, i.e. an exchange relationship, rather than as isolated and detached acts of benevolence. It is also worth considering the behavioural effect on the employee of being paid as opposed to not being paid. Being paid (i.e. rewarded through pay) may not elicit any obvious behavioural consequences. It might generate a sense of reassurance; it might reinforce the degree to which the individual identifies with the organization; it might create a sense of obligation to those in control. But these effects can be difficult to discern and may not be obviously expressed in what the employee does or in how he or she performs at work. Ask yourself the question: 'What motivational effect follows from opening the monthly wage or salary pay slip?'

KEY CONCEPT **Reciprocation**

Reciprocation relates to the effect that certain kinds of rewards generate. This can take the form of an obligation or predisposition to give something back to the person or organization responsible for the original reward. Reciprocation also suggests that rewards are never simply one person giving to another, but represent a more complex, and often unspoken, exchange that has positive outcomes for both parties. The concept emphasizes the idea that the act of rewarding, particularly if rewards are discretionary, valued and represent genuine motives, can, in turn, result in the recipient rewarding the giver, albeit in different, but no less important, ways.

What is more predictable, however, is the effect on the employee's behaviour of not being paid, not being paid on time or not being paid the right amount, and of not being given the benefits to which he or she is entitled. Failing to deliver rewards that have the status of rights will almost certainly generate a much more obvious, and potentially damaging, response simply because these rewards are both expected and contractually determined.

Rewards that are conditional or contingent

Within the employment relationship, many rewards made available to employees are additional to those prescribed in the employment contract. This means that they are linked to, and dependent on, certain conditions being met. These might involve acquiring new competencies, for which extra pay would be given, achieving agreed levels of output or production, meeting sales targets or meeting personal and business objectives. It would be too restrictive to suggest that this type of reward is only associated with performance criteria, but many of the reward schemes that are based on the 'conditionality principle' are associated with some measure of job performance and are frequently linked to what is generally understood as performance-related pay.

The point about this category of rewards is that they are not 'freestanding', in the sense that they are acquired simply as a result of being employed, but are related to some measure of how we actually behave or perform at work, and are experienced only if predetermined conditions and criteria are met. An incentive is a particular kind of reward that, according to Armstrong (2002), can be understood to be the promise of a specified reward that only becomes realizable after the achievement of previously set and known targets. He makes the following important distinction:

> **Financial incentives aim to motivate people to achieve their objectives by focussing on predetermined specific targets and priorities ... Financial rewards provide financial recognition for achievement.**

Certain kinds of rewards can, therefore, take the form of promises of what will, or might, be experienced by employees at some future date. While many promises provide a clear understanding of what the employee has to do or achieve for the reward to be given, some are more ambiguous.

Consider, for example, an employer who is struggling to make money in difficult trading conditions and who pays his staff below market rates for the jobs they are doing, on the grounds that he 'can't afford to pay more', but with 'promises' to increase pay when conditions and profitability improve. In this case, it is the employer who decides when levels of profitability justify increased pay and, despite the reasonable expectations of his employees, the pay increases may never materialize, with fairly predictable consequences for the quality of relationships between those employees and management.

305

Rewards that are discretionary

These are rewards that are neither based on contractual rights nor on meeting specified conditions, but which result from managers and employees deciding to reward others in ways that only make sense in the context of their own particular circumstances and working environment. For example, without it being part of any formal agreement or incentive scheme, an owner of a business might, in the light of a good year's results, decide to give his or her staff a week's fully paid holiday in the Mediterranean. Alternatively, he or she might provide a one-off payment to reflect the contribution of the workforce to the organization's success, as was the case with the American Shoe Corporation (see HRM Insight 12.2). There is no promise of repeating the reward and, even if the company achieves similar results in the future, the owner may decide to invest the sum potentially available as a bonus, in new capital equipment or even pay it as dividends to the shareholders. Discretionary rewards are often not planned and, therefore, employees have no expectation of receiving them. Discretionary rewards that become regular and predictable can, however, increase employee's expectation that they will receive them, with predictable consequences when they cease.

STUDENT ACTIVITY 12.2

1. In groups, list all of the rewards that members have experienced throughout their working experiences.

2. Consider the effects that the different rewards had on their behaviour and performance.

3. Present your findings to the class and be prepared to discuss the implications of your results for the management of rewards.

Issues in paying employees

Notwithstanding the importance of the conceptual and psychological dimensions of rewards, managers and HR professionals have to make practical decisions that relate to:

- the amount to pay people;
- the basis or the criteria used to pay them;
- the techniques or instruments used to help them 'manage pay' better;
- the need to minimize disagreement and conflict over pay issues.

Pay remains, for many people, at the heart of the reward function. What follows represents some of the key issues and practices associated with managing pay.

Payment frequency

The interval at which an employee is paid varies between different organizations and positions within an organization. Many organizations pay their more senior people, and those in office-based positions, an annual amount, paid as a monthly salary, that does not vary in relation to attendance at work, except in circumstances of long-term sickness absence. Often those employees in lower skilled or less senior posts will be paid weekly and only for the hours they have worked during the previous week. The advantages to the organization of paying employees a salary each month include that the amount remains fixed, simplifying administration of the payroll; the employee enjoys a regular income and can arrange his or her own personal finances around this predictable monthly payment.

This system may not suit positions in which overtime – i.e. time worked that is additional to the contracted level – varies and forms a significant proportion of the wage earned. Paid overtime working, at premium hourly rates, tends to be associated with hourly rates of pay and weekly pay cheques or bank transfers. If employees are also paid according to the time they are at work but are not for time not worked (e.g. if late or absent), their pay will be reduced proportionately.

For salaried employees, there will be a day nominated each month as the 'pay day'. This is usually in the middle, or towards the end, of the month and the earlier in the month the date, the more likely that an overpayment will occur in the event of an employee either leaving without working notice or taking unpaid leave at short notice. For this reason, in more transient types of work, it may be more appropriate to pay weekly, based on an hourly rate.

There are also other payment frequencies that are less common, such as paying every four weeks or, if contracts for service are involved, payment may be staggered over the contract period to correspond to work completed.

A recent development that changes the traditional pattern of weekly payment relates to what are called 'annualized hours'. As the term implies, an annual hours approach to work and payment involves calculating working time on an annual, rather than a weekly, basis. The increasing numbers of employees now covered by annual hours contracts, driven by the need for greater resource flexibility and control over labour costs (annual hours effectively removes the need for more expensive overtime working), suggests that this trend is likely to continue (Waring, 1992). As Blyton (1995) points out, however, this development is not unproblematical and raises, among other matters, the question of appropriate payments for working at different times.

Discriminating between employees in terms of pay frequency and security has been a characteristic of UK employment practices for many years. As a result of organizations moving towards the harmonization of rewards and conditions of employment, however, more employees now enjoy, if not the same level of pay, the same or similar conditions of employment. A report into ways of building better relations between employees and management found a strong case for extending harmonization agreements and for creating high-commitment workplaces. The IPA (1997) concluded that:

> Resolving reward issues around pay, hours and conditions would appear to be a more important contributor to partnership than profit sharing arrangements. If these fundamental issues are not resolved they can act as a barrier to the resolution of other key parts of the partnership agenda such as the security/flexibility trade off or the building of high commitment workplace behaviours.

It also found that:

> Harmonization removes these barriers and sends important signals to staff about how they are valued. Any organization which claims that 'our people are our greatest asset' will be measured by how far the principles of single status are applied in the business.

Determining pay

A great deal of effort goes into determining the level at which to pay employees. Pay too much and the organization may suffer due to not being competitive in its marketplace: being over budget may result in management being unable to employ sufficient numbers of people to carry out the required work. Pay too little, however, and this can lead to an inability to recruit and retain the necessary calibre of employees, and can result in disputes over pay. Determining pay properly in the first place might involve activities as simple as a short investigation into the appropriate rates, by scanning through the jobs pages in the local press, or might involve complex systems of evaluating a job, involving examining its content and the skills required to be able to carry out the tasks and responsibilities of the post. This is known as 'job evaluation'.

The rate of pay that the organization chooses to pay will also be determined by external factors, such as the levels of unemployment and typical rates of pay locally. If unemployment is very low, this will usually drive pay rates higher. In the UK, for example, rates of pay for similar positions will typically be higher in the south-east of the country. There may also be regional differences due to variations in the availability of labour.

Typical hourly payment systems

Flat rate

Most payment systems are based on a flat rate or have a flat rate element to them. A flat rate is that under which an employee is given a fixed amount for a fixed period of time. This might be an hourly rate (e.g. £7 per hour), an annual amount (e.g. £20,000 per annum) or a set amount for any period between these two. There are also a variety of payment systems that are designed to improve the productivity of the workers to whom they are paid. The so-called 'market rate' helps organizations to fix hourly rates and many salary levels. Differences in skills and competencies also help to explain differences in basic pay levels.

Figure 12.1 shows the relationship between the level of skill and the band into which market rates fall. The more skilled a position, the higher the rate of pay and the broader the range of pay rates applied to the position in the marketplace.

The model in Figure 12.2 shows a typical distribution of rates of pay across different organizations for jobs of a similar value. By comparing rates of pay within an organization to those paid in others, it is possible to determine whether or not employees are overpaid or underpaid against market rates. There are no wrong or right answers for an organization about the level at which to pay compared to market rate. If the employer has a good reputation and a relatively stable workforce, along with other benefits for employees, then being at the lower end may not result in recruitment and retention problems. A highly profitable organization may, however, choose to pay at the top end to give wider choice in attracting and selecting the very best candidates.

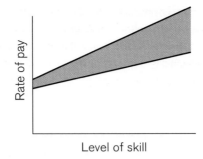

Figure 12.1 Relationship between pay and skills

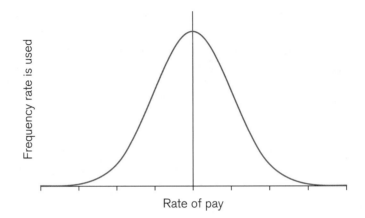

Figure 12.2 Distribution of pay rates

Piece rates

A piece rate is that under which an employee is paid for each item of work completed. Piece rates were more commonly found in manufacturing before the 1980s, but versions of piece rates still exist today. An example of an industry using a piece rate might be garment manufacture, in which each task is divided up into components and is timed, to establish how long it should take to carry out that particular task. The employee can then increase their rate of pay when carrying out these tasks by working at a faster rate than is average. Often this is capped at a maximum of, for example, 20 per cent extra.

While it can be argued that this system does enhance productivity, there are many factors that have led to its demise. Modern manufacturing techniques have increasingly favoured more flexible manufacturing. Piece rates become more complicated, the more component parts there are, and the administration of these schemes can be excessive. Many organizations have adopted cellular manufacturing systems, within which one item is taken through to completion before the next is started, to avoid having a large amount of expensive stock as work in progress and to avoid having leftover obsolete stock if orders change. There is also no doubt that a large part of the reduction in the use of the piece rate is due to the decline of manufacturing in the UK, with a large proportion of manufactured goods, including electrical goods, toys, and textiles now being imported from China and the Far East.

Piece rate systems encourage workers to try to stick to the jobs that they can do best and naturally tend to make employees reluctant to do work that does not attract the higher rates. Staff can therefore be reluctant to participate in off-the-job training or meetings to help improve productivity, because of the loss of wages that this involves. Production changes may not be welcomed because these can result in tasks being retimed at less favourable rates; staff may be tempted to compromise on both quality and health and safety, in order to maximize their output to achieve higher rates of pay. Repeating the same task over a long period of time can cause medical conditions known as upper limb disorders or repetitive strain injuries. Regularly rotating people around different tasks and allowing employees to take regular breaks can reduce the risk of this type of injury, but piece rate systems can make it harder to implement measures to minimize the risk of employees developing these types of problem at work.

Group/team bonus

Another payment system, frequently used to encourage employees to complete more work in the time given, is a group bonus. Schemes vary depending on the organization, the nature of the work and the number of people employed, but typically involve measuring the performance of a group of people and awarding a payment to the group for increased output. The group either receives an equal portion of the bonus or pro rata payments that reflect different contributions. For example, certain team members may receive 100 per cent of the bonus, while others are paid 80 per cent. Different factors can affect the success of these schemes. If the group to which it is applied is too large, then there may be little personal reward for extra effort from the individual so effectiveness may be reliant on the quality of supervision rather than on the efforts of any one individual. Other factors can be linked to payment in addition to output levels. These can include, for example, the team's health and safety record, quality achievements or the team's attendance records. The more factors that are included in the calculation of the team or group bonus, however, the more complicated pay administration becomes.

Rates for skills, shift premium and overtime premium

We have already established that higher skilled positions attract higher rates of pay. In addition to determining the basic hourly rate, an employer should also consider the time by which the work needs to be carried out and the possibility that additional hours might be required to complete the job/work in progress, for which 'premium' payments may need to be paid.

If employees are required to work at unusual times of the day, then 'shift' pay may be included as a pay item. For example, employees may work only at night, which can attract an additional payment that is typically in the region of 25 to 35 per cent of their normal rate. This is often expressed as a separate pay item, but may be incorporated into an employee's basic wage. There may be payments for early starts or late finishes, or a combination of payments if hours vary on a rotating basis.

There may also be extra payments above the normal rate of pay for extra hours worked either at the end or beginning of a working day, or on days that are not normally worked, i.e. overtime. A typical payment for overtime on a normal working day might be 'time and a half' after eight hours (i.e. an extra 50 per cent on top of the normal hourly rate). Working at weekends, if this is not the normal working pattern, may typically attract time and a half on Saturday and double time (i.e. 100 per cent on top of the normal hourly rate) on a Sunday.

STUDENT ACTIVITY 12.3

Overtime working has a long tradition in UK industry, particularly in manufacturing. Yet many organizations, such as Rolls Royce, are abandoning systematic overtime payments, instead moving towards paying increased hourly rates and annualized hours. After researching the literature available and looking at changes in company practices, answer the following questions.

1. What does 'institutionalized' overtime mean and how does this come about?
2. What are the disadvantages of excessive overtime?
3. What adverse behavioural and performance effects does it have?
4. What might be the effects of reducing or withdrawing overtime completely?
5. What strategies are available to management to maintain production in the absence of overtime?

309

Performance-related pay (PRP)

Earlier in the chapter, we explored the arguments for and against the use of financial incentives to reward employees. Here, we will consider rewards to drive performance from a more practical perspective.

Performance-related pay uses financial incentives to link an individual's pay to his or her performance. Rather than simply awarding a bonus payment, performance-related pay usually refers to the system used to calculate the pay rise awarded to an individual, which is linked to a measure of his or her performance over a given time period. Pay rises tend to be awarded annually for salaried and professional staff, but might be awarded at other intervals depending on the schemes in place. The performance element might be the whole of the award or an additional amount over and above the standard cost-of-living award.

Often, performance-related pay is linked to performance objectives set for the individual as part of an annual appraisal process. The goals for the entire organization are broken down by department and by seniority, and each employee on the performance-related pay scheme is set a number of objectives to achieve in a given period. Measures are put in place and these are then reviewed at the end of the period to determine the extent to which they have been achieved. The pay award reflects the extent to which the measures are met. A key requirement in the employment of PRP is therefore, the ability to measure accurately and consistently what performance is defined as.

> → Signpost to Chapter 9: HR Planning and Measurement, for insight into measuring the HR function

Incentive schemes and commission payments, as examples of the PRP principle, potentially apply to all categories of employee. Consider, for example, commission payments, which are frequently used for sales staff. The sales representative or manager will be given a target, usually an amount that he or she must sell or a profit level that he or she must achieve over a given period. The amount of commission earned during the period will depend on the extra sales or profit achieved above a minimum target. For example, a sales representative may be able to earn up to an extra 25 per cent of his or her salary at the end of the year as a bonus payment, if he or she can sell more than 10 per cent above the minimum target set.

Bonus schemes can also apply to senior executives in an organization. In a private company, this might be linked to the profit levels, sales and cash generated by the business or might relate to achievement of objectives or budgets (Blanchflower, 1991).

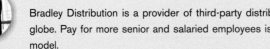

HRM INSIGHT 12.3 The case of Bradley Distribution

Bradley Distribution is a provider of third-party distribution services, with locations across the globe. Pay for more senior and salaried employees is performance-related, using the following model.

Behavioural rating

Performance rating		1	2	3
	A	4.5 – 6.5%		4%
	B	2.5 – 3.5%		2%
	C	0 – 2%		0%

Employees' performance is described in terms of their performance against last year's objectives, with 'A performers' exceeding their objectives, 'B performers' meeting their objectives and 'C performers' not meeting their objectives. The behavioural style ratings from '1' to '3' represent the way in which the individual goes about meeting his or her objectives, with '1' representing 'always follows the required behaviour', to '3' representing 'rarely displays the required behaviour'. Under this model, the organization asserts that 20 per cent of all employees should fall into the 'A' category, 70 per cent into the 'B' category and 10 per cent into the 'C' category.

The overall budget set for pay reviews is 4.5 per cent and the actual amount paid is at the discretion of the departmental manager within the bands set, dependent on the employee's rating in the matrix.

Questions

1. What advantages might be achieved by an organization in implementing this model?

2. What might the disadvantages be in terms of cost, and in terms of the impact on the employees and managers of the organization?

3. Consider a typical salary within an organization with which you are familiar. Work out the difference in annual salary for an A2 and a B3 performer in this model. Consider the positive motivational impact of receiving this extra payment and the potential demotivational impact of receiving the lower payment.

4. Consider the above model from the point of view of a manager of team of twenty versus a manager of only two people. What dilemmas might each manager face if asked to rate his or her team against this model?

5. What are the legal, moral and ethical implications of using this system to identify the poorest performing 10 per cent of the senior salaried workforce, given the intention not to award any pay increase at all to up to 10 per cent of the workforce each year?

Signpost to Chapter 11: Managing Performance, for more detail on performance rating scales

Incremental pay schemes

The defining feature of this type of pay scheme is the way in which length of service drives pay increases, in addition to annual increases linked to cost-of-living adjustments. Incremental awards are generally limited to salaried employees, particularly those who work in the public sector. Such increases, according to Brown and Armstrong (1999):

> ... inevitably seem to generate into automatic progression.

Such increases are less popular among private sector employers for the simple reason that increases in pay have nothing to do with performance, contribution or any appropriate criteria other than length of service. Upward movement from one point in a salary grade to the next is relatively unproblematical, although so-called 'bars' are sometimes applied to progression to the top of the grade. 'Going through the bar' can, however, be relatively easy, if meeting the criteria for progression is not difficult to achieve. Teachers, lecturers, civil servants and local government officials are most closely associated with payment structures that provide for annual incremental increases. Since the introduction of legislation on age discrimination in 2006, however, rewards relating to service levels exceeding five years are potentially unlawful, particularly if these relate to remuneration.

Signpost to Chapter 6: Equality in Employment, for more information on age discrimination

Job evaluation

Job evaluation is a process or technique whereby the relative value or worth of a job can be determined in a systematic and transparent manner, although whether the additional claim for objectivity made by its supporters is as convincing is more controversial.

There are various techniques available to establish this worth, from simple subjective judgement, to more complex analysis using points and weightings for different factors. The process looks at the actual job and its content, and not at the jobholder. It is therefore designed to provide a fair basis for determining the level of pay or grade of individual workers, relative to others whose jobs are rated higher or lower. The outcome of the evaluation exercise, whichever of the following methods is used, is usually a ranking of jobs based on their relative values – known as a 'job structure' – which then becomes the basis for pay rates or salary levels, which is described as a 'pay structure'.

Non-analytical methods

The simplest methods of determining the relative worth of a job involve considering the overall job content and making a judgement about the role. 'Job ranking' involves deciding the order of jobs, from the highest worth to the lowest. While this simple technique is subjective and carries the danger of ranking based on known pay levels, it may be attractive to a smaller organization, for example, in which there are no disputes or disagreements over pay and for which a guideline is required to determine the appropriate level of pay to offer to a new recruit. 'Paired comparison' is another, similar, technique under which each job is considered relative to each other job and is given a simple score of '0', '1' or '2', depending on whether it is of lower, similar or higher value.

Analytical methods

If a more objective means of determining the worth of a job is required, organizations usually use a points-based system, whereby the job is considered against a predetermined set of criteria and is scored against each of the criteria. Sometimes the criteria are also weighted and some elements may therefore be given more points due to their importance to the organization.

The criteria used can either be designed specifically for the organization or there are a number of 'off-the-shelf' job evaluation packages in use. Unless there is in-house expertise and resource with which to design a robust system, the organization may need to pay for the services of an external body to design a system or it may need to pay for an existing product. While this can be expensive, it carries the advantage of being ready for immediate use; clients can also usually access the provider's data on pay levels to help to benchmark their own levels of pay against other rates locally and within the market for positions of similar value.

One of the most well-known analytical methodologies has been developed by the Hay Group (www.haygroup.com), and involves evaluating and allocating points to each job using the following factors.

- Know-how
  - The depth and range of practical, technical, specialist, professional and general skills needed to deliver job objectives
  - The degree of planning, organizing, supervising, coordinating, and integrating that the job involves
  - The extent of interpersonal skills required

- Problem solving
  - The extent to which thinking is constrained by its context (business environment, organization policies and procedures, and legislation) and the level of flexibility permitted in applying them
  - The complexity and intensity of problems arising in the job and the amount of analysis, judgement, and innovation involved in arriving at conclusions

- Accountability
  - The degree of authority and discretion vested in the job and the degree of answerability for the exercise of it
  - The scale of the areas of activity on which the job is expected to have an impact and the nature of that impact

Whilst the total points score derived is important for grading and pay purposes, the Hay Group method is unique in two ways. The points scale used increases in percentage steps so gaps and relationships between jobs can be analysed in a meaningful way. The weighting between the three factors is not constant and changes to reflect the nature (shape) of the job. These combine to give a tool that is useful for organization analysis and design.

ACAS publishes useful guidelines on both job evaluation and performance-related pay on its website (**www.acas.org.uk**).

A current example of strategic change in reward systems, based on a national system of job evaluation, can be found in the NHS' Agenda for Change programme. An overview of this programme can be found on the Department for Health's website (**www.dh.gov.uk**).

Equal pay

Legal challenges to the outcome of payment decisions are increasingly in the form of claims of unequal pay or of work of equal value not being reflected in both men and women's pay. Such claims, if successful, can result in large compensation payments and may be made if an employee of one sex believes that another employee in the same organization of the opposite sex is paid at a higher rate for carrying out work of similar value. It should be noted that, under current legislation, equal value claims can only be brought about if the employee to whom the claimant is comparing themselves is of the opposite sex. There is no legal redress if two people of the same sex earn different amounts for what is felt to be work of a similar value.

In order to defend an equal value claim, the organization needs to be able objectively to demonstrate that the posts in question have different value to the organization. It is unlikely that anything other than a robust points-based job evaluation scheme will enable the employer to be able to do this. Other means of establishing pay levels that are more subjective, such as ranking, will be less likely to stand up to a legal challenge.

It should also be noted that employees can now submit an equal value questionnaire to their employer to assist them with submitting this claim. This includes questions about the rate of pay of colleagues of the opposite sex (see **www.eoc.org.uk**).

313

Moving from one payment system to another

Moving from one payment system to another is usually a complex and challenging exercise for any organization. If HR believes that the payment system currently in use needs to be replaced, the first step is to consider carefully exactly what is wrong with the current system and the criteria that a new system would have to meet. There are a number of reasons why it might be necessary to change. Perhaps the organization has been subjected to equal value claims or grievances from employees who feel that they are underpaid. There may also be a perception that the productivity or effectiveness of the workforce might be improved by changing the pay system. Alternatively, it might simply be the case that, due to changes in market rates over time, the pay scheme is now out of date and some employees are being paid too much for their contribution, while others are being underpaid or are proving difficult to recruit and retain under the rates given in the existing scheme.

The difficult balance to achieve when altering pay is to keep costs under control while implementing new rates. Any organization would find it hard to get employees to accept a reduction in their rate of pay and, if disputes are to be avoided, such a change will usually involve most people receiving an increase against their current remuneration. It may be possible to pay for this by increasing productivity, but, if employees are feeling unsettled or unfairly treated, this may be difficult to achieve. Organizations should therefore think carefully before embarking upon a project to change pay structures, and should be clear about the benefits versus the disruption and effort required to bring about the change.

For those whose job is valued at a lower figure than that being paid, there are a number of options for changing the employee's contractual rate of pay. It should be noted that the employee's current rate of pay forms part of his or her contact of employment, so a change to pay would involve a change to the contract. There would, in this situation, consequently be a legal requirement to consult with those affected.

Signpost to Chapter 4: Managing Employee Relations, for further information on consultation and pay bargaining

The simplest way to address a situation in which an employee's pay is too high is to 'red circle' an employee's pay, effectively preventing him or her from receiving any further pay increase until those identified as having similar value jobs have caught up. This can take a considerable amount of time, particularly if the difference is significant and the organization is unlikely to be giving large increases in the foreseeable future. Other options might include 'buying out' the difference, by offering a one-off payment as compensation, or retraining the employee to increase his or her value to match his or her current rate.

There may also be circumstances under which the employee's rate of pay is altered simply by issuing the appropriate notice, but care needs to be taken to have justifiable reasons for this and to consult fully if a claim for unfair dismissal is not to follow as a result.

HRM INSIGHT 12.4 Oakholme Furniture

You have been asked to give advice to a friend of the family about her business. The business employs thirty people in three teams in a workshop, which manufactures self-assembly furniture. These packs are sold to a larger manufacturer, which supplies to retail and trade outlets. The business is growing rapidly and the main limit to what it can sell is how much product it can make. The basic rate of pay for all of the staff is the National Minimum Wage, but each person can earn a team-based bonus, based on the productivity improvement for the team as a whole compared to that of last year. This bonus is shared out, taking into account the amount of product each individual makes and his or her level of attendance. The bonus has worked so well in the panel assembly department that production has increased by 50 per cent and members of the team now earn, on average, an extra 50 per cent of their basic pay on top. They have asked if some of this can be converted into an increase in basic pay. The extra volume has meant that the machining department has more work to do, but has had to take on extra staff as well as undertaking a lot of overtime, because its productivity has only increased by 10 per cent. The parts department, which has experienced no significant increase in productivity mainly due to the layout of the department and poor supervision, is worried that its wages will fall behind. To complicate matters, this department employs mostly women, while the other two departments employ mostly men.

Questions

1. Consider what advice you would give to the family friend.

2. What factors should the owner take into consideration when deciding what new bonus schemes to put into place?

3. What are the pros and cons associated with the owner's options?

4. How should the owner handle the change?

Reward practices

The final section in this chapter provides an overview of the reward practices and priorities associated with a survey of 477 companies across all sectors and employing some 1.5 million employees (CIPD, 2005). National surveys are useful indicators of what organizations are actually doing and, assuming that they are broadly representative, they also provide insights into the reward agendas with which organizations are engaged.

The CIPD survey (2005) found the following:

- the relationship between reward strategies, wider business strategy and specific organizational object-ives is seen as critical by reward specialists, with many emphasizing the importance of using rewards to support what the business is trying to do (an example of achieving the vertical integration of HR activities);

- the importance of using rewards specifically to support an organization's need to recruit and retain high performers was also identified;

- the costs of rewards, particularly pay costs, is an important consideration;

- the concept of 'total rewards' has been adopted by around 33 per cent of employers, but all sectors believe that there is still a problem with getting front-line managers to implement this approach;

- a wide variety of approaches have been adopted in determining base pay, with annual pay awards reflecting organizational performance, the 'going rate', keeping pace with inflation and changes in market rates;

- interestingly, despite the criticisms of Kohn (1993a), there was widespread use of cash bonuses and incentive schemes, particularly in the private sector, with the range of bonus payments extending from 6 to 20 per cent of base pay;

- service-related benefits and pay are common to many organizations, as is the use of equal pay reviews;

- a wide variety of approaches are adopted by organizations to structure and manage pay, indicating that there is no single 'correct' approach.

STUDENT ACTIVITY 12.4

1. Working in groups, and using the findings of the CIPD Reward Management survey report (2005), present summaries of the findings from the following sections of the survey and be prepared to discuss their implications.

- The views from the 'front line'
- The relationship between service and rewards
- Developments in equal pay issues
- The use of bonuses and incentives
- The determination of base pay

2. What do the findings you have summarized tell us about the business strategies and organizational objectives that reward practices and strategies are supporting?

Summary

Rewards and how they are managed constitute an important part of what HR professionals are respons-ible for, and this importance is likely to grow as the new class of knowledge workers applies different requirements and priorities to what they want their employers to provide for them. Managing rewards has never been particularly easy; it is certainly becoming more challenging as employers have to meet the reward expectations of an increasingly diverse labour force. Inevitably, this means that reward packages and 'solutions' will become more individualized, rather than be the product of collective negotiations, and will reflect changes in personal circumstances.

The evidence suggests that rewards that meet an individual's intrinsic needs, i.e. those that connect to his or her 'humanness', have a stronger and longer lasting effect on his or her perception and behaviour than do those that are essentially materialistic in nature, which are used by managers in an instrumental way. Many of these rewards are generated in the working environment, and are given and received in an often informal and hidden (from HR) way. Examples of these might include praise from a manager, colleague or customer, recognition for achievement and opportunities to learn new skills. The psychological environment is, once again, identified as the context in which major influences on how an employee feels and behaves are located.

As far as the formal reward arena is concerned, pay and benefits continue to remain contentious issues for management and this is, in an era of increasing competition and outsourcing of production and jobs, much to do with costs as well as the effectiveness of different pay practices. The concept of flexibility, which is so critical to management, theoretically means that pay can go down, for all or certain employees, as well as up. But this does not mean that the value of rewards has to fall as well as rise. One of the challenges facing HR and line management is to increase the overall value of the reward package without increasing its cost and this is being achieved by those who understand the value of non-financial rewards.

 Visit the Online Resource Centre that accompanies this book for self-test questions, weblinks, and more information on the topics covered in this chapter.
www.oxfordtextbooks.co.uk/orc/banfield_kay/

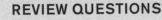

REVIEW QUESTIONS

1. Why do organizations use job evaluation as the basis for their pay structures? What are the advantages and disadvantages of paying people according to the job they do?

2. What is performance-related pay, and what are the pros and cons of implementing a performance-related pay system?

3. How do intrinsic and extrinsic rewards differ, and why is this distinction important?

4. Why have organizations moved away from the piece rate pay systems that were so popular in the 1970s?

5. What reward strategies are contemporary organizations using and what are the objectives to which these strategies relate?

CASE STUDY
The Star Hotel

The Star Group of hotels has 26 hotels throughout the UK, operating in the business, conference and banqueting markets. While there is a London-based corporate headquarters, hotel general managers have considerable discretion for deciding on wage and salary levels, and over any incentive/bonus schemes they may wish to introduce.

Strict financial controls are established through the budgeting process, and managers have to produce monthly revenue and expenditure forecasts for head office. The expectation is that agreed budgets will be met, because this allows HQ to be confident about revenue and cash flows. Strict control over staff and employment costs are expected to be in place and maintained, which should not exceed an agreed percentage of each hotel's monthly turnover figure.

Beating the performance standards represented by the monthly and annual budgets is seen by managers as the way in which to demonstrate to senior management that the hotel is being well managed and is financially successful. Equally important is the need to ensure that customers are satisfied with the services they receive when they use the hotel. This helps to ensure a strong customer base and long-term prosperity. Increasing the proportion of 'repeat business', as well as finding new business, is a key role played by the conference and banqueting department and by reception/reservations.

The Sheffield Star Hotel is located on the edge of the city, which is itself seeing a growth in the number of hotels operating within the city limits. The growth in competition without a corresponding increase in overall demand for hotel facilities might be a potential threat to the Sheffield Star and its general manager is keen to find ways of responding to this. He is also under pressure to increase bottom-line performance and is considering different cost reduction strategies to achieve this. He is, however, convinced that increasing revenue and cash flow has to be the main way forward, because most obvious areas for cost savings have already been explored.

The following information summarizes the hotel's key financial, employment and operational situation.

Annual sales turnover	£6m
Gross profit	£1.2m
Employee WTEs	48
Annual payroll	£1.4m
Average monthly wage/salary bill	£278,000
Average room occupancy rate	69%
Average monthly sales ledger, i.e. outstanding debt	£187,000
Average monthly restaurant sales	£89,000
Average monthly conference and banqueting sales	£215,000

The hotel has the following departments and related numbers of employees:

Department	Numbers	FT	PT
Housekeeping	15	3	12
Reception, including telesales	7	7	0
Restaurant, including waiting staff	28	7	21
Sales and banqueting	5	5	0
Bar staff	11	3	8
Finance	3	3	0
Secretarial and admin	5	3	2
General manager	1	1	0
Operations manager	1	1	0
Maintenance	1	1	0
Total	77		

Note: A significant proportion of the bar and restaurant staff are casual workers. The remaining staff are either on part-time or full-time contracts.

The task

The general manager believes that the way forward is to incentivize his staff to perform at higher levels of effectiveness and holds the view that, if the right kind of incentive schemes can be designed, most of his employees will respond positively. He has invited your company of reward management consultants to work with him on this task.

These are the guidelines you have been given:

- as many employees as is practical to be included;
- individual, functional/departmental and organizational schemes can be considered;
- a close relationship between changes in employee performance and contribution to the bottom line should be established;
- schemes should be based on the ability to measure changes in performance;
- the expectation is that benefits, in all cases, should exceed costs;
- different incentive schemes for different groups of employees can be considered.

The task is to prepare a presentation to the general manager, in which you outline your ideas for incentivizing the hotel's employees. The presentation should include details on the following:

- who should be and who should not be considered for incentivizing, with reasons;
- your ideas/plans for incentivizing any two groups of employees, showing clearly how you would measure the performance of each group (note that a group can even be one person or all of the employees);
- the problems that the hotel might encounter, in general, from its attempts to incentivize staff and the specific problems that might be experienced in the two schemes considered as part of the above point.

 Insights & Outcomes: visit the Online Resource Centre at www.oxfordtextbooks.co.uk/orc/banfield_kay/ for examples of incentive schemes that were developed by the hotel's management.

FURTHER READING

IRS (2001) 'The new reward agenda', *IRS Management Review*, Issue 22.

Marsden, D (2004) 'The "network economy" and models of the employment contract', *British Journal of Industrial Relations*, 42:4, pp 659–84.

Marsden, D, French, S and Kubo, K (2001) *Does Pay De-Motivate, And Does It Matter?* Centre for Economic Performance.

Rousseau, D (1995) *Psychological Contracts in Organizations: Understanding Written and Unwritten Agreements*, Sage.

Thorpe, R and Homan, G (2000) *Strategic Reward Systems*, FT/Prentice Hall.

Wilson, TB (2003) *Innovative Reward Systems for the Changing Workplace*, McGraw-Hill.

Zingheim, PK and Schuster, JR (2000) *Pay People Right*, Jossey-Bass.

REFERENCES

Arkin, A (2005) 'Eyes on the prize', *People Management*, 10 February, p 28.

Armstrong, M (2002) *Employee Rewards*, CIPD.

Bennett Stewart, G, Appelbaum, E, Beer, M and Lebby, AM (1993) 'Rethinking rewards', *Harvard Business Review*, 71:6, pp 37–49.

Blanchflower, DG (1991) 'The economic effects of profit sharing in Britain', *International Journal of Manpower*, 12:1, pp 3–9.

Blyton, P (1995) *The Development of Annual Working Hours in the United Kingdom*, International Labour Office.

Brown, D and Armstrong, M (1999) *Paying for Contribution*, Kogan.

Chartered Institute of Personnel and Development (2005) *Reward Management*, CIPD survey report, available online at www.cipd.co.uk.

Daniels, AC (2000) *Bringing Out the Best in People*, McGraw Hill.

Deeks, E (2000) 'Mates lighten workload', *People Management*, 12 October, p 9.

Department of Health (2004) *Agenda for Change: What Will it Mean for You? A Guide for Staff*, DoH guidance document, available online at www.dh.gov.uk.

Gouldner, A (1954) *Wildcat Strike*, Antioch Press.

Herzberg, F (2003) 'One more time: how do you motivate people?', *Harvard Business Review*, 81:1, pp 87–96.

IPA (1997) *Towards Industrial Partnership: New Ways of Working in British Companies*, IPA report, executive summary available online at www.ipa-involve.com.

Kohn, A (1993a) *Punished by Rewards*, Houghton Mifflin Co.

Kohn, A (1993b) 'Why incentive plans cannot work', *Harvard Business Review*, 71:5, pp 54–63.

Kohn, A (1995) 'Punished by rewards? A conversation with Alfie Kohn', *Educational Leadership*, 53:1, pp 13–16.

Pfeffer, J (1998) *The Human Equation: Building Profits by Putting People First*, Harvard Business School Press.

Taylor, FW (1998) *The Principles of Scientific Management*, Dover Publications.

Thompson, P (2002) *Total Reward*, CIPD.

Waring, A (1992) 'Working arrangements and patterns of working hours in Britain', *Employment Gazette*, March, pp 88–100.

Case Studies

4

Case Study: HR and the New Opening

13

Key Terms

Organizational structure This relates to aspects of the formal organization, particularly the roles and responsibilities that people have, the hierarchy and reporting lines, the different departments and sections within the organization and how they are connected, formal communication channels and the way in which power and authority are distributed. Organizational structure is analogous to the human skeleton or the framework of a new building: it is what gives the organization shape and influences how it operates.

Induction This needs to be understood as a multistaged process rather than as a single,

course-based event. It represents the introduction of new employees into the organization, into the department in which they work and into the job they have to do, although it can also relate to the transfer and promotion of existing employees. It should introduce the employee to the social environment, the technical aspects of work, and the rules and procedures of employment.

Blended learning This technique uses several different but complementary learning methods, which, when used together, are considered to be more effective at generating the required learning outcomes than the one method alone.

Learning Objectives

As a result of reading this chapter and using the Online Resource Centre, you should be able to:

- understand the HR issues and requirements associated with opening a new productive facility;

- appreciate the role that HR plays in supporting the business;

- be aware of the way in which operational pressures and demands drives HR in a competitive, customer-focused environment;

- contribute actively to the delivery of key HR outcomes linked to 'new openings', particularly in recruitment and selection, organizational and job design, induction, skills training, and performance review and appraisal.

Introduction

The first of the three integrated HR case studies that comprise this part of the text focuses on the activities and challenges associated with the role of HR when organizations expand or open new facilities. In this particular case, it involves opening a new hotel, and ensuring that is staffed and ready to open on time. The term 'greenfield site' is sometimes used to describe a new plant in a new location, for which nothing is inherited other than the company's existing philosophy and operating systems. The specific example used to illustrate HR's role in supporting such a new opening is based on the recently developed Robinson Hotel, located in the centre of Birmingham. The following section provides details about the company, the hotel and labour market conditions; before we move onto this, it is important to understand that, while this chapter and the following two share some features with those found in the preceding chapters, these chapters are different from them in important ways.

Because they are based on real events and because much of the content is based on interviews with the HR practitioners who were closely involved, they represent unique insights into the pressures and challenges that these practitioners faced – and how they dealt with them. All three chapters provide examples of HR making important contributions to the 'business', and of HR professionals who have a very clear conception of what is expected of HR and of what they have to do to meet these expectations. The chapters are about 'delivering', to use Ulrich's (1996) word, but also demonstrate what and how things were done to achieve the required outcomes. In addition, the three chapters show how important it is to link different activities together and to approach the practice of HR with a very clear understanding of the importance of maintaining an integrated and holistic perspective on what needs to done. They also give a sense of the operational and strategic value of these activities.

In this chapter, particular emphasis is given to employing staff, inducting and training them, and using performance reviews and appraisals. This appears not only in the context of how these activities contribute to better employee performance, but also in that of ensuring that the employees themselves value and benefit from these being carried out in the most effective ways possible. The case study shows that a competent, efficient and motivated workforce, possessing the right attitude and performing to the required standards, is one of the key determinants of organizational success, and this is where HR can add value – through its ability consistently to deliver these outcomes.

The approach taken:

- provides information on the location, organizational context and specific requirements associated with meeting all staffing requirements leading up to, and shortly after, the opening of the hotel;
- offers academic insights into key HR activities and responsibilities, using appropriate research and literature contributions to provide an academic perspective on these activities;
- provides realistic exercises that reflect the tasks and challenges faced by the HR practitioner involved;
- offers insights into the actual experiences of the people involved in the project and, through this, allows the student to understand more realistically the pressures, dilemmas, successes and failures of those involved, and what they learnt from their experiences;
- puts the student in the key role of HR manager and other stakeholders;
- provides extensive opportunities to research and practise important aspects of the HR function.

The background

Robinson Hotels & Resorts is the UK's largest independently owned hotel group, with over sixty properties spread throughout the UK. It operates within the four-star deluxe sector of the market, and is committed to providing a full range of services and facilities to its customers. As a result of its strategy of growing organically rather than through mergers and acquisitions, it acquired a site in the heart of Birmingham and developed plans for a brand new, 120-bedroom hotel, with an opening date of November 2005. Failure to meet this deadline had obvious implications for the ability of the general manager (GM) to take advantage of the busy Christmas and New Year period, and would have affected his planned revenue budget.

The GM, Daniel Martin, was appointed in January 2005, followed in June by Marjory Hughes and Claire Wilson, sales director and HR manager respectively. Claire's initial tasks during this six months' pre-opening period were to:

- design the organizational structure, and prepare job descriptions and person specifications for each job;
- agree the headcount and workforce budget;
- recruit and select staff for all posts;
- plan for induction and skills training;
- devise an effective performance review and appraisal system.

Designing the organizational structure

The ability to meet the November opening deadline was heavily dependent on having a fully staffed and trained workforce in place by that time, but before any recruitment could begin, agreement had to be reached over the hotel's establishment numbers and its internal structure. In thinking through the implications of structure building, it is worth noting the comment that:

> **The design of jobs and work structures should not only take into account the nature of the work and the characteristics of personnel; it also has to be consistent with the philosophy of management that is being followed. The structuring of jobs needs to be matched by an appropriate design of organisational systems and an appropriate managerial style.**
> (Child, 1984)

This way of conceptualizing structure suggests that it is more than simply a technical task, involving creating roles, jobs, relationships and lines of accountability; decisions on these issues also reflect something about the beliefs and values of the organization's senior managers, and about the functional requirements associated with delivering a specified level of service to meet customer expectations and service standards. Structure is also, as Watson (2002) argues, about:

> ...the regular or persisting patterns of action that give shape and predictability to an organisation.

This means that the hotel's structure of work and jobs needed to deliver behavioural patterns and standards that were known and understood, regularly repeated, and fit for purpose.

At the time of opening, the hotel employed 160 people from 17 different national groups, although not all of these were full-time employees. The management structure reflected the industry's traditional emphasis on heads of departments reporting to functional heads, who, in turn, reported to the general manager, as indicated in Figure 13.1.

The first three senior management appointments had responsibility for appointing the remaining functional heads and, with these in post, the heads of department. The people who filled these three positions were clearly critical to all subsequent employment decisions, and to the effective and profitable operation of the hotel.

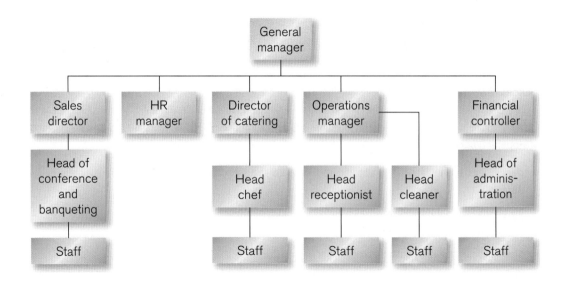

Figure 13.1 The structure of the Birmingham Robinson Hotel

STUDENT ACTIVITY 13.1 Preparing job descriptions and person specifications

1. Either individually or in groups, prepare job descriptions for the general manager and HR manager. The structure and content of these should be sufficiently detailed to allow for the following tasks to be completed.

2. Produce person specifications for each position, detailing the necessary and desirable features that applicants should possess, and specifying, where appropriate, the level of attainment or standard.

3. Design an advertisement for the post of HR manager and indicate what your recruitment strategy would be.

4. Design an assessment and selection strategy for the HR post, based on a shortlist of six applicants, indicating clearly the chosen assessment methods and key criteria, with weightings, if considered appropriate.

Note: You should explore all opportunities to collect data on both roles and validate the outcome of this exercise by arranging feedback from practising managers.

Once in post, the focus of the management team in the pre-opening phase was agreeing the establishment numbers, allocating jobs to departments and recruiting staff. Staffing models used in other hotels influenced the numbers of posts agreed upon, but particular use was also made of the following.

● Ratios

For example, the number of bedrooms that might be cleaned to standard in one shift divided by the number of bedrooms, subject to a projected occupancy rate. With 120 rooms, with one cleaner able to clean six bedrooms per shift at an average projected occupancy of 80 per cent, the number of WTE cleaners needed would be calculated as follows.

$$\frac{120}{6} \times 0.80 = 19$$

● Size of facilities

For example, the range of facilities offered in the leisure centre would indicate not only the numbers of staff needed, but their different jobs and skill sets.

- Projected usage rates

    The number of guests and visitors expected to use the restaurant, for example, would inform decisions on the number and variety of restaurant/bar posts needed.

Because of uncertainties over actual occupancy and usage rates, the hotel's management could only agree on permanent establishment numbers, both full and part time. Variations in demand due to seasonal differences and the effects of sales promotions were met by recruiting casual staff, usually students and other young people, to work in the bar, restaurant and banqueting facilities.

STUDENT ACTIVITY 13.2 Annual hours contracts

In order to achieve the required level of flexibility, many organizations are turning to annual hours and zero hours contracts.

1. Research the use of annual and zero hours contracts, and report on the available evidence of the experiences of both employers and employees.

2. Explain how annual hours contracts differ from zero hours contracts.

3. In the case of the Birmingham Robinson Hotel, consider the advantages and disadvantages of guaranteeing a minimum number of hours/shifts per month to its casual workers (CIPD, 2005).

Staffing the hotel

Unlike established workplaces, with a new opening, there are no opportunities to draw upon the internal labour force as a source of labour supply. All recruitment had to be based on the external labour market, which effectively meant the Birmingham region for the majority of employees. The bulk of the pre-opening budget of £300,000 was allocated for staffing purposes, compared to a starting budget of £2m. The difference between the two is explained by the fact that recruitment to the full establishment figure gradually took place over the full pre-opening period. The recruitment strategy was based on four elements:

- unsolicited CVs sent in on a speculative basis;

- the use of online applications and processing, using the hotel's electronic database and search facilities. The CIPD has found that the trend for online recruitment is growing, with almost two-thirds of organizations using technology to support this activity (CIPD, 2006b, p 3);

- local advertising and the use of industry-specific publications;

- recruitment agencies, but limited to posts that required specialist skills and experience.

Selection for senior managers was based on interviews, with the HR manager undertaking the first and the GM, the second interviews. Interestingly, psychometric tests were not used for any position, the emphasis being placed instead on a person's CV, experience and ability to 'fit' the hotel environment. This involved having the required skill set, being flexible and adaptive, being able to work under pressure and understanding the need to meet customer expectations.

For all other positions, responsibility for selection was devolved to the appropriate head of department, with the HR manager conducting the initial assessment of applications and then agreeing with the appropriate head of function/department which candidates would be invited for interview. Effectively, the criteria used in deciding on this and the subsequent decision whether to offer a job or not were related to the following factors.

- The employability of the applicant

    This was based on a review of his or her work record, education and qualifications, and experience.

327

- **The legal status of the applicant**

  This involved reviewing any criminal records that an applicant might have and reaching a judgement on whether this disbarred him or her from working in the hotel. It also included establishing the candidate's right to work, defined in terms of his or her national status.

- **The technical skills of the applicant**

  This was particularly important in recruiting to areas such as bars, restaurant, leisure club and conference/banqueting.

Three other features of the hotel's recruitment strategy deserve mention:

- building and maintaining links with institutions that represent a long-term source of labour supply. In this case, one of the two Birmingham universities provided, via its course in hotel and leisure management, a regular supply of casual and part-time workers, many of who came from abroad and had previous experience of the hotel industry;

- the development of a 'talent bank' of applications and CVs that might be used to fill new vacancies as they came on stream or to provide replacements for those who left;

- the decision to pay above the local labour market rate for hourly paid staff. This may have cost more in one sense, but attracted better quality applicants, which, in turn, allowed the hotel to deliver a 'deluxe' level of service.

Induction

According to the CIPD (2006a):

> Every organisation, large or small, should have a well-considered induction programme Although the Institute claim that designing an appropriate and cost-effective induction package is a complex task, it need not be, and in the context of a hotel, the induction experience is driven by two requirements.
>
> 1. The need to meet legal requirements surrounding employment. This involves communicating information on issues such as pay and benefits, sick pay, holidays and conditions, company rules and health and safety procedures. This might be termed the formal dimension of induction.
>
> 2. Job induction. This is a dimension of induction covering duties and responsibilities, working location, reporting lines and job standards.

The CIPD claims that:

> ... [an] induction programme has to provide all the information that new employees and others need, and are able to assimilate, without being overwhelming or diverting them from the essential process of integration into a team.

Conceptually, induction needs to be seen as a process rather than as a discrete event, and as multifaceted. This is consistent with Mullin's view that 'orientation' (as he describes it) is basically a natural extension of the recruitment and selection process (Mullins, 1995).

It might also be argued that, from the perspective of line managers working under considerable financial and production pressures, induction needs to be delivered without compromising operational requirements. Realistically, of course, there will always be tension between the need to provide a comprehensive and satisfactory induction experience that goes beyond the basics, and operational pressures. This tension may help to explain some of the frustrations and disappointments that new employees sometimes experience with the way in which they are inducted into an organization.

In explaining why the hotel suffered from a higher than expected level of turnover, Claire Wilson offered the opinion that some new employees came with unrealistic expectations of what hotel work was like, i.e. tending to imagine it as glamorous, when in reality, it was hard work and demanded a high level of commitment. In their book on the hospitality industry, Boella and Goss-Turner (2005, p 94) similarly emphasize the potential importance of misplaced expectations that are built up during the recruitment and selection process. Not only are these expectations important in understanding subsequent behaviour, but so too are the first impressions that are created as a result of starting to work. According to Boella and Goss-Turner:

> **First impressions are often the most lasting impressions, and the first impressions formed by many employees upon starting employment with a new employer may not be good ones ... The first hours and days are critical and if properly dealt with can create the right relationship that contributes to employees staying with an employer.**

Figure 13.2 offers a more realistic insight into the induction experience and the challenges that this presents to the HR professional.

The so-called 'induction crisis', a term used to explain the higher levels of wastage among newly recruited employees, helps to explain the relationship between unrealistic expectations, ineffective induction practices and the propensity to leave. Such losses are not only costly, but often unnecessary: the individual might not have left if the induction experience had created a positive, rather than a negative, impact on the person's 'feelings' about the organization and job (Ramsay-Smith, 2004; Cheng and Brown, 1998).

This view is supported by the experience of Claire Wilson, who saw a clear correlation between the people who left full-time posts and the inadequacy of their induction, training and development – limitations that created a feeling of not being valued on the part of the employee. But not all situations in which wastage rates appear to be higher than expected indicate weaknesses in the way induction has been experienced, as is explained later in this chapter.

Party with responsibility for provision	Legal aspects of employment	Company procedures and rules	Organizational culture– values and expectations	Working environment and job performance	Social and informal environment
HR professionals	✓	✓	✓		
Senior manager(s)			✓		
Line/ departmental manager				✓	✓
Co-workers				✓	✓

First day/week ←———— Timeframe ————→ First month

Figure 13.2 The induction process

What Figure 13.2 doesn't offer is an answer to the 'how' question: how is induction to be structured and experienced so that employees don't simply learn about the organization and their job, but do so in a way that connects with their affective domain (their attitudes and what they feel), and begins to build a relationship between the employee and the organization? This is the challenge that is found in this set of activities, which can be undertaken either individually or in groups.

1. Design a one-day induction experience for 15 new, hourly paid, employees working as cleaners, bar staff and receptionists, and who have been employed three weeks before opening.

2. Design an induction experience for the head chef, head receptionist and head of operations, all of which began work eight weeks before opening.

3. Discuss the role of employee feedback in induction and give examples of how this can be built into the induction experience.

Training

Responsibility for training is shared between different stakeholders and, for the majority of employees, follows on from induction. The Robinson Hotel Group, as a whole, provides a centralized training facility available to all of its hotels, offering course-based training in key areas of the business, such as food preparation, hygiene and 'back office' procedures. Hotel staff can be nominated for these courses. Suppliers of equipment and products also have an important contribution to make, offering on-site training in the use and maintenance of equipment, as well as product knowledge training. Heads of department, as the key line managers, carry out operational training covering specific procedures, techniques and performance standards. This is provided in the form of on-the-job training, and is designed to provide staff with the necessary skills and knowledge to perform their jobs to the required standards and to display appropriate customer service behaviours. Finally, the HR manager is responsible for meeting statutory training requirements that all staff must meet, particularly in the fields of discrimination in employment and health and safety. This is the only form of what might be described as 'awareness training'; much more emphasis and time is given to specific and job-orientated training that supports operational requirements. The distinction between 'knowing about' and 'being able to do' is important, particularly in understanding training priorities and the appropriateness and effectiveness of different training methods. Training in hotels does reflect statutory requirements, but is primarily driven by what employees need to know and to be able to do, i.e. it is business focused.

Given the difficulties of taking staff away from their work to experience classroom-based training, the prominence of on-the-job training methods is understandable, although not all of the things that staff must learn can be acquired in such a way. This is particularly the case with the knowledge that has to be acquired about the legislative framework within which both managers and employees are required to work. Training for this is based on the use of CDs and laptop computers. These are made available to new employees, who can progress through the specially designed structured training programme at their own pace and in their own chosen location. The package has a self-assessment element and staff can complete this when they feel that they are ready. An external verifier then checks the submitted assessments and the result is communicated to each individual. Certificates of attainment are sent to successful candidates, and the HR manager updates their personal records and the hotel's training records. The advantage of using this form of e-learning lies in its potential to provide a consistent level of training whenever, and wherever, needed (IDS, 2006).

The use of a mix of training approaches and methods that fit different and changing requirements is consistent with the idea of blended learning.

In the hospitality industry, much of the work of staff is performed in direct contact with customers, and the behaviours and skills needed to be effective cannot easily be taught using conventional course-based learning, but must be learnt through direct experience or simulation. According to Boella and Goss-Turner (2005, p 123), on-the-job training, if handled correctly, can be particularly effective for learning manual and social skills, but much depends on the technical skills of the instructor/manager and his or her ability to deal sympathetically with the difficulties experienced by staff in learning new skills in a pressurized environment.

One of the more challenging tasks faced by Claire Wilson was training the hotel's heads of department in appraisal skills. Because this is a common requirement for all of the hotels in the group, Claire has discussed with Ahmad Khan, the group HR manager, the idea of designing a programme open to managers from other hotels. He is keen to promote more centralized training, if this makes sense and can be justified, and has asked Claire to meet with him to explore how this can be achieved. He is bringing an open mind to this challenge and is looking for some practical, realistic ideas. This is the background to the next student activity.

STUDENT ACTIVITY 13.4 Training managers in appraisal skills

This exercise can be done in a number of different ways, but is more productive if students take the roles of Claire Wilson and Ahmad Khan, and work together to complete the following.

1. Design the outline of a one-day, course-based appraisal training programme for heads of departments, assuming around twenty attendees in the first group, showing very clearly how you would spend the time and the learning activities that you would include. You should agree learning outcomes and specific behavioural competences that you want each participant to achieve. You need to consider how these outcomes and competences can be realistically assessed and where, and what pre- and post-course activities you want participants to commit to. The training will be carried out in hotel conference facilities.

2. One of the elements of the training programme you design must include a session on 'giving and receiving effective feedback'. Research this subject and explain how you would develop this capability.

3. Produce a training budget for the course and any associated activities.

4. Devise an evaluation strategy to establish the effectiveness of the training.

Performance review and appraisal

The need 'to know' whether an employee is meeting reasonable expectations of his or her performance and establishing whether the employee 'fits' into the organization are not the same thing, but each is important for both employee and manager. A formal system of appraising employees is used by many public sector organizations and larger private sector businesses, but more flexible and informal systems for answering these two questions are increasingly being explored as the limitations and disadvantages of traditional performance appraisal methods are better understood.

As far as the Birmingham Robinson Hotel is concerned, the approach taken to appraisal was practical and realistic. All employee contracts contained a provision relating to a three-month probationary period, at which point the contract could be terminated if job performance or general behaviour failed to meet expectations. At weeks four and eight, employees participated in a performance review with their head of department. This was a relatively informal exchange between the two parties to establish how each one 'felt about how things were going', with the results of the exchange recorded and placed in the employee's personal file. The 12-week exchange was, according to Claire Wilson, 'more of a performance appraisal', in the sense that it followed a clearer structure and confirmed continuation (or otherwise) of employment. Criteria used to establish whether the employee was performing at an acceptable level included:

- punctuality;
- customer service skills;
- attendance.

What is rarely, if ever, considered under the performance appraisal heading is the significance of an equivalent process involving the employee appraising management and the organization. By this, we mean that employees go through a similar, if more individual and unstructured, process of reaching decisions about how well the organization has performed in relation to the promises it made, i.e. the expectations that employees had of how they would be treated and rewarded, in the light of the actual experience of working and being managed. The decision by some people to leave – and this is probably the main reason for the majority of voluntary quits – is that they feel disappointed, let down or badly treated: the performance of the organization and its managers has, in the perception of those leaving, been consistently below reasonable standards. The frequently referred-to aphorism that 'people leave their managers not their jobs' strongly suggests that the process of reaching judgements about performance is not one-sided.

At the Birmingham Robinson, managers received a performance appraisal, based on a formal interview with their line manager, both after three months in post and just before 12 months. The second is significant in the sense that, after 12 months, all employees acquire employment protection rights, and cannot have their contracts terminated without good reason and in the absence of a proper procedure. After this, appraisals were held annually, and involved a formal interview and completion of an appraisal form.

STUDENT ACTIVITY 13.5 How to appraise the performance of managers in the hotel

This activity requires students to design an appraisal instrument that reflects the context and requirements of a hotel environment.

1. Design an appraisal matrix that has two dimensions. Identify on the left-hand side the appraisal criteria and, along the top, you need to have a scale that reflects the extent to which each criteria has been met. You may wish to consider weighting the criteria and quantitatively assessing these to produce an overall rating or assessment score, with a minimum achievement level, below which performance would be considered deficient or unacceptable.

2. Identify the kind of evidence you would need to use to allow proper decisions to be made in reaching conclusions about managers' performance and where this might be found.

3. Consider what action would be appropriate to deal with situations of:
   - excellent performance;
   - average performance;
   - unsatisfactory performance.

   Highlight the possible implications of each action.

In carrying out these tasks, remember the points made in Chapters 2 and 11 about the general problems that managers and employees experience with performance appraisals.

Signpost to Chapters 2 and 11: HRM: An Academic and Professional Perspective and Managing Performance

According to Claire Wilson, the effectiveness and value of reviews and appraisals – they mean the same thing in different organizations – depends very much on who is involved as the appraiser and how appraisals are carried out, particularly how feedback is given and received. This means that the skills of the appraiser and appraisee may be important factors in determining the extent to which the experience of appraising and being appraised is positive and functional, rather than negative and unhelpful. As was pointed out in Chapters 2 and 11, simply having an appraisal scheme or system does not, in itself, mean that it will generate the desired outcomes. In considering the key features of an effective appraisal scheme, ACAS (2006) suggests that the following are desirable:

- written records of the appraisal to provide feedback and to allow more managers to monitor the effectiveness of appraisals;
- a job description that focuses attention on the employee's performance at work, thus ensuring that assessments are based on objectively verifiable requirements rather than on the person;
- the use of a rating system, under which categories of performance can be numerically scored;
- the use of assessments based on objectives, standards or other reasonable and agreed criteria, thus reducing the degree of subjectivity (note that it would be unrealistic to expect to eliminate subjectivity completely);
- the provision of a genuine procedure that allows people to be able to appeal against their assessment.

Summary

In reviewing the experiences of the six-month period prior to opening the Birmingham Robinson Hotel, the following are some of the key learning points that the HR manager made.

- Much more training might have been carried out during the pre-opening phase to prepare staff for the pressures and demands on their skills and knowledge that would arise once the hotel became fully functional. The general point here is that operational pressures *do* interfere with employee training and it is often difficult to undertake required training when such pressures take priority. It might be argued that the HR practitioner must find creative, effective solutions to this tension rather than force managers to release staff for training when this causes operational problems.
- The heads of department might have used the pre-opening time more effectively to build their teams, and to create a better understanding of operating procedures and standards. This may be about the important role that line managers play in building the social organization of the business, under which employees' feelings and attitudes towards their work, and towards their work group, is a key variable in determining how they actually perform their jobs. It's not only about having the technical skills, but about wanting to use them.
- There was a degree of over-recruitment in the pre-opening phase, partly because of the successful recruitment campaign, and as the headcount was reduced through non-renewal of casual and temporary contracts and through voluntary quits, the impact on wastage rates created the impression that there 'was a problem here'. The point to note is that any measure of HR – in this case, wastage and turnover – can be misunderstood in terms of its seriousness or cause. What was a natural adjustment to a temporary oversupply situation might have been interpreted by people taking the statistics in isolation as some kind of problem that needed a solution, as well as a failure on the part of management.
- The departure of two heads of department, who left the hotel during its first eight months of operation, was not a surprise and, according to Claire Wilson, she realistically knew at the time that the two appointments might be problematical. The decision to employ was heavily influenced by the urgent need to make appointments and to fill key posts. Her comment that 'you need to have the confidence to hold off' reinforces the point made in Chapter 3 that it is better to resist short-term pressures to recruit, if at all possible, particularly if key managerial jobs are involved, and to make sure that the 'right'

manager is in place from day one. It is just as important *not* to recruit if there is real doubt about the suitability of the applicant.

→ Signpost to Chapter 3: Recruitment and Selection

- Finally, the experiences of managing the HR dimension of the new opening offer persuasive support for those arguing that a link does exist between what HR does and organizational performance. Claire Wilson made this clear when she remarked that the staff that had left had been those whose induction, training and development had not been satisfactory; in general, those that stayed had benefited from more positive and supportive experiences in these key areas of HR.

@
online
resource
centre
Visit the Online Resource Centre that accompanies this book for self-test questions, weblinks, and more information on the topics covered in this chapter.
www.oxfordtextbooks.co.uk/orc/banfield_kay/

CASE STUDIES

The final part of this chapter gives students the opportunity to consider how to address the types of issue that arise when managing projects of this sort. Due to the different pressures facing organizations in this type of situation, the response to staffing issues can vary from that which appears appropriate in a more stable environment. In the following mini case studies, students can use their knowledge and judgement to offer practical solutions that will overcome the challenges described.

Joe's case

Joe was interviewed for the position of head chef. As an Australian national, he noted during his interview that, if offered the post, he would require the support of the hotel in obtaining a permit to work in the UK. He explained that he already had a work permit to work at a different organization and that it should be relatively easy to get a permit for the new hotel. Joe had a very impressive CV and had extensive experience in similar positions at different hotels, both UK-based and elsewhere in the world. The director of catering felt that Joe was, by far, the best candidate for the post and, despite the delay expected in obtaining a work permit and the associated cost, was still keen to offer the position to Joe. He was therefore offered the post, conditional on eligibility to work in the UK. As part of the application process for a work permit, the hotel asked Joe to supply supporting documents, including his passport and current work permit. It transpired that he did not have a work permit and that his visa granting permission to work in the UK had expired some months before. The HR manager explained to the catering director that it would be much more difficult to get a work permit in these circumstances, due to the strict requirements to employ a resident worker.

Questions

1. What options might the HR manager and catering director have considered?
2. Investigate the rules on employing migrant workers in the UK. What would be the potential penalty for employing Joe without eligibility to work in the UK?
3. How should the catering director and HR manager have handled the situation, given this problem?

Cathy's case

Cathy was appointed as a waitress and bar attendant at the hotel when it first opened. Although, when at work, she proved to be a real asset, being both efficient and capable, and establishing good relationships with her customers, her attendance and timekeeping were a real problem. During her first few weeks, she was absent with a cold for two days, took one day off when her car broke down and took two further separate days due to a migraine. She was also late for her allotted shifts on four different occasions. Ordinarily, she would have failed her initial four-month probationary period, but due to her excellent performance when at work, and the fact that staff turnover had made it exceptionally difficult to recruit and train a replacement, Cathy's probationary period was extended. When challenged about her absence, she mentioned problems at home, including a recent breakdown in her marriage, and problems with childcare, including having to rely on family members to look after her children when she worked in the evenings.

Questions

1. What were the pros and cons of continuing Cathy's employment beyond her probationary period?
2. To what extent do you feel that attendance and timekeeping issues were relevant to her probationary period?
3. What options might the hotel have considered? What action would you have taken?

Ben's case

Ben was employed as a hotel porter and, during his probationary period, demonstrated that he was extremely keen and conscientious. He also had an exemplary timekeeping and attendance record. He did, however, find it difficult to pick up new tasks and, despite being shown by his supervisor on numerous occasions exactly what he was required to do, he kept forgetting many instructions and making simple mistakes. Prior to taking the job, he was out of work for a long time and he got very nervous during any meetings with his supervisor to discuss the difficulties he had in learning new tasks. He failed to pass his probationary period and, although this was extended, he became very agitated and upset: he was very concerned that he might lose his job because he enjoyed the work at the hotel and really needed the money.

Questions

1. What were the potential implications to the hotel in continuing Ben's employment?
2. What options might the hotel have employed to help Ben to learn more systematically the required tasks in the role?
3. What was the likelihood of Ben's difficulties proving to be a problem in the long term?

Allegations of bullying

During recruitment, the hotel worked closely with a recruitment agency to provide large numbers of staff, particularly to the lower paid positions in the hotel. During the initial weeks after opening, the agency continued to supply staff to replace those who decided to leave. As part of its efforts to re-employ some of those who left the hotel, the agency obviously discussed the reasons why these people left and raised a delicate issue with the hotel, concerning the reasons why some of the staff left. In a discussion over staffing requirements, the agency informed the hotel that bullying might be a problem among some of the cleaning staff and that three of those who left had raised this as being a problem. For reasons of confidentiality, it could not disclose more information because those who had informed them of the issue had specifically asked not to be named, but the agency felt that it might help the hotel to raise the issue so that steps could be taken to ensure that this did not continue to be a problem in the future.

Questions

1. How might the hotel have investigated these allegations?
2. How might the hotel have gone about establishing the opinions of the remaining staff about their employment?
3. What recommendations would you have made to reduce the risks of bullying and harassment among staff?
4. How might the hotel have gone about gathering information from those that had left to help to reduce staff turnover?

REFERENCES

Advisory Conciliation and Arbitration Service (2006) *Employee Appraisal*, ACAS advisory booklet, available online at www.acas.org.uk.

Boella, M and Goss-Turner, S (2005) *Human Resource Management in the Hospitality Industry*, Elsevier Butterworth Heinemann.

Chartered Institute of Personnel and Development (2005) *Flexible Working: The Implementation Challenge*, CIPD report, available online at www.cipd.co.uk.

Chartered Institute of Personnel and Development (2006a) *Induction*, CIPD factsheet, available online at www.cipd.co.uk.

Chartered Institute of Personnel and Development (2006b) *Recruitment, Retention and Turnover*, CIPD survey report, available online at www.cipd.co.uk.

Cheng, A and Brown, A (1998) 'HRM strategies and labour turnover in the hotel industry: a comparative study of Australia and Singapore', *International Journal of Human Resource Management*, 9:1, pp 136–54.

Child, J (1984) *Organisation: A Guide to Problems and Practice*, Harper Row.

Incomes Data Services (2006) *e-learning*, IDS HR Study 818, summary available online at www.incomesdata.co.uk.

Mullins, LJ (1995) *Hospitality Management: A Human Resources Approach*, Pitman.

Ramsay-Smith, G (2004) 'Employee turnover: the real cost', *Strategic HR Review*, 3:4, p 7.

Ulrich, D (1996) *Human Resource Champions*, Harvard Business School Press.

Watson, TJ (2002) *Organising and Managing Work*, FT/Prentice Hall.

Case Study: The Role of HR in Closing a Factory

14

Key Terms

Collective redundancy This arises when an organization intends to dismiss, because of redundancy, 20 or more employees at one establishment within a 90-day period. In such cases, dismissal is not related to individual performance or behaviour, but is for business reasons, such as plant closure, reorganization or reallocation of work.

Consultation A process that can be individual and collective, and involves managers and employees, or their representatives, jointly examining and talking about issues of mutual concern. There is also an expectation that the discussions will seek to produce jointly acceptable solutions through a genuine exchange of views and ideas (Dix and Oxenbridge, 2003).

Learning Objectives

As a result of reading this chapter and using the Online Resource Centre, you should be able to:

- plan a closure and understand how the role of HR fits in with the project plan;

- understand what is involved in the communication processes relating to a closure and the options for managing this process;

- identify and contribute to the management of the different HR activities needed to promote continuing performance during, and following, a closure;

- understand the legal and ethical issues facing managers in a closure situation.

Introduction

This chapter has two general aims. The first is to provide insights into what is involved in closing a manufacturing unit, although the closure 'principles' and requirements are broadly similar whatever the sector/industry. The second is to facilitate, through a series of integrated tasks, the development of the knowledge and competences needed to participate in, and contribute to, this type of project. Participation in closing an operating unit, particularly one that has been in existence for many years, takes the HR professional out of his or her 'normal', and often routinized, world. It requires the HR professional to operate in a context full of new, and often unpredictable, challenges – a world in which measures of success and failure are much more obvious and known, and in which there are very clear expectations about what HR needs to deliver.

From a practitioner perspective, the textbook world of neatly packaged and sequentially arranged HR activities, devoid of context, complications and pressure, is at odds with organizational reality. During closure situations, in addition to maintaining core HR activities, the HR professional must work across functional boundaries, plan and deliver HR outcomes that are scheduled sequentially and in parallel, and cope with conflicting and changing priorities. Particularly at more senior levels, the boundary between HR management and what might be described as 'general management' can become less clear, and, frequently, HR is only one element of a team of 'managers' grappling with the demands of the challenges set by the organization. Professional and functional boundaries become blurred as people come together to plan, solve problems and achieve objectives.

The exercises built into the chapter are closely related to those in which the HR professionals assigned to the closure were actually involved. All can be done individually, but the tasks are better undertaken as group activities. The learning experience is enriched even more if all of the activities and tasks are undertaken as part of a skills development study block, into which learning experience opportunities for research, presentation, reflection and feedback can be built.

In trying to make the case study as experiential as possible, we have tried to strike a healthy balance between providing information on what is involved in closing an operational unit and leaving important areas of information to be researched by the student. While much background information is provided and explanations of processes are given, the emphasis is on students working together to make their own decisions and to provide answers to the tasks set.

 Signpost to Chapter 10: Learning and Development

There are additional exercises that concentrate on more specific situations that developed during the period of planned closure. These exercises provide opportunities to solve the kinds of specific problem that emerged as a result of implementing agreed policies on how redundancies and transfers were going to be managed.

Background to Standard Tools

Standard Tools is an American-owned manufacturing company, with factories and distribution units located throughout the USA and Europe. It manufactures and sells a wide range of hand tools, hardware and DIY products. It has annual European sales of $2.7bn, of which $150m is generated in the UK. Its UK sites are as follows.

- Northton Central

  This site employs the following staff:

  - 150 employees in tool manufacturing;
  - 20 engineering and design staff;
  - 20 IT support staff;
  - 20 finance and administrative staff.

- Northton (outskirts) *(seven miles from Northton Central)*

  This site employs the following staff:

  - 50 employees in garden furniture manufacturing;
  - 50 commercial and customer service employees;
  - 50 field sales representatives, selling doors, tools and decorating products.

- Bramham *(15 miles from Northton Central)*

  This site employs 350 staff in tool manufacturing, along with managerial and administrative staff.

- Beechford *(40 miles from Northton)*

  This site employs 150 staff in gardening products and distribution.

- Midsleigh *(200 miles from Northton)*

  This site employs the following staff:

  - 100 distribution employees;
  - 50 customer service and commercial sales staff.

Union involvement

Amicus is recognized at the Northton Central and Bramham sites for the purposes of procedural representation of salaried staff and the negotiation of terms and conditions of employment for hourly paid employees (manual workers). Shop stewards are an accepted part of the recognition agreement and have regular meetings with management as part of their representational role. The full-time district officer may become involved in negotiations if disputes cannot be resolved internally. The other sites are non-unionized.

The company has a severance agreement with the union in the event of compulsory job losses. Any employee made redundant, or volunteering for redundancy, receives twice the statutory entitlement without a cap on weekly earnings level, inclusive of all statutory and notice entitlements. The agreement states that, in the event of redundancy, volunteers will be sought in the first instance. A performance-based selection method has been agreed for salaried staff in the event of redundancy, but no agreed selection method exists for hourly paid employees.

Background to the decision to close

Standard Tools' parent company is registered on the New York Stock Exchange and its headquarters is in Columbus, Ohio. The CEO and his vice presidents take strategic business decisions for manufacturing and human resources. The problem for the HR team in the UK is that the approach taken by American-based companies in closing factories and the legal framework that regulates such actions are different to the UK. In the USA, the decision to close comes first and, once it is announced, there follows a period of 'impact bargaining' to lessen the impact of the closure on employees. There is therefore little understanding or appreciation within corporate headquarters of the UK requirements for consultation and of other legal requirements. The CEO simply wants the closure to be announced and completed within the shortest possible time, and is not too interested in the protestations of the UK managers charged with achieving this objective.

The reasons for closing Northton Central are entirely business driven and directly relate to the economics of production. Employment and production costs, as well as overheads, are much higher for two manufacturing units than for one, and it has been obvious for some time that significant cost savings might be made by closing the much older, and less efficient, Northton Central site, transferring production and employees to the newer factory in Bramham.

Production requirements for both Bramham and Northton Central sites (only 15 miles from each other) have reduced in recent years, due to what is referred to as 'strategic sourcing from low-cost countries'. Not only might costs be saved by closing one of the sites and concentrating all activity on the other, but the land and buildings might be sold to release cash, which can either be invested back into the business or used to fund other projects, such as acquisitions. Unless these efficiencies are delivered, the ability to compete with low-cost producers in the Far East will be undermined, which might mean the end of manufacturing in the UK.

The possibility of closing the Northton Central site has been an agenda item at senior meetings for a number of years. In terms of priorities, it took this time for it to reach a point at which the decision was made to investigate the feasibility of closing the site. The information-gathering team involved manufacturing, sourcing, financial and engineering representatives from around the world, along with key UK-based managers, including the HR manager. This team worked in the UK for three days at the end of January 2006 to gather all of the necessary details and to establish a cost-effective closure plan. This was presented, two days later, to the US executive board in order that it might make a decision.

The decision was made to close the site. The company wants the estimated savings of £1m per year to be released quickly and all activity to be completed within five months from the end of January 2006. In addition to estimated closure costs, including redundancy, of £1m, every week that the site remains occupied after the five-month period incurs costs of approximately £20,000 per week.

From a legal point of view, it has been accepted by the UK management team that the outcome of the executive board meeting was a proposal subject to consultation, rather than a final decision to close, although as far as the Americans are concerned, it is a final decision. The UK HR team has been given responsibility for producing the HR plan and for ensuring that this is in line with the operational plans for the closure.

Implications

The detailed implications of the closure decision are as follows:

- 90 manufacturing jobs will be transferred to the Bramham factory;
- 60 manufacturing jobs will become redundant because the manufacture of certain products will be outsourced;
- 20 design and engineering staff will transfer to Bramham;
- 30 manufacturing jobs at the Bramham factory will become redundant because the manufacture of certain products will be transferred to the company's French plant;
- the 40 non-manual employees at Northton Central will be transferred to a new administration building on the outskirts of Northton, two miles away from the garden furniture plant.

Responsibility for managing the HR part of the closure project is in the hands of the HR department that is based at the Bramham site. The team consists of the HR manager and two HR officers, all of whom are permanent, full-time staff. They have been required to commit 50 per cent of their time for the next six months to support the project.

Other managers at Bramham and Central Northton can be used to provide additional resources to support the project, as long as the demands made on them are not excessive. The sum of £25,000 has been allocated from the total project budget to help to resource HR activities, for which existing resources are not available. This money can be spent on anything to do with the HR project plan and is controlled by the HR manager.

STUDENT ACTIVITY 14.1

In working on this activity, you can draw upon other resources that might be available to help deliver or support certain activities, but you cannot spend more than £25,000. You can also make any reasonable assumptions about the company, its workforce and its environment, if these help you to undertake the different activities associated with the project.

Produce a project plan covering all of the HR issues relating to closing the factory, transferring staff to Bramham and dealing with possible redundancies. This plan must identify and schedule all of the key activities that need to be undertaken to achieve the objective of a successful closure within the five-month timeframe. The plan should not include activities that are to do with production transfers, plant movement or other non-HR matters, although, in reality, the HR activities would be integrated within a comprehensive project plan.

The project plan can be constructed in one of two ways.

There are different software packages that can be used to produce the plan, with Microsoft Project being the most well known and available of these. The ability to use a software-based system is dependent on possessing certain basic skills, but these can be acquired with a minimum of three hours' training provided by someone experienced in using the software.

Alternatively, a paper-based approach can be used. The same principles and techniques incorporated into project-planning software are used in a manual approach and either will be suitable, provided proper preparation and training are given. It is recommended that, if possible, a software-based approach is adopted, because this will provide opportunities for significant skill development in project management.

Project management

Projects, of different types and complexities, are becoming increasingly common in HR and represent a different kind of challenge to the more discrete approach to HR work. Projects, and the ability to manage them, require new and different skills that many HR professionals lack. Not only are these skills an essential part of an HR professional's 'toolkit', however, but they also represent a prerequisite for being able to work across functional boundaries.

According to Bee and Bee (1997), projects can be differentiated from other activities because they:

- are goal-oriented, with specific and clear objectives;
- require members of project teams to work cross-functionally;
- involve careful coordination of interrelated activities, requiring accurate scheduling;
- are of a finite duration, with start and finish times;
- are usually unique in terms of context and experience.

Invariably projects, although differing widely in size and scale, involve a team of people working together, under the direction of a project leader or manager, and the ability to meet the project's objectives is closely related to the way in which the project team works together. These members not only have the responsibility of directly delivering individual parts of the project plan, but are also required to organize and coordinate the contributions of other internal stakeholders and external resource providers.

Projects tend to have a distinctive life cycle, with five recognized phases, as follows.

1. Project definition, with agreed aims and objectives.

2. Planning and resourcing, using either computer software or paper-based systems.

3. Implementation, with ongoing learning and adaptation. This is, arguably, the most intensive part of the project and involves:

   - devising a detailed list of tasks and activities that contribute to the achievement of the project's objectives;

   - agreeing on timescales for the carrying out and completion of activities, including milestones. 'Milestones' are important points in the life of the project and represent key achievements;

   - agreeing on the resources that the project needs to complete all activities on time. Resources can include time, money, skills/knowledge and facilities;

   - agreeing on the roles and responsibilities of team members.

3. Project completion.

4. A post-completion stage, at which features of the new situation need to be managed.

Working as a team

The ability to work effectively as a project team member is closely related to being sensitive to the internal dynamics within the team itself. A useful model that can help to explain what these dynamics are and how they develop was developed by Bruce Tuckman in 1965 and revised in the 1970s (Tuckman and Jensen, 1977). Tuckman's model is based on the premise that teams go through the following different phases and activities before they reach full effectiveness.

- Forming

  The team comes together with little clear understanding of its structure and leadership or team roles. Relatively high levels of uncertainty will be experienced over how the team will function and its priorities.

- Storming

  There is an increase in the degree of clarity about the purpose of the team, but some uncertainty remains. Competition for leadership roles may be experienced, and energy can be expended on relationship and emotional issues at the expense of project objectives. Decision making is often difficult and compromises may be required to facilitate progress.

- Norming

  Agreement and consensus emerges, and the roles of leader(s) and member(s) are accepted. Emerging commitment to each other and to project objectives develops, with team members engaging in social activities. More open discussion about how the team functions take place.

- Performing

  There is growth in the level of confidence among team members and a strong commitment to deliver against project objectives. There will be more independent working within a framework of understanding and agreement. Decisions about how the team functions are taken collectively.

- Adjourning

  This is the stage at which the team breaks up after the end of the project. This is more to do with the well being of the team members and their relationships with each other and the organization, than it is about the project itself. Nevertheless, how people feel about their experiences will affect their future roles and status.

Communicating the decision to close

If a reorganization involves the possibility of redundancies and the consequent legal requirements for consultation, it important to express any initial announcement as a proposal rather than as a plan. This avoids the criticism that consultation is not meaningful and preserves the integrity of the consultation process. Representatives of employees affected by these changes are likely to attempt to challenge the decision to close and, again to meet legal requirements, it is necessary to avoid giving the impression that the decision has already been made. For example, moving towards seeking volunteers for redundancy at an early stage might be inferred as evidence that the company is refusing to engage in meaningful consultation.

Announcements that are sympathetic, to a point, and indicate the next step in the process will be better than those that are ambiguous, uncaring and complicated. For example, you can announce what the proposal is, why this has come about and state that the process of consultation will be commencing at the earliest opportunity. You can also express support for those who may be affected by the proposals and give a commitment to consider all alternatives put forward. It is not helpful, in the early stages, to make promises that might compromise the company, raise unrealistic expectations among the workforce about the size of any redundancy package or misrepresent the number of people who might be faced with compulsory redundancy.

Careful consideration should be given to when the initial announcement is made and the way in which this is carried out. It is also important to consider who should be the person to make the announcement to the workforce. Announcing a closure is very daunting: the person standing at the front of the workforce needs to be sufficiently senior be able to shoulder the responsibility and take questions, without making commitments beyond the intention to consult. On the other hand, it is better to have someone as close to the workforce as possible to provide reassurance to those who may be affected. In the case of Standard Tools, while US leaders offered to read out announcements, it was felt that this would be unnecessarily inflammatory and the decision was made that the plant manager of the central site should take personal responsibility.

Press release

If the press picks up on a good story then it will report it and an organization can do little to prevent this. All that an organization can hope to do is to give factually correct information to ensure that what is written in the press is representative of the company's viewpoint. If incorrect information is reported, while court action can be taken to sue the newspaper responsible, this will usually only make the organization look worse and generate negative publicity, as well as incurring significant legal costs. It can also become a distraction to management. Perhaps the best course of action is to prepare a brief press release that is either sent 'proactively' to local newspapers or held as a 'reactive' statement, for release in the event of enquiries.

Public relations (PR) agencies can handle media interest on behalf of the company and this can help it to focus its own attention on managing internal processes, rather than getting embroiled with answering questions from the media. This is often represented in the media as: 'A spokesperson for the company said…' It may also be helpful to nominate one person to deal with queries from outside.

STUDENT ACTIVITY 14.3

1. Prepare a written announcement outlining the company's proposals to close the central Northton factory. This would be read out by the factory manager to the workforce as part of the initial announcement of the closure and then distributed to all employees. The document should not exceed 300 words.

2. Prepare a press release to be sent to local and regional newspapers, with title, presenting the company case for the closure and reorganization. Think of the press release as the actual article that would be published. It should not exceed 250 words.

In completing both of these tasks, give particular regard to the different audiences that each will be communicating to and the objectives associated with each of the two documents.

The consultation process

There is a legal responsibility to consult at the earliest opportunity with individuals affected and, if appropriate, their representatives. There must also be a proposal against which to consult, however, and pulling together these proposals takes time. Herein lies the first dilemma, because there is a degree of contradiction between these requirements. At what point should consultation start for it to be fair and meaningful? Legally, this should be as soon as the possibility of closure is a serious possibility, but in reality, this can only be once the company is prepared and ready to initiate the process. Confidentiality and the careful management of information are of the utmost importance during this early period, prior to the full proposal being formulated.

Employees and their representatives are entitled to receive sufficient information about the management's proposals to be able to take a useful and constructive role in the process of consultation. In law, the purpose of consultation is to try to avoid redundancies or dismissals, or, if this cannot be achieved, to reduce the number of dismissals involved and to mitigate the effects of any dismissals. Consultations need, therefore, to be seen to be genuine and must be undertaken with a view to reaching agreement with the employees' representatives. The expectation is that management and employees, together with representatives, will work to try to find common solutions (Lewis and Sargeant, 2004).

Management teams engaged in reorganizations of the kind in which Standard Tools is involved, are only likely to change their plans fundamentally in exceptional circumstances. This means that, while the details over the number of redundancies and the terms under which these are announced might change as a result of the consultation process, the principal decision itself is unlikely to be rescinded. This is because it is difficult to see how representatives and individuals can put forward alternatives that can deliver the objectives that managers are seeking to achieve. In reality, the process of consultation predominantly serves the purpose of mitigating the consequences, rather than of providing any worthwhile challenge to the strategy – although representatives often feel that this is their role in earlier stages of consultation.

Following on from the previous point, consultation needs to be expressed in terms of responding to a proposal and not to a plan, and herein lies the second dilemma. From a managerial perspective, consultation cannot commence until there is sufficient clarity over management's intentions that it can present at least an outline of what it intends to do. To avoid the criticism of not engaging in meaningful consultation, however, management cannot be seen to be submitting a complete plan. It is difficult to demonstrate that consultation is meaningful unless something has changed as a result of it having taken place. While it is essential for managers to have a plan, it can only be presented as a draft that is sufficiently flexible to allow for meaningful consultation to take place.

STUDENT ACTIVITY 14.4

Devise a detailed communication and consultation strategy, covering the period from the point at which the first announcement is made to the closure of the factory.

Collective redundancy

According to ACAS (www.acas.org.gov), a collective redundancy situation arises if an employer proposes to dismiss as redundant 20 or more employees at one establishment within a 90-day period. Such a situation might occur if a business or plant closes down, or if an employer no longer needs as many employees to carry out a particular task. It might also occur if dismissals are to take place in a reorganization or reallocation of work. This latter case applies to the situation in which Standard Tools finds itself. Redundancies can also exist if there are job losses in one section, but, because of new recruitment in a different section with different skill requirements, there is no overall reduction in the number of people employed.

If these conditions are met, an employer is required to consult in advance with representatives of the affected employees and to notify the projected redundancies to the Department of Trade and Industry (since 2007 now the Department of Business, Enterprise and Regulatory Reform). Consultation must be completed before any notices of dismissal are issued to employees. Employees, or their representatives, may bring a complaint to an employment tribunal if they feel that an employer has failed to comply with these requirements. Any complaint must normally be brought within three months of the last of the dismissals.

The obligation to consult may apply even when an employer intends to offer alternative employment on different terms and conditions to some, or all, of the employees, with the result that the number actually dismissed is less than 20. This will be the case if employees are to be redeployed on such different terms and conditions that accepting the new posts amounts to dismissal and re-engagement.

The obligations apply particularly to situations in which compulsory redundancies are likely, but may, in some circumstances, also apply to 'voluntary' redundancies if an employee has no real choice about whether to stay or to leave. If, in the case of Standard Tools, management believes that 20 or more redundancies may result from the intended changes, but is not sure whether there will be sufficient volunteers for redundancy or whether some of the redundancies can be avoided, the obligation to consult employees and to notify the Department of Trade and Industry still applies.

The management at Standard Tools would not be under any specific legal obligation to consult employee representatives or notify the Department if they were to believe that less than 20 employees would need to be made redundant. They would, however, be at risk of successful unfair dismissal claims if they were to fail to warn and consult individual employees who might be dismissed, fail to apply dispute resolution procedures if required, and fail to adopt a fair basis for selection or to take reasonable steps to redeploy such employees.

The Information and Consultation of Employees Regulations 2004 (ICE), introduced in April 2005, apply to organizations with 50 or more employees (with effect from April 2008). The Regulations give employees the right to:

- be informed about the organization's economic situation;

- be informed and consulted about its future employment prospects;

- be informed and consulted about any decisions it might contemplate making that could lead to significant changes in the way in which work is undertaken, changes in contractual issues, and to redundancies and transfers.

STUDENT ACTIVITY 14.5

Identify and discuss all of the legal implications of the closure and transfer of staff to Bramham, and those arising from any possible redundancies.

Managing and selecting for redundancy

The majority of HR professionals will, at some stage in their careers, be involved in managing job losses. A reduction in the number of jobs does not necessarily mean that the jobholders will have to be made redundant, however, although this is often the case. Whenever a closure or reorganization announcement is made, the employees directly affected, as well as those whose jobs may be preserved, are likely to experience a range of emotional reactions. According to the CIPD (2007):

> Redundancy is one of the most traumatic events an employee may experience. Announcement of redundancies will invariably have an adverse impact on morale, motivation and productivity, but the negative effects can be reduced by sensitive handling of redundant employees and those remaining.

This is the general view on the effects of redundancy on employees, but it fails to reflect the complex and changing reactions that employees go through when faced with the enforced loss of their jobs. To help them to develop the 'right' strategies, HR professionals need to understand the following matters.

- Not all employees will react in the same way, although, initially, all are likely to feel the negative effects identified by the CIPD. The loss of one's job can be perceived as a direct threat to one's self-esteem, self-identity and standard of living, but while this might be an initial reaction, it is unlikely to be a permanent one for all of those affected.

- Different employees will be in different situations regarding age, length of service and employability. Those who are relatively young, with limited service and marketable skills, are likely to take control over their own destiny and seek employment elsewhere at an early stage. Those coming towards the end of their working lives and with many years' service are in a different position. They may well come to view the prospect of redundancy in a more positive light, as they contemplate the attractiveness of what might be a generous, tax-free redundancy payment.

- Employees are unlikely to remain passive in the face of management attempts to keep control of the situation. Even those not affected by the threat of redundancy may well decide that they no longer wish to remain with a company whose future seems unsure and leave. Retaining important employees can often run in parallel with making others redundant!

- Future recruitment requirements can be made more difficult to achieve as a result of the publicity over the closure and uncertainty over the long-term future of the company.

While the experience of redundancies is likely to involve negative emotions, these will vary between people, with many employees moving from one emotional state to another as the situation evolves and as individual positions become clearer. Critically, from a company perspective, these negative emotions and reactions need to be managed, as far as possible, to ensure that they do not undermine the economic well being of the company or its ability to continue to meet customer requirements during the transitional period.

The key stages of the redundancy process

Most redundancy situations share common features, although all are unique. As was pointed out earlier, a reduction in jobs does not necessarily mean that the same number of employees will have their employment terminated. Some will decide to leave, over time; natural wastage will reduce the number as employees leave who do not need to be replaced; casual or agency staff can bear the brunt of job losses; internal transfers may be possible. Much depends on the timescale of the planned changes and the extent to which management has the ability to reduce the labour force without having to make employees redundant. If a complete closure of a facility is planned, however, it is likely that either voluntary and/or compulsory redundancies will be experienced. Decisions on redundancies need to be based on:

- planning and scoping the numbers likely to be involved;
- agreeing on the financial terms and level of redundancy payments, including statutory rights;
- inviting employees to volunteer for redundancy;
- agreeing on the use of objective selection criteria and the way in which these will be applied;
- identifying and notifying those selected for redundancy;
- creating opportunity for appeals;
- allowing opportuntity to seek alternative employment;
- calculating redundancy payment;
- helping redundant employees obtain training or alternative work.

Selecting for redundancy

Arguably, the task of reaching agreement on the choice and application of criteria for selecting employees for redundancy represents the most challenging part of the whole process. Whatever the choice of criteria, they must be objectively fair and consistently applied. If they are not, then the whole process can be compromised, with the possibility of delays in completing the project.

Selection criteria should also be reasonably applied in the light of individual circumstances. The Disability Discrimination Act 1995 makes it unlawful for an employer to treat a disabled person less favourably because of a reason relating to their disability that cannot be justified. Reasonable adjustments to working conditions or the workplace, if that would help to accommodate a particular disabled person, may need to be considered. Care also needs to be taken to ensure that the criteria are neither directly nor indirectly discriminatory on grounds of sex, marital status, race, disability, sexual orientation, religion or belief or age.

➡ Signpost to Chapter 6: Equality in Employment

As a result of the Employment Equality (Age) Regulations 2006, which came into force on 1 December 2006, employers now need to take even more care to ensure that their choice of objective criteria for redundancy selection is non-discriminatory. The use of 'last in, first out' (LIFO), one of the more commonly used selection methods in the 1970s and 1980s, was effectively made unlawful in most cases due to the relative advantage it gives to older workers.

STUDENT ACTIVITY 14.6

Devise a strategy for handling redundancies at Standard Tools and specifically develop a mechanism for selecting employees for redundancy.

@ See the Online Resource Centre for an example of a selection matrix that can be used to help to select employees for redundancy.

Managing the transfer of employees from the old to the new location

In addition to managing the factory closure and redundancies, Standard Tools' HR team also has to ensure, together with other members of the project team, that the company experiences minimum disruption to its production targets, despite the many changes associated with the closure. Critical to achieving this is the retention and transfer of designated staff from the Northton to the Bramham site. The company may know what it wants, but it still has to develop practices that ensure that the employees involved become committed to their transfer and trial periods, if these are involved. The following is an account of how this was achieved.

The 90-day consultation period with the company over the closure of the old factory ended on 2 June 2006. After this date, the company began to serve notice on employees who wished to transfer to the new site and made redundant those employees who had been selected for compulsory redundancy (in addition to those volunteers who had already been released earlier at their own request). Employees transferring to the new site were entitled to a week's notice for every year of service, up to a maximum of 12 weeks, before they transferred.

Because many of those involved in the move had asked that the situation be resolved as quickly as possible and because of the financial benefits that the company would enjoy if people moved earlier, the decision was taken to try to expedite the transfer process. To achieve this, it was decided that, if employees were willing to move early on a date set by the company (which would be no earlier than 29 April and, in most cases, would be in July), the company was prepared to offer the following options:

● £100 per employee payable on the date on which they started working at the new site; free transport for 12 months by bus from, and to, the old site if they worked on the day shift; transport from, and to, the old site at a subsidized cost of £12.50 per week for a further six months. Employees would have to commit to this for at least 12 months;

OR

● £300 per employee payable on the date on which they started working at the new site; subsidized transport for 18 months by bus at a cost of £12.50 per week for those ten employees at the old site who had already stated that they wished to transfer, but had no other means of transport to the new site than the company bus. These employees would have to commit to this for at least 12 months;

OR

● £350 per employee − other than those in engineering, who would get £200 each − payable on the date on which they started working at the new site.

The company also agreed that, if the above were to be accepted, they would extend the trial period to eight weeks (from the statutory four weeks) and gave assurances that, should any employee in the seventh week of their trial period declare a genuine reason why their position at the new site were not suitable, they would be granted redundancy within a further three months of the end of the trial period. This request for redundancy could only then be rescinded at the company's discretion due to recruitment commitments that might subsequently be made. The union supported the company's concern that finding other employment would not count as a genuine reason.

The above is another example of the kinds of creative solution with which the HR team needed to come up to ensure that the project went according to plan and that key workers were not lost to the company.

The final student activity involves looking forward to the six-month period after the closure of the Northton site and the implementation of the planned changes for Bramham.

STUDENT ACTIVITY 14.7

Consider all of the other HR issues and requirements that need to be managed during the post-closure phase of the project.

It is important to recognize that the work of HR continues after the formal completion of the project and this task provides an opportunity of 'seeing' what needs to be done in the post-completion phase.

Summary

Handling the closure of a business is a complex challenge facing both line managers and HR. This complexity is often further complicated if another part of the business is to remain operational and if it is necessary to transfer employees from one area of the business to another. The process required is time-consuming and the overriding issue of impending redundancies can affect other HR activity that occurs during this time.

Legal requirements must be met if the business is to avoid the potential of excessive costs of unfair dismissal and other legal claims that may arise as a result of poorly managed redundancies. The legally required consultation process can be an effective framework to help maintain morale and productivity through constructive two-way dialogue with those whose jobs are at risk.

Those who are not made redundant can also be adversely affected either by facing a period of personal uncertainty and evaluation or by working in close proximity to those affected. Businesses need to consider carefully what can be done to support these people to ensure that they remain motivated and feel secure following redundancies elsewhere. Retaining 'survivors' can be critical to future success, and their retention can be encouraged by ensuring a fair and flexible approach is taken from the beginning, and by comprehensively communicating accurate and timely information, and by acting upon feedback throughout the process.

Visit the Online Resource Centre that accompanies this book for self-test questions, weblinks, and more information on the topics covered in this chapter.
online resource centre www.oxfordtextbooks.co.uk/orc/banfield_kay/

The final part of this chapter offers students the opportunity to deal with four situations that emerged during the transfer of staff from Northton to Bramham. In these four mini case studies, don't try to guess what the HR team actually did to resolve the situations, but use your own knowledge and judgement to produce 'the best possible solutions'.

The team leader

A team leader in one of the redundant team leader positions makes the decision to transfer to the new plant in a non-managerial position, on a job with which he is not familiar and in a different department. He has also worked in a supervisory position at Standard Tools.

During his first few weeks, he learns the job quickly but expresses concern to the HR department that he is finding it extremely difficult to adjust to being in a non-supervisory role. He is reluctant to share his feelings with his new supervisor because they used to be colleagues previously and he does not want to appear to be either uncooperative or awkward. At the end of his trial period, he decides to stay and take advantage of the generous red circling arrangements in place. (Essentially, this is an agreement that his old salary will be preserved.) One week later, he approaches the HR department again requesting redundancy. There has been an incident between him and his new supervisor, who has accused him of wandering off the job without permission and who has told him he is not happy with his performance, and he regards this as being the last straw. He does not have a job to go to and is really unhappy about his situation.

Questions

1. What is the legal position with regards to the company's obligation to consider this request?

2. What options might be open to the company and the supervisor, and what are the pros and cons associated with each option?

3. What actions should the HR team recommend to best resolve the present situation?

The warehouse operative

A warehouse operative, whose position is redundant, has requested to be released early and be made redundant before the company had planned to lose his position, because he has another job to go to. He requests to be released at least three weeks prior to the date on which his work ceases. He was to be required to stay beyond the actual date in which manufacturing ceased, to help count stock and ship out remaining stock, and to help to clear the other items on site, such as furniture files and obsolete machinery. He is 59 years old and extremely concerned about his ability to get another job if he is not released.

Questions

1. What is the legal and ethical position of the company, given this request?

2. What options are open to the company, given this request, and what pros and cons are associated with each course of action?

3. What steps might the company consider to resolve the situation?

The key manager who drives

A key manager in the business has requested voluntary redundancy because she does not want to transfer to the new site. She has stated that her childcare arrangements rely on her being able to get to and
from work within 15 minutes. Although she drives and earns a reasonable salary, and can afford the extra
cost of transport, she does not wish to alter her existing childcare arrangements. She has critical plant
and process knowledge, and the company believes that losing her at the time of transfer of production
would be extremely detrimental to the ongoing efficiency of the Bramham factory.

Questions

1. What options might the company consider to encourage the manager to transfer to the new plan?
2. Is there any legal argument that might be used to refuse to grant the manager's request for voluntary
   redundancy?
3. What might the implications be of refusing the request?
4. What options might be available to reach a compromise in this situation?

The key manager who cycles

Another key manager who lives very close to the site that is closing currently cycles to and from work. His
responsibilities cover both plants and, because he can drive, he has begun to use a pool car to get from
the old site to the new site to cover these duties. He is not, however, willing to buy a car or to pay the tax
on a company vehicle that he would be obliged to pay if he were to be allocated a car in which to travel to
the new plant.

Questions

1. What options might the company consider, and which would you consider to be 'the best' and why?
2. What implications would the decision taken have, with regard to the preferred way of dealing with this
   situation and with regards to other people at different levels whose jobs are to be transferred and who do
   not have *any* means of transport to get to and from the new site?

REFERENCES

Bee, F and Bee, R (1997) *Project Management*, CIPD.

Chartered Institute of Personnel and Development (2007) *Redundancy*, CIPD factsheet, available online at
www.cipd.co.uk.

Dix, G and Oxenbridge, S (2003) *Information and Challenges at Work: From Challenges to Good Practice*,
ACAS research paper, available online at www.acas.org.uk.

Lewis, D and Sargeant, M (2004) *Essentials of Employment Law*, 8th edn, CIPD.

Tuckman, BW and Jensen, MAC (1977) 'Stages of small group development revisited', *Group and Organizational Studies*, 2:4, pp 419–27.

15 Case Study: Reforming the HR Function

Key Terms

Organizational capability This refers to an organization's ability to create, mobilize and utilize its key resources to maximum effect. The concept is important because it helps to redefine what HR represents; it is seen less as a series of activities and responsibilities, and more in terms of a resource and capability builder.

Learning Objectives

As a result of reading this chapter and using the Online Resource Centre, you should be able to:

- understand the challenges that HR managers face in changing an HR department;

- understand the concept of organizational capabilities and contribute to their development;

- recognize weaknesses in existing HR provision and identify ways in which this can be improved;

- understand the importance of the 'human dimension' in bringing about successful change.

Introduction

The last of the three case study chapters deals with another important and increasingly experienced aspect of HR: the need to reform and improve the operation and contribution of the HR department. While it shares many of the features and the approach of the previous two chapters, it has one major difference. It is presented more as a narrative and is based on conversations with a senior HR professional who, in his last full-time job, was required to transform a relatively conservative and ineffective personnel department into one that reflected the needs and requirements of a rapidly changing organization. Many of the observations, comments and views expressed in this chapter are based directly on conversations with him or reflect his general views on, and experiences of, managing people. Additional contributions come from other managers who have offered their experiences of changing 'the way things are done' and in the critical area of staffing in HR.

The supporting literature lends authority to many of the comments and observations included in this chapter. Its objective is not, however, to 'prove' any theoretical position or validate a conceptual model; rather it is to engage with the experiences and reflections of HR professionals, to learn from these and to relate them to aspects of HR theory in such a way as to establish the usefulness of that theory. It is through this dialectical process that greater insights and a deeper understanding of HR, in both its theoretical and applied forms, is likely to emerge.

The adoption of a more narrative-led approach in this chapter compared with those preceding it is intended to allow the reader to gain as much as possible from the collective experiences of those who have contributed to it. The student activities encourage the reader to face the kinds of personal and professional challenges associated with leading change, and with reorganizing the way in which HR is structured and staffed. One of the themes that emerges, and one that was raised in Chapter 2, is that of the potential that exists within individual employees for improved performance, subject to the right environmental conditions and management, and the role that HR can play in facilitating this. But what this particular case demonstrates is that this key facilitating role is often dependent and conditional on the HR function itself being transformed and made 'fit for purpose'.

→ Signpost to Chapter 2: HRM: An Academic and Professional Perspective

In certain cases, change can originate from within but, as far as HR is concerned, the likelihood is that the catalyst for change will be linked to new appointments, more often than not at the head of the function. The chapter is therefore very much about two kinds of change:

- that which can be described as *enabling* change – the change that needs to be made to allow other things to happen and to be done differently. This kind of change is associated with changes in culture, attitudes, mindset, philosophy, and, above all, of the key decision makers and organizational shapers;
- the changes in how things are done, the behaviour of people and improvements in performance that can only be realized after the enabling changes have been made.

The importance of understanding the significance of change to improved performance cannot be underestimated and is captured in the following statement:

If you do what you always did, you get what you always got.

In its very simplicity, this captures the importance of change as a precursor and precondition for improvement. The 18-handicap golfer referred to in Chapter 11 is unlikely to become the next Tiger Woods – innate talent and technique will tend to be the main reason why golfers perform at different levels – but knowing that performance can be improved by linking the fundamental aspects of stance, swing and temperament with the known consequences, and making changes in these, is the only basis upon which any golfer can make permanent improvements to his or her performance. One might argue that, despite obvious differences between changing an individual, the HR function or an organization, fundamentally, the same principles apply, i.e. linking what is done and how it is done to the immediate effect and longer term consequences.

Improving the performance of HR has to be based on having a clear understanding of the relationship between the activities in which HR is engaged, how these are carried out and the consequences of these activities, in terms of their perceived value and contribution to organizational objectives. The ability to validate these activities and approaches, by reference to the value given to them by different stakeholders, is vital in knowing what needs to be done differently to achieve a better outcome. Doing things differently means change. (For a detailed exploration of how change can be conceptualized and modelled, see Burnes (2004a; 2004b).)

Understanding the changing environment

This case study and its associated student activities are based largely on the experiences of a senior NHS HR executive in one of the country's largest Trust hospitals. Its central focus is in the challenges that he and other managers faced in turning around what might be accurately described as a 'traditional' HR department. The department was struggling to deliver the services and contributions required by the key organizational stakeholders as they themselves moved to adapt to the new environment within which public sector healthcare provision was now being delivered.

What emerges from his experiences is the realization that simply having an HR department, in whatever form this might take, is not the key to effective people management, as acknowledged in Chapter 2. Rather, it is the appropriateness, the value and the impact that the function makes that determines its status and whether others see it as worthy of a 'seat at the top table'. Although admittedly simplistic and contextually determined, the notion of 'effective' and 'ineffective' HR is a central theme both of this case study and of the whole book. The HR department that has become an inward-looking and inflexible institution, unable or unwilling to change, can be contrasted with that which is adaptive and flexible, and which works strategically to deliver valued outcomes and to build organizational capability. But how is this transformation achieved?

The point about changing environments is that they render existing capabilities and contributions less relevant than they used to be. This point was emphasized by Patricia Hewitt, Secretary of State for Health, who, speaking at a conference in September 2006 and referring to the NHS, is reported to have said:

> **The structures that were right in the 1960s, when the model for the district general hospital was defined, aren't right today.**

Logically, it might be argued that the HR function that evolved to serve the institutional delivery model of the 1960s is also inappropriate to meet the very different contributions that the reforming NHS requires in the twenty-first century.

A frequently made criticism of HR is that it can become very good at doing the wrong things or, at least, at spending disproportionate amounts of time and resources on activities that add little or no value. In extreme cases, it can become dysfunctional and undermine organizational interests (Hammonds, 2005). The Trust hospital upon which this case is based provides a very good example of how changes in an organization's economic and political environments can raise questions about the contribution of HR, if it fails to adapt itself to the demands of the new situation.

The impact of organizational change on HR is twofold.

- Firstly, it is not enough for HR simply to adapt to the new situation by changing the way in which it is structured and organized; it has to acquire new capabilities that are more appropriate to its new role. Reorganizing itself without acquiring new capabilities is unlikely to be a successful change strategy.

- Secondly, HR has to question and change the way it thinks about how it operates and the kind of contributions it needs to make, either to retain or regain its credibility and status with key organizational stakeholders. This is about acquiring 'a new HR mindset'.

In this case, the Trust was not in a budgetary deficit and had a reasonably good reputation for financial management, but the chief executive felt that it had become somewhat complacent. She wanted the organization to 'move up several gears' in response to potentially threatening changes in its operating environment.

The main environmental changes impacting on the Trust were:

- the introduction of hospital financing based on the 'payment by results' principle. This meant that funding would be based on numbers of patients, and of procedures and services that were actually delivered;

- the introduction of patient choice meant that people requiring elective procedures could choose from a number of 'providers' rather than being forced to accept treatment at their local hospital;

- the introduction of an internal market, enforced competition and a minimum of 18 per cent private sector provision meant that staff and unit performance was critical in attracting business, delivering an excellent service and, through this, maintaining a healthy financial position.

All hospitals needed to confront these changes by changing the way in which they operated, particularly in the context of staff expectations and contributions, and this greater emphasis on commercial issues meant that those seeking Foundation Trust status really needed to function as independent businesses. As a result of this new orientation, the challenge faced by the Trust's senior management team, but particularly by the director of HR, was:

How do you take an organization that thinks it's already successful, and therefore isn't inclined to accept radical change, and get it to move in a new direction?

(For a detailed analysis of HR's role in reorganization and planned change, see CIPD (2004).)

Organizational capability

As defined at the start of this chapter, 'organizational capability' refers to an organization's ability to create, mobilize and utilize its key resources – in this case, its human resources – to maximum effect. The concept emphasizes the key strategic role that HR can, and must, play if the organization is to optimize the contribution from all its employees. The concept is important because it helps to redefine what HR represents: it is seen less as a series of activities and responsibilities, and more in terms of a resource and capability builder. This is a view very much consistent with the resource-based view of the firm explored in Chapter 2.

 Signpost to Chapter 2: HRM: An Academic and Professional Perspective

Figure 15.1 represents a way of linking the following strategically important capabilities with the key personnel and professional competences of the HR professional, particularly those charged with leading the function, and the following points represent what key stakeholders might expect from those working in HR:

- aligning HR with the business;

- achieving high performance;

- creating new solutions and being innovative;

- building partnerships.

One way of understanding organizational capability is to relate it very clearly to human capability, i.e. the quality of the people that the organization employs. The premise that is presented here is that the HR function's status and perceived effectiveness reflects the quality of the people who lead and staff

Figure 15.1 Human resources capability model

Source: Australian Public Services Commission, 2003, copyright Commonwealth of Australia, reproduced by permisson.

the function, other variables being of secondary importance. These personal traits and characteristics are key to understanding:

● the status that the HR department enjoys among organizational stakeholders;

● the extent to which it operates at the strategic, as well as operational and administrative, levels;

● the contribution that it makes to the 'bottom line';

● improvements in employee behaviour and performance.

The following two simple, but powerful, statements focus attention on the importance of the human dimension of HR in relation to its functional contribution:

> **It's only behaviour that counts.**

> **Get the right people, with the right skills, in the right place at the right time.**
> (Buckingham and Elliot, 1993)

This way of making sense of what really makes a difference to organizational performance is supported by powerful and influential contributions from some of the most influential writers on management and organization. We have already made reference to the work of Charles O'Reillly and Jeffrey Pfeffer in several chapters of this book (especially in Chapter 1), but it is worth recalling some of their most important observations.

At the very beginning of their book, *Hidden Value* (2000), O'Reilly and Pfeffer ask the question:

The 'right' people or the 'right' organization?

They answer this by suggesting that, while companies need talented people, with the obvious implications this has for recruitment, selection and retention, these companies also need environments in which the very best and talented people can actually use and apply their talents in the interests of the organization. Companies also need management practices that bring the best out in everyone. The point that O'Reilly and Pfeffer are making is that success and effectiveness is not simply a matter of recruiting and retaining talented people, but that it is equally important to understand that the kinds of environment to which they refer don't emerge by accident. These types of environment are often constructed and maintained by managers who understand their value and importance; without talented managers, these environments might not exist.

The importance to the organization of the quality of key decision makers is also a feature of the work of Jim Collins (2001). He begins his third chapter with the statement:

First who ... then what.

He goes on to explain that the companies who were transformed from being simply 'good' to being 'great' did not achieve this status by having a clear vision of where they wanted to go, but rather shared the common characteristic of deciding who the key people were that would take them forward. The direction and strategies that were adopted *followed* the selection of key people. As he said:

> **No, they first got the right people on the bus (and the wrong people off the bus), and then figured out where to drive it.**
> (Collins, 2001, p 41)

In pursuing this theme of 'people first', Collins makes three other important points:

- if you begin with 'who' rather than 'what', it is much easier to adapt to a changing environment – the 'wrong' people are often wrong because of their inflexibility and refusal to come to terms with a changing world;

- the 'right' people often attract others precisely because of what these leaders represent – they inspire and others continue to follow, even when the direction of the organization or department changes;

- having a vision of what needs to be done and developing strategies that take you where you want to be are irrelevant if you do not have the right people in the first place.

This case study confirms the views and arguments of those writers who emphasize the importance of the quality and characteristics of the people who occupy key roles within organizations. In this particular case, these are the leading professionals who occupied key roles in the Trust's HR department. Their ability to visualize the changes needed, in the way in which HR operated and the contributions it needed to make to reflect changing requirements and new challenges, is directly linked to the creation of new capability at the individual and organizational level. How this is achieved is the heart of the story that follows.

Background

Midshire Hospital Trust (MHT) delivers a range of acute and specialist health service provision to 250,000 people in the south of England. It consists of one large district general hospital and several smaller mental health and geriatric units, spread throughout the region. The Trust employed around 7,000 people, 60 per cent of whom were medics and nurses, 30 per cent support and ancillary staff, and the remainder occupied administrative and managerial roles. Despite the many organizational changes that affected the NHS in the 1990s, the MHT was still, in many ways, a very traditional hospital, particularly in relation to its working culture and employees' expectations of what their jobs involved. Despite several waves of reform, little had changed in the way in which many of the administrative and managerial employees thought about their work, and there was still resistance, albeit passive, to attempts by senior management to change attitudes and working practices. This was particularly the case with members of the 20-strong personnel department, many of whom had worked there for over twenty years. They had, in the view of several senior managers, '*become part of the woodwork*'.

The department was organized along traditional lines, reflecting the historical importance given to collective employment relations, recruitment and formalized training. More recently, increasing time and resources had been committed to issues of equality and diversity, a shift in emphasis that reflected the more general trend in public sector personnel to prioritize these issues; for those concerned with service provision and the need to increase hospital efficiency and productivity, this emphasis was 'not service driven'. Staff within the department tended to operate in isolation from each other, with very little cross-fertilization and cooperation within the department, which had effectively become disconnected from the Trust's key stakeholders.

The fundamental problem was that the approach taken by personnel reflected what it was good at, rather than what the Trust needed it to do, and become, in order to support managers and staff who were now being forced to confront a situation in which external competitive challenges and internal economic pressures were threatening the reputation and financial health of the Trust. This 'alienation' from the strategic and operational priorities that the Trust was facing was expressed in the way in which the department preferred to operate, which was process driven. Whatever the issue, whether insignificant in relation to the wider context or of major importance, the default mechanism was to apply the appropriate personnel procedure in the genuine belief that, if you went through the right procedure, the right answer would come out at the other end.

The Trust's chief executive, Dr Anne Sloman, had realized for some time that the personnel department was as much part of the problem as it was the potential source of many of the solutions with which the Trust needed to come up if it were to survive and prosper in the new environment. An opportunity to address this issue arose in the summer of 2004, when the head of personnel retired. The choice of a replacement was now more important than ever, and Dr Sloman arranged a meeting with her executive team to discuss the kind of person for whom they were looking and how to find him or her.

STUDENT ACTIVITY 15.1 Recruiting the new head of personnel/HR

The tasks associated with this activity generate more learning and insights if they are done in groups/teams, with decisions being made after considerable discussion and debate. It adds value to the exercise if people also play senior management roles. Representing the hospital's executive group, you are required to undertake the following.

1. Write a job description that reflects the challenges facing the new appointee.

2. Construct a person specification for the post of director of personnel/HR, having regard for the personal qualities, leadership abilities and experience needed for this key job.

3. Consider the relative merits and costs of recruiting the 'right' person using:

   ● headhunters;

   ● personal networks and contacts;

   ● advertising in the professional and national press.

4. Devise an assessment and selection strategy that will lead to the final decision to appoint, or otherwise. Fundamentally, what would you be looking for to identify the outstanding candidate and where might the evidence be found that would help to identify the 'right' person for the job?

The appointment

As a result of the process adopted, the Trust made the decision to appoint an experienced HR professional called John Harper, who started work on 1 November 2004. His first exposure to the culture of the personnel department came as a result of participating, with other new starters, in an induction day run by his own department. According to John, this experience confirmed what the chief executive had told him about its preoccupation with process. In order to liven up one of the sessions, one of the presenting personnel officers decided to introduce a little quiz. The exchange went something like this:

'How many personnel policies has the Trust got?'

'6?'

'Oh no...'

'12?'

'Not even warm... We have 64!'

John noted that the personnel officer was quite proud of this claim because, for her, it demonstrated the department had got everything covered. The position being represented was:

... you will not find a problem that we haven't a solution to.

The real point was that the solution was seen to lie in the existence of policies and procedures themselves. They had acquired the status of both means and ends, and no one in the department appeared to see the danger in this. On the contrary, the multiplicity of procedures was seen to be a source of strength rather than a systemic weakness.

Based on his experience and approach to HR, John's view on the role of procedures differed fundamentally from that of the current personnel staff. In his view, procedures can be helpful and should not be ignored – when they contribute to constructing solutions and point towards the 'right way' of responding to a situation. But, for John, it is questionable whether there is even a 'right' way of doing things. He believes that HR professionals need constantly to ask themselves:

What is the solution we are looking for to solve this problem or respond to this challenge?

The task is *then* to deploy resources to support the solution, but the key to moving HR to what is effectively a different mindset is shifting its approach, from being procedurally determined to solution-led and driven.

If procedures represent a predetermined course of action that is triggered by particular actions, behaviours and requirements, then a policy can be thought of as a statement of intent, or a position on a particular issue or subject. Policies set out, in an explicit form, the organization's standpoint in relation to key aspects of HR and establish expectations of how people should behave at work. For example, a recruitment policy might state that, wherever possible, vacancies will be filled from within the ranks of existing employees; a reward policy might state that the pay differential between the highest paid and lowest paid employee should never exceed a factor of 10; and so on.

John's view is that many traditional personnel departments have too many policies, which, in turn, spawn numerous procedures that give life and meaning to each policy. According to John:

The principle I have operated under for many years is that HR policies should be a bit like the Ten Commandments – you shouldn't have more than ten and they should be expressed as absolutes.

Taking equal opportunities as an example, he argues that the creation of numerous and lengthy written procedures that present detailed prescriptions of what is acceptable and unacceptable behaviour is unnecessary. All that is required is a simple, but powerful, policy statement that needs little in the way of procedural support. He argues that the statement '*we do not discriminate in this organization other than on grounds of merit*' *is* the policy. It is unambiguous, simple and easy to understand, and has the power to inform everything else that the organization does. The recruitment and selection practices, access to training, decisions on reward and promotion, etc. should then reflect this policy without the kind of procedural overkill that still characterizes many organizations.

Essentially, what he is saying is that HR needs to question the prevalence and value of extensive procedural regulation, and move towards developing and embedding the organization's HR philosophy within the organization's culture, so that it becomes part of 'the way we do things here'.

STUDENT ACTIVITY 15.2 Evaluating the use and effectiveness of procedures in HR

To adopt a more evaluative stance towards the use of procedures in HR is not to challenge their potential to contribute to required or desired solutions, but it is to ask questions about their utility and functionality. The case of the hospital consultant suspended for allegedly taking food without paying for it, which we mentioned in Chapter 5, might be considered an example of procedural regulation becoming dysfunctional, resulting in the creation of more problems, rather than effective solutions to existing ones. On the other hand, relying less on procedures, and more on values and brief statements of policy, is not without risks.

This activity requires students to look carefully at the use of procedures in HR and, through researching their use and analysing the evidence collected, reach an informed position on their role and value. The tasks associated with this activity, again, should be undertaken collaboratively and, if possible, be based on talking to HR professionals and line managers about their views and experiences of procedures in HR.

1. Compare the relative advantages and disadvantages of procedures.

2. Evaluate the influence of context on procedural use.

3. The use of procedures implies there is only 'one way' of handling a given situation. Consider whether this also means that there is only one 'right solution', and consider whether this inevitably conflicts with the need to build flexibility into how HR acts and reacts to the challenges it faces.

4. Explore generally the possibility of relying more on principles and values, rather than on detailed and comprehensive rules and prescriptions to influence people's behaviour.

5. Explore the above possibility in the context of individual casework relating, for example, to disciplinary cases. You can do this by thinking of similar core belief and value statements to that offered on discrimination.

The discussion about the overuse of procedures in HR and ideas about capability building naturally leads to the question:

What kind of HR do we need/want?

Table 15.1 has an obvious connection to ideas developed in Chapter 2, but, despite the dangers of oversimplification, tries to represent HR in terms of categories or choices, with associated issues and implications.

Table 15.1 is useful in understanding the extensive differences between the way in which HR is practised and conceived, but the mistake to avoid is that of seeing these differences in terms of alternatives or polar choices, in the sense of this model or that. While the emphasis given to all five conceptions of HR will inevitably vary, in response to different and changing environment factors, there is a strong case to be made for an HR function that contains elements of all five.

Developing an HR strategy

Any strategy for improving the status and effectiveness of the HR function has to be based on changes, many of which are often significant and extend beyond the superficial to affect structures, roles and responsibilities, approaches and, crucially, people. In the case of Midshire Hospital Trust, what kind of changes needed to be made to transform its capability and contribution?

Table 15.1 Ways of conceptualizing the role and purpose of HR

Requirement	Label	Problems	Consequences	Justifications
To care for the physical, psychological and emotional well being of employees	The welfare role and function	Can focus too narrowly on employee interests – no explicit recognition of 'business interests'	HR seen as 'soft' and 'woolly'; seen by line managers as of little relevance	Continues to be of fundamental importance in how people are managed and how they behave or perform at work
To solve problems and fix things	The fire-fighting role	Largely a reactive role – involves HR dealing with symptoms, rather than addressing underlying causes and problems	HR is often 'busy', but its agenda and focus is limited and misses out on other important areas of contribution	Fixing problems and 'putting out fires' is important: small 'fires' can develop into larger, and more threatening, situations
To maintain systems and procedures, with an emphasis on administrative conformity	The conservative and process role	Can focus too narrowly, with little regard for outcomes; HR seen as coercive and reactionary	HR has negative reputation – seen as adding little value and becomes marginalized	Efficient administration is always important and a certain level of procedural regulation is legally prescribed
To build capability	HR's strategic contribution and strategic alignment	Can lose sight of the importance of efficient administrative and effective operational interventions	Associated with outsourcing of non-strategic functions and devolvement of many key operational responsibilities to line managers	Easily spoken about and more often than not aspirational; requires different mindsets and skill sets on the part of HR professionals working in this way
To support the business and line managers	The 'business partner' role	Requires specialist skills and wider business experience to be effective	Raises questions about the 'professional' dimension of HR	Often ignores tensions between business and professional interests; is 'being good for the business' the only reference point for HR professionals to use to justify their actions?

Interestingly, the first change that John Harper made was to persuade the CEO to change the name of the department from 'personnel' to 'HR' (equates to HRM). According to John:

> **There is a fundamental difference between 'personnel' and 'HR' – it's not a question of old wine in new bottles.**

The new name was also an important tactical opportunity to flag up a change in the approach to HR and represented a way of engaging with people in the changes being planned that would not have been possible under the old 'personnel' banner. The 'new flag' of HR represented a powerful symbol of, and for, change and became a new focus for people's allegiance (Mach, 1993).

John Harper was very insistent about the differences between the two approaches to managing people and justified his position by arguing that:

- there is a community and body of knowledge that is distinctive to HRM that can be used and deployed for whatever the organization needs to achieve. In this sense, HR represents a different kind of 'resource' to that represented by 'personnel';

- HR represents a stronger and closer alignment with business objectives and can be contrasted with the more limited, introspective and detached positioning of 'personnel';

- the language of HRM differs in important respects to that of Personnel Management, with a much stronger emphasis given to matters of finance, efficiency, results and resource utilization;

- essentially, HR is much beyond what 'personnel' represents to many organizational stakeholders;

- those associated with this more 'traditional' personnel model can almost be antagonistic to 'the business', expressed in such statements as 'we are independent' and 'we are between the organization and the employees' as some kind of neutral, third party.

According to Harper, the idea that a function charged with employing and managing people can, or should be, somehow independent is unacceptable and unsustainable. His view is that the function and those who work in it:

> ... must be fundamentally part of the foundations of that business.

Harper's position on the relationship between Personnel Management and HRM enjoys a degree of literary support, but as explained in greater depth in Chapter 2, there is a lack of unanimity on this key conceptual issue; indeed, certain popular textbooks fail to address it at all.

 Signpost to Chapter 2: HRM: An Academic and Professional Perspective

Torrington ot al (2005) bogin their exploration of the meaning of Human Resource Management by saying that the term 'is not easy to define'. This is because it is used to describe an academic area of study and also as way of describing a particular approach to the management of people. It is claimed that, in important respects, it is distinct from Personnel Management. This is essentially, the way in which John Harper understands and uses the term. According to Torrington et al:

> **Used in this way, HRM signifies more than an updating of the label: it also suggests a distinctive philosophy towards carrying out people-orientated organizational activities: one which is held to serve the modern business more effectively than traditional personnel management.**

On the other hand, in their latest edition of *Introducing Human Resource Management*, Foot and Hook (2005) introduce the subject by listing '*the main activities of personnel/human resource management*'. They seem to have accepted that the two terms carry the same meaning and can be used interchangeably, although later in the chapter they refer to research that suggests actual people management practices do vary, with some of the differences linked to the use of the two different designations (see Hoque and Noon, 2001). Whatever the outcome of the academic debate on designations and meanings, from a student and professional perspective, the lack of clarity about the philosophical and practical relationship between Personnel Management and HRM can be, at best, irritating, and, at worst, unhelpful and confusing.

The importance of being comfortable with definitions and conceptual distinctions has more than academic significance, however; it also has important practical implications. In the case of Midshire Hospital Trust, it helped to shape the recruitment and selection strategy adopted by John Harper as, over time, he needed to replace HR staff who left. Given the new business orientation of HR, the job descriptions and person specifications were substantially different from those used previously, with much more emphasis on line management experience, the ability to understand financial matters and a results orientation. The 'business partner' concept, if not used explicitly, certainly became the template against which new appointments were made (CIPD, 2006).

The second strategic initiative undertaken by the new director of HR was to generate insights into how the department had been operating and what needed to change if it was 'to engage with the business' in an effective way. There are different ways in which this can be done, but the approach adopted in this case was to commission a client/customer survey, involving all key stakeholders. The thinking behind this was that this kind of survey not only produces useful information and insights into what stakeholders think of HR and its contributions, but actively engages respondents in the process of reshaping what HR does and how it does those things. It also, through establishing better communications, builds relationships, and creates opportunities for each party to influence the other and, in turn, be influenced. This client–provider interface represents what might be described as the 'political dimension of HR'.

STUDENT ACTIVITY 15.3 Carrying out a stakeholder survey

This is a design exercise and benefits from being done with others in order to generate maximum creative output.

1. Identify the main customers/clients of the HR department.

2. Agree on what each would expect from HR, in terms of the services and contributions it provides.

3. Agree on a strategy for collecting information and the most effective way in which the department might engage with each of the customer/client groups.

4. Design a questionnaire that might be used to collect useful data about the client group's perceptions of the effectiveness of the department.

(Hirsch et al, 1995)

The view expressed by Harper was that change should not be imposed, but should reflect the building of relations, and that, through this ability to 'see' the world as others see it, change will emerge. He also emphasized that it does not necessarily follow that you will do everything that people want you to do, but it does mean:

> ... checking out what people value and what they don't and the feedback we got back was that they liked the people and thought them conscientious, but they weren't getting the solutions they wanted. In fact they often found that they were deterred from dealing with issues because of the time Personnel took to sort it out. There was also a problem of availability and access which led to delays in getting things done.

The belief, represented by Harper, that HR should be a catalyst for change and should have the competences to 'make change happen' is consistent with Ulrich's (1996) business partner model of HR that was explored in Chapter 2. In advocating this role of 'change agent', it is important to remember that the changes that HR promotes and leads must be 'doable'. They must be realistic in terms of existing capabilities, the strength of resisting forces and in relation to the costs of forcing change onto an unwilling group of people.

→ Signpost to Chapter 2: HRM: An Academic and Professional Perspective

Harper also holds the view that the search for credibility and influence also requires HR to set an example, and to conform to those standards that it might be trying to apply to, or impose on, other parts of the organization. One of his strongest criticisms of personnel departments generally is that:

> ... they are very good at telling the rest of the organization what's good for them but very poor at taking that medicine themselves.

From a practical perspective, this means that, as a matter of principle, he needs to demonstrate to the rest of the organization that HR has sorted its own problems out first, in terms of attendance, performance problems and the conduct of its own staff, as a basis for setting a clear example to others, and to demonstrate to line management that HR has experienced the same kinds of problems with which line management are having to deal and has tried to solve them. According to Harper:

HR should be the exemplar of the willingness and competence to manage change successfully.

Formulating the new HR strategy

The MHT knew that its commitment to achieving independent trust status would be difficult to deliver in the absence of a credible HR strategy, and the decision to appoint John Harper was based largely on the belief that he could develop and lead a strategy that would significantly contribute to this objective. The strategy he inherited consisted of a list of laudable things to do, but none were aligned to the organization's operational and strategic objectives – the strategy was effectively disconnected from any strategic objectives and needs of the Trust.

Essentially, there was no clear link between the old strategy and the movement towards Foundation status and this is a serious, but according to Harper not uncommon, omission in the way in which many HR strategies are formulated. Realistically, whatever the rhetoric, they often represent little more than a list of things that people would like to do; in the absence of any clear understanding of how to align different elements of the strategy to what the organization values and wants, such strategies are unlikely to have any significant practical impact. In a hospital context, the following are examples of aligning activities and initiatives to valued outcomes and improvements in bottom-line performance:

- reducing and eliminating financial deficit;
- reducing level and cost of absence;
- reducing spend on locums and agency staff;
- increasing productivity;
- questioning and reducing the money and resources spent on ineffective and inefficient people management practices.

In summary, an HR strategy can be seen in terms of the following three requirements:

- creating and aligning activities to desired outcomes;
- having the skills and capability to deliver the strategy;
- removing or reducing the impact of current activities and forces that will, if left unchanged and unchallenged, undermine the new strategy and way of working.

But what are the elements or main features that represent an answer to the 'how' question? *How* will the strategy actually work?

In this particular case, the strategy developed by Harper involved:

- a high level of innovative thinking, leading to agreement on new ways of working; reliance on tradition, the 'old ways' of acting, the conservative mindset and the centralized way of doing things were obstacles that had to be overcome; innovation and flexibility were seen as long-term strategic objectives;
- an emphasis on rewards, based on the belief that the right kind of rewards, used in appropriate ways, reinforce the values of the organization and encourage required patterns of behaviour among employees. At a practical level, this meant that the Trust opted out of the national Agenda for Change programme that imposed a centralized pay structure, and developed its own terms and conditions of employment. Somewhat surprisingly, the trade unions in MHT supported this local solution, because they could see that it was in their members' interests to have pay and conditions aligned to the environment in which they were operating;
- recognition that all of the Trust's employees represented important assets that had to be renewed. This meant an extensive programme of investment in training and development, to generate higher

levels of skill throughout the Trust. This became a way of creating the capabilities to be, and do, more and was a key enabling mechanism for making employees more productive, efficient and effective. It also meant that they behaved more flexibly and responded more quickly to the changing health needs of the community;

● the creation of a physically and emotionally secure working environment, in which employees felt able to make the higher levels of contribution expected of them without fearing the consequences. According to Harper, this is not about 'mollycoddling' staff, but is rather about *delivering the employer's part of the psychological contract in practice*.

One of the central themes of this book has been the emphasis given to the importance of creating the right working environment as a precondition for liberating people's potential to perform at higher levels. The important role given to the environment in Harper's strategy lends further weight to the significance of this factor for the way people are managed at work.

This importance is also reflected in the work of writers such as, particularly, Pfeffer and O'Reilly (2000) and, more recently, Markides (2006). According to Markides, while an organization's strategy has the potential to energize people and get them excited about whom they work for and what they do, the internal environment plays a crucial role in translating that strategy into changed behaviour. He claims that:

> **If you want your company's strategy to be implemented properly, you need to ask the question: 'What organizational environment must I create internally to elicit the employee behaviour that will support the strategy?'**

As a way of understanding what this involves, Markides breaks the internal environment down into four distinctive parts:

● the measurement and incentive systems of the company;

● its culture, values and norms;

● its structure and processes;

● its people and their skills, mindsets and attitudes.

He argues that:

> **People will not change what they do because we tell them to; they will change only if we put in place the right incentives and the right culture and values – in short, the right organization.** (Markides, 2006)

STUDENT ACTIVITY 15.4 Designing the working environment

Arguably one of the most difficult challenges facing the HR professional is shaping the working environment(s) in ways that are consistent with the ideas of Markides (2006). This activity offers students an opportunity to identify the kind of environment that would generate the behaviours required by MHT and, particularly, how HR might contribute to this.

1. Identify what should be measured and how this should be done to encourage appropriate employee behaviours. You should concentrate here on measurements associated with the HR function.

2. What kind of incentives should be present in this environment and how should they be used?

3. Give examples of social values and standards of behaviour that you would want to see embedded in the hospital's working environment.

4. Describe the ideal mindset of employees, in terms of their attitudes to work, job-related behaviour and general behaviour at work.

5. What would line managers contribute to this environment?

Strategy implementation

Implementing the new HR strategy at MHT was as much of a challenge as was developing the strategy itself. It involved:

- stopping doing certain things that were not working and which had become institutionalized and dysfunctional. For example, reducing and simplifying the number of policies and procedures in use, and moving away from the idea that they provide solutions to problems – they only represent a way of processing them;

- moving away from 'a one size fits all' approach to HR policies and practices. Difference and diversity within an organization require tailored solutions that fit the situation and context;

- developing flexible working arrangements that liberated talent and potential. This resulted in significant financial savings, by reducing the number of locums and agency staff needed;

- active engagement with line managers by HR professionals. This helped to reinforce the change message, and provided authority and reassurance to those who were trying to 'buy in' to the new ways of doing things.

In order to develop the right attitudes and capabilities within his own staff, John Harper made the following changes that collectively reshaped and re-energized the department.

1. After carrying out performance reviews and discussing their future with John, all four of his senior HR staff left within the following six months of Harper taking over as director. This was done amicably and it served the best interests of both parties. The inability of certain people to adjust to the new ways of working and the changed HR mindset required of them led to a parting of the ways, with those who couldn't, or wouldn't, change deciding to retire or to seek work elsewhere. This provided an opportunity to recruit people from outside the NHS, who would bring experiences of the private sector into the hospital. The aphorism 'if you can't change the people, change the people' is particularly resonant in relation to the strategy that Harper was trying to deliver.

2. Within weeks of taking over, new staff workshops were established for people in HR who had never been involved in full departmental meetings before. These were then held every six weeks, as part of a process of involvement, communication and motivation. Other workshops, concentrating on the business plan, improving business-related skills and on interpreting the HR strategy in relation to individual contributions, were also held. The idea behind these workshops, was to:

   > ... **get them to see a picture of the future that was materially different from the one they currently had.**

3. All HR staff spent at least a day a year out in the wards and working with porters. This was intended to give them first-hand experience of how the hospital was functioning, and helped to overcome the narrow specialisms and limited experiences of many of his staff. But it also had a symbolic significance: it sent a message to front-line staff that HR was interested in what they were doing and in the kinds of problems that they were experiencing.

Summary

Many of the initiatives introduced by Harper were directed at creating a kind of paradigm change in the attitude towards HR, both from within and outside the function. This type of shift inevitably demands time before the intended outcomes can be identified and measured. Certain positive outcomes have, however, already been seen.

- HR is now accepted within the Trust as an important function that is central to facilitating the transition in attitudes and behaviours of hospital staff. It has acquired a seat 'at the top table', in the sense that Harper reports on HR's activities and successes at the regular senior management review meetings. He is also listened to.

- The high levels of absence among nursing staff have been reduced to a level that is approaching the best in the country. This has come about because of the new abilities to measure the cost of absence, to create different expectations about what is acceptable and what is not acceptable in terms of absence, and to follow these through with vigour and fairness.

- Through new flexible working, significant savings have been made in labour costs.

- New HR capabilities have been introduced as a result of the adoption of a very different approach to HR recruitment and selection.

- Because of the adoption of a client-centred HR approach, the credibility of the function has been raised with line managers.

Of course, such successes have not been achieved without tension and conflict, and the need to replace people who were unable to adapt to the new situation or who had consistently put their personal interests above those of the Trust. But what the case study does show is that HR can make a difference and that, with the right people implementing an appropriate strategy, this difference can be both significant and positive.

 Visit the Online Resource Centre that accompanies this book for self-test questions, weblinks, and more information on the topics covered in this chapter.

online resource centre

www.oxfordtextbooks.co.uk/orc/banfield_kay/

REFERENCES

Buckingham, G and Elliot, G (1993) 'Profile of a successful personnel manager', *Personnel Management*, 25:8, pp 27–31.

Burnes, B (2004a) 'Kurt Lewin and the planned approach to change: a reappraisal', *Journal of Management Studies*, 41:6, pp 977–1002.

Burnes, B (2004b) *Managing Change: A Strategic Approach to Managing Organisational Dynamics*, 4th edn, Pearson Professional Education.

Chartered Institute of Personnel and Development (2004) *Reorganising for Success: A Survey of HR's Role in Change*, CIPD survey report, available online at www.cipd.co.uk.

Chartered Institute of Personnel and Development (2006) *HR Business Partnering*, CIPD factsheet, available online at www.cipd.co.uk.

Collins, J (2001) *From Good to Great*, Random House, ch 3.

Foot, M and Hook, C (2005) *Introducing Human Resource Management*, 4th edn, FT/Prentice Hall.

Hammonds, K (2005) 'Why we hate HR', *Fast Company*, Issue 97, pp 40–8, available online at www.fastcompany.com.

Hirsh, W, Bevan, S and Barber, L (1995) Measuring the Personnel Function, IES Report 286, summary available online at www.employment-studies.co.uk.

Hoque, K and Noon, M (2001) 'Counting angels: a comparison of personnel and HR specialists', *Human Resource Management*, 11:3, pp 5–22.

Mach, Z (1993) *Symbols, Conflict and Identity: Essays in Political Anthropology*, State University of New York Press, ch 2.

Markides, C (2006) 'Hidden agenda', *People Management*, 28 September, p 36.

Mathews, BP and Redman, T (1996) 'Getting personal in personnel recruitment', *Employee Relations*, 18:1, pp 68–78.

O'Reilly, CA and Pfeffer, J (2000) *Hidden Value*, Harvard Business School Press.

Torrington, D, Hall, L and Taylor, S (2005) *Human Resource Management*, 6th edn, FT/Prentice Hall.

Ulrich, D (1996) *Human Resource Champions*, Harvard Business School Press.

Glossary

Accident An unplanned event that causes, or may have caused, injury or harm to people, equipment or property.

Assessment The tools and techniques used by an organization to identify and measure, either qualitatively or quantitatively, the skills, knowledge and potential of applicants.

Balanced scorecard A specific model for measuring business outcomes, devised by management theorists Kaplan and Norton, that allows managers to balance the financial perspective with those of the customer, internal processes, and innovation and learning. The model has been adapted and applied for use within the HR function.

Benefit Normally contractually agreed 'additions' to the wage or salary, provided by an employer as part of the overall employment package.

Bonus An additional, but variable, payment associated with individual, group or organizational performance.

Bullying The abuse of power, or of physical or mental strength, by someone in a position of authority towards a person (or group of people), resulting in harmful stress and undermined self-confidence.

Collective agreement A written statement defining the arrangements agreed between a union and employer, and the terms that will apply. Such agreements are only legally enforceable if this is expressly stated or if the collective agreement is referred to in individual written terms and conditions of employment.

Collective bargaining The process of negotiation between trade union representatives and employers, or employer representatives, to establish by agreement the terms and conditions of employment of a group of employees.

Collective redundancy This arises when an organization intends to dismiss, because of redundancy, 20 or more employees at one establishment within a 90-day period. In such cases, dismissal is not related to individual performance or behaviour, but is for business reasons, such as plant closure, reorganization or reallocation of work.

Competence The combination of skills, knowledge and experience that results in a person's ability to carry out specific tasks and procedures to a required standard. Can be equated to 'know-how' (Gladstone, 2000). A specific competency can also be understood as an underlying characteristic of a person, i.e. a trait, a belief, an ability or an attitude, that distinguishes one person from another and explains differences in job performance (Rothwell, 2004).

Consultation A process that can be individual and collective, and involves managers and employees, or their representatives, jointly examining and talking about issues of mutual concern. There is also an expectation that the discussions will seek to produce jointly acceptable solutions through a genuine exchange of views and ideas (Dix and Oxenbridge, 2003).

Contributory negligence If an injury is partly due to lack of reasonable care on behalf of the individual bringing about the claim, then the damages received may be reduced due to the claimant's own contribution towards the incident.

Development A term often used to describe changes in the whole person and what that person is, as well as what they can do. It reflects the belief that all people have the potential to be more and do more, and that this potential needs to be developed as well as utilized. People can develop to a limited degree through training, but development implies the employment of a much wider range of learning experiences and methods, such as coaching and mentoring, not all of which are necessarily connected to the working environment (cf **Learning**; **Training**).

Dialectics The tension that arises between conflicting ideas, interacting forces or competing interests. The term can also be used to explain the process of reconciling opposing opinions or facts by means of argument and discussion.

Discipline The formal measures taken, sanctions applied and outcomes achieved by management in response to perceived acts of misconduct.

Discrimination Treating a person or group of people less favourably compared to another person or group of people.

Diversity A multifaceted approach to the management of employees, reflecting the changing social and demographic characteristics of the workforce. The approach reflects the belief that maximizing the potential and contribution of all organizational stakeholders is inextricably linked to recognizing and valuing difference, and to treating people with respect.

Due diligence Written documentary evidence that all reasonably practicable steps have been taken to ensure the health and safety of an individual or group of individuals.

Equal opportunity The process of ensuring that employment practices in an organization are fair and unbiased, and do not breach any of the legislative provisions that are in place to protect workers from unlawful discrimination.

Ethnocentric A way of looking at the world primarily from the perspective of one's own culture and experience, which are perceived as being superior or more important than those of others (cf **Polycentric**).

Expatriate worker An employee deployed overseas, usually sourced from his or her country of origin.

External recruitment The process of identifying and attracting potential employees to an organization to fill current or future vacancies (cf **Internal recruitment**).

Global organization An organization that employs a workforce in different countries throughout the world, with a view to maximizing performance by sourcing or providing goods and/or services in a globally based market, and in which decisions are driven by markets rather than by geography.

Grievance The formalization of a claim that one or more persons, either co-workers or management, have acted wrongly towards another person(s) and, as a consequence, inflicted physical or psychological harm on that person, or others. This may involve an act, or acts, of misconduct.

Harassment Any unwelcome attention or behaviour from another that a person finds offensive or unacceptable and which results in the person feeling offended, uncomfortable or threatened, and leads to a loss of dignity or self-worth.

Hazard Anything that has the potential to cause harm or injury to people, equipment or property.

Hiring or employing The overall process of taking on new staff from outside the organization.

Human resource development This term came into usage in the late 1980s and early 1990s, and is used by many writers, but fewer practitioners, in preference to training. Its relationship to training is similar to that between Human Resource Management and Personnel Management, in that it represents a more holistic and strategic approach to learning than does training (Walton, 1999; cf **Training**).

Human Resource Management (HRM) A more recent approach to the management of employees, which sees people as a key organizational resource that needs to be developed and utilized to support the organization's operational and strategic objectives (cf **Personnel Management**).

Human resource planning (HRP) Originally known as 'manpower planning', this is concerned with planning and controlling the quantity and quality of labour available to an organization.

Human Resources (HR) An alternative to 'people' and also the name used by many organizations to describe the specialized department that deals with the administration and management of employees (cf **Human Resource Management**; **Personnel Management**).

Incentive The prospect or promise of a reward that is conditional upon an agreed outcome being achieved.

Induction This needs to be understood as a multistaged process rather than as a single, course-based event. It represents the introduction of new employees into the organization, into the department in which they work and into the job they have to do, although it can also relate to the transfer and promotion of existing employees. It should introduce the employee to the social environment, the technical aspects of work, and the rules and procedures of employment.

Internal recruitment The process of identifying current employees who may be suitable for newly created vacancies or for replacing staff who leave (cf **External recruitment**).

Learning A fundamental and natural human process involving growth and change. Learning is about behavioural modification. It cannot be seen, but is inferred from differences in what we know, believe and can do. Learning is the way in which we can improve and be different from that which we were. Learning needs to be understood as both a process and an outcome (cf **Training**; **Development**).

Metrics Relates to what and how something is measured. HR metrics focus on key aspects of the labour force, its behaviours, and its costs and contributions. The use of measures is increasingly associated with important features of the HR function, as part of the process of evaluating its efficiency and effectiveness.

Misconduct Behaviour that transgresses contractual arrangements, work rules, established norms of performance or other standards that can be seen as reasonable and necessary for the effective employment and management of people at work; behaviour that is deemed to be unacceptable by reference to formally established norms.

MNCs Multinational companies that have a national base, but which operate and trade multinationally.

Organizational capability This refers to an organization's ability to create, mobilize and utilize its key resources to maximum effect. The concept is important because it helps to redefine what HR represents; it is seen less as a series of activities and responsibilities, and more in terms of a resource and capability builder.

Organizational structure This relates to aspects of the formal organization, particularly the roles and responsibilities that people have, the hierarchy and reporting lines, the different departments and sections within the organization and how they are connected, formal communication channels and the way in which power and authority are distributed. Organizational structure is analogous to the human skeleton or the framework of a new building: it is what gives the organization shape and influences how it operates.

Pay Regular and contractually agreed monetary rewards, usually linked to position or job and paid as a wage or salary.

Performance Can be interpreted as expressing the relationship between a person's capabilities and what the person actually achieves, usually related to a person's job.

Performance appraisal A process for reviewing the past performance of an employee, and agreeing future objectives and development activities. It can be seen as '…*the process of evaluating and judging the way in which someone is functioning…*' (Coens and Jenkins, 2000).

Performance management '…*A broad term that has come to stand for the set of practices through which work is defined and reviewed, capabilities are developed, and rewards are distributed…*' (Morhman and Morhman, 1995).

'…*A strategic and integrated approach to delivering sustained success to organizations by improving the performance of the people who work in them and by developing the capabilities of team and individual contributions …*' (Armstrong and Baron, 1998).

Personnel Management The name given to the specialized management function responsible for an organization's employees (cf **Human Resource Management**).

Planning Can be understood as a set of techniques, an approach and a mindset, all of which relate to achieving specified objectives.

It should be understood as a process, rather than a time-constrained event.

Polycentric A way of looking at the world that recognizes and accepts difference, and the legitimacy of different values and systems (cf **Ethnocentric**).

Psychological contract The obligations that an employer and an employee, or group of employees, perceive to exist between each other as part of the employment relationship, comprising both expectations of each other and promises made to each other.

Rewards Can be both material and symbolic in form, and are outcomes of the employment and psychological contracts.

Reward system All of the practices, procedures and methods of rewarding employees either in use by, or potentially available to, management.

Risk The likelihood that harm or injury will occur.

Selection The process, culminating in the decision to offer employment or fill a vacancy from internal or external applicants, used by the organization to choose the most suitable candidate from a pool of applicants.

Trade union An organization that is independent of an employer and funded by member contributions, the function of which is to represent worker interests in relations between workers and employers.

Training Can best be understood as planned, structured and often formalized learning experiences that seek to develop specific skills and knowledge needed for effective job performance. Historically, employees have learnt many of the competences they need to perform effectively by being trained (cf **Learning; Development**).

Vicarious liability An employer can be liable for the acts of an employee towards another. This can arise if there is an employment relationship and if the employee commits a civil wrong during the course of their employment.

Index